Name of publication: THE FIRST REVIEW OF SPECIAL EDUCATION
Published by: Buttonwood Farms, Inc.
Office of publication: 3515 Woodhaven Road, Philadelphia, Pennsylvania 19154
Editorial Offices: 443 South Gulph Road, King of Prussia, Pennsylvania 19406.

JSE Press series in special education

The First Review
of
Special Education

LESTER MANN, *Editor*
Montgomery County Intermediate Unit
Bluebell, Pennsylvania

DAVID A. SABATINO, *Editor*
The Pennsylvania State University
University Park, Pennsylvania

Volume 2

JSE Press
Philadelphia, Pennsylvania
1973

Composition and Printing by STUDIO II
B-5 Benson East, Jenkintown, Pa. 19046

CONTENTS

Editor's note

Volume 2 is the second of the twins that comprise *The First Review of Special Education.* The first volume is the more "basic" of the two; this, the second, the more "applied." The reader is referred to the Introduction to the first volume for further discussion of this division.

SPECIFIC READING RETARDATION

Michael Rutter, M.D.
William Yule, M.A.

Institute of Psychiatry, University of London

Inconsistencies in terminology and definition abound in the literature on reading difficulties. Despite this, there is general agreement on one basic point — the need to differentiate between those children who, irrespective of ability, are at the bottom end of a continuum of reading attainment (*backward readers*) and those who are underachieving in relation to their chronological age (CA) and level of general intelligence. The latter group has a specific educational handicap and, on the whole, a roughly average IQ. It is this group with *specific reading retardation* with which this review is concerned. Two issues discussed are the extent to which the concept is valid, and how far the latter group differs from that of generally backward readers. Attention is mainly confined to epidemiologically based studies; but within these confines, the review aims to be comprehensive and to provide an up-to-date appraisal of the present state of knowledge.

Much of the confusion in the literature on specific reading retardation stems from the fact that most investigators have examined highly selected groups of children. The type of problems seen at any one clinic naturally reflects the biases influencing referral to that clinic and the kind of services that it provides. It is hardly surprising that retarded readers referred to a neurologist are rather different from those referred to a child psychiatrist or to a remedial teacher or speech therapist or educational psychologist. Biases influencing referral can only be avoided by epidemiological investigations of *total* child populations (Rutter, Yule, Tizard, & Graham, 1967). The effect of such biases is illustrated by the Warrington studies of reading retardation. On the basis of a study of a small selected group of children attending a neurological clinic, it was suggested that visuospatial difficulties commonly accompany reading difficulty (Kinsbourne & Warrington, 1963). A later, larger study of a somewhat more representative group showed that, on the contrary, visuospatial difficulties are quite uncommon among retarded readers and, at most, account for a very small proportion of children with reading difficulties (Warrington, 1967). For this reason, the present chapter focuses on epidemiologically based studies and only brings in other investigations as pointers to possible associations, when epidemiological data are lacking.

DEFINITION OF SPECIFIC READING RETARDATION

The first point to be made is that reading retardation is a comparative concept.[1] A child is deemed a poor reader if he is reading significantly below what is "expected" of him. For the purposes of general reading backwardness, expectation is based on the average level achieved by children of the same age or school grade. For the purposes of specific reading retardation, expectation is based on the average level achieved by children of the same age (or grade) and degree of general intelligence. There is little dispute on these three elements (age, intelligence, and length of formal schooling). By and large, one expects a 12-year-old child to be a better reader than a 7-year-old, a bright child to read better than an intellectually dull child of the same age; and the whole educational system is based on the belief that schooling influences attainment. Confusion arises from variation in *how* these elements are taken into account and *what* degree of retardation is required for a diagnosis of specific reading retardation.

The commonest way of categorizing a child as a poor reader is to compare his score on a standardized reading test with the scores of his same-aged peers in the standardization sample. In Britain such tests are constructed to produce "reading ages"; in the United States they yield "reading grades"; but both are ultimately linked to CA. If the child's reading score is lower than that of his age group by some arbitrary amount, he is considered a backward reader. Following Schonell (1942) and Burt (1950), it has become customary in Britain to consider a pupil as backward in reading if, at age 10 years, he has a reading age of 8½ years or less on a standardized test. By extension, reading backwardness has come to mean reading at a level 18 months (or sometimes 2 years) below expectation.

There are many problems in this approach; the most important is that the same level of backwardness means different things at different ages. As Chall (1970) pointed out, 1½ years' backwardness at age 8 years is more serious than 1½ years' backwardness at age 14 years. Common sense suggests that the units of reading attainment are not equal at different points on the scale. Lyle (1969) attempted to deal with this problem by defining reading retardation as 6 months' retardation at grade 1, 1 year at grade 2, 1½ years at grade 3, and so on. However, there are no data given to demonstrate that, in fact, 6 months' retardation at grade 1 is equivalent to 1½ years' retardation at grade 3. Without information on the spread of reading abilities at each age, this kind of adjustment is quite arbitrary and potentially misleading.

The difficulties increase sharply when specific reading retardation is considered, with the consequent need to take IQ into account. Perhaps the commonest method

---

[1] In theory, one could devise an absolute level of reading. For example, there could be a measure of the child's absolute level of phonic decoding skills, or the number of phonically irregular words whose meaning he knows. But this would be a complex psychometric task, and so far it has not been done.

2

has been to define reading retardation in terms of a reading level 18 months to 2 years (or one and a half to two grades) below average, and then to exclude children with an IQ below 80 or 85 or 90 or some other arbitrary point.

This selection of a single IQ cutoff point has unfortunate consequences. It automatically means that reading retardation can only occur in children above a certain IQ – a totally unjustified assumption and, again, liable to have misleading consequences. The higher the IQ cutoff point, the worse the distortion. Second, such a definition still allows the inclusion of children who are reading at a level equivalent to their mental age (MA) and therefore do not have specific reading retardation. Thus, if reading retardation is defined as 18 months' retardation at age 10 years in children of IQ 80 or more, children of IQ 80 to 85 with reading ages at the same level will be included. This defect in definition is most marked with older children or where a low IQ cutoff point is used.

These defects are sufficiently serious to make a definition of this sort unsuitable for any but the most rough and ready comparisons. In order to overcome these difficulties and to provide a means of taking IQ into account in a more precise and standardized way, the *achievement ratio* was devised by Franzen (1920) in the United States. The achievement ratio for reading is derived from the following equation:

$$\text{achievement ratio} = \frac{\text{reading age}}{\text{mental age}} \times 100$$

The idea as expressed by Burt (1950) was: "If a child's achievement ratio is exactly one hundred, then teaching is keeping pace with mental growth; the child, it may be inferred, is learning his lessons up to the full limit of his born capacity [p. 34]." Similar notions underlie Monroe's (1932) reading index and Myklebust's (1968) use of the learning quotient, in which the achievement age is divided by the expectancy age. The expectancy age is simply the sum of the MA, CA, and grade age divided by 3.

Several assumptions are implicit in this approach. First, there is the view that MA measures innate intelligence. That genetic factors are important in the development of intelligence is indisputable, but there is abundant evidence that the IQ is *not* a pure measure of innate ability. Second, there is the belief that children rarely, if ever, achieve at a level above their MA (Burt, 1950; 1970). Again, there is ample evidence that this is not the case (Crame, 1959; Graham, 1970; Yule, Rutter, Berger, & Thompson, 1973). Overachievement is probably as frequent as underachievement. However, these conceptual issues are less important than serious statistical objections to the procedure (Thorndike, 1963; Vernon, 1958), the most important of which stem from the *regression effect:* Wherever the correlation between measures (such as MA and reading age) is less than perfect, the children who are well *above* average on one measure will be less superior on the other, and those who are well *below* average on the first measure will be less inferior on the second (Thorndike, 1963). In other words, the mean reading age of 10-year-olds with an average MA of 13 years will *not* be 13 years; it will be more like 12 years. Only in the middle of the distribution will the two variables be identical. For these and other reasons, the achievement ratio has become a discredited statistic.

Yet this leaves the problem of how to determine what reading attainment can be expected of a child, taking into account his CA and IQ. A (multiple) regression analysis provides the only satisfactory technique for doing this. If one knows the correlation between predictor variables (in this case, CA and IQ) and the criterion variable (in this case, reading attainment), it is possible to calculate the expected value of reading attainment for any predictor value. On this basis, one can then determine whether the child scores above, at, or below this predicted value. Moreover, it is possible to determine the statistical probability for any deviation from the expected value, thus reducing the arbitrariness of the cutoff point in defining what level of retardation is necessary to diagnose specific reading retardation.

This technique of regression analysis has long been available, but only rarely applied. One of the earliest applications was that of Ravenette (1961), who predicted children's reading ages on Schonell's Graded Word Reading Test (GWRT) from their scores on a vocabulary test. Fransella and Gerver (1965) extended the technique to a multiple-regression analysis, predicting Schonell GWRT scores from the Wechsler Intelligence Scale for Children (WISC) verbal scale IQ, and CA. However, this study suffered from basing the analysis on data collected at a psychiatric clinic. Yule (1967) refined the procedure by using data from an epidemiologically based study, and Levy and Tucker (1972) went on to note sex differences in regression slopes.

Interestingly, all of these applications were British. Yet, much the clearest exposition of the need to apply regression analyses to the study of reading retardation was in Thorndike's (1963) book written for educators — a book which has been sadly neglected. He discussed clearly and simply the factors which require attention in studying underachievement and argued convincingly that regression procedures are the only satisfactory way of estimating discrepancies between expected and actual achievement. Strictly speaking, therefore, the present review should be restricted to studies employing this technique. However, the paucity of investigations using the regression method make such a limitation impractical. An attempt has been made to confine attention to studies using definitions which minimized systematic bias, but most are less than wholly satisfactory in this respect.

CONCEPTS

Specific reading retardation

The concept of a syndrome characterized by a severe and specific difficulty in learning to read has been the subject of much controversy, and many educationalists have denied that it exists. To some extent, this denial refers to the additional concept that such a syndrome is neurologically determined — as implied by the term "dyslexia." The issue is discussed below; but before considering the nature and causes of such a disorder, it is necessary to consider the evidence for and against its existence.

The arguments against a syndrome of specific reading retardation have often been more emotional than scientific, but two main themes can be identified: First, there is the view that reading skills constitute a normal distribution. Just as some people are tall and some short, so some read well and some read badly; there is no point in differentiating the poor readers, as they are merely the inevitable tail on a Gaussian curve. Second, there is the view that even if such a syndrome can be delineated, it is a meaningless distinction, since specific reading retardation is no different in quality from general backwardness. Both these arguments would have considerable force if their basic assumptions were correct. Until very recently, there has been no evidence upon which to judge these assumptions, but Rutter and Yule (1973) have now presented findings from two epidemiological inquiries which allow some decision on the question.

Before the subject of normal distribution can be considered, it is necessary to define the problem more precisely. Critchley (1970) suggested that, as in the case of IQ, there is a hump in the distribution of reading abilities which can be attributed to the presence of dyslexic children. Actually, the existence of such a hump has not been shown, but even if it does exist (as it may well), it is irrelevant to the present issue, since it can be explained in terms of mental subnormality (because reading and IQ are positively correlated). What is needed is information on the distribution of *specific* reading retardation, as defined above. If there is no meaning to the concept, the proportion of children in the general population with specific reading retardation should be just that predicted on the basis of a normal distribution. This has been tested by Yule, Rutter, Berger, and Thompson (1973) with respect to 10-year-old children on the Isle of Wight and in an inner London borough. Because a narrow (1 year) age range was being studied, and because within that range there was a zero correlation between age and reading, a simple regression of reading on WISC IQ was used to define the predicted level of reading. Children whose reading on the Neale Analysis of Reading Ability (1958)[2] was at a level at least 2 standard deviations (in fact, 30 months) below prediction were categorized as having specific reading retardation. On this definition exactly 2.28% of children should have such a categorization. In fact, in the Isle of Wight population, there were 3.1% of children with a specific retardation on reading accuracy and 3.6% on reading comprehension. Both figures differ significantly from 2.28% ($p < .02$). It should be noted that although 3.1% and 3.6% are known to be underestimates (because they depend on imperfect screening of the total population, using group reading tests), both figures are appreciably above the expected 2.28%.

The differences in the London study were even more striking. There were 6.3% of children with specific reading retardation, using reading accuracy as the criterion,

---

[2]The Neale test is a well-standardized, individually administered British prose-reading test which gives rise to scores of reading accuracy, rate, and comprehension.

and 9.3% using reading comprehension. In all cases, the groups of children with specific reading retardation had a roughly average level of intelligence. It may be concluded that there is a sizable abnormal hump on the normal distribution, caused by the presence of a group of children of normal intelligence with severe reading difficulties. That group is larger in size than expected on the basis of the known regression of reading on IQ in the same population.

The syndrome exists then, but does it have any meaning? As Davis and Cashdan (1963) pointed out, for the syndrome to have any usefulness, it must be shown to differ from ordinary reading backwardness in some other respects. In this connection little is known, but some limited findings from the Isle of Wight study (Rutter & Yule, 1973) suggested the existence of important differences. Children with specific reading retardation were compared with children whose reading was equally poor, but whose reading was not significantly below that expected on the basis of the children's age and IQ. This group of children with general reading backwardness were, for this reason, of much lower IQ. Perhaps the most striking difference between the groups concerns the sex ratio, which was 3.3 to 1 (boys to girls) in the specific group but only 1.3 to 1 in the general group. This is in keeping with several previous studies which have all shown that specific reading retardation is much more common in boys, whereas general reading backwardness is only slightly more common in boys or even of similar frequency in the two sexes (e.g., Clark, 1970; Leeds Education Committee, 1953; Middlesborough Head Teachers Association, 1953).

There were also differences in background factors of probable etiological significance. None of the specific group showed hard signs of overt neurological disorder (such as cerebral palsy), whereas 11.4% of the general group did so. Impairment of neurodevelopmental functions (so-called soft signs) was more frequent in both groups but was, again, more common in the general group. Ingram, Mason, and Blackburn (1970) obtained similar findings comparing children underachieving in reading and spelling only ("specifics") and those underachieving in arithmetic as well ("generals"). Their definition differed from that used in the Isle of Wight study, and the sample was highly selective, consisting of children who had attended neurological or speech clinics; but the groups in the two studies probably had something in common. Ingram et al. (1970) found that neurological abnormalities were much more common in their general group than in the specific group.

In terms of specific neurodevelopmental functions in the Isle of Wight study, the "specifics" were similar to the "generals" with respect to speech delay (also family history of speech delay) and choreiform movements. However, motor incoordination (measured both clinically and by a modification of the Oseretsky test), constructional difficulties, and motor impersistence were over twice as common in the children with general reading backwardness. A family history of reading difficulties was equally common in the two groups. In short, specific reading retardation seemed to be specifically associated with speech and language difficulties, whereas general backwardness was related to developmental delay in a much wider range of functions. Ingram's finding (Ingram et al., 1970) – that his "specifics" had a much higher rate of audiophonic difficulties than did his "generals" – is in keeping with this conclusion.

Specific reading retardation has usually been thought to be associated with severe spelling difficulties; but the implication has been that difficulties in other school subjects are less marked. This was borne out in the Isle of Wight study. The children with specific reading retardation had equally marked spelling difficulties, whereas this particular association was not found in the general-reading-backwardness group (see "Spelling" section below).

It seems that in outcome, too, the children with specific reading retardation differ from those with general reading backwardness. The Isle of Wight children with reading difficulties were followed from age 10 to 14½, and the progress of "specifics" and "generals" was compared (Yule, 1973). Originally the groups were comparable in the severity of their reading and spelling difficulties, but at follow-up the "specifics" had made *less* progress in spite of their much higher IQ; their reading accuracy lagged 7 months behind that of the "generals," and their spelling was 8 months worse. In contrast, the "specifics" had reached a *higher* level of achievement in arithmetic than did the "generals." The significance of these findings, based on a straightforward comparison of means, were confirmed by multivariant analysis of variance. Whether the groups also require different methods of teaching remains unknown.

Replication of all these findings is obviously required; but the evidence to date provides substantial support for the concept of specific reading retardation as a syndrome characterized by severe reading difficulties not accountable in terms of low intelligence nor explicable merely in terms of the lower end of a normal distribution of reading skills.

Dyslexia

The concept of specific reading retardation carries no implications concerning type of etiology, nor does it imply any type of unitary causation. However, the related concept of dyslexia (at least as put forward by some psychologists and by neurologists primarily treating adults, e.g., Miles, 1971) usually carries these connotations. Critchley (1962) said that dyslexia is a specific, constitutional, genetically determined disorder distinguished from other forms of reading disability by its gravity and purity. The characteristics of dyslexia have usually been described in terms of a family history of reading difficulties, disorders in speech and language (particular spelling difficulties), clumsiness, right-left confusion, and a variety of other developmental difficulties (Critchley, 1962, 1970; Gallagher, 1962; Hallgren, 1950; Hermann, 1959; Money, 1962; Orton, 1937; Shankweiler, 1964; Vernon, 1962).

That children with these characteristics exist is not in doubt. If you look long enough, any combination of features can be found in some child. The question is, Does the syndrome mean anything (Rutter, 1969)? Two issues have given rise to controversy in this connection: First, there is the question of whether these developmental abnormalities described above are either important or common causes of severe reading retardation (Daniels, 1962; Houghton, 1967; Pond, 1967). It has

7

been suggested that they are so rarely important in practice that they can be largely ignored. Second, there is the question of the homogeneity of the syndrome as a single, specific, genetically determined neurological condition which arises independently of environmental circumstances (Critchley, 1970).

The strong and consistent association between speech and language impairment, right-left disorientation, motor impersistence, spelling difficulties, motor incoordination, a family history of reading difficulties, and specific reading retardation is described in other sections of this chapter. With the single exception of mixed-handedness, all the features said to be characteristic of dyslexia have been found to be associated with specific reading retardation. Correlations can never prove causation, but it seems reasonable to infer from these findings that developmental abnormalities are both common and important causes of failure to learn to read (Rutter, 1969). Thus, one of the two chief objections to the concept of dyslexia runs counter to the available evidence and can be dismissed.

On the other hand, objections concerning the homogeneity of the syndrome appear much more soundly based. The same group of children who show the developmental characteristics associated with dyslexia also come from backgrounds suggesting the operation of social and psychological factors in the causation of reading difficulties (see relevant sections of this chapter). Biological factors are certainly important in pathogenesis, but environmental influences also play a part. It seems that severe reading retardation is often overdetermined, in that several different causes have been operative, although only one may be primary (Rutter, 1969).

The concept of dyslexia also implies a clustering of the neurological characteristics. This was examined in the Isle of Wight study in relation to speech and language abnormalities, motor incoordination, constructional difficulties, motor impersistence, and right-left confusion (Rutter, 1969). It was found that the associations between the various developmental abnormalities were of a low order and offered no support for a single dyslexia syndrome. Margaret Clark (1970) also commented (on the basis of her Dunbartonshire survey) that there was a diversity of disabilities and not an underlying pattern common to the group. Similar findings were reported by Naidoo (1972) in a study of a highly selected clinic sample. Whether there are several distinct types of "specific dyslexia" which possess clear differentiating features, or whether, on the other hand, reading difficulties develop as the result of an interaction between only weakly related factors without any specific meaningful syndromes cannot be determined on the available data.

This lack of unity in the syndrome has led a recent British governmental advisory committee to reject the use of the term "dyslexia" (Deparment of Education and Science, 1972). Insofar as the term implies a single condition with a single cause, this rejection is undoubtedly justified. However, the above evidence does not support the further view that specific reading retardation is merely the lower end of a continuum, nor does it support those who deny the importance of developmental factors. In rejecting the narrow, classical, neurological notion of dyslexia and the mystique associated with it, it is important not to overlook the reality of the problem, multifactorially determined though it probably is (Lansdown, 1972). The view that specific reading retardation is a meaningful designation, but one that includes a variety of syndromes and a variety of causal factors, is entirely in keeping with Ingram's (1970, 1971) thoughtful appraisal of dyslexia from the viewpoint of a modern pediatric neurologist.

PREVALENCE

All general population surveys have shown a high frequency of reading difficulties, and it has been clear that this frequency applies to specific reading retardation as well as to general reading backwardness, where the distinction has been made. For example, MacMeeken (1939), in a study of Edinburgh children aged 7 to 10 years, found that 9% had a reading-accomplishment quotient of 85 or less. A survey of Middlesborough 11-year-olds showed that 8 to 11% of children had a reading age at least 18 months below their MA, and that about 3% had a reading age at least 36 months below MA (Middlesborough Head Teachers Association, 1953). About the same time, a survey of 9- to 10-year-old children in Leeds found that 8½% had reading ages at least 2 years below their MA (Leeds Education Committee, 1953). The rate in Burton-on-Trent was still higher (Birch, 1950). More recently, Barker, Fee, and Sturrock (1967), in a survey in Dundee, Scotland, found that among 9-year-olds with an IQ of 90 or more, 1% had a reading age of 6½ years or less. Clark's (1970) study in Dunbartonshire produced a similar figure, but a further 5% of those with an IQ of 90 or more were between 1 and 2 years below the level expected for 9-year-old children. Malmqvist (1958), studying Swedish children aged 7 years-9 months, found that 8½% of those with an IQ of 90 or more had a reading attainment at least 1 standard deviation below normal. Miller, Margolin, and Yolles (1957) found that 11% of third-grade children with an IQ of 90 or more, living in a county just outside Washington, D.C., were reading 1.3 years or more below their grade. Frisk, Holmström, and Wasz-Höckert (1967) used writing difficulties as an index of dyslexia and found a prevalence of 12% in grade 3, 8% in grade 5, and 3 to 4% in grade 7. Unfortunately, all these studies suffered from the defects in definition noted above, and it is not possible to make any comparisons between studies.

A variety of investigations has shown that there are marked differences in reading attainment over both time and place. For example, between 1938 and 1948, the average reading age for 11-year-olds in England and Wales dropped by nearly a year (Ministry of Education, 1950); between 1948 and 1964, there was a progressive improvement, totaling some 17 months overall; and since 1964, there may have been a slight drop once more (Start & Wells, 1972). Similar changes were found in illiteracy rates. Eisenberg (1966), using group reading tests in the United States, showed that there were major differences in reading attainment between children in a large city, those in a suburb immediately outside the city, and those in a more distant commuter area. Morris (1959, 1966), studying children in an English county, found important differences in reading attainment according to the characteristics of the schools which the children attended. The British National Child Development Study (Davie, Butler, & Goldstein, 1972; Pringle, Butler, & Davie, 1966) showed that reading standards were considerably higher in Scotland than in England (although arithmetic standards showed the reverse trend). Kerdel-Vegas (1968), studying letter reversal among children in Caracas, found the prevalence much higher in children from lower socioeconomic groups. However, all these studies were concerned with either average reading attainment or general reading backwardness, rather than specific reading retardation.

For information on the prevalence of specific reading retardation alone, it is necessary to turn to recent surveys in the Isle of Wight (Rutter, Tizard & Whitmore, 1970) and in London (Berger, Yule, & Rutter, 1973).[3] In the Isle of Wight survey of 9- to 10-year-old children, reading retardation was defined as an attainment on either reading accuracy or reading comprehension (on the Neale Analysis of Reading Ability) which was 28 months or more below the level predicted on the basis of each child's age and short WISC IQ (using a multiple-regression equation derived from a random selected sample of the general population). On this definition, there was a minimum prevalence of specific reading retardation of just under 4%. A directly comparable study was undertaken of 10-year-old children living in one of London's inner boroughs, and the findings were contrasted with those for the Isle of Wight 10-year-olds. In this narrower age range, the correlation between CA and reading attainment did not differ from zero, so a single regression of reading on IQ was used for prediction. The correlations between IQ and reading were closely similar in the two areas, and there was no significant difference in mean IQ between London and Isle of Wight children; therefore, the same regression equation was used to predict reading in both populations. It was found that the prevalence of specific reading retardation was more than twice as high in London as on the Isle of Wight. In both areas, the reading-retarded children had a mean IQ of close to 100. As the same methods were used in the two studies, it may be concluded that there are real differences in prevalence. Specific reading retardation (equivalent to 28 months' retardation in 10-year-olds) runs at a rate varying between 4 and 10%. As already noted, this rate is well above that expected on the basis of a normal distribution. It means that although in the general population there is a linear regression of reading on IQ, there is a sizeable subgroup whose reading is unrelated to their general intelligence and who constitute the group with specific reading retardation. The fact that there is such a large difference in prevalence between two parts of Britain makes it very unlikely that specific reading retardation can be regarded simply as a genetically determined condition, as suggested by the proponents of the concept of dyslexia (Critchley,

---

[3] Faglioni, Gatti, Pagamoni, and Robutti (1969) also used a multiple-regression technique to define dyslexia in a study of Italian children, but the numbers involved (13) were too small for the estimation of prevalence.

1970). Conditions in the home, community, or school have been shown to differ markedly between London and the Isle of Wight (Rutter, Yule, Quinton, Rowlands, Yule, & Berger, 1972), but which of these conditions are responsible for the difference in prevalence of specific reading retardation remains to be determined.

Cross-cultural differences

Specific reading retardation has been reported in children from a wide variety of European countries; there are also reports of Japanese, Israeli, and Arab children with the disorder (Critchley, 1970). Makita (1968), on the basis of a study using questionnaires completed by teachers, reported a rate of less than 1% for Japanese children with reading difficulties; he suggested that reading disability might be much rarer in Japan than in English-speaking countries. However, there are no systematic comparative studies, and it remains unknown whether the prevalence of specific reading retardation varies with different languages.

SEX DISTRIBUTION

Although there is little difference between boys and girls in the average level of reading (Clark, 1970; Morris, 1966; Start & Wells, 1972), boys greatly outnumber girls with respect to specific reading retardation in all epidemiologically based studies. Ratios of 3 or 4 to 1 were reported by Clark (1970), Rutter, Tizard, and Whitmore (1970) and Berger, Yule, and Rutter (1973); and 2 to 1 by MacMeeken (1939), Barker et al. (1967), Malmqvist (1958), and the studies in Middlesborough and Leeds referred to above. Specific reading retardation has always been found to have a male-to-female sex ratio (when sex ratio has been measured) about double that of general reading backwardness (see above). Because this distinction has not been clearly made in the above studies with sex ratios of about 2 to 1, it seems probable that the true sex ratio of specific reading retardation lies nearer 3 or 4 to 1.

Because male preponderance has been a feature of all epidemiologically based inquiries into sex distribution in specific reading retardation, it is quite clear that male preponderance is a real difference which cannot be explained in terms of referral biases, as once thought (Hallgren, 1950). Nevertheless, the reason for the difference remains a matter for speculation. The sex difference applies to all specific developmental disorders (especially speech and language delay, to which reading is linked; see below) as well as to delays in the acquisition of motor, bowel, and bladder control (Rutter, Tizard, & Whitmore, 1970). Accordingly, it is necessary to search for reasons why boys should show a higher rate of specific developmental delays, rather than just a higher rate of specific reading retardation. It may be relevant that boys are generally slower in biological maturation and are more susceptible to all kinds of biological stresses, and possibly to psychological stresses as well (Rutter, Tizard, & Whitmore, 1970; Rutter, 1972). However, how – or if – these are related to reading difficulties remains unknown.

SPELLING

Spelling errors have long been regarded as a special feature of dyslexia; it has been claimed that "the spelling mistakes in the writings of dyslexics differ in many respects from the errors made by normal uneducated subjects or by dullards [Critchley, 1970, p. 41]." Numerous case reports have indicated that spelling errors are very frequent in the writing of individuals with specific difficulties in reading. However, spelling and reading are closely correlated in the general population, so it would be expected that poor readers should also be poor spellers. Unfortunately, this has very rarely been taken into account. Most studies have compared retarded readers (or so-called dyslexics) with normal children of the same age whose reading is necessarily superior, thus negating the point of the comparison. Two main questions require attention: Is the rate of spelling difficulties shown by children with specific reading retardation higher than would be expected from the correlation between spelling and reading skills in the general population? Do retarded readers tend to make special types of spelling errors different from those made by normal children at the time both groups begin learning to read?

If there is no *specific* association between spelling errors and specific reading retardation, then children identified on the basis of specific reading retardation should be poor in spelling but worse in reading (based on the regression effect [Thorndike, 1963] and the reading-spelling correlation in the general population). This is what is found with arithmetic and reading in the specific-reading-retardation group, suggesting that difficulties in arithmetic are not a particular feature of specific reading retardation (Rutter, Tizard, & Whitmore, 1970). Reading-retarded children in the Isle of Wight study performed in reading nearly 2 standard deviations below that of the control children, but their arithmetic was less than 1½ standard deviations below. However, the findings for spelling were different. Spelling was as retarded as reading; this association persisted as the children grew older. At age 14, the children with specific reading retardation were still 2 standard deviations below the mean in spelling, whereas they were only 1.2 standard deviations below the mean in arithmetic (Yule, 1973). That spelling difficulties are associated with specific reading retardation is evident from the comparison with data concerning reading-backward children in the Isle of Wight (Yule, 1973). The reading-backward children, when originally identified at age 9 to 10 years, showed reading difficulties of similar severity of those of the reading-retarded. At follow-up at 14 years, their reading was still very poor, although not quite so poor as that of the reading-retarded. However, unlike the children with specific reading retardation, those with general reading backwardness had roughly comparable achievements in spelling and arithmetic (1.7 and 1.5 standard deviations below the mean, respectively.)

A similar comparison between reading and spelling can be drawn from Clark's (1970) investigation in Scotland. As part of an epidemiological inquiry, a group of

8-year-old children of average intelligence but with severe reading difficulties had been identified. These were followed up at age 10 years when tests of reading and spelling were given. At this time, 49 of the 96 children were still at least 2 years backward, and 19 at least 3 years backward. In other words, although the group had been identified on the basis of poor reading, their spelling was actually worse than their reading. As in the Isle of Wight study, this is out of keeping with the expectation from the correlation between reading and spelling in the population at large. Again, the findings suggest a *specific* association between spelling difficulties and specific reading retardation. Other studies have not yielded results in a form allowing comparison between the degree of spelling retardation and the degree of reading retardation. Nevertheless, all epidemiological investigations which have examined the question have found a very high rate of spelling difficulties in children identified because of reading problems (Malmqvist, 1958). When these data are taken in conjunction with the Scottish and Isle of Wight findings, it may be concluded, in answer to the first question, that the rate of spelling difficulties shown by children with specific reading retardation probably *is* above that expected from the correlation between spelling and reading skills in the general population; i.e., there is a specific association over and above the correlation between the two skills found in the general population. However, before this conclusion can be firm, replication of the findings is required.

The question of whether reading-retarded children show a special type of spelling error is more difficult to answer. Most studies have simply compared the rates of different types of error with those of normal children. Unfortunately, this type of comparison is useless without close matching on reading and spelling skills, because (*a*) there may be a different distribution of types of errors at different levels of reading ability; and (*b*) children of different spelling ability will be tested for errors on their spelling of different words, and individual words differ in the types of spelling errors they are likely to suggest. These methodological considerations cast serious doubt on Malmqvist's (1958) comparison of spelling errors in good and poor readers, for example, which showed that vowel omission was specifically characteristic of poor readers. Malmqvist's finding is certainly in keeping with views based on clinic studies (Hermann, 1959) and therefore well worth investigating, but it could be just an artifact of the differences in level of spelling ability.

A further difficulty lies in the problems involved in classifying spelling errors. Numerous schemes have been proposed (Scottish Council for Research in Education, 1961; Spache, 1940a, b), but none has received universal acceptance, and most are of dubious reliability. Because of differences in classification, comparisons between different studies are liable to be misleading.

One of the few studies to compare reading-retarded children with normal (but younger) children of similar reading age was reported by Frank (1936). She investigated types of spelling errors in 35 children aged 7 to 11½, of roughly average intelligence but very poor reading ability, and in 350 normal 4- to 7-year-olds. She reported that the types of errors were similar in the two groups; unfortunately, no figures were given.

More recently, Tordrup (1966) compared 130 retarded readers in grades 4 to 7 with 92 normal readers from grade 2 (thus, of younger age but comparable reading skills). It was found that reversals (one of the errors reputedly associated with dyslexia) was equally frequent in the two groups, suggesting that reversals were a function of level of reading reached and were *not* specifically associated with reading retardation. A study of dictation errors with two other groups also showed a very similar pattern of errors (using a 12-category classification) in retarded readers and normal children. Similarly, the Scottish Council for Research in Education (1961) found that poor spellers made the same types of errors in the same relative proportions as good spellers.

In neither Frank's nor Tordrup's study was there any definition of reading retardation, making it uncertain whether children with specific reading retardation were studied. Other investigations have failed to equate for spelling and reading ability, so that any differences found may be artifacts of differences in level. Malmqvist's finding that vowel omission was characteristic of poor readers has already been noted. Hermann (1959) compared the spelling errors of children attending the Word Blind Institute with those in Noesgaard's (1945) sample of normal children. He found that although the frequency of spelling errors was much higher in the Institute children, the proportion of errors which were reversals was *not* higher. (In fact, it was somewhat lower.)

So far, there is no sound evidence that specific reading retardation is associated with particular types of spelling errors, but it must be said that the matter has not been adequately investigated. All the spelling errors associated with "dyslexia" have been reported in normal children just learning to read; if differences exist, they must be quantitative rather than qualitative. The issue merits further study.

WISC VERBAL-PERFORMANCE DISCREPANCIES

The pattern of scores on the WISC has been widely studied with respect to reading difficulties. The WISC is a downward extension of the earlier Wechsler scales for adults. It includes 10 short subtests divided into two groups, providing a verbal-scale IQ and a performance-scale IQ. The division of subtests was somewhat arbitrary, but later factor-analytic studies (Cohen, 1959; Maxwell, 1959) provided some support.

The literature on verbal-performance discrepancies and reading retardation is not satisfactory (see review by Huelsman, 1970) because of selective sampling, poor definitions of reading retardation, and psychometric näivety in the assessment of the significance of discrepancies of varying sizes. Arbitrary cutoff points have been used in many studies, in spite of published tables giving the frequencies of different verbal-performance discrepancies (Field, 1960; Seashore, 1951).

Nevertheless, epidemiological studies have been unanimous in findings that the verbal IQ tends to be lower than the performance IQ in children with specific reading retardation. Belmont and Birch (1966) found that the verbal-scale IQ was, on the average, 7 points lower than the performance-scale IQ among poor readers of normal intelligence, whereas there was a 5-point difference in the reverse direction for the controls. Similar results for backward readers were reported by Clark (1970). Among her backward readers, 31% had a performance score exceeding the verbal score by at least 10 points, as against 11% with a similar-sized discrepancy in the opposite direction. Rutter, Tizard, and Whitmore (1970) showed that 13% of retarded readers had a verbal score significantly less than the performance score (at the 5% level), compared with only 5% of the controls (as expected). Similar results have been reported from most clinic studies with large samples (Doehring, 1968; Huelsman, 1970; Warrington, 1967).

It may be concluded that there is a well-established tendency for retarded readers to be impaired in their verbal skills, as assessed on the WISC. This is important in the light that it throws on handicaps associated with reading retardation. But it needs to be emphasized that, although there is a definite and significant trend for the verbal IQ to be lower than the performance IQ, there are too many exceptions for the discrepancy to be of much predictive value in an individual case. There are some retarded readers with large discrepancies in the opposite direction. This is particularly the case in children with severe clumsiness (see "Motor Incoordination" below), and it may also be true, to a small extent, of the minority of retarded readers with overt neurological disorder (Rutter, Graham, & Yule, 1970).

HANDEDNESS, EYEDNESS, AND FOOTEDNESS

Following Orton (1925, 1937), numerous writers have associated specific reading retardation with left-handedness, left-eyedness, or mixed laterality and have gone on to argue that the reading difficulties were caused by impaired cerebral dominance. This argument is poorly based, in view of the rather limited association between handedness and cerebral dominance (Benton, 1965; Mountcastle, 1962; Zangwill, 1960, 1962). There is a positive correlation, but it is far from invariable. The link between cerebral dominance and eyedness is even more tenuous, since each eye has bilateral representation in the brain.

However, the argument is probably irrelevant, as there seems to be no association between laterality, as measured in any way, and specific reading retardation. Although there have been some positive clinic-based studies, there are more negative ones; *all* the epidemiologically based studies are negative. Belmont and Birch (1965), studying 150 reading-retarded 9- and 10-year-old boys in Aberdeen, Scotland, found that they did not differ from controls with respect to eyedness, handedness, or hand-eye codominance. Malmqvist (1958) found no association between poor reading and either left-handedness or mixed-handedness. Clark (1970), studying Scottish children, found no association between reading retardation and any measure of laterality. Similarly, in the Isle of Wight study (Rutter, Tizard, & Whitmore, 1970), specific reading retardation was unassociated with differences in handedness, footedness, eyedness, hand-foot-dominance discrepancy, or hand-eye-dominance discrepancy. In the British National Survey, Douglas, Ross, and Cooper (1967) found no association between handedness and attainment (specific reading retardation as such was not studied). Helveston, Billips, and Weber (1970), studying the entire third, fourth, and fifth grades of a suburban Indianapolis public school, together with 67 children referred to a dyslexia clinic, found no association with laterality of hand or eye or with the controlling eye (assessed by stereovision cards).

It may safely be concluded that specific reading retardation as a whole is *not* associated with any particular pattern of handedness, eyedness, or footedness.

DEVELOPMENTAL DELAY

More than any other factor, a delay in the development of certain cortical functions has been held to be the cause of specific reading retardation (Vernon, 1971). As will be shown, there is strong evidence in favor of this supposition. The controversy largely concerns two subissues: (*a*) *which* cortical functions are delayed or impaired in their development; and (*b*) whether the delay is due to a slowing of otherwise normal maturation, or to damage or defect which will not be outgrown with age. These issues are considered in turn.

Speech and language

All epidemiological studies have found a strong association between speech and language delay and specific reading retardation. Thus, in the Isle of Wight study (Rutter, Tizard, & Whitmore, 1970), 11% of retarded readers had not spoken their first words by 2 years, compared with 2% of the controls. By 30 months, 15% were not using phrases, as against 4% of the controls. Even on current examination at 9 to 10 years, 14% had an articulation defect (compared with 7% in the controls), 15% showed syntactic immaturity (compared with 6% in the controls), and 9% were impaired in their ability to use spoken language to give an adequate description (compared with 2% in the controls). Current speech defects were also a feature of the backward readers studied by Clark (1970). She found, too, that reading difficulties were associated with poor auditory discrimination (assessed on the Wepman test) and low scores on the Illinois Test of Psycholinguistic Abilities (ITPA). Wussler and Barclay (1970), in a study of clinic children, also found low ITPA scores in children with reading disability. Belmont and Birch (1966), in their epidemiological study of Aberdeen boys, found that the average WISC vocabulary score of poor readers was well below that of matched controls. Lovell, Gray, and Oliver (1964) and Lovell, Shapton, and Warren (1964) found the same in retarded readers of both 10 years and 15 years. Malmqvist (1958), using retrospective reports, found that 21% of his poor readers had speech defects in the preschool period, compared with 12% of medium readers and 8% of good readers. Morris (1966) also found that speech defects and poor language development were associated with reading difficulties. Similarly, Lyle (1970) found that speech delay and speech defects were associated with reading retardation. Equally strong associations have been reported from investigations of clinic populations (Doehring, 1968; Hallgren, 1950).

The validity of the association between speech delay and reading retardation was confirmed in a follow-up study by Ingram (Ingram, 1970; Mason, 1967) of children with speech delay. Two years after starting school, a third of the speech-retarded children were backward in reading and spelling, compared with only 1 to 6% of the controls. The reading difficulties occurred both in children with a true delay in spoken language and in children with just an articulation defect. The same was found in Crookes and Greene's study (1963). Poor language was also a feature of the children with reading difficulties in de Hirsch's predictive study (de Hirsch, Jansky, & Langford, 1966b). The prevalence of language impairment among reading-retarded children is also shown by the pattern of verbal-performance discrepancies in which a verbal deficit is often found (see "WISC Verbal-Performance Discrepancies" above).

It may be concluded that speech and/or language delay is strongly associated with specific reading retardation. The consistency with which this is found, both in studies of reading-retarded children and in follow-up studies of children with speech delay, indicates that the association is basic and probably reflects causal influences. This is scarcely surprising, since reading concerns written language and speaking involves spoken language; an impairment in one form of language is likely to be associated with impairment in other forms. Nevertheless, it should be noted that the association also seems to apply to children with articulation defects who have no overt impairment in spoken-language skills. These cases may reflect different psychological mechanisms.

Audiovisual integration and sequencing

In an epidemiologically based sample of backward readers with an IQ of 80 or more, Birch and Belmont (1964) found that the poor readers did less well than controls on a task requiring the matching of an auditory tap pattern to a visual dot pattern. They suggested that a defect in cross-modal intersensory integration might be one important factor contributing to reading disability. It was further shown that skills in audiovisual integration were correlated with reading ability in the normal population (Birch & Belmont, 1965; Kahn & Birch, 1968). These findings have been broadly confirmed in a variety of other studies of both clinic children and ordinary school children (Beery, 1967; Blank & Bridger, 1966; Blank, Weider, & Bridger, 1968; Clark, 1970; Ford, 1967; Reilly, 1971), but there has been controversy over the mechanisms involved. Blank and her colleagues (Blank & Bridger, 1966; Blank et al., 1968) showed that retarded readers were equally poor at tasks which involved matching of two visual patterns, so that the cross-modal element did not appear to be essential. They noted that the most common method used by the children in the pattern-matching tasks was some kind of verbal coding. Differences between retarded readers and controls were less (and statistically insignificant) on a task involving

17

rhythm perception (but no coding of sequences). On this basis, they argued that a *verbal*-coding deficiency with respect to sequencing tasks was likely to be the basic handicap, rather than the perceptual deficit suggested by Birch and Belmont. This would be in keeping with Doehring's (1968) finding that impaired language skills and impaired sequential processing were the most characteristic deficits associated with reading retardation. Belmont, Birch, and Belmont (1968) showed that verbal skills were not correlated with audiovisual integrative performance in brain-damaged *adults*, some of whom were aphasic. This certainly means that audiovisual processing is not necessarily mediated verbally; but loss of language in an adult is not the same as failure to gain language in a child, and it does not follow that it is not a language defect which leads to poor processing in retarded readers.

Sterritt and Rudnick (1966) found that scores on the Birch-Belmont procedure were not related to reading independently of IQ. Testing using a pure auditory rhythm was so related; testing using pure light stimuli was not. On this basis, they argued that it was auditory perception, rather than intersensory processing, which was related to reading. However, this was studied within the normal range of reading skills and not in a reading-retarded group; it has been found that the factors associated with reading in the general population are not quite the same as those in a reading-retarded group (Lovell & Gorton, 1968).

It is evident that several skills may underlie performance of the pattern-matching task. These include language, auditory and visual perception, sequencing, and cross-modal intersensory integration. Which of these basic skills is most commonly defective in retarded readers cannot be determined from the published studies of pattern matching.

Right-left awareness

Although handedness has generally been found to follow a normal distribution among retarded readers (see "Handedness, Eyedness, and Footedness" above), right-left *awareness* has been found to be markedly impaired in epidemiological studies. Rutter, Tizard, and Whitmore (1970) found that twice as many retarded readers as controls (16% versus 8%) scored poorly on a test of right-left differentiation. Larger differences were reported by Belmont and Birch (1965) in their study of Aberdeen 9- and 10-year-olds, but right-left differentiation difficulties were not so marked in Clark's (1970) survey. Rosenberger (1970) also found laterality awareness impaired in children with poor reading. Harris (1957), in a study of clinic children, found confusion between right and left associated with reading disability at age 7, but not at age 9. Lovell, Gray, and Oliver (1964) found right-left confusion in 9- and 10-year-old retarded readers, but the difference from controls was quite small. Poor right-left discrimination has also been reported in several studies of "dyslexic" children attending clinics (see review by Vernon, 1971).

The nature of the disability underlying directional confusion remains uncertain. Benton and Kemble (1960) suggested that right-left orientation might be a function of verbal facility, but neither Belmont and Birch (1965) nor Rosenberger (1970) found that difficulties in laterality awareness were associated with low verbal IQ, so this factor does not seem to be an adequate explanation.

Perceptual difficulties

In order to be able to read, a child must be able to make perceptual distinctions involving both a differentiation of letter shapes (e.g., *s* from *t*) and of letter rotations (e.g., *b* from *p* and *d*). These perceptual skills systematically improve with age, as shown in a series of elegant studies by Gibson (1965), and it might be supposed that children with impaired visual perception would have difficulty in learning to read. Certainly, various types of visual-perceptual difficulties have been reported in "dyslexic" children (see review by Vernon, 1971) and in children with reading backwardness (Malmqvist, 1958); but such difficulties, at least in older children, seem less important than language impairment as causes of reading retardation, once IQ effects have been partialed out.

In the Isle of Wight study (Rutter, Tizard, & Whitmore, 1970) retarded readers tended to have poorer constructional abilities than controls, but this nonsignificant difference was lost if IQ was taken into account. Clark (1970) found that low scores on the Bender-Gestalt (B-G) test were associated with reading difficulties. Lachmann (1960) found this only in younger children. Lovell, Gray, and Oliver (1964) and Lovell, Shapton, and Warren (1964) showed that visual-perception difficulties were greater in younger retarded readers. Keogh (1965) and Keogh and Smith (1967) found that low B-G scores correlated with reading achievement, but the correlation was reduced to an insignificant level if IQ was held constant. In an epidemiological study of children in Hawaii, Werner, Simonion, and Smith (1967) found that reading was impaired in children with low verbal-comprehension scores, but the B-G did *not* add to the prediction of reading skills at 10 to 11 years. Visual-discrimination skills were found to be associated with reading difficulties by Whipple and Kodman (1969) and by Lyle and Goyen (1968), but not by Bonsall and Dornbush (1969). Lyle and Goyen (1968) found that perceptual skills were most impaired in the young children with reading difficulties. Olson (1966) found that scores on the Frostig tests of visual perception correlated as highly with IQ as with reading. Malmqvist (1958) found that visual perception correlated more highly with IQ than with reading. Golden and Steiner (1969), Bruininks (1969), and Lingren (1969) found that poor readers were more impaired in auditory than in visual functions. Finger agnosia has been said to be characteristic of dyslexics, but Lyle (1969) did not find it so. Doehring (1968) and Rosenberger (1970) found that visual-perceptual difficulties in children with reading disability primarily involved difficulties in sequencing, which would seem to put the defect more in the group of factors associated with linguistic skills.

The evidence is somewhat contradictory, and very few of the studies used epidemilogically based samples of read-retarded children. However, it may be suggested that visual-perceptual difficulties are not consistently associated with reading retardation in older children, although they may be more important in younger children.

Motor incoordination

Clumsiness has been noted in several clinical studies of "dyslexic" children (Critchley, 1970; Rabinovitch, Drew, De Jong, Ingram, & Withey, 1954), and was found to be associated with specific reading retardation in the Isle of Wight studies (Rutter, Tizard, & Whitmore, 1970). Conversely, children identified because of a severe coordination difficulty often have educational difficulties (Brenner & Gillman, 1966; Gubbay, Ellis, Walton, & Court, 1965). These educational difficulties are as great in other attainments as in reading, or greater. This is in keeping with the finding (see above) that motor difficulties are more strongly associated with general reading backwardness than with specific reading retardation. It would appear that problems in motor coordination show some association with reading skills, but the association is neither very strong nor very specific; however, it may be important in individual children.

Motor impersistence

Motor impersistence is a term that has been used to denote an inability to sustain a voluntary motor act that has been initiated on verbal command. The developmental phenomenon known as *motor persistence* is age-related and tends to be impaired by brain damage (Rutter, Graham, & Yule, 1970). In the Isle of Wight studies (Rutter, Tizard, & Whitmore, 1970), three times as many reading-retarded children as control children obtained low scores on the motor-impersistence test devised by Garfield (1964). The nature of the phenomenon is ill-understood, but it seems to be related to distractibility, short attention span, and poor motor control.

Choreiform movements

The term *choreiform movements* was coined by Prechtl and Stemmer (1962) to describe certain slight, jerky movements, sudden and of short duration, which occurred quite irregularly and arrhythmically in different muscles. It was suggested that these movements were associated with reading difficulties; Wolff and Hurwitz (1966) reported a high prevalence among neurotic and borderline psychotic children attending a psychiatric clinic for learning difficulties. However, this association was not found in the Aberdeen (Rutter, Graham, & Birch, 1966), Isle of Wight (Rutter, Tizard, & Whitmore, 1970), or Dutch (Stemmer, 1964) epidemiological studies, so that the association is almost certainly an artifact or referral biases to clinics.

Specific developmental functions associated with reading retardation

It is evident that quite a wide range of cortical functions are associated with reading skills, and a variety of impairments have been associated with specific reading retardation. It is also clear that there is no one unitary syndrome of developmental impairment which underlies reading retardation. Speech and language difficulties and problems in sequencing are those manifestations most strongly and consistently associated with reading retardation, but right-left confusion, motor impersistence, weak sensory integration, and poor motor coordination are also important to a lesser degree; visual-perceptual difficulties may also be influential, perhaps especially in younger children with reading retardation.

"Maturational delay"

It is commonly suggested that specific reading retardation is due to a relative failure in the normal maturation of certain specific functions of the cerebral cortex (Critchley, 1970; Vernon, 1971). The chief evidence in support of this view is that most of the developmental disabilities associated with reading retardation are normal in younger children; there is a characteristic increase in competence with age. The limited evidence also suggests that these developmental disabilities also lessen in reading-retarded children as they grow older, but it is uncertain whether normal competence in the developmental functions is always achieved. Against the maturational-delay hypothesis is the general finding that reading-retarded children rarely become fluent readers, and many are left with persistent spelling difficulties. However, the continuation of reading difficulties, in spite of the diminution in developmental disabilities, might be partially a function of inadequate education at that point in later childhood when developmental problems have diminished. The presence of overt neurological disorders and a history of perinatal complications in some reading-retarded children suggests that actual dysfunction of the brain is involved in this minority subgroup. However, brain dysfunction accounts for only a few children with specific reading retardation. The presence of adverse social factors in some reading-retarded children also suggests that the developmental delay may have been due, at least in part, and in these cases, to inadequate environmental stimulation rather than an organic slowing of brain development.

The findings are far from conclusive, and the supposed delay in brain maturation is purely hypothetical at the moment, since maturation cannot be directly measured in living subjects. Nevertheless, the hypothesis that particular brain functions might be specifically delayed, in spite of normal development of the rest of the brain, would be consonant with what is known of brain growth. The brain does not normally develop at a uniform rate (Marshall, 1968). Normally, some parts are advanced in maturation over others, and it would only be an extension of this observation to postulate that abnormal delays might also involve only certain specific brain functions. It is unknown whether, in fact, this happens.

NEUROLOGICAL ASPECTS

Neurological disorder

Very few children with specific reading retardation have frank neurological disorders such as cerebral palsy. There were no cases of definite disorders of this type among the 86 children with specific reading retardation in the Isle of Wight total population study of 9- and 10-year-old children (Rutter, Tizard, & Whitmore, 1970). All subjects received a standardized neurological assessment. Even in Ingram's selected sample of children referred to neurological or speech clinics, only 5% of those with specific reading difficulties had cerebral palsy or epilepsy (Ingram et al., 1970). It has already been noted that overt neurological disorder is *less* frequently associated

21

with specific reading retardation than with general reading backwardness.

Nevertheless, it would be wrong to conclude that there is no association between neurological disorder and specific reading retardation. In a total population survey of 5- to 15-year-old children (also on the Isle of Wight), it was found that 18% of epileptic children and 40% of those with cerebral palsy or other brain conditions had a specific reading retardation of at least 24 months below prediction – a rate several times that of the control group (Rutter, Graham, & Yule, 1970). At first, this seems inconsistent with the above finding that few children with specific reading retardation have cerebral palsy. The explanation lies in the relative frequency of cerebral palsy and specific reading retardation, and in the IQ distribution of children with cerebral palsy. Specific reading retardation (of 24 months' severity) occurred in 68 children per 1,000 on the Isle of Wight,[4] compared with a rate of only 2.9 per 1,000 for cerebral palsy. Thus, specific reading retardation is 23 times as common as cerebral palsy. As an IQ of at least 70 is necessary for children to have specific reading retardation (as so defined), and as only about half of cerebral palsied children have an IQ above this, it follows that even if *all* cerebral palsied children of IQ 70 or more had specific reading retardation (and in fact less than half do), this would still only amount to less than 2 children out of 86 (the number of children with specific reading retardation in the Isle of Wight study). Thus, the correct conclusion, although it sounds paradoxical, is that scarcely any children with specific reading retardation have cerebral palsy, but that specific reading retardation is very common in cerebral palsied children!

Minor neurological signs

Minor, or soft, neurological signs, as distinct from overt neurological abnormality, are much more common in reading-retarded children, but it is doubtful whether the designation is very meaningful. The signs seem to fall into three distinct groups, the pooling of which can only lead to confusion (Rutter, Graham, & Yule, 1970). The first group consists of signs of developmental delay in functions such as speech language, motor coordination, perception, right-left differentiation, and the like. For the most part, these signs can be reliably identified and quantified; they are not equivocal, and they do not necessarily concern minor abnormalities; but they are often best assessed by psychometric rather than neurological methods. Developmental delays of this sort are strongly associated with specific reading retardation and have been considered separately above under appropriate headings. The second group of soft signs consists of those in which the abnormality may be due to either neurological or nonneurological factors (e.g., nystagmus, strabismus). As far as is known, these signs are not particularly associated with specific reading retardation (Rutter, Tizard, & Whitmore, 1970). The third group consists of slight abnormalities

---

[4]This is a higher figure than that given in the "Prevalence" section because a 24-month rather than a 28-month cutoff was used for examining associations with cerebral palsy.

which are difficult to detect, such as slight asymmetries of tone or reflexes. The softness of these signs resides in the demonstrated unreliability of judgments concerning their presence (Rutter, Graham, & Yule, 1970). Because of their unreliability, these signs will not be discussed further with respect to specific reading retardation.

Electroencephalographic (EEG) findings

There are no published studies of EEG findings for an epidemiologically based sample of children with specific reading retardation, and no specific association between EEG characteristics and specific reading retardation has been unequivocally demonstrated (Benton & Bird, 1963; Hughes, 1968). A variety of uncontrolled clinical studies of selected groups have suggested that 6- and 14-per-second positive spikes and excessive posterior slow activity are particularly associated with reading difficulties, but in the absence of controls and "blind" evaluation of records (i.e., without knowledge of whether the EEG is from a case or control), little can be concluded from these observations. Ayers and Torres (1967) reported one of the few controlled studies with "blind" reading of the EEG. Children of normal IQ with reading difficulties who attended a clinic and a similar group in remedial-reading classes were compared with controls. About half the children with reading difficulties had an abnormal EEG, compared with 29% in the controls. That the finding may have some meaning is indicated by a similar difference between the best and worst readers within the *control* group. On the other hand, Hughes's (1968) EEG study of a mixed group of clinic children with learning difficulties showed that within this group, low scores in reading and spelling were significantly associated with a *normal* EEG. Similarly, Muehl, Knott, and Benton (1965) found that within a group of children attending a reading clinic, abnormal EEGs were more common in those with the *least* reading retardation. No conclusions are possible on the association between EEG findings and specific reading retardation; this remains an area where research is badly needed.

Perinatal complications

Kawi and Pasamanick (1959) reported that boys of IQ 85 or more with reading disorders had a rate of perinatal abnormalities several times that of their control group. They argued on this basis that reproductive complications played a major role in the cause of reading problems; however, only a proportion of the children had specific reading retardation. The population was clinic-based, and it was not possible to take social influences into account. For all these reasons, caution is necessary in generalizing from Kawi and Pasamanick's findings, particularly as other studies have found a much weaker association between perinatal complications and specific reading retardation. In the Isle of Wight study (Rutter, Tizard, & Whitmore, 1970), children with specific reading retardation included a higher proportion of premature babies than the controls (16% born at 37 weeks or earlier, compared with 10%), more of low birth weight (12% below 5½ pounds, compared with 7%), and more who were small in relation to gestational age (6% as against 4%); but none of the differences reached the .05 level of statistical significance. The data were derived from parental report and thereby subject to some error. Malmqvist (1958) also found an association between low birth weight and poor reading — the difference between poor readers (9% under 2,500 gm), medium readers (3%), and good readers (2%) being significant at the .05 level. There were similar differences for birth before 38 weeks of gestation. Lyle (1970) found no significant association between birth weight (or other perinatal complications) and reading retardation.

Follow-up studies of children of low birth weight have shown that a disproportionate number are intellectually backward (Birch & Gussow, 1970), but the association with reading difficulties appeared less strong (Barker & Edwards, 1967; de Hirsch et al., 1966a). In the British National Child Development Study (Davie et al., 1972), there was a significant association at age 7 years between low birth weight and reading attainment, but it accounted for far less of the variance than did social factors; IQ was not taken into account. The evidence is not altogether satisfactory, as so few studies have been specifically concerned with reading retardation. Most have examined reading levels in relation to perinatal factors, without first partialing out the (known) association with general intelligence. Taken overall, the findings suggest a weak (but possibly meaningful) association between low birth weight and specific reading retardation. To some extent this may reflect neurological abnormality, but low birth weight tends to be accompanied by a variety of adverse social circumstances, and it is quite uncertain to what extent the former represents neurological dysfunction or social handicap.

Postnatal disease

Some early studies (Burt, 1950; Eames, 1948) suggested that minor ill health was more common among children with educational difficulties than in the general population, but this has not been found in more recent studies of reading-retarded children (Malmqvist, 1958; Rutter, Tizard, & Whitmore, 1970). Severe illnesses involving possible brain damage may contribute to reading retardation in some cases, but considering the group as a whole, a history of such an illness is quite rare. In the Isle of Wight study (Rutter, Tizard, & Whitmore, 1970), no reading-retarded children had had meningitis, and only 2.4% (compared with 1.4% in the controls) had had an incident involving loss of consciousness for 10 minutes or more (excluding fits). Malmqvist (1958) also found no difference between good and poor readers with respect to either neurological diseases or head injuries. In a follow-up study of children who had had meningitis, Lawson, Metcalfe, and Pampiglione (1965) found that of those who had had nonbacterial meningitis, half had school attainments (not necessarily in reading) which were judged below expectation on the basis of IQ, compared with a quarter of those who had had bacterial meningitis. This implies that poor school attainment may sometimes be a sequel to meningitis, but the epidemiological studies noted above suggest that meningitis is a very unusual cause of specific reading retardation.

Although encephalitis is a rare complication of measles, some studies have suggested that there may sometimes be subclinical damage to the brain, leading to later reading difficulties. This possibility was recently examined in a systematic set of epidemiological studies in New Haven, Conn.; New York State; and a suburb in the state of Washington (Black & Davis, 1968; Black, Fox, Elveback, Kogon, 1968; Fox, Black, Elveback, Kogon, Hall, Turgeon, & Abruzzi, 1968; Fox, Black, & Kogon, 1968; Kogon, Hall, Cooney, & Fox, 1968). Measles was assessed both serologically and by history, and reading-readiness tests were given to children at the end of the kindergarten year. There was a small but significant impairment of reading-readiness score associated with measles in two out of the three studies, but circumstantial evidence suggested that even the small difference in the first two studies may have been an artifact due to associations between measles and environmental influences. An earlier British study (Douglas, 1964) had shown no connection between measles and school attainment. Neither set of studies dealt with specific reading retardation, but the findings, together with Malmqvist's (1958) failure to find any association between childhood exanthemata and reading difficulties, suggest that measles or any other postnatal disease plays little if any part in the genesis of specific reading retardation.

Delayed physical maturation

Interest in the concept of specific maturational delay (see above) has led some workers to assess the general physical maturation of retarded readers. One method of assessment is an X ray of the wrist and hand in order to determine the developmental stage of the small bones in this region. It is thus possible to obtain a bone-age score reflecting skeletal maturity. In the Isle of Wight study (Rutter, Tizard, & Whitmore, 1970), 19% of reading-retarded boys had a score below the 10th percentile for children of that age, compared with 8% of controls. This difference fell short of statistical significance, but in view of a similar finding based on a clinic population (Frisk, Wegelius, Tenhunen, Widholm, & Hortling, 1967; Frisk, Holström, & Wasz-Höckert, 1967), the matter warrants further investigation.

VISUAL AND OCULAR FACTORS

In both the Swedish (Malmqvist, 1958) and Isle of Wight (Rutter, Tizard, & Whitmore, 1970) studies, reading-retarded children had vision as good as vision in children from the general population. These negative findings are entirely consonant with the clinic studies which have also failed to find any association between reading retardation and impaired acuity, refractive errors, or orthoptic disorders (Flax, 1967; Lawson, 1968; Norn, Rindziunski, & Skydsgaard, 1969).

The question of eye movements has also aroused some interest (Gaarder, 1970; Tinker, 1958); it has been suggested that impaired control of eye movements might lead to difficulties in learning to read (Prechtl & Stemmer, 1962). There seems to be some association between irregularity of eye movements and difficulty in reading, but it is doubtful whether the irregularity in eye movements is in any sense causal. The control of eye movements is related to both CA and MA, and control is often impaired in cerebral palsied subjects (Abercrombie, Davis, & Shackel, 1963). In the Abercrombie study, movements were unrelated to reading attainment in the cerebral palsy group but were related in the normal group. This suggests that abnormal eye movements as such do not lead to reading difficulties. Peterson (1969), using a tachistoscope with third-grade children, found no association between patterns of eye movements and reading comprehension. Goldberg and Arnott (1970) reported that within a group of dyslexic children, eye movements were normal when the children read words within their capacity but were abnormal when they read words which they found difficult; unfortunately, no details of findings were given. Again, there is a lack of studies on children with specific reading retardation; but investigations of children with a wider range of reading difficulties suggest that although there may be some association between eye movements and reading skills, it is unlikely that impaired eye movements play a significant role in the etiology of the condition.

GENETICS

Although "constitutional origin" forms part of the definition of "specific developmental dyslexia" (Critchley, 1970), surprisingly little is known about genetic influences in dyslexia or in any other variety of specific reading retardation. This question may best be examined by studies of twins. There have been a few isolated case reports of twins with reading retardation (see Hallgren, 1950), but the only substantial series were those collected by Norrie and Hallgren and brought together by Hermann (1959). There was 100% concordance in the 12 monozygotic pairs and 33% concordance in the 33 dizygotic pairs. This appears to be strong evidence for hereditary influences, but there are difficulties in interpretation. First, for the finding to have any validity, it is essential that the collection of twins be both unselective and comprehensive; otherwise selective biases may seriously distort the results (Shields & Slater, 1960). It is unclear how far this was the case in the published series. Second, reading difficulties are on a continuum; therefore, explicit and unambiguous diagnostic criteria are essential. Unfortunately, they were not provided. Third, twin studies do not allow the differentiation between a single gene inheritance of a *condition* and the polygenic inheritance of a *skill*. In other words, is it the normally distributed reading ability which is inherited, or is it the abnormal condition of specific reading retardation? There is abundant evidence of an important genetic component in the development of reading ability (Jensen, 1969; Mittler, 1971), but a lack of evidence on the question of the separate inheritance of a specific *dis*ability in reading.

Other evidence is provided by family studies. Most reports have emphasised the frequency with which several family members, apart from the child being studied, suffer from specific reading difficulties (Critchley, 1970; Vernon, 1971). Particular emphasis has usually been laid on Hallgren's thorough study of "dyslexic" individuals (1950). He found that 88% of his cases had relatives with similar reading difficulties.

About two-fifths of the parents and a similar proportion of the siblings had "specific dyslexia." Unfortunately, this finding means little in the absence of a control group and diagnostic criteria (in particular, the lack of any guide as to the severity of reading difficulties required for the diagnosis). That biases entered the findings is suggested by the sex distribution of "dyslexia" in the relatives. Whereas boys greatly predominated among the cases (as in virtually all other studies; see "Dyslexia" above), dyslexia in the relatives occurred with approximately the same frequency in both sexes. As this is so dissonant with all that is known on the sex distribution of specific reading retardation or dyslexia, the probable explanation lies in reporting or diagnostic biases.

Better evidence is provided by studies using control groups. Doehring (1968) reported reading problems in parents or siblings in 22 out of 37 cases of reading retardation, compared with only 8 such problems out of 36 cases in the control group. Similarly, in the Isle of Wight study (Rutter, Tizard, & Whitmore, 1970), 34% of the children with specific reading retardation had parents or siblings with reading difficulties, compared with 9% of controls. Put another way, 7½% of the individual members of retarded readers' families reported reading difficulties, compared with 2½% among the family members of controls. Unfortunately, when it is necessary to rely on parents' memory of their schooling, it is not possible to differentiate adequately between *specific* reading difficulties and *general* learning difficulties. Thus, in the Isle of Wight study, a similar difference between cases and controls was found for general backwardness. Accordingly, whereas it may safely be concluded that there is frequently a family history of difficulties in learning to read, it remains uncertain how much these difficulties in relatives are due to specific reading retardation and how much to more general cognitive or motivational problems.

Furthermore, it is unclear how far the family history represents a biological inheritance and how far a social transmission. For example, parents who themselves read badly may inculcate in the child a negative attitude toward reading, may be unable to instruct the child in how to read, may provide inadequate verbal or other stimulation, and may not establish a milieu in which books are available and libraries are visited. That this kind of social transmission does indeed account for part of the association between individual and family histories of reading difficulties is suggested by the finding that a family history of reading difficulties was much more common in children from large families (Rutter, Tizard, & Whitmore, 1970). There is no straightforward genetic reason to account for that finding, whereas there are possible social explanations (see section below).

In short, the evidence on genetic factors is disappointingly inconclusive. Both the twin and family studies suggest the probability of some type of hereditary influence, but it is unknown how far reading skills in general are inherited and how far there is inheritance of a specific condition of reading retardation. It appears that the high rate of reading difficulties in the parents acts in part through its social influence on parent-child interaction, but it is unclear how much of the association is explicable in this way.

SOCIAL AND FAMILIAL INFLUENCES

Because most studies of specific reading retardation have used a neurological concept of dyslexia and thus ignored sociofamilial influences, and because most studies of social and familial factors have failed to differentiate specific reading retardation from general reading backwardness, there is a regrettable lack of information on this topic. However, some data are available in several areas.

Family size

The Isle of Wight study found a strong association between large family size and specific reading retardation (Rutter, Tizard, & Whitmore, 1970). Of the reading-retarded children, 58% came from families with four or more children, compared with only 33% of the controls. The percentage differences in Malmqvist's investigation (1958) and in the London study (Sturge, 1972) were in the same direction but much less marked and short of statistical significance. Many other epidemiological studies showed marked associations between large family size and poor reading attainment, but most have not partialed out the effect of general intelligence. In her study of Kent primary school children, Morris (1966) found that 22% of the poor readers had more than three siblings, compared with only 5% of the good readers. In his large national sample, Douglas (Douglas, 1964; Douglas, Ross, & Simpson, 1968) showed that large family size was associated with lower mean scores on vocabulary and reading. This association held even within social-class groupings. Nisbet (Nisbet, 1953; Nisbet & Entwistle, 1967) also showed that the association with family size was greater for verbal than for nonverbal abilities. This was implied, too, by the British National Child Development Study finding (Davie et al., 1972) that large family size is strongly associated with attainment in reading (at age 7), but only very slightly with attainment in arithmetic.

That family size is quite strongly associated with reading attainment and verbal skills can be taken as well established. It appears likely that it is also associated with specific reading retardation, but this is less certain and needs confirmation. The mechanism underlying the association remains in doubt. Oldman, Bytheway, and Horobin (1971) argued that family size was important only through its association with deviant parental characteristics. Unfortunately, their analysis was based on associations between family size and nonverbal IQ; these associations, as already noted, are neither so strong nor so consistent as associations with reading and verbal skills. Nisbet (1953) and Douglas (Douglas, Ross, & Simpson, 1968) argued that the influence of family size is probably felt through language, on the grounds that the association of family size and verbal skills is so marked; that the effect is maximal by age 8; and that the adverse effects of family size are increased by the presence of younger children in the home. The last finding was also confirmed by Davie et al. (1972). It was suggested that verbal development is affected by the extent to which children, when learning to talk, come into contact with other preschool children whose vocabularies and elementary grammar offer little verbal stimulation, rather than with adults whose language is richer and more varied. On the other hand, it may be the clarity and meaningfulness of stimuli, rather than the complexity of stimulation, which are most important (Rutter, 1972). The probably greater amount of conflicting cross-talk when a large family is gathered together may make it difficult for the young child to make sense of what is being said.

Social class

There are a host of studies (e.g., Davie et al., 1972; Douglas, Ross, & Simpson, 1968; Kelsall & Kelsall, 1971) showing that working-class children have, on the average, lower scholastic attainments than do middle-class children. This effect is most marked at the bottom of the occupational range (i.e., the offspring of laborers and semiskilled workers), with smaller differences in the middle of the social-class distribution. It is questionable whether this association of class and scholastic attainment applies to any marked extent to specific reading retardation. Certainly the pattern of associations differs from that found with family size. Whereas large family size is particularly associated with reading and verbal skills, low social class is associated with low scores on IQ tests and *all* types of attainment tests; but the association of class with reading is much less specific. Morris (1959) found that when the correlation between social class and nonverbal IQ was partialed out, only a low and nonsignificant correlation between social class and reading was left. Malmqvist (1958) found an association between reading ability and social group but did not partial out the effect of low IQ. The Isle of Wight (Rutter, Tizard, & Whitmore, 1970) and London (Sturge, 1972) studies found only a slight association between occupation of the father and specific reading retardation. Moreover, the difference that was found referred to a paucity of parents with nonmanual jobs and an excess of *skilled* manual jobs, rather than an excess at the lower end of the scale. The association was only with current social class; there was no association with social origins of the parents. This also tended to be the case in the British National Child Development Study (Davie et al., 1972).

The matter remains unsettled. There may be a slight tendency for specific reading retardation to be less common in the children of nonmanual workers, but the association is probably not very strong and not specifically with reading skills.

Educational interest and opportunities in the home

There have been many studies showing that children with general reading backwardness often come from homes with a paucity of books and other reading material; the parents show slight interest in their children's school programs and do little to aid learning (Davie et al., 1972; Douglas, 1964; Malmqvist, 1958; Morris, 1966; Wiseman, 1964, 1967). It is uncertain to what extent these factors are associated with specific reading retardation. Sturge (1972) found that a scarcity of books in the home was associated with specific reading retardation only when the children showed antisocial behavior as well. The variables were not included in the Isle of Wight study.

While it seems reasonable to suppose that a lack of educational interests and opportunities at home might predispose a child to specific reading retardation, there is no adequate evidence to support or reject the hypothesis.

Family disruption

Broken homes were found to have no association with specific reading retardation in the Isle of Wight study (Rutter, Tizard, & Whitmore, 1970), and no association was found between broken homes and reading difficulties in studies by Malmqvist (1958) and Morris (1966). In the British National Child Development Study (Davie et al., 1972), broken homes showed a slight association with reading attainment in the upper social group, but not at all in the children of semiskilled or unskilled workers. Clinic studies vary widely in their findings on family characteristics, presumably reflecting differing referral policies. Specific patterns of family relationships have been said to be associated with reading disability (e.g., Miller & Westman, 1964), but in the absence of controlled studies of representative populations, it is not possible to draw any conclusions. On the extremely limited evidence available, it appears that broken homes are probably not particularly associated with specific reading retardation, but it is impossible to say whether or not there are other aspects of family relationships which are important in this connection.

Family history of reading difficulties

The section on genetics (above) outlined the evidence that children with specific reading retardation frequently have parents who also had difficulties learning to read. It is mentioned here only as a reminder that social as well as a biological factors are involved. Parents who themselves are poor readers are less likely to be able to help their children to read and may readily convey an attitude that reading is difficult and unrewarding, thus influencing the child's attitude toward learning.

SCHOOL INFLUENCES

There have been many studies which examined associations between school characteristics and reading attainments of children. (Coleman, Campbell, Hobson, McPortland, Mood, Weinfeld, & York, 1966; Davie et al., 1972; Malmqvist, 1958; Morris, 1966; Rutter, Yule, Quinton, Rowlands, Yule, & Berger, 1973; Wiseman, 1964, 1967). It has been found, for example, that the social mix of pupils, amount of teacher and child turnover, and caliber and experience of the teachers are all influential. Curiously, large class size is, if anything, associated with better reading attainment in the children (Davie, 1971; Davie et al., 1972; Little, Mabey, & Russell, 1971; Morris, 1966); therefore, although it is desirable for other reasons to reduce class sizes, this is unlikely in itself to improve reading standards. If the reduction in class size is to benefit reading, it is probably necessary for the teacher to provide more individual help.

Specific teaching skills are also likely to be important. A preliminary study by Yule and Rigley (1970) showed that the in-service training of elementary school teachers (of 7-year-old children) resulted in the children making 2 months' greater progress in reading than the children in control classes. On the whole, the precise method of teaching reading is less important, but an emphasis on phonic methods at the start seems to lead to fewer serious reading problems (Chall, 1967). These findings are important, but they do not refer to children with specific reading retardation. They certainly indicate the great likelihood that school influences will prove to be important with reading-retarded children, but this possibility needs to be specifically investigated.

TEMPERAMENTAL CHARACTERISTICS

All investigators who have looked for associations between children's temperamental attributes and specific reading retardation have found them to be strong. In the Isle of Wight study (Rutter, Tizard, & Whitmore, 1970), the trait most characteristic of the reading-retarded children was poor concentration; this was reported in the majority of such children, the rate being over twice that found in the controls. Overactivity and fidgetiness were also common, the rate being again twice that in the controls. Exactly the same findings emerged from the London study of boys with specific reading retardation (Sturge, 1972). As these traits are also fairly common in antisocial children, it is important to note that both investigations found poor concentration to be more strongly associated with reading retardation than with antisocial disorder. Furthermore, poor concentration was still a feature of the reading-retarded boys who had *no* antisocial problems. Of course, it could be argued that the children concentrated poorly because of their difficulty in reading, rather than the other way around. While this could well account for the teacher's reports of poor concentration and fidgetiness, it is unlikely to account for judgments made at a psychiatric interview (which involved no reading) and ratings based on parent interviews about the children's concentration on the tasks they enjoyed (Rutter, Tizard, & Whitmore, 1970; Sturge, 1972).

Malmqvist (1958) found that the traits of concentration, persistence, self-confidence, and dominance were correlated with reading ability (correlations of .3 to .5) in a general population sample. De Hirsch et al. (1966b) found that the characteristics of "hyperactive, distractible, impulsive, and disinhibited" were associated with poor reading in their predictive study. In neither of these studies was IQ taken into account. In a study of children attending one village primary school, Gregory (1965), too, found that restlessness was strongly associated with poor reading. As the association was as marked at 6 to 7 years of age as at 8 to 10 years, he suggested that the restlessness was probably not a response to reading failure but possibly a contributory cause of reading failure. Kagan (1965) found that 6-year-old children who were impulsive and quick to jump to conclusions read less well than reflective, more deliberate children.

The origin of these temperamental attributes remains uncertain, and the mechanism by which they are associated with specific reading retardation is also ill understood. However, as Chall (1970) pointed out, attention is an important part of learning to read (as with any other learning task), and pupils who have difficulty maintaining their attention because of impulsiveness, restlessness, distractibility, or short attention span are likely to be impaired in their reading skills.

ASSOCIATION OF READING PROBLEMS WITH ANTISOCIAL BEHAVIOR

It has long been known that maladjustment and delinquency are frequently accompanied by severe reading difficulties (see, for example Burt, 1925; Burt & Howard, 1952; Chazan, 1969; Critchley, 1968; Fendrick & Bond, 1936; Gibbens, 1963; Glueck & Glueck, 1950; Millar, 1969; Roe, 1965; Rutter, Tizard, & Whitmore, 1970; Sampson, 1966). Many writers have commented on the emotional problems shown by many reading-retarded children (Gates, 1968; Hallgren, 1950). However, until recently there has been surprisingly little interest in the association between reading retardation and antisocial disorder.

Several issues arise from these observations. Many of the reports concerned clinic or institutional groups, so that the association of antisocial behavior and reading problems might be seen as a function of referral biases. However, this is not the case. Several epidemiological studies of the general population clearly showed a strong association between educational difficulties and behavioral problems (Clark, 1970; Douglas, 1964; Douglas, Ross, & Simpson, 1968; Malmqvist, 1958; Morris, 1966; Rutter, 1970b). As the average IQ of delinquents is only a little below that of the general population (Woodward, 1955a, b), these findings imply that delinquency is associated with specific reading retardation and not just general backwardness. That this is indeed the case was shown in the Isle of Wight study (Rutter, Tizard, & Whitmore, 1970). Of the children with specific reading retardation, one-quarter showed antisocial behavior as measured on a questionnaire completed by teachers (Rutter, 1967) — a rate several times that in the population at large. Similarly, of the children showing antisocial disorder (diagnosed on the basis of information from parents, teachers, and the children themselves), one-third were at least 28 months retarded in their reading (after IQ was partialed out), compared with 4% in the general population.

The question arises whether the association of behavior and reading problems specifically refers to antisocial disorders or to all types of emotional or behavioral disturbance. Both the Dunbartonshire (Clark, 1970) and Isle of Wight surveys (Rutter, Tizard, & Whitmore, 1970) found that although there was a tendency among reading-retarded children to an increased rate of emotional disturbance, much the stronger association was with reading retardation and antisocial behavior. It was notable that the association was not just with delinquency. Reading retardation was as common among antisocial and aggressive children who were *not* overtly delinquent as among those who had transgressed the law (Rutter, Tizard, & Whitmore, 1970).

Perhaps the most important question concerns the nature of the association. Opinions abound, but there is a remarkable lack of clear-cut evidence. Various methods have been employed to tackle the problem. First, there is the matter of timing. Retrospective information indicates that antisocial problems often begin after the child has fallen behind in reading (Malmqvist, 1958; Rutter, Tizard, & Whitmore, 1970); but such information is unreliable. Prospective studies of preschool children are needed. An alternative approach is to see the effects on behavior of improving reading by remedial techniques; little has been achieved in this connection. Gates and Bond (1936) reported a study which claimed to show that coaching in reading led to better conduct and classroom adjustment. Unfortunately, too few details were given for an adequate evaluation of the study. In another study of a very small group of children, Margolin, Roman, & Harai (1955) suggested that delinquents with reading retardation made somewhat better progress when they received both remedial reading and psychotherapy then when they had either alone. However, the numbers were small and the differences not statistically significant. The only two systematic and controlled comparisons were somewhat at variance. Schiffman (1962) found that remedial reading was more effective than psychotherapy in improving reading achievement. Conversely, Lawrence (1971) found that counseling was more effective than remedial reading, in terms of greater gains in reading. Neither study was particularly concerned with specific reading retardation, and further work is obviously needed.

The most fruitful approach was a study of children with both specific reading retardation and antisocial disorder, to determine if they had more in common with purely antisocial children or with purely reading-retarded children. This technique was used in the Isle of Wight survey by Rutter, Tizard, & Whitmore (1970) and in the London survey by Sturge (1972). In the former, pure reading retardation was associated with large family size, a family history of reading difficulties, speech delay, poor right-left differentiation, and very poor concentration. In all these respects, the antisocial retarded readers were closely similar to the pure retarded readers. On the other hand, pure antisocial behavior was associated with a broken home, but this association was not found with either pure reading retardation or a mixture of reading retardation and antisocial behavior. In other words, the antisocial retarded readers were much more like the pure retarded readers than the pure antisocial children. On these grounds, it was suggested that in some cases, antisocial disorder might arise as a result of educational failure. With status and satisfaction denied him through school work, the reading-retarded child might rebel and seek satisfaction in activities running counter to everything for which the school stood. If this tentative suggestion should be proved accurate, correct teaching at the appropriate time might help prevent the development of some forms of delinquent behavior.

While there is some circumstantial evidence in support of this being one mechanism involved in the association between reading retardation and antisocial behavior, the London findings clearly indicated that it is unlikely to be the *only* mechanism. The London analysis was complicated by the fact that there was not so clear a demarcation between factors leading to reading retardation and factors leading to antisocial behavior. However, poor concentration and motor restlessness were strongly associated with pure reading retardation. As in the Isle of Wight study, this was also the case with reading retardation when it occurred together with antisocial behavior, but not with pure antisocial behavior. Broken homes, family discord, and criminal behavior in the father were strongly associated with antisocial disorder in the sons, but there was also a similar although lesser association of the above-mentioned family factors with pure reading retardation. In this case, reading retardation in conjunction with antisocial disorder occupied an intermediate position, which seems to rule out antisocial disorder arising solely as a reaction to educational failure. Curiously, one factor shown in several previous studies to be associated with reading difficulties — namely, a lack of books in the home — was strongly associated with reading retardation plus antisocial disorder, but not with pure reading retardation.

The findings are complex, and it is likely that the mechanisms underlying the association of antisocial behavior and reading retardation are equally complex. Taken altogether, the findings suggest that at least three processes are operating: First, at least in a big-city population, family influences leading to reading retardation overlap considerably with family influences leading to antisocial behavior. The association between reading retardation and antisocial behavior, in this case, is merely a function of the underlying association between background factors. This is another example of the truism that a depriving environment tends to be depriving in many respects — not just in one element necessary for normal child development (Rutter, 1972). Second, there are probably features of the child which tend to lead to both types of handicap (i.e., reading retardation and antisocial disorder). To some extent, the temperamental features leading to behavioral difficulties (Graham & George, 1972; Rutter, Birch, Thomas, & Chess, 1964; Thomas, Chess, & Birch, 1968) probably overlap with those which predispose to difficulties in learning to read. Furthermore, it is known that organic brain dysfunction predisposes to both reading retardation and behavioral disorder (Rutter, Graham, & Yule, 1970); insofar as organic brain dysfunction is a factor in the causation of some cases of specific reading retardation, this, too, would lead to the association with antisocial disorder. Third, because reading is an essential skill in schooling, reading failure itself may be a potent source of discouragement, loss of self-esteem, and antagonism, which in some cases may contribute to the development of delinquent activities.

COURSE AND FOLLOW-UP

Specific reading retardation tends to be a persistent handicap. Of the 86 reading-retarded children identified at 9 to 10 years in the Isle of Wight study (Rutter, Tizard, & Whitmore, 1970), all but 1 were at least 2 years behind in reading when followed up at 12 years. During the intervening 28 months, the average progress in reading accuracy was only 10 months! *All* the children were still reading at below age level. The situation at age 14 was only slightly better (Yule, 1973). Eleven children were reading within 1 standard deviation below the mean, and the average reading-accuracy attainment was still only 8 years-10 months. Of Morris's (1966) group of poor readers (identified at age 9), over half were still semiliterate or markedly backward when they reached school-leaving age. Of Clark's (1970) 7-year-old backward readers, half were still at least 2 years backward at age 10.

Morris (1966) found that poor home circumstances tended to impede progress, but otherwise none of the studies has found clear distinguishing features between the retarded readers who continue to read poorly and those who progress. Silver and Hagin (1964) reported that organic factors of a neurological kind tended to be associated with a worse prognosis in a clinic group, but their findings were not reported in a way which allowed a differentiation between organic factors and more severe reading retardation (which also led to a worse outcome). Lytton (1968) compared eight boys who made good progress with remedial teaching with eight who made little progress. The poor achievers were differentiated by a more severe reading retardation initially, less drive to achieve, a history of delayed speech development, a family history of reading difficulties, a greater number of serious illnesses, and more maladjustment. The limited range of investigations so far does not allow more than a tentative conclusion that the more severely handicapped retarded readers tend to make less progress.

Little is known about the occupational performance of reading-retarded children after they leave school. Rawson (1968) followed into middle life a mixed group of boys who had attended one particular school. Some of these were "dyslexic," and although some continued to have reading and spelling difficulties, many went on to higher education. A lack of adequate documentation of the children's reading skills makes this study (unusual in its apparently good outcome) impossible to evaluate.

It is clear that, in general, most reading-retarded children who are not given effective treatment continue to be severely handicapped in reading. Most studies of remedial treatment have not differentiated children with specific reading retardation, so that little can be concluded about the ways in which treatment may modify the otherwise poor prognosis. One can say that remedial help provided on a small-group basis leads to some modest short-term gains; but unless help is continued, the improvement is short-lived (Cashdan & Pumfrey, 1969; Chazan, 1967; Collins, 1961; Lovell, Byrne, & Richardson, 1963; Lovell, Johnson, & Platts, 1962; Shearer, 1967). Whether more individualized coaching would have greater benefit is not known.

SPECIFIC REMEDIAL TREATMENT

Much has been written about methods of teaching "dyslexic" children (e.g., Franklin & Naidoo, 1970; Miles, 1970; Money, 1966), but evaluation of different techniques is lacking, and very little is known about the merits and demerits of each approach. Most attention has focused on various types of perceptual training, on the rationale that if perceptual defects underlie reading problems, then alleviation of the perceptual difficulties should improve reading. This is the principle of the perceptual stimulation advocated by Silver, Hagin, & Hersh (1967), the perceptual training in the Frostig program (Frostig, 1968), and the Doman-Delacato patterning method (see review by Cohen, Birch, & Taft, 1970). The rationale has rightly come in for some trenchant criticism (Mann, 1970), but the real test is whether it works. Studies of perceptual training have generally shown that the training could, and usually did, improve scores on tests of perception, but the effects on reading were no better than more conventional direct teaching of reading itself (Elkind & Deblinger, 1969; Feldmann, Schmidt, & Deutsch, 1968; Horn & Quarmby, 1970; Robbins, 1967; Rosen, 1966, 1967). It has also been often assumed that children with different perceptual handicaps should be taught through different sensory channels, but again the results of one study designed to test this hypothesis were negative (Bateman, 1969). While the studies were far from conclusive, varied in the rigor of their methodology, and were not conducted with children suffering only from specific reading retardation, they serve to emphasize that the presence of perceptual or other handicaps does not necessarily mean that teaching methods should be based on them. Moreover, insofar as teaching should be so based, it remains uncertain whether instruction should concentrate on the child's strengths or his weaknesses (Berger & Yule, 1972). The same issues arise with respect to other approaches, such as programmed learning (Winsberg, 1969), operant techniques (Staats, 1970), or the Initial Teaching Alphabet (Warburton & Southgate, 1969). They have their value, but whether they work any *differently* with reading-retarded children is not known. Information on the differences and similarities between children with specific reading retardation and other children, with respect to their response to different teaching methods, might well throw light on the nature of the syndrome; so far, this information is lacking.

CONCLUSIONS

The whole of this review has been bedeviled by the great variety of definitions of reading disability, making comparisons between different studies hazardous and uncertain. Many of the definitions used have been unsatisfactory, both conceptually and statistically. Greater rigor and uniformity in definition are much needed.

The concept of specific reading retardation (as a disorder in which children are reading at a level much below that expected on the basis of CA and IQ) has proved controversial in the past. However, there is now substantial evidence for its validity and usefulness. Evidence for the existence of such a disorder is the finding that the prevalence of specific reading retardation is appreciably above that which would be expected on the basis of the correlation between IQ and reading in the general population. The validity of the differentiations between specific reading retardation and general reading backwardness is shown by the finding that the two conditions differ with respect to sex distribution, neurological disorder, neurodevelopmental functions, other educational attainments, and prognosis. These findings need to be replicated, but meanwhile it is important to make a careful distinction between the two types of reading disability. The use of multiple-regression equations to define specific reading retardation seems the most satisfactory procedure at the present time.

However, while the syndrome of specific reading retardation appears valid, it is not homogeneous in the way implied by some concepts of dyslexia. Reading is a complex skill, involving cognition, language, and perception. Up to now, most emphasis has been placed on the biological basis required for the development of this skill. It has been found that a wide range of neurodevelopmental functions tend to be impaired in retarded readers. These do not constitute a specific pattern, but speech and language difficulties and problems in sequencing are those most strongly and consistently associated with reading retardation. Right-left confusion, motor impersistence, and weak intersensory integration are also important to a lesser extent. Visual-perceptual difficulties and poor motor coordination may also be influential — perhaps especially in younger children. Many of these developmental functions are interrelated; further research is required to determine which are most clearly associated with specific reading retardation.

The exact cause of the developmental impairment remains uncertain, but most likely it is multifactorial. In some cases, there may be a relative failure in the normal maturation of certain special functions of the cerebral cortex; in others, there may be some neurological damage; and in yet others, the developmental retardation may stem from a lack of suitable environmental stimulation. Genetic factors probably also play a part, but by what mechanism is not known. It would be worthwhile to have investigations to determine whether social and biological influences lead to reading retardation by the same route. It is noteworthy that large family size is the social variable most consistently associated with reading retardation. In this case, the mechanism seems to be that large families often do not provide the right kind of opportunities for the optimal development of language, and that it is the verbal deficit which leads to reading difficulties. Language impairment is also the "biological" factor most strongly associated with reading retardation. Is a language deficit the crucial mediating factor in both cases? Is so, is the language deficit stemming from environmental privation the same as that stemming from organic factors?

Reading, like any other skill, requires not only a biological capacity but also concentration, motivation, and teaching. Family circumstances may be important in this connection, but so also may be the child's individual characteristics. Temperamental features involving poor concentration, restlessness, and impulsiveness are commonly found in children with specific reading retardation. School influences seem to be important with respect to educational attainment generally, but further research is needed to determine their importance in the genesis of specific reading retardation. The strong association between reading retardation and antisocial disorder has been generally neglected. Several mechanisms probably underlie this association, but research is needed to assess the relative importance of each.

The rate of reading retardation in the general population obviously depends on the severity cutoff point which is used, but evidently it is a common disorder. Some 4%

to 10% of children are reading at a level more than 2 standard deviations below prediction. This is equivalent to 30 months' retardation at 10 years of age. The disorder is very much commoner in boys, with a ratio of 3-4 to 1.

The prognosis for retarded readers during the school years is not good, but how far this reflects inadequate educational provision is uncertain. Group methods of teaching have not proved very beneficial, and an exploration and evaluation of individual approaches to teaching is indicated. It has been suggested that specific remedial techniques are needed in treatment, but supporting evidence for this proposition is lacking, and research is required. Finally, surprisingly little is known about what happens to retarded readers after they leave school; research into their later careers would be rewarding.

References

Abercrombie, M.L.J., Davis, J.R., & Shackel, B. Pilot study of version movements of eyes in cerebral palsied and other children. *Vision Research,* 1963, **3**, 135-153.

Ayers, F.W., & Torres, F. The incidence of E.E.G. abnormalities in a dyslexic and a control group. *Journal of Clinical Psychology,* 1967, **23**, 334-336.

Barker, D.J.P., & Edwards, J.H. Obstetric complications and school performance. *British Medical Journal,* 1967, **3**, 695-699.

Barker, P., Fee, R., & Sturrock, G.W. A note on retarded readers in Dundee. *Journal of Child Psychology and Psychiatry,* 1967, **8**, 227-232.

Bateman, B. Reading, a controversial view: Research and rationale. In L. Tarnopol (Ed.), *Learning disabilities: Introduction to educational and medical management.* Springfield, Ill.: Charles C Thomas, 1969.

Beery, J.W. Matching of auditory and visual stimuli by average and retarded readers. *Child Development,* 1967, **38**, 827-833.

Belmont, L., & Birch, H.G. Lateral dominance, lateral awareness and reading disability. *Child Development,* 1965, **36**, 57-71.

Belmont, L., & Birch, H.G. The intellectual profile of retarded readers. *Perceptual and Motor Skills,* 1966, **22**(6), 787-816.

Belmont, L., Birch, H.G., & Belmont, I. Auditory-visual intersensory processing and verbal mediation. *Journal of Nervous and Mental Disease,* 1968, **147**, 562-569.

Benton, A.L. The problem of cerebral dominance. *Canadian Psychologist,* 1965, **6a**, 332-348.

Benton, A.L., & Bird, J.W. The E.E.G. and reading disability. *American Journal of Orthopsychiatry,* 1963, **33**, 529-531.

Benton, A.L., & Kemble, J.D. Right-left orientation and reading disability. *Psychiatria et Neurologia,* 1960, **139**, 49-60.

Berger, M., & Yule, W. Cognitive assessment in young children with language delay. In M. Rutter & J.A.M. Martin (Eds.), *The child with delayed speech. Clinics in developmental medicine.* London: Heineman, 1972.

Berger, M., Yule, W., & Rutter, M. Attainment and adjustment in two geographic areas: 2. The prevalance of specific reading retardation. Unpublished manuscript, 1973.

Birch, H.G., & Belmont, L. Auditory-visual integration in normal and retarded readers. *American Journal of Orthopsychiatry,* 1964, **34**, 852-861.

Birch, H.G., & Belmont, L. Auditory-visual integration, intelligence and reading ability in school children. *Perceptual and Motor Skills,* 1965, **20**, 295-305.

Birch, H.G., & Gussow, J.D. *Disadvantaged children: Health, nutrition and school failure.* New York: Harcourt Brace Jovanovitch, 1970.

Birch, L.B. The improvement of reading ability. *British Journal of Educational Psychology,* 1950, **20**, 73-76.

Black, F.L., & Davis, E.M. Measles and readiness for reading and learning. II. New Haven Study. *American Journal of Epidemiology,* 1968, **88**, 337-344.

Black, F.L., Fox, J.P., Elveback, L., & Kogon, A. Measles and readiness for reading and learning. I. Background, purpose and general methodology. *American Journal of Epidemiology,* 1968, **88**, 333-336.

Blank, M., & Bridger, W.H. Deficiencies in verbal labeling in retarded readers. *American Journal of Orthopsychiatry,* 1966, **36**, 840-847.

Blank, M., Weider, S., & Bridger, W.H. Verbal deficiencies in abstract thinking in early reading retardation. *American Journal of Orthopsychiatry,* 1968, **38**, 823-834.

Bonsall, C., & Dornbush, R.L. Visual perception and reading ability. *Journal of Educational Psychology,* 1969, **60**, 294-299.

Brenner, M.W., & Gillman, S. Visuomotor ability in school children – a survey. *Developmental Medicine and Child Neurology,* 1966, **8**, 686-703.

Bruininks, R.H. Auditory and visual perceptual skills related to the reading performance of disadvantaged boys. *Perceptual and Motor Skills,* 1969, **29**, 179-186.

Burt, C. *The young delinquent.* London: University of London Press, 1925.

Burt, C. *The backward child.* (3rd ed.) London: University of London Press, 1950.

Burt, C. The concept of intelligence. In *Association of Educational Psychology Journal and News Letter: Modern Concepts of Intelligence,* 1970, 16-38.

Burt, C., & Howard, M. The nature and causes of maladjustment among children of school age. *British Journal of Psychology,* 1952, **5**, 39-59.

Cashdan, A., & Pumfrey, P.D. Some effects of the remedial teaching of reading. *Educational Research,* 1969, **11**, 138-142.

Chall, J.S. *Learning to read: The great debate.* New York: McGraw-Hill, 1967.

Chall, J.S. Learning and not learning to read: Current issues and trends. In F.A. Young & D.B. Lindsley (Eds.), *Early experience and visual information. Processing in perceptual and reading disorders.* Washington, D.C.: National Academy of Sciences, 1970.

Chazan, M. The effects of remedial teaching in reading: A review of research. *Remedial Education,* 1967, **2**, 4-12.

Chazan, M. Maladjustment and reading difficulties: I. Recent research and experiments. *Remedial Education,* 1969, **4**, 119-123.

Clark, M.M. *Reading difficulties in schools.* Harmondsworth, Eng.: Penguin Books, 1970.

Cohen, H.J., Birch, H.G., & Taft, L.T. Some considerations for evaluating the Doman-Delacato "patterning" method. *Pediatrics,* 1970, **45**, 302-314.

Cohen, J. The factorial structure of the WISC at ages 7.6, 10.6 and 13.6. *Journal of Consulting Psychology,* 1959, **23**, 285-299.

Coleman, J.S., Campbell, E.Q., Hobson, C.J., McPortland, J., Mood, A.M., Weinfeld, F.D., & York, R.L. *Equality of educational opportunity.* Washington, D.C.: United States Government Printing Office, 1966.

Collins, J.E. *The effects of remedial education.* London: Oliver & Boyd, 1961.

Crane, A.R. An historical and critical account of the accomplishment quotient idea. *British Journal of Educational Psychology,* 1959, **29**, 252-259.

Critchley, E.M.R. Reading retardation, dyslexia and delinquency. *British Journal of Psychiatry,* 1968, **115**, 1537-1547.

Critchley, M. Developmental dyslexia: A constitutional dyssymbolia. In A.W. Franklin (Ed.), *Word blindness or specific developmental dyslexia.* London: Pitman, 1962.

Critchley, M. *The dyslexic child.* Springfield, Ill.: Charles C Thomas, 1970.

Crookes, T.G., & Greene, M.C.L. Some characteristics of children with two types of speech disorder. *British Journal of Educational Psychology,* 1963, **33**, 31-40.

Daniels, J.C. Reading difficulty and aural training. In A.N. Franklin (Ed.), *Word blindness or specific developmental dyslexia.* London: Pitman, 1962.

Davie, R. Size of class, educational attainment and adjustment. *Concern,* 1971, **7**, 2-8.

Davie, R., Butler, N.R., & Goldstein, H. *From birth to seven.* London: Longmans, 1972.

Davis, R.D., & Cashdan, A. Specific dyslexia. *British Journal of Educational Psychology,* 1963, **33**, 80.

De Hirsch, K., Jansky, J. J., & Langford, W. S. Comparisons between prematurely and maturely born children at three age levels. *American Journal of Orthopsychiatry,* 1966, **36**, 616-628. (a)

De Hirsch, K., Jansky, J. J., & Langford, W. S. *Predicting reading failure.* New York: Harper, 1966. (b)

Department of Education and Science. Children with specific reading difficulties: Report of the Advisory Committee on Handicapped Children. London: Her Majesty's Stationer's Office, 1972.

Doehring, D.G. *Patterns of impairment in specific reading disability.* Bloomington, Ind.: Indiana University Press, 1968.

Douglas, J.W.B. *The home and the school.* London: Macgibbon & Kee, 1964.

Douglas, J.W.B., Ross, J.M., & Cooper, J.E. The relationship between handedness, attainment and adjustment in a national sample of school children. *Educational Research,* 1967, **9**, 223-233.

Douglas, J.W.B., Ross, J.M., & Simpson, H.R. *All our future.* London: Peter Davies, 1968.

Eames, T.H. Incidence of diseases among reading failures and non-failures. *Journal of Pediatrics,* 1948, **33**, 614-617.

Eisenberg, L. Reading retardation: I. Psychiatric and sociologic aspects. *Pediatrics,* 1966, **37**, 352-365.

Elkind, D., & Deblinger, J.A. Perceptual training and reading achievement in disadvantaged children. *Child Development,* 1969, **40**, 11-19.

Faglioni, P., Gatti, B., Pagamoni, A.M., & Robutti, A. A psychometric evaluation of developmental dyslexia in Italian children. *Cortex,* 1969, **5**, 15-26.

Feldmann, S.C., Schmidt, D.E., & Deutsch, C.P. Effect of auditory training on reading skills of retarded readers. *Perceptual and Motor Skills,* 1968, **26**, 467-480.

Fendrick, P., & Bond, G. Delinquency and reading. *Pedagogical Seminary and Journal of Genetic Psychology,* 1936, **48**, 236-43.

Field, J.G. The performance-verbal IQ discrepancy in a group of sociopaths. *Journal of Clinical Psychology,* 1960, **16**, 321-322.

Flax, N. Visual function in dyslexia. *American Journal of Optometry,* 1967, **45**, 574-587.

Ford, M.P. Auditory-visual and tactual-visual integrations in relation to reading ability. *Perceptual and Motor Skills,* 1967, **24**, 831-841.

Fox, J.P., Black, F.L., Elveback, L., Kogon, A., Hall, C.E., Turgeon, L., & Abruzzi, W. Measles and readiness for reading and learning. III. Wappingers Central School District study. *American Journal of Epidemiology,* 1968, **88**, 345-350.

Fox, J.P., Black, F.L., & Kogon, A. Measles and readiness for reading and learning. V. Evaluative comparison of the studies and overall conclusions. *American Journal of Epidemiology,* 1968, **88**, 359-367.

Frank, H. 'Word-blindness' in school children. *Transactions of the Ophthalmological Society of the United Kingdom,* 1936, **56**, 231-238.

Franklin, A.W., & Naidoo, S. *Assessment and teaching of dyslexic children.* London: Invalid Children's Aid Association, 1970.

Fransella, F., & Gerver, D. Multiple regression equations for predicting reading age from chronological age and WISC verbal I.Q. *British Journal of Educational Psychology,* 1965, **35**, 86-89.

Franzen, R.H. The accomplishment quotient. *Teacher's College Record,* 1920, **21**, 432-440.

Frisk, M., Holmström, G., & Wasz-Höckert, O. Writing difficulties and the problem of dyslexia among secondary school students. *Sosiaalilääketieteelinen Aikakaus-lehti,* 1967, **1**, 33-38.

Frisk, M., Wegelius, E., Tenhunen, T., Widholm, O., & Hortling, H. The problem of dyslexia in teenage. *Acta Paediatrica Scandinavica,* 1967, **56**, 333-343.

Frostig, M. Education for children with learning disabilities. In H.R. Myklebust (Ed.), *Progress in learning disabilities.* New York: Grune & Stratton, 1968.

Gaarder, K.R. Eye movements and perception. In F.A. Young & D.B. Lindsley (Eds.), *Early experience and visual information processing in perceptual and reading disorders.* Washington, D.C.: National Academy of Sciences, 1970.

Gallagher, J.R. Word-blindness (reading disability; dyslexia): Its diagnosis and treatment. In A.W. Franklin (Ed.), *Word-blindness or specific developmental dyslexia.* London: Pitman, 1962.

Garfield, J.C. Motor impersistence in normal and brain-damaged children. *Neurology,* 1964, **14**, 623-630.

Gates, A.I. The role of personality maladjustment in reading disability. In G. Natchez (Ed.), *Children with reading problems.* New York: Basic Books, 1968.

Gates, A.I., & Bond, G.L. Failure in reading and social maladjustment. *National Education Association Journal*, 1936, **25**, 205-206.

Gibbens, T.C.N. Psychiatric studies of Borstal lads. *Maudsley Monograph No. 11*. London: Oxford University Press, 1963.

Gibson, E.J. Learning to read. *Science*, 1965, **148**, 1066-1072.

Glueck, S., & Glueck, E. *Unraveling juvenile delinquency*. New York: New York Commonwealth Fund, 1950.

Goldberg, H.K., & Arnott, W. Ocular motility in learning disabilities. *Journal of Learning Disabilities*, 1970, **3**, 40-42.

Golden, N.E., & Steiner, S.R. Auditory and visual functions in good and poor readers. *Journal of Learning Disabilities*, 1969, **2**, 476-481.

Graham, C. The relation between ability and attainment tests. In *Association of Educational Psychology Journal and News Letter: Modern Concepts of Intelligence*, 1970, 53-59.

Graham, P., & George, S. Children's responses to parental illness: Individual differences. *Journal of Psychosomatic Research*, 1972, **16**, 251-255.

Gregory, R.E. Unsettledness, maladjustment and reading failure: A village study. *British Journal of Educational Psychology*, 1965, **35**, 63-68.

Gubbay, S.S., Ellis, E., Walton, J.N., & Court, S.D.M. Clumsy children. A study of apraxic and agnosic defects in 21 children. *Brain*, 1965, **88**, 295-312.

Hallgren, B. Specific dyslexia: A clinical and genetic study. *Acta Psychiatrica Scandinavica Supplementum*, 1950, **65**.

Harris, A.J. Lateral dominance, directional confusion and reading disability. *Journal of Psychology*, 1957, **44**, 283-294.

Helveston, E.M., Billips, W.C., & Weber, J.C. Controlling eye-dominant hemisphere relationship as a factor in reading ability. *American Journal of Ophthalmology*, 1970, **70**, 96-100.

Hermann, K. *Reading disability: A medical study of word-blindness and related handicaps*. Copenhagen: Munksgaard, 1959.

Horn, J., & Quarmby, D. The problem of the older non-readers. *Special Education*, 1970, **59**, 23-25.

Houghton, V.P. Why dyslexia? In J. Downing & A.L. Brown (Eds.), *The second international reading symposium*. London: Cassell, 1967.

Huelsman, C.B. The WISC subtest syndrome for disabled readers. *Perceptual and Motor Skills*, 1970, **30**, 535-550.

Hughes, J.R. Electroencephalography and learning. In H.R. Myklebust (Ed.), *Progress in learning disabilities I*. New York: Grune & Stratton, 1968.

Ingram, T.T.S. The nature of dyslexia. In F.A. Young & D.B. Lindsley (Eds.), *Early experience and visual information processing in perceptual and reading disorders*. Washington, D.C.: National Academy of Sciences, 1970.

Ingram, T.T.S. Specific learning disabilities in childhood: A medical point of view. *British Journal of Educational Psychology*, 1971, **41**, 6-13.

Ingram, T.T.S., Mason, A.W., & Blackburn, I. A retrospective study of 82 children with reading disability. *Developmental Medicine and Child Neurology*, 1970, **12**, 271-281.

Jensen, A.R. How much can we boost IQ and scholastic achievement? *Harvard Educational Review*, 1969, **39**, 1-123.

Kagan, J. Reflection – impulsivity and reading ability in primary grade children. *Child Development*, 1965, **36**, 609-628.

Kahn, D., & Birch, H.G. Development of auditory-visual integration and reading achievement. *Perceptual and Motor Skills*, 1968, **27**, 459-468.

Kawi, A.A., & Pasamanick, B. Prenatal and paranatal factors in the development of childhood reading disorders. *Society for Research in Child Development*, 1959, **24**(4).

Kelsall, R.K., & Kelsall, H.M. *Social disadvantage and educational opportunity.* London: Holt, 1971.

Kendall, B.S. A note on the relation of reading to performance on a memory-for-designs test. *Journal of Educational Psychology*, 1948, **39**, 370-373.

Keogh, B.K. The Bender-Gestalt as a predictive and diagnostic test of reading performance. *Journal of Consulting Psychology*, 1965, **29**, 83-84.

Keogh, B.K., & Smith, C.E. Visuo-motor ability for school prediction: A seven year study. *Perceptual and Motor Skills*, 1967, **25**, 101-110.

Kerdel-Vegas, O. Strephosymbolia (incidence in the school sectors of Caracas). *Diseases of the Nervous System*, 1968, **29**, 548-549.

Kinsbourne, M., & Warrington, E.K. Developmental factors in reading and writing backwardness. *British Journal of Psychology*, 1963, **54**, 145-156.

Kogon, A., Hall, C.E., Cooney, M.K., & Fox, J.P. Measles and readiness for reading and learning. IV. Shoreline School District study. *American Journal of Epidemiology*, 1968, **88**, 351-358.

Lachmann, F.M. Perceptual-motor development in children retarded in reading ability. *Journal of Consulting Psychology*, 1960, **24**, 427-431.

Lansdown, R. Problems of reading: The psychology. *New Society*, 1972, **496**, 645-646.

Lawrence, D. The effects of counselling on retarded readers. *Educational Research*, 1971, **13**, 119-124.

Lawson, D., Metcalfe, M., & Pampiglione, G. Meningitis in childhood. *British Medical Journal*, 1965, **1**, 557-562.

Lawson, L.J. Ophthalmological factors in learning disabilities. In H.R. Myklebust (Ed.), *Progress in learning disabilities.* New York: Grune & Stratton, 1968.

Leeds Education Committee. Report on a survey of reading ability. Leeds, Eng.: Education Department, 1953.

Levy, P., & Tucker, J. Differential effects of streaming on primary attainment. *British Journal of Educational Psychology*, 1972, **42**, 75-79.

Lingren, R.H. Performance of disabled and normal readers on the Bender-Gestalt, Auditory Discrimination Test and Visual-Motor Matching. *Perceptual and Motor Skills,* 1969, **29**, 152-154.

Little, A., Mabey, C., & Russell, J. Do small classes help a pupil? *New Society,* 1971, **473**, 769-771.

Lovell, K., Byrne, C., & Richardson, B. A further study of the educational progress of children who had received remedial education. *British Journal of Educational Psychology,* 1963, **33**, 3-9.

Lovell, K., & Gorton, A. A study of some differences between backward and normal readers of average intelligence. *British Journal of Educational Psychology,* 1968, **38**, 240-248.

Lovell, K., Gray, E.A., & Oliver, D.E. A further study of some cognitive and other disabilities in backward readers of average non-verbal reasoning scores. *British Journal of Educational Psychology,* 1964, **34**, 275-279.

Lovell, K., Johnson, E., & Platts, D. A summary of a study of the reading ages of children who had been given remedial teaching. *British Journal of Educational Psychology,* 1962, **32**, 66-71.

Lovell, K., Shapton, D., & Warren, N.S. A study of some cognitive and other disabilities in backward readers of average intelligence as assessed by a non-verbal test. *British Journal of Educational Psychology,* 1964, **34**, 58-64.

Lyle, J.C. Reading retardation and reversal tendency: A factorial study. *Child Development,* 1969, **40**, 833-843.

Lyle, J.C. Certain antenatal, perinatal and developmental variables and reading retardation in middle-class boys. *Child Development,* 1970, **41**, 481-491.

Lyle, J.C., & Goyen, J. Visual recognition, developmental lag and strephosymbolia in reading retardation. *Journal of Abnormal Psychology,* 1968, **73**, 25-29.

Lytton, H. Some psychological and sociological characteristics of "good" and "poor" achievers" (boys) in remedial reading groups: Clinical case studies. *Human Development,* 1968, **11**, 260-276.

MacMeeken, M. *Ocular dominance in relation to developmental aphasia.* London: University of London Press, 1939.

Makita, K. The rarity of reading disability in Japanese children. *American Journal of Orthopsychiatry,* 1968, **38**, 599-614.

Malmqvist, E. *Factors related to reading disabilities in the first grade of elementary school.* Stockholm: Almqvist & Wiksell, 1958.

Mann, L. Perceptual training: Misdirections and redirections. *American Journal of Orthopsychiatry,* 1970, **40**, 30-38.

Margolin, J.B., Roman, M., & Harari, C. Reading disability in the delinquent child: A microcosm of psychosocial pathology. *American Journal of Orthopsychiatry,* 1955, **25**, 25-35.

Marshall, W.A. *Development of the brain.* Edinburgh: Oliver & Boyd, 1968.

Mason, A.W. Specific (developmental) dyslexia. *Developmental Medicine and Child Neurology,* 1967, **8**, 149-159.

Maxwell, A.E. A factor analysis of the Wechsler Intelligence Scale for Children. *British Journal of Educational Psychology,* 1959, **29**, 237-241.

Middlesborough Head Teachers Association. Report of a survey of reading ability. Middlesborough, Eng.: Education Committee, 1953.

Miles, T.R. *On helping the dyslexic child.* London: Methuen, 1970.

Miles, T.R. More on dyslexia. *British Journal of Educational Psychology,* 1971, **41**, 1-5.

Millar, T.P. Some observations concerning reading retardation and delinquency. *Connecticut Medicine,* 1969, **33**, 457-463.

Miller, A.D., Margolin, J.B., & Yolles, S.F. Epidemiology of reading disabilities: Some methodologic considerations and early findings. *American Journal of Public Health,* 1957, **47**, 1250-1256.

Miller, D.R., & Westman, J.C. Reading disability as a condition of family stability. *Family Process,* 1964, **3**, 66-76.

Ministry of Education. *Reading ability: Some suggestions for helping the backward.* London: Her Majesty's Stationer's Office, 1950.

Mittler, P. *The study of twins.* Harmondsworth, Eng.: Penguin Books, 1971.

Money, J. (Ed.) *Reading disability: Progress and research needs in dyslexia.* Baltimore: Johns Hopkins Press, 1962.

Money, J. *The disabled reader.* Baltimore: Johns Hopkins Press, 1966.

Monroe, M. *Children who cannot read.* Chicago: University of Chicago Press, 1932.

Morris, J.M. *Reading in the primary school.* London: Newnes, 1959.

Morris, J.M. *Standards and progress in reading.* Slough, Bucks., Eng.: National Foundation for Educational Research, 1966.

Mountcastle, V.B. (Ed.) *Interhemispheric relations and cerebral dominance.* Baltimore: Johns Hopkins Press, 1962.

Muehl, S., Knott, J.R., & Benton, A.L. EEG abnormality and psychological test performance in reading disability. *Cortex,* 1965, **1**, 434-440.

Myklebust, H.R. Learning disabilities: Definition and overview. In H.R. Myklebust (Ed.), *Progress in learning disabilities.* New York: Grune & Stratton, 1968.

Naidoo, S. *Specific dyslexia.* London: Pitman, 1972.

Neale, M.D. *Manual: Neale Analysis of Reading Ability.* New York: Macmillan, 1958.

Nisbet, J.D. Family environment and intelligence. *Eugenics Review,* 1953, **45**, 31-40.

Nisbet, J.D., & Entwistle, N.J. Intelligence and family size 1949-1965. *British Journal of Educational Psychology,* 1967, **37**, 188-193.

Noesgaard, A. Fejltyper i dansk retskrivning, Copenhagen, 1945. Cited by Knud Hermann in *Reading disability: A medical study of word-blindness and related handicaps.* Copenhagen: Munkegaard, 1959.

Norn, M.S., Rindziunski, E., & Skydsgaard, H. Ophthalmologic and orthoptic examinations of dyslectics. *Acta Ophthalmologica,* 1969, **47**, 147-160.

Oldman, D., Bytheway, B., & Horobin, G. Family structure and educational achievement. *Journal of Biosocial Science Supplement,* 1971, **3**, 81-91.

Olson, A.V. Relation of achievement test scores and specific reading abilities to the Frostig Developmental Test of Visual Perception. *Perceptual and Motor Skills,* 1966, **22**, 179-184.

Orton, S.T. 'Word-blindness' in school children. *Archives of Neurology and Psychiatry,* 1925, **14**, 581-615.

Orton, S.T. *Reading, writing and speech problems in children.* New York: Norton, 1937.

Peck, H.B., Zwerling, I., Rabban, M., & Mendelsohn, M. Reading disability and community psychiatry. *American Journal of Orthopsychiatry,* 1966, **36**, 420-433.

Peterson, R.P. Patterns of eye movements in rapid symbol identification and their relation to reading achievement. *Perceptual and Motor Skills,* 1969, **28**, 307-310.

Pond, D. Communication disorders in brain-damaged children. *Proceedings of the Royal Society of Medicine,* 1967, **60**, 343-348.

Prechtl, H.F.R., & Stemmer, C.J. The choreiform syndrome in children. *Developmental Medicine and Child Neurology,* 1962, **4**, 119-127.

Pringle, M.L. K., Butler, N., & Davie, R. *11,000 seven-year-olds.* London: Longmans, 1966.

Rabinovitch, R.D., Drew, A.L., De Jong, R.N., Ingram, W., & Withey, L. A research approach to reading retardation. *Research Publication of the Association for Research in Nervous and Mental Diseases,* 1954, **34**, 363-396.

Ravenette, A.T. Vocabulary level and reading attainment: An empirical approach to the assessment of reading retardation. *British Journal of Educational Psychology,* 1961, **31**, 96-103.

Rawson, M.B. *Developmental language disability.* Baltimore: Johns Hopkins Press, 1968.

Reilly, D.H. Auditory-visual integration, sex and reading achievement. *Journal of Educational Psychology,* 1971, **62**, 482-486.

Robbins, M.P. Test of the Doman-Delacato rationale with retarded readers. *Journal of the American Medical Association,* 1967, **202**, 389-393.

Roe, M. *Survey into progress of maladjusted pupils.* London: Inner London Education Authority, 1965.

Rosen, C.L. An experimental study of visual perceptual training and reading achievement in first grade. *Perceptual and Motor Skills,* 1966, **22**, 979-986.

Rosen, C.L. An investigation of perceptual training and reading achievement in first grade. *American Journal of Optometry,* 1967, **45**, 322-332.

Rosenberger, P.B. Visual matching and clinical findings among good and poor readers. *American Journal of Diseases of Children,* 1970, **119**, 103-110.

Rutter, M. A children's behaviour questionnaire for completion by teachers: Preliminary findings. *Journal of Child Psychology and Psychiatry,* 1967, **8**, 1-11.

Rutter, M. The concept of "dyslexia." In P. Wolff & R.C. MacKeith (Eds.), *Planning for better learning. Clinics in developmental medicine, 33.* London: Heinemann Medical Books, 1969.

Rutter, M. *Maternal deprivation reassessed.* Harmondsworth, Eng.: Penguin Books, 1972.

Rutter, M., Birch, H.G., Thomas, A., & Chess, S. Temperamental characteristics in infancy and the later development of behavioural disorders. *British Journal of Psychiatry,* 1964, **110**, 651-661.

Rutter, M., Graham, P., & Birch, H.G. Interrelations between the choreiform syndrome, reading disability and psychiatric disorder in children of 8-11 years. *Developmental Medicine and Child Neurology,* 1966, **8**, 149-159.

Rutter, M., Graham, P., & Yule, W. *A neuropsychiatric study in childhood. Clinics in developmental medicine 35/36.* London: Heinemann Medical Books, 1970. (a)

Rutter, M., Tizard, J., & Whitmore, K. (Eds.) *Education, Health and Behaviour.* London: Longmans, 1970 (b)

Rutter, M., & Yule, W. The concept of specific reading retardation. Unpublished manuscript, 1973.

Rutter, M., Yule, B.A., Quinton, D., Rowlands, O., Yule, W., & Berger, M. Attainment and adjustment in two geographical areas. 3. Some factors accounting for cross-community differences. Unpublished manuscript, 1973.

Rutter, M., Yule, W., Tizard, J., & Graham, P. Severe reading retardation: Its relationship to maladjustment, epilepsy and neurological disorders. *Proceedings of the First International Conference of the Association for Special Education,* 1967, **1**.

Sampson, O.C. Reading and adjustment: A review of the literature. *Educational Research,* 1966, **8**, 184-190.

Schiffman, G. Dyslexia as an educational phenomenon: Its recognition and treatment. In J. Money (Ed.), *Reading disability: Progress and research needs in dyslexia.* Baltimore: Johns Hopkins Press, 1962.

Schonell, F.J. *Backwardness in the basic subjects.* Edinburgh: Oliver & Boyd, 1942.

Scottish Council for Research in Education. *Studies in spelling.* London: University of London Press, 1961.

Seashore, H.G. Differences between verbal and performance IQ in the Wechsler Intelligence Scale for Children. *Journal of Consulting Psychology,* 1951, **15**, 62-67.

Shankweiler, D. Developmental dyslexia: A critique and review of recent evidence. *Cortex,* 1964, **1**, 53-62.

Shearer, E. The long-term effects of remedial education. *Educational Research,* 1967, **9**, 219-222.

Shields, J., & Slater, E. Heredity and psychological abnormality. In H.J. Eysenck (Ed.), *Handbook of abnormal psychology: An experimental approach.* New York: Basic Books, 1960.

Silver, A.A., & Hagin, R.A. Specific reading disability: Follow-up studies. *American Journal of Orthopsychiatry*, 1964, **34**, 95-102.

Silver, A.A., Hagin, R.A., & Hersh, M.F. Reading disability: Teaching through stimulation of deficit perceptual areas. *American Journal of Orthopsychiatry*, 1967, **37**, 744-752.

Spache, G. A critical analysis of various methods of classifying spelling errors. I. *Journal of Educational Psychology*, 1940, **31**, 111-134. (a)

Spache, G. Validity and reliability of the proposed classification of spelling errors. II. *Journal of Educational Psychology*, 1940, **31**, 204-214. (b)

Staats, A.W. *Learning, language and cognition*. London: Holt, 1970.

Start, K.B., & Wells, B.K. *The trend of reading standards*. Slough, Bucks., Eng.: National Foundation for Educational Research, 1972.

Stemmer, C.J. Choreatiforme bewegungsonrust. Unpublished doctoral dissertation, University of Groningen, Germany, 1964.

Sterritt, G.M., & Rudnick, M. Auditory and visual rhythm perception in relation to reading ability in 4th grade boys. *Perceptual and Motor Skills*, 1966, **22**, 849-864.

Sturge, C. Reading retardation and antisocial behavior. Unpublished M. Phil. thesis, University of London, 1972.

Thomas, A., Chess, S., & Birch, H.G. *Temperament and behaviour disorders in children*. London: University of London Press, 1968.

Thorndike, R.L. *The concepts of over- and under-achievement*. New York: Bureau of Publications, Teachers College, Columbia University, 1963.

Tinker, M.A. Recent studies of eye movements in reading. *Psychological Bulletin*, 1958, **55**, 215-231.

Tordrup, S.A. Reversals in reading and spelling. *The Slow Learning Child*, 1966, **12**, 173-183.

Vernon, M.D. Specific dyslexia. *British Journal of Educational Psychology*, 1962, **32**, 143-150.

Vernon, M.D. *Reading and its difficulties*. Cambridge, Eng.: Cambridge University Press, 1971.

Vernon, P.E. The relation of intelligence to educational backwardness. *Educational Review*, 1958, **11**, 7-10.

Warburton, F.W., & Southgate, V. *I.T.A.: An independent evaluation*. London: Murray & Chambers, 1969.

Warrington, E.K. The incidence of verbal disability associated with reading retardation. *Neuropsychologia*, 1967, **5**, 175-179.

Wechsler, D. *Manual: Wechsler Intelligence Scale for Children*. New York: Psychological Corporation, 1949.

Werner, E.E., Simonian, K., & Smith, R.S. Reading achievement, language functioning and perceptual-motor development of 10- and 11-year olds. *Perceptual and Motor Skills*, 1967, **25**, 409-420.

Whipple, C.I., & Kodman, F. A study of discrimination and perceptual learning with retarded readers. *Journal of Educational Psychology*, 1969, **60**, 1-5.

Winsberg, B.G. Programmed learning, teaching machines and dyslexia. *American Journal of Orthopsychiatry*, 1969, **39**, 418-427.

Wiseman, S. *Education and environment.* Manchester: Manchester University Press, 1964.

Wiseman, S. The Manchester survey. In *Children and their primary schools: A report of the Central Advisory Council for Education. Research and survey.* Vol. 2. London: Her Majesty's Stationer's Office, 1967.

Wolff, P.H., & Hurwitz, I. The choreiform symdrome. *Developmental Medicine and Child Neurology*, 1966, **8**, 160-165.

Woodward, M. *Low intelligence and delinquency.* London: Institute for the Study and Treatment of Delinquency, 1955. (a)

Woodward, M. The role of low intelligence in delinquency. *British Journal of Delinquency*, 1955, **5**, 281-303. (b)

Wussler, M., & Barcley, A. Cerebral dominance, psycholinguistic skills and reading disability. *Perceptual and Motor Skills*, 1970, **31**, 419-425.

Yule, W. Predicting reading ages on Neale's analysis of reading ability. *British Journal of Educational Psychology*, 1967, **37**, 252-255.

Yule, W. Differential prognosis of reading backwardness and specific reading retardation. *British Journal of Educational Psychology*, 1973, in press.

Yule, W., & Rigley, L.V. A four-year follow-up of severely backward readers into adolescence. In M.M. Clark & S.M. Maxwell (Eds.), *Reading: Influences on progress. Proceedings of the Fifth Annual Study Congress of The United Kingdom Reading Association, Edinburgh, 1967/68*, 1970, **5**.

Yule, W., Rutter, M., Berger, M., & Thompson, J. Over- and under-achievement in reading: Distribution in the general population. Unpublished manuscript, 1973.

Zangwill, O.L. *Cerebral dominance and its relation to psychological function.* Edinburgh: Oliver & Boyd, 1960.

Zangwill, O.L. Dyslexia in relation to cerebral dominance. In J. Money (Ed.), *Reading disability: Progress and research needs in dyslexia.* Baltimore: Johns Hopkins Press, 1962.

BEHAVIOR MODIFICATION IN SPECIAL EDUCATION

Alan E. Kazdin, Ph.D.
W. Edward Craighead, Ph.D.

The Pennsylvania State University

Behavior modification in special education encompasses a variety of procedures. The procedures have a primary commonality, i.e., their derivation from theoretical and empirical work in the psychology of learning. Procedures are divisible according to whether they are based on classical conditioning or operant conditioning. Although techniques derived from both models have been used to effect behavioral change with special education populations, operant conditioning has conspicuously dominated the area. This is the case because the type of behaviors usually of interest in special education are considered to be operant and are a function of their consequences. Operant conditioning, as applied to a variety of populations in diverse settings, will be the focus of this chapter.

It is the operant approach primarily that has engendered avid enthusiasts and critics in the field of education. While operant conditioning itself may be elucidated with relatively few principles, the use of the procedures for training, education, and rehabilitation represents a philosophical stance as well. There are several aspects implicit in the use of operant procedures which need to be examined, for some of them account for educators' resistance to the approach.

Behavior modification represents a departure from several traditional presuppositions and methods of dealing with special education problems. Traditional views of children in special educational settings have focused on diagnosing emotional problems, perceptual-motor deficits, organic impairments, and similar approaches which attempt to provide information as to the etiology of the behavioral problem. The implicit assumption in these formulations is that behavior can be best understood and altered in terms of subject variables or the characteristics inherent in the individuals (Bandura, 1968). In this context, diagnostic labels are given to denote the child's disorder or problem. It is implicit that this sort of diagnosis determines the procedures employed to ameliorate the condition. In fact, the focus on subject variables and etiology of behavior has not had much specific educational value. Diagnosis has not created effective training procedures. Few practical recommendations have been made on this basis to alter the condition of the child. Certainly, some typical labels (e.g., mental retardation) remove any optimism in developing training procedures to alter behavior.

In contrast to the traditional strategy, the behavioral approach focuses on stimulus situations or environmental events as a major source of problems. The focus of treatment or change in behavior modification is not on a problem in the child, but rather on the environment which fails to support certain adaptive behaviors. Behavior modification focuses on present behavior and, to a large extent, ignores etiological speculations of problem behavior. The child is observed in the context in which his behavior is deficient or problematic, and changes are attempted in this context. Rather than search for appropriate trait labels to characterize the child, the behavioral view concerns itself with the *behaviors* for which that label is applied. In the process, if there is any diagnosis made, it includes the environment in which the child functions. In the typical case, behaviors to be increased or decreased are identified in the child. In addition, the consequences which may precede and follow behaviors are arranged to effect these changes. The arrangement of environmental events is used to alter the frequency of certain responses.

Claiming that traditional diagnoses are avoided is not tantamount to saying that a given child is indistinguishable in some way from "normal." Lindsley (1964) emphasized these points in the case of "retarded" children by claiming that "children are not retarded. Only their *behavior* in average environments is sometimes retarded. In fact, it is modern science's ability to design suitable environments for these children that are retarded. [p. 62]." Lindsley showed that with the careful design of environments, the behavior of retardates can be brought under careful control (Barrett & Lindsley, 1962; Lindsley, 1958).

The present chapter focuses on the behavior-modification techniques which have been used rather extensively to alter behavior. In a large measure, the material covered describes improvements in the technology which have been used to arrange environments so as to maximize behavior change.

Although educators and other professionals systematically applied the principles of behavior modification slowly and reluctantly, the increase in the number of research reports indicates a more frequent and broader use of those principles, especially in the area of special education. Perhaps one reason for the increased employment of the behavioral approach is that for the first time psychology has offered educators something other than an IQ test or an impractical theory; instead, the principles of behavior modification present a practically oriented (sometimes oversold) conceptual framework by which the effectiveness of special education procedures may be enhanced.

This chapter briefly reviews the principles of operant approaches to behavior modification (see Skinner, 1953). Although the research to date in this area has been largely operant in nature, it is not to be assumed that operant conditioning and behavior modification are synonymous. While such a view has been voiced occasionally, even a cursory examination of Bandura (1969) indicates that the term "behavior modification" is much more encompassing than the term "operant conditioning" and includes such areas as vicarious learning, self-control, and other covert (or generally labeled "cognitive") procedures.

One other cautionary note is appropriate. While the principles of behavior modification, especially operant ones, may seem simplistic (and, in fact, are frequently criticized for being overly simplistic), it has been the authors' experience that the employment of these principles in applied settings requires a much greater facility with them, as well as with research in the area, than is sometimes assumed. In fact, naive applications by well-intentioned professionals have created rather than ameliorated problems.

Principles of operant conditioning

As indicated earlier, most of the research in the application of behavior modification in special education has employed the principles of operant conditioning; only the most basic operant principles are presented here. (For a more extensive review of these principles and their methods of application, the reader may wish to consult the contemporary review by O'Leary and O'Leary, 1972, as well as Honig, 1966, and Reynolds, 1968. For an exhaustive review of all behavior-modification approaches, the reader is referred to Bandura, 1969.) One of the characteristics of this approach is a clear specification of the behavior, usually an observable response, to be modified. This is labeled the "target behavior"; it may be one or more behaviors. In terms of modification, one may wish to change the frequency, intensity, or rate of learning of a behavior (Bijou & Baer, 1961). *Frequency* of the target behavior is the variable most often chosen for change. Thus, with the target behavior(s) specified, what are the principles used for modification?

Five basic principles may be employed and may best be conceptualized in terms of their consequences. Two of the principles (positive and negative reinforcement) may be employed to strengthen a target behavior, and three of the principles (punishment by application, punishment by removal, and extinction) may be used to weaken it. These principles are based on the Skinnerian S-R (stimulus-response) model, which specifies that the response R is determined by the antecedent and consequent stimuli to that response; more clearly, we might refer to it as the S-R-S model. The preceding, or antecedent, stimulus does not elicit the response but simply marks the time or place when reinforcement will or will not occur. This preceding stimulus is known as the discriminative stimulus. When reinforcement will occur, the discriminative stimulus is designated as S^D; when reinforcement will *not* occur, the discriminative stimulus is designated as S^Δ. The stimulus that follows the behavior, or "consequence" stimulus, has been viewed as the more significant in modifying the response. (More recent research has demonstrated the significance of the antecedent stimulus in modifying behavior.) This consequence stimulus may be positive or aversive in nature.

If a response results in a positive stimulus (positive reinforcement) or the

53

disappearance of an aversive stimulus (negative reinforcement), then the probability of that response occurring in the future in that stimulus situation is increased; in other words, the response has been strengthened. On the other hand, if a response results in an aversive stimulus (punishment by application) or the disappearance of a positive stimulus (punishment by removal), then the probability of that response occurring in the future in that stimulus situation is decreased; the response has been weakened.

Extinction is the process whereby a response which has been reinforced is no longer reinforced (Reynolds, 1968) and thus the response decreases in frequency, or *extinguishes.* Special notice should be paid to two characteristics of this latter procedure: (*a*) The change generally is gradual; and (*b*) the response may slow an initial increase immediately after the beginning of extinction, and then a gradual decrease. It is particularly important to be aware of the second characteristic because many attempts at behavioral change have been aborted by a lack of understanding of this "extinction burst."

Reinforcement can follow a response according to any one of several different schedules; in addition, schedules may be combined. (For a detailed discussion of simple and complex schedules of reinforcement, consult Reynolds, 1968, or Honig, 1966; only simple schedules are defined here.) If a response is reinforced every time it occurs, then a *continuous schedule* is being employed. One may choose to reinforce some, but not all, occurrences of a response, in which case an *intermittent schedule* of reinforcement is being employed. Intermittent schedules may be divided into those arranged according to time (*interval schedule*), or according to number of occurrences of a response (*ratio schedule*). If a response is reinforced the first time it occurs after a set interval of time, a *fixed interval schedule* is being employed. If, however, a response is reinforced the first time it occurs after a specified interval of time, but with that specified interval varying around some average interval of time, then a *variable interval schedule* is being employed. If a response is reinforced the first time it occurs after a set number of correct responses, then a *fixed ratio schedule* is being employed. If a response is reinforced the first time it occurs after a specified number of correct responses, but with that specified number varying around some average number of responses, then a *variable ratio schedule* is being employed. A continuous schedule usually results in a faster rate of learning, while an intermittent variable ratio schedule is most resistant to extinction.

Shaping, or learning by successive approximations, refers to the process whereby a new response may be taught. At first, a subject is reinforced for making a response that may only be slightly or partially like the target response. Then, after successful trials with that response, the subject is reinforced only for responses that are slightly more similar to the target response. Thus, by selective and successive reinforcing of those responses which are more and more similar to the target response, the experiment teaches the subject to emit the target response. Once several responses are taught, they may be *chained* together. Chaining is more effective if the first two responses to be chained are the last two responses to be included in the chain; in other words, it is done from end to beginning so that reinforcement always follows the terminal response in the chain.

In order to facilitate learning, one may wish to demonstrate the correct response that the subject is to emit. Such a demonstration is called *modeling*; when a modeled response is emitted by the subject, it is called *imitation.* Learning by this process may be labeled *observational learning* (Bandura, 1969).

Another principle of some importance has been named for the psychologist Premack, who first made note of it (Premack, 1965). The Premack principle states that a high-probability behavior can serve as a reinforcer for a low-probability behavior. For example, a student may work continuously at his desk for 10 minutes in order to engage in 10 minutes of play time.

Two other terms, *discrimination* and *generalization,* need to be defined before beginning a discussion of the applications of the above principles. A discriminative stimulus has been defined above as a stimulus which marks the time and place that reinforcement (or punishment) will occur; thus discrimination is the process whereby a response is brought under discriminative-stimulus control (Bijou & Baer, 1961). A person learns what stimuli have preceded the response on the trials in which that response has been strengthened or weakened; to the extent that he emits the response only in the presence of those stimuli, discrimination has occurred. Generalization may be conceptualized as the failure of discrimination to occur and is used to describe the occurrence of the response (target behavior) in the presence of stimuli other than those which served as training discriminative stimuli.

How have these principles – and the various procedures derived from them – been employed to modify behavior in special education settings? The rest of this chapter is designed to answer that question.

DEVELOPMENT OF A BEHAVIOR-MODIFICATION PROGRAM

In spite of the diversity of behavioral programs employed in special education, there are three essential steps in developing a program: (*a*) identification of the behavior(s) to be altered, (*b*) identification of the events which will consequate performance of the behavior, and (*c*) a set of rules which specify the relationship between behavior and the consequating events. Each of these steps can be easily exemplified in developing a reinforcement program, the behavior modification most frequently used.

The first step, identification of the behaviors, requires careful specification of those responses for which reinforcement is to be delivered and for which data are to be collected. The behaviors which are the focus in the program are the target responses. The specification of target responses must include specific behaviors, rather than global traits or general diagnostic labels. For example, cleanliness as a general trait would be an inappropriate target response for a behavioral program unless response manifestations were enumerated, such as absence of dirt spots on face, hands, and clothes. Even with these latter specified responses, further information is needed to determine what constitutes a dirt spot, and so on. The behaviors need to be well specified for at least two reasons: First, if the response is to be reinforced consistently, there needs to be agreement as to when it is performed. This is best achieved by specifying in advance what is included and excluded from the response category. Second, specification of the response class is essential for gathering data to determine the rate of the behavior before, during, and after the program. These data will be required to determine the efficacy of the program. Only if the behavior is reliably assessed can the data reflect changes resulting from the program. To specify the behavior, investigators will typically define the response in a careful manner and have observers independently record the target behavior. If occurrence of the target behavior can be agreed upon by independent observers, the response is sufficiently specified (see Bijou, Peterson, Harris, Allen & Johnston, 1969).

The second step in developing a behavioral program is selection of the consequating events which will alter the frequency of the target response(s). In the case of a reinforcement program, events are selected which will increase the performance of the behavior they follow. Of course, the reinforcing events depend upon the type of population and individual(s) for whom the program is devised. Several sorts of events have been used as reinforcers, including preferred activities; the distribution of food (candy, meals, snacks), trinkets (toys, prizes, gadgets), tokens (points, stars, check marks, tickets, poker chips, money); and praise and approval. Tokens are considered generalized reinforcers because they can be used to purchase other reinforcers. Token reinforcement is often preferred because it is usually more powerful than any single reinforcer; furthermore, it is not subject to deprivation and satiation effects associated with items such as food. Several additional advantages of token reinforcers have been elaborated elsewhere (Ayllon & Azrin, 1968; Kazdin & Bootzin, 1972).

If the goal of a behavioral program is to suppress behaviors, aversive events may be chosen to consequate performance of an undesirable target response. Such events frequently used include time-out from reinforcement (isolation or removal of reinforcers for a period of time) and aversive events, e.g., disapproval, reprimands, administration of electric shock, and removal of tokens.

The third basic step for developing a behavioral program is to set the guidelines relating performance of the target response(s) to the consequating events. This relationship is referred to as the *contingency*. Several contingencies are available; e.g., whenever the response is performed, the reinforcer is delivered. There may be qualification; e.g., when the response is performed in this situation, it is to be reinforced, but it is not to be reinforced in other situations. On the other hand, if intermittent reinforcement is employed, a certain number of responses may be required before reinforcement is given. In short, the rules must relate the reinforcement to behavior. Where token reinforcers are used, rules have to be invoked which specify the exchange between tokens and back-up reinforcers. It is necessary to spell out when tokens can be spent, what they can purchase, and what the exchange rate is for back-up reinforcers.

After the steps for the development of the behavior-modification program have been completed, it is essential that some means are provided for a careful evaluation of the contingencies designed to alter the target behavior. This requirement is simply an extension of Step 1 described above. After the response is specified, the frequency with which it is performed needs to be determined prior to implementing the behavior modification program so as to clarify the extent of the problem. The frequency of the target response prior to the implementation of the program is referred to as *baseline data*. Obviously, it is important to determine the extent of response performance without the program in effect, so that it can be compared with behavior while the contingency is operating. Once the contingency has been implemented, the frequency of the target response should change. When there are clear data indicating that the target response has changed, it may be important to ensure that contingencies were responsible for this, rather than extraneous factors that covaried with the contingency. To this end, investigators frequently withdraw reinforcement for a short period after the behavior has changed. If behavior returns to the baseline level or approximates baseline when the contingency is removed, it is assumed that the contingency controlled the behavior. Of course, it is frequently undesirable to even temporarily remove the program and allow behavioral gains to deteriorate while the efficacy of the contingencies is assessed. Other procedures, beyond the scope of the present discussion, have been suggested to demonstrate the controlling effect of reinforcement without the withdrawal of the contingencies (Baer, Wolf, & Risley, 1968; Kazdin, 1973b).

The data obtained during the program may indicate that performance of the target response is unaltered, or even becomes worse, during the program. These data provide valuable and immediate feedback indicating one or a combination of alternative explanations: (*a*) The contingency is not being carried out correctly; (*b*) the consequating events are not sufficiently motivating; (*c*) competing influences in the environment are maintaining the present level of performance; and (*d*) other alternatives are operating which may be peculiar to the situation in which the program is conducted. Further investigation is required to determine precisely which of these factors has interfered with the effect of the contingency. When one of the alternatives seems reasonable, a change is made in the contingency to determine its effect on behavior.

It can be seen that the use of data offers the investigator, teacher, or administrator immediate feedback regarding the efficacy of the program. The collection of data for program evaluation in large measure distinguishes operant procedures from several other programs used in special education. Often a program is based on a sound theoretical rationale and is carried out dutifully. Nevertheless, there may be no objective evaluation as to whether the program is accomplishing what it is supposed to accomplish. The behavioral approach attempts to avoid this by systematically evaluating the effect of the contingencies.

THE MENTALLY RETARDED

Behavior modification has been applied in a variety of settings for the mentally retarded (MR) for several different types of behaviors. The behaviors altered or developed depend upon the goals of the particular type of setting and the pretraining skills of the child. With the severely and profoundly retarded, self-care skills are frequently trained. With the moderately or mildly retarded, training may include work skills or academic activities.

Self-care behaviors

The focus of the majority of institutional programs has been the development of such self-care behaviors as toilet training, dressing, grooming, and feeding among the severely and profoundly retarded. Operant techniques are well suited to these groups because language skills are unnecessary for their effective use. Of the self-care behaviors, toilet training has received a great deal of attention. Dayan (1964) had severely retarded children placed on the toilet every 2 hours. Reinforcement was delivered for eliminating during these periods. Training over 6 months resulted in a dramatic decrease in the quantity of dirty diapers. Hundziak, Maurer, and Watson (1965) compared reinforcement, conventional training, and no training in developing toileting among severely retarded boys. The reinforcement group received food, a light, and tone for desired behavior, whereas the conventional-training subjects were taken to the bathroom periodically. The reinforcement group showed significant improvements in toileting, whereas the conventional-training group did not. An important finding is that the toilet training developed in the special training unit transferred to the institutional setting. Minge and Ball (1967) trained six profoundly retarded children in toileting. Food reinforcement and praise for appropriate toileting led to significant improvements on a situational test, compared with the control situation in which reinforcement was not administered.

Giles and Wolf (1966) used both positive and negative reinforcement to develop toileting behavior in five severely and profoundly retarded children. Positive reinforcement (e.g., extra desserts, meals, social attention) was used to develop elimination on the toilet. Since this was ineffective by itself, aversive stimuli were introduced into training. Children were tied to the toilet or confined for short periods, contingent upon failure to toilet properly. The aversive conditions were reduced or removed entirely when elimination was appropriate. These procedures, even though used for a short time, were effective in developing appropriate toileting. Ultimately, the behaviors were maintained by social reinforcement. Watson (1968) used an automated toilet trainer which administered reinforcement when a child defecated or urinated into the toilet. Although toileting improved in several retardates using this device, some soiling and wetting remained. Azrin, Bugle, and O'Brien (1971) reported two relatively simple devices (pants alarm and toilet-signal apparatus), which were used to train toileting in profoundly retarded subjects. Through the use of these devices along with certain procedures (modeling, artifically increasing frequency of urinations, presenting food and social reinforcement for urinating correctly or staying dry, reprimands and time-out for soiling, shaping self-initiation of toileting), nine profoundly retarded adults were trained in a median time of 4 days per person (Azrin & Foxx, 1971). Most important, procedures were used to ensure long-term maintenance of toileting behaviors. Toilet-training programs have been effective in training these behaviors in several additional studies using reinforcement, chaining and shaping of responses, prompting, and punishment (Baumeister & Klosowski, 1965; Kimbrell, Luckey, Barbuto, & Love, 1967; Mahoney, VanWagenen, & Meyerson, 1971; VanWagenen, Meyerson, Kerr, & Mahoney, 1969). In some studies, when the specific training program was terminated, the children were often not trained to use the toilet as a response to appropriate bowel and bladder cues; that is, there was inadequate stimulus control over the behavior. The children may have learned to go to the toilet when prompted, but not when they felt physiological cues (Hundziak et al., 1965; Mahoney et al., 1971). Toilet training needs to be extended to develop the appropriate response under physiological stimuli to ensure that the behaviors are maintained. With few exceptions (Mahoney et al., 1971), little follow-up data have been reported on the long-term effects of a toilet-training program. It is assumed that once developed, toileting skills are self-rewarding because the child will perform appropriately to avoid soiling. However, it is unlikely that these skills are automatically maintained after they are trained.

Training in other self-care behaviors, e.g., feeding and grooming, has been frequent in institutions for the retarded. Feeding programs have involved individualized training, where attendants try to shape behavior with a single child; or a more extensive program, where eating behaviors do not have to be so carefully shaped. Training feeding behaviors automatically uses a power reinforcer — food.

Gorton and Hollis (1965) described steps used to shape feeding skills. Increasingly greater demands were made until the children could take food to a table, feed themselves, and use proper utensils. Bensberg, Colwell, and Cassel (1965) used food (cereal, cookies, and candy) to train six severely retarded boys in toileting, dressing, and appropriate eating skills. Training was conducted individually in 15- to 30-minute sessions for 4 to 5 months. Reinforcement was given for successive approximations of the final target responses. Improvement was noted for all six subjects on a modified version of the Vineland Social Maturity Scale (VSMS), with the major gains being made in the first month. The authors noted that it was not possible to determine from these data if the improvements were due to reinforcement or simply to increased attention by the staff. However, Roos and Oliver (1969) compared operant techniques in developing self-help skills among institutionalized retardates with a group that received classroom training and a no-training control group. Primary and social reinforcement for desirable behaviors and time-out from reinforcement were used for the operant group. Ratings on a version of the VSMS prior to, 6 months after, and 1 year after the training program indicated that only the operant group showed significant gains. Increased staff attention was insufficient to account for these gains. Using punishment, Barton, Guess, Garcia, and Baer (1970) developed appropriate mealtime behavior in severely and profoundly retarded subjects. The aversive event was time-out from reinforcement, consisting of removal of the subject from the meal or a temporary removal of the food tray. Several behaviors (e.g., stealing food from others, using fingers, pushing food off the dish) were altered sequentially by time-out. When a particular undesirable behavior was suppressed, time-out was extended to include another behavior until all inappropriate meal responses were included into the contingency. The procedure was markedly effective.

Token reinforcement has been employed extensively in institutional settings. Girardeau and Spradlin (1964) used this method with severely and moderately retarded girls. Tokens were delivered for a variety of self-care, grooming, and social behaviors including making beds, washing hair, and being on time for activities. For a few children, individualized contingencies were used to develop persistence at a task, cooperative play, and academic skills. The program emphasized individual improvement in behaviors rather than performance of a predetermined response. The tokens delivered for these behaviors were exchangeable for food, clothing, jewelry, and other items displayed at a "store." Marked gains were reported 4½ months after the inception of the program. In subsequent reports of this program (Lent, 1967, 1968) residents were effectively reinforced by check marks for clearly specified behaviors related to personal appearance, occupational skills, academic skills, and social behaviors. Moreover, when token reinforcement was discontinued, social reinforcement (praise) maintained or increased these initial improvements. A 1-year follow-up after the token program showed significant group improvement in self-care, personal appearance, and walking and sitting behaviors. However, social skills and verbal behaviors did not reliably improve over baseline.

Hunt, Fitzhugh, and Fitzhugh (1968) used token reinforcement to improve the personal appearance of 12 retardates. Initially, continuous reinforcement was given when the subjects met the criterion for personal appearance. Subsequently, reinforcement was given intermittently. The Ss improved under the reinforcement program and showed the highest gains under intermittent reinforcement. When reinforcement was withdrawn, personal appearance deteriorated.

Ray and Shelton (1968) reported that 77% of 42 adolescent retardates improved in self-care behaviors, dining-room activities, and meal routines when contingent token reinforcement was used. Interestingly, over a 2-year period 13% of the Ss who passed through the program were unaffected by token reinforcement. Because this report did not include a control group or information about periods in which reinforcement was not delivered, it is unclear that the improvements were due to the reinforcement.

Several other investigators reported improvements in work behaviors, grooming, instruction following, and social skills, with adult retardates receiving token reinforcement in institutional settings (Anderson, Morrow, & Schleisinger, 1967; Bourgeois, 1968; Brierton, Garms, & Metzger, 1969; Musick & Luckey, 1970; Roberts & Perry, 1970). However, in these reports, data were not presented that rigorously demonstrated the specific control of token reinforcement.

Disruptive and destructive behaviors

Disruptive behaviors are often problems in institutional settings. To suppress such behaviors, punishment is frequently used either by itself or in conjunction with reinforcement for appropriate behaviors.

White, Nielsen, and Johnson (1972) compared different durations of time-out from reinforcement to suppress aggressive, self-injurious, and tantrum behaviors with 20 moderately and severely retarded children. Time-out consisted of placing a subject in a small room. The results showed that time-out effectively reduced the disruptive behaviors. Time-out durations of 15 and 30 minutes generally were more effective than a period of only 1 minute. Other investigators showed the effectiveness of time-out in reducing aggressive behaviors in institutionalized retardates (Hamilton, Stephens, & Allen, 1967). Reinforcement has been used with time-out in order to increase the period of time in which the client does not engage in the disruptive behaviors (Becker, Thomas, & Carnine, 1971; Bostow & Bailey, 1969; Vukelich & Hake, 1971; Wiesen & Watson, 1967).

For severe destructive behaviors, stimuli stronger than isolation have been used. Birnbrauer (1968) used electric shock to stop a profoundly retarded adolescent from biting others and destroying objects on the ward. A laboratory setting was developed which provided stimuli objects for the subject to destroy, for which he could be punished. Candy and token reinforcement were delivered for nondestructive behavior. These procedures were extended to the ward. Improvements in several behaviors were noted, although some punished behaviors persisted. The effects of punishment were specific to particular target responses and did not automatically generalize to other destructive behaviors.

Destructive and aggressive behaviors may not always victimize others, but rather may be self-inflicted. Various procedures have been used to control self-destructive behaviors. Tate and Baroff (1966) used electric shock to suppress self-injurious behavior in a retarded boy. After 1 day of treatment, self-injurious behaviors decreased from 2 per minute to .06. This behavior was completely eliminated by the end of treatment. If it had not been suppressed, the child might have sustained permanent retinal damage.

Lovaas and Simmons (1969) studied three severely retarded children who banged their heads. Removal of adult attention (extinction) was shown to gradually reduce self-destructive behaviors. However, several responses were performed in the process. Also, the extinction effect was specific to the setting (a single room) in which it was carried out. Punishment in the form of a brief electric shock rapidly reduced

61

self-destructive behavior and was associated with favorable side effects (e.g., less avoidance of an attendant nurse). Additional shocks were required to suppress behavior in locations not initially used in treatment. Similarly, Corte, Wolf, and Locke (1971) compared extinction (removal of social consequences), reinforcement for non-self-injurious behavior, and punishment (electric shock) in suppressing self-destructive behavior in four profoundly retarded adolescents. Punishment was the most effective procedure, although the effects were usually specific to the situation in which the shock was used. The authors discussed procedures to program generalization of punishment effects across several situations.

Language development

Developing language skills in the retarded includes shaping fundamental speech patterns or reinstating speech in mute individuals, developing specific word-class responses, and suppressing inappropriate speech patterns. Linguistic skills represent an important focus because restricted language usage and reliance upon gestures are often evident in this population; furthermore, verbal skills may deteriorate as a function of length of institutionalization.

As for the development of vocalization in nonverbal retardates, Kerr, Meyerson, and Michael (1965) used reinforcement (physical contact) to increase vocalizations (under control of the experimenter) in a severely retarded, mute 3-year-old girl. Peine, Gregerson, and Sloane (1970) increased the vocabulary and spontaneous speech in a severely retarded girl, using token and social reinforcement; initially, speech was prompted but eventually was performed spontaneously. Hamilton and Stephens (1967) reinstated speech in a mute 19-year-old retardate who exhibited social isolation and autistic behaviors. Using prompting and fading of prompts, verbal behaviors of an increasingly complex nature were reinforced. At the end of the study, spontaneous nonreinforced verbalizations were performed and social isolation decreased.

A great deal of research has focused upon modification of existing verbal repertoires in the retarded. MacCubrey (1971) used verbal conditioning procedures (using food and social reinforcement) to improve language skills in children with Down's syndrome. After 7 weeks of conditioning, the children showed significant improvements in language, as measured by the Stanford-Binet and a social rating scale, relative to similar groups who did not receive the conditioning. In two aggressive adolescent retardates, Doubros (1966) verbally reinforced socially acceptable talk and verbalizations describing nonaggressive social interactions. Follow-up data indicated that cooperative behaviors increased following alteration of verbal behaviors. Barton (1970) altered bizarre speech in a severely retarded boy by reinforcing appropriate responses to questions with candy. Inappropriate verbal responses resulted in time-out (withdrawal of social interaction and the magazine stimuli materials on which questions were based). Appropriate responses increased dramatically under this regime and decreased when the contingencies were withdrawn. Kazdin (1971a) suppressed psychotic talk in a prepsychotic retardate by subtracting tokens for bizarre verbalizations. Kircher, Pear, and Martin (1971) used token reinforcement and electric shock to develop appropriate picture-naming responses in two retarded children. The results showed that more words were learned and less inattentive behaviors occurred when shock was used than when the word "no" followed incorrect responses.

Guess and Baer (Baer & Guess, 1971; Guess, 1969; Guess, Sailor, Rutherford, & Baer, 1968) trained severely and moderately retarded children to make auditory discriminations of singular and plural words, to distinguish comparative and superlative adjective usage, and to generate or express plural morphemes indicating correct naming of objects after training in imitative speech. Sailor, Guess, Rutherford, and Baer (1968) controlled tantrum behavior in a retarded girl while training increasingly difficult imitative speech. Presenting difficult stimulus materials contingent upon disruptive behaviors decreased the rate of these behaviors. Investigators have used imitation training and reinforcement to produce present and past tenses of verbs in response to requests (Schumacher & Sherman, 1970) and to develop the use of complete sentences (Wheeler & Sulzer, 1970). In both of these studies, the effect of training generalized to stimuli material not specifically used in training.

Classroom behavior

Several studies have developed academic or appropriate classroom behaviors in the retarded. Token reinforcement has been relied upon extensively to alter classroom behavior. A series of investigations was reported on a 3-year program at Rainier School in Washington with retarded children whose IQs ranged from 39 to 93 (*M*=63). In the first report (Birnbrauer & Lawler, 1964), severely retarded children were reinforced with candy for entering the classroom quietly, hanging up coats, sitting attentively, and working on the task. Eventually, tokens (exchangeable for candy and prizes) were used. Of the 41 students, 37 were reported as improved on behavioral criteria. In subsequent reports of this program (Bijou, Birnbrauer, Kidder, & Tague, 1966; Birnbrauer, Wolf, Kidder, & Tague, 1965), token reinforcement was delivered for academic and cooperative responses. Individually programmed materials were used to develop vocabulary, arithmetic, comprehension, and writing skills. Aside from token reinforcement, other procedures were used. For example, time-out (removal from the classroom) was used to suppress disruptive behavior. Also, fines (loss of tokens) were used to decrease the number of errors on academic assignments below the level achieved through token reinforcement. Birnbrauer et al. (1965) reported that removal of token reinforcement led to decrements in academic performance for 10 of 15 subjects. Apparently, some of the subjects depended upon token reinforcement, whereas others sustained high levels of performance under social approval alone.

Zimmerman, Zimmerman, and Russell (1969) used token reinforcement for retarded boys who were disruptive in class. Token reinforcement and praise were alternated with praise alone over the 7 weeks of the study. For four of seven subjects, token reinforcement led to higher frequencies of instruction-following behavior than praise alone. The remaining subjects either did not differentially respond to the contingencies or did not respond at all throughout the study.

To control aggressive and disruptive behaviors in a preschool setting, Perline and Levinsky (1968) employed token reinforcement for appropriate behavior. Instances of inappropriate behavior resulted in time-out (physical restraint) or the loss of a token. Over a 5-day period of token reinforcement, aggressive and disruptive behaviors decreased relative to the previous 5 days of baseline. This effect obtained for each of the four subjects.

Sulzbacher and Houser (1968) used a punishment procedure in a class of 14 educably retarded children to suppress use of the "naughty finger" or verbal references to it. Out of a possible 10 points for the class as a whole, 1 point was lost for each instance of the behavior. Points remaining at the end of the day (the number was visible at the front of the room) could each be used for a minute of recess. This fining procedure significantly reduced the behavior over baseline when no program was invoked. However, removal of the punishment procedure resulted in an increase of the undesirable behavior. In seven different studies, Clark and Walberg (1969) used reinforcement (primarily praise) in classrooms for slow learners (including educable retarded students). Spelling and reading abilities, vocational aspirations, aspirations in performing simple tasks, and attitudes toward teacher and parents – as well as teacher attitudes toward students – were shown to improve or become more favorable as a result of reinforcement for classroom behaviors. This report demonstrated the range of changes that can be effected through reinforcement in classroom settings.

In general, proportionately few studies have focused on academic and classroom behaviors – as compared with other behaviors, e.g., self-care – for those traditionally classified as MR. Where such attempts have been made, however, the results have been favorable.

Occupational and work-related behaviors

Programs developing occupationally relevant behaviors in retardates have been carried out in sheltered workshops and institutional settings. Various reports have outlined how sheltered workshop activities may be programmed so that responses of retarded Ss can be shaped (Crosson, 1969; Tate & Baroff, 1967). Recently, excellent research has become available in this area.

Zimmerman, Stuckey, Garlick, and Miller (1969) used token reinforcement to alter productivity of 16 multiply handicapped retarded Ss. After baseline data were gathered on production rates, the subjects were trained in the use of tokens and could "practice" earning tokens without actually receiving them. Feedback was given by explaining how many tokens would have been earned. Eventually, tokens (exchangeable for activities, refreshments, and tangible rewards) were given out for improvements in production. At the end of the study, "practice" days (no tokens) and token reinforcement were alternated daily. Practice alone effectively increased production over baseline. Improvements were even greater when tokens were given. The removal of tokens at the end of the study resulted in a decrease in work rates.

Zimmerman, Overpeck, Eisenberg, and Garlick (1969a) reported a different procedure which resulted in long-lasting behavioral change after the contingencies were removed. Using 13 retarded *S*s, an avoidance procedure was employed to alter productivity. Individually, *S*s were instructed that in order for them to work at a table with other trainees, an improvement in production was required. Each day an individualized criterion was set for each *S*. If the production goal was not met on a given day, the trainee had to work the next day isolated from the group. With several *S*s, the avoidance procedure was alternated with baseline periods in which no avoidance contingency was used. The avoidance procedure consistently improved performance. Interestingly, when the avoidance contingencies were finally withdrawn completely, gains in production were maintained up to 2 weeks and did not return to initial baseline levels. Further data are needed to support the superiority of avoidance procedures to token reinforcement in effecting long-term changes.

Hunt and Zimmerman (1969) used token reinforcement for institutionalized retardates in a simulated workshop. After baseline rates of production were assessed, 14 *S*s were told that increases in production (specified individually) would be rewarded with coupons redeemable for items in a canteen. During experimental sessions, hours of coupon payment for high work rates were alternated with hours of no coupon payment. The results showed higher production rates in coupon-payment periods than in no-payment periods. When the coupon was no longer given out at the end of the study, rates remained significantly higher than the initial baseline rates.

Evans and Spradlin (1966) compared different incentive conditions in altering work rates of moderately retarded adolescent males. Each of 12 *S*s received piece-rate (contingent) reinforcement and salary (noncontingent reinforcement) over 20 sessions. Tokens (light flash and points on a counter) were each backed by a penny. A comparison of means indicated that the subjects responded more frequently under piece-rate or ratio reinforcement than under noncontingent reinforcement. Further, noncontingent token reinforcement led to greater response rates than when tokens were not given at all.

Aside from tokens, social reinforcers have been used to alter work behaviors. Logan, Kinsinger, Shelton, and Brown (1971) compared the effects of token reinforcement (backed by money) and systematic praise together with token reinforcement (stars which served as feedback) in increasing production in six moderately retarded adolescents. The subjects receiving praise and feedback for improvements in work rates improved to a greater extent than those receiving tokens backed by money.

In a simulated sheltered workshop in a public school, Brown and Pearce (1970) used teacher praise and feedback to alter the production rates of five moderately retarded clients. Reinforcement appeared to increase production, although these results could have been due to practice. Simply observing a model receive reinforcement for productivity increased performance in two *S*s. In this latter study, appropriate reversals of experimental conditions were used. The study is interesting because it demonstrated that vicarious reinforcement (observing others receive reinforcement) resulted in behavior change.

Jens and Shores (1969) evaluated the effect of feedback (graphic display indicating the number of work units completed) on the performance of three trainable retarded subjects. In a reversal design in which the experimental condition was presented, withdrawn, and re-presented, productivity increased with feedback. These results demonstrated the efficacy of nontangible reinforcement in altering work performance.

Social responses

Behavior-modification programs, particularly in institutions, often include, as part of the contingencies, reinforcement for some social responses, e.g., group play, participation in activities, and interaction with peers and adults (Girardeau & Spradlin, 1964; Musick & Luckey, 1970; Roos & Oliver, 1969). A few investigations concentrated on developing different types of social responses and provided data demonstrating the efficacy of the procedures.

Hopkins (1968) used candy and social reinforcement to develop smiling in two retarded boys. For both children, candy reinforcement was shown to control the frequency of smiling. Subsequently, a sign was worn by each child saying "If I smile—talk to me. If I look sad—ignore me." Persons at the school were told to follow the instructions of the sign. The smiling responses were relatively frequent under this regime and did not extinguish when the sign was no longer worn. At the end of the experiment, the children continued to smile at almost everyone encountered.

Redd (1969) altered the cooperative play behavior of two severely retarded boys. Three adults, each delivering reinforcement according to a different schedule, gave M & M candies to each child as he played with other children. The results showed that cooperative behavior was controlled by the discriminative stimulus value of the adult; the presence of the adult who reinforced cooperative play contingently led to cooperative play, whereas this was not the case for the adult who reinforced the children noncontingently. The children also differentially responded to an adult when that adult reinforced contingently and non-contingently at different times. These results demonstrated that cooperative behaviors were under control of the adult who served as a discriminative stimulus for the contingency in effect. Using food reinforcement and praise, Whitman, Mercurio, and Caponigri (1970) developed social responses in two severely retarded children. The presentation and withdrawal of reinforcement respectively increased and decreased interactive play. Social responses generalized to periods in which reinforcement was not given and to children who were not included in the training session. The type of social responses developed also generalized beyond those responses specifically reinforced. At the end of the study, the children remained more interactive than they had been at previous baseline rates.

THE EMOTIONALLY DISTURBED

The use of behavior-modification procedures with children who might be considered emotionally disturbed has been extensive. In spite of the problems in delineating precisely what emotional disturbance entails (Phillips, 1967) and the disdain of behavior modifers for such labels (Stuart, 1970), particular behavior problems are usually included, e.g., hyperactivity, socially withdrawn behavior, hyperaggressiveness, distractibility (Phillips, 1967). Each of these traditionally has been considered a reflection of "disturbed emotions." Of course, the behavioral approach views the behaviors as problematic in themselves, without necessarily reflecting disturbed emotions (whatever those would be). In any case, the treatment approach alters the behaviors for which the label was devised.

Hyperactivity

A variety of behaviors included under the rubric of hyperactivity have been altered with behavior-modification techniques. Homme, DeBaca, DeVine, Steinhorst, and Rickert (1963) used the Premack principle to change the behavior of hyperactive 3-year-olds in a classroom situation. High-probability behaviors were extremely disruptive classroom activities such as throwing and kicking things, running, and screaming. Low-probability behaviors included sitting quietly and working on tasks. An area was set aside where high-probability behaviors could be performed after a certain amount of time of performing low-probability behaviors. The procedure rapidly increased appropriate behaviors. Gradually, the requirements for engaging in high-probability behaviors were increased.

Patterson (1965a) employed reinforcement to control the behavior of a hyperactive child in the classroom. After baseline observations of behavior, an apparatus was put in front of the child. The apparatus lighted and made a click, when he had been attending to his work. This was immediately followed by an M & M or a penny. These back-up rewards were recorded on a counter and, at the end of each day, divided by the entire class. This procedure effectively controlled inappropriate classroom behaviors and the child was much quieter.

Risley (1968) used punishment to control a hyperactive child. Frequent climbing (into trees, furniture, and houses) was a source of injury to the child and anxiety to the parents. Time-out in the home and reinforcement (food and praise) for incompatible behaviors failed to change the behavior. Punishment with electric shock — first in the laboratory and then at home — decreased climbing. The effects were associated specifically with the presence of particular stimuli (e.g., experimenter). Side effects were noted when the behaviors were suppressed (e.g., performance of other nonpunished forms of climbing). A similar specificity of effects was noted for the punishment of the child for autistic rocking.

Wahler (1969a, b) developed reinforcement contingencies in the homes of four deviant boys. Parental approval for appropriate behaviors (compliant or study) and

67

time-out (isolation in the bedroom) for oppositional behavior effectively altered these children in the home. Changes made in the home did not generalize to the school setting, where data on similar behaviors were gathered. When similar contingency procedures also were used at school, behavior improved as it had at home (Wahler, 1969a). Zeilberger, Sampen, and Sloane (1968) instructed a parent to use social reinforcement and time-out to control aggressive behaviors in the home. In these studies showing the effect of behavior modification in the home, observers collected data indicating the frequency of the deviant (target) behaviors.

Ramp, Ulrich, and Dulaney (1971) used a delayed time-out procedure to control a severely disruptive child in an elementary school classroom. Occurrences of disruptive behavior resulted in a small light going on to signal that gym or recess time later in the day would be lost and that the student would go into isolation. This resulted in a marked reduction of inappropriate behavior.

Kubany, Weiss, and Sloggett (1971) combined time-out and token reinforcement to control oppositional and hyperactive behaviors of a boy in a first-grade classroom. Accumulated time (on a large clock) of appropriate behavior earned treats for the class. Disruptive behavior terminated the clock (time-out). This procedure controlled disruptive behavior. In addition, the child's punctuality improved as a side effect of the program.

Using contingency contracts (written agreements associating reinforcing events with response requirements), Cantrell, Cantrell, Huddleston, and Wooldridge (1969) used parents and teachers to control deviant underachieving students manifesting such behavior as truancy, hyperaggression, and school phobia. A few cases suggested the effectiveness of this procedure. Advantages of contingency contracting include the reliance on reinforcers already present in the person's environment (e.g., privileges, activities).

Social behaviors

Aside from hyperactive, hyperaggressive, tantrum, and other behaviors often considered indicative of emotional disturbance, asocial, isolate, and withdrawn behaviors are also important. Although the latter behaviors often draw less attention than acting out, they have great significance for adjustment and later social intercourse.

Hart, Reynolds, Baer, Brawley, and Harris (1968) demonstrated that teacher attention reinforcing social and cooperative play with peers increased these responses in a nonsocial and uncooperative child. Patterson (1965b) treated a school-phobic child by reinforcing verbal responses with candy in the context of doll play with the experimenter. In the structured play situation, the experimenter first used dolls to enact the child's fears of being separated from his mother. Reinforcement was given when the child answered questions related to the doll situation indicating that the "doll" was not afraid in various situations. The child went to school, the experimenter presence was gradually withdrawn, and school adjustment was restored.

Allen, Hart, Buell, Harris, and Wolf (1964) used social reinforcement (teacher reinforcement) to increase peer interactions in a socially withdrawn girl. Time spent with peers came under control of reinforcement. Brown and Elliott (1965) had a teacher attend to cooperative behaviors in nursery school children to control physical and verbal aggression. After 2 weeks of treatment, aggression was significantly reduced. A 3-week follow-up after withdrawal of the program indicated that physical agression had increased, whereas verbal aggression continued to decline. Both types of aggression were further reduced by a subsequent reinstatement of attention contingent upon cooperative behaviors. Kirby and Toler (1970) used an interesting procedure to develop social interaction with a preschool child who failed to interact with peers. The child was made responsible for passing out candy to classmates. This resulted in a marked increase in social interaction.

MacDonald, Gallimore, and MacDonald (1970) had counselors make contingency contracts with six high school students who had high rates of truancy. Individuals in the community who controlled reinforcement for the students (relatives, relatives of a girl friend, store proprietor) were used to deliver reinforcement contingent upon attendance at school. The results showed that as the contingencies ("deals") were presented, withdrawn, and reinstated, attendance was controlled by reinforcement. Other investigators have reported numerous cases where contingency contracting altered a wide range of behaviors (Tharp & Wetzel, 1969; Thorne, Tharp, & Wetzel, 1971).

Classroom behaviors

Often children who are special education problems are easily distracted and spend a great deal of time attending to stimuli irrelevant to the academic tasks. These children need not necessarily qualify as hyperactive; many are simply inattentive. Several investigators have studied attentiveness in behavioral programs.

O'Leary and Becker (1967) dramatically reduced high rates of disruptive behavior in an adjustment class by reinforcing attentive behaviors with tokens. As the program progressed, the number of periods of token reinforcement and token exchange for back-up rewards were decreased without a loss of attentive behaviors. Anecdotally, generalization of desirable behaviors across situations was noted. Kuypers, Becker, and O'Leary (1968) demonstrated a reduction in the deviant classroom behaviors of an adjustment class of third and fourth graders. The behaviors decreased during reinforcement and increased when the contingencies were withdrawn. Improved behavior during the morning class sessions (when the token program was in effect) did not generalize to afternoon sessions (when the program was not in effect).

In six classrooms for "emotionally disturbed" elementary school children, Hewett, Taylor, and Artuso (1968) used token reinforcement to increase attentive behaviors and academic functioning in reading and arithmetic. Classes received one of the following programs over 34 weeks: E (experimental period, using token reinforcement, C (control period, using no tokens), CE (17 weeks of no tokens, followed by 17 weeks of tokens), and EC (17 weeks of tokens, followed by 17 weeks of no tokens). A comparison of E and C classes demonstrated the effectiveness of token reinforcement in altering attentive behaviors. An interesting finding obtained in two classes receiving the EC condition was that attentive behavior increased slightly when the token programs were withdrawn. Gains in achievement and achievement scores also resulted from the program.

Barrish, Saunders, and Wolf (1969) divided a class including several problem students into two teams. Deviant behavior (out of seat or talking) by an individual resulted in a point for his team. The team with the fewest points would earn several rewards (e.g., privileges, victory tags). The effect of this contingency was demonstrated for one period of the day (during mathematics) and did not generalize to another period (reading) until both periods were included into the contingency.

Coleman (1970) selected elementary school students who were behavior problems in four different classes. A contingency was used whereby feedback for good behavior was given to the behavior-problem child in the form of an audible click from a counter. Each click earned a piece of candy; the candy was accumulated and was divided among the classmates. This procedure resulted in behavior change. Dividing reinforcement among classmates maximized social and peer support for behavior change.

Also using social reinforcement for appropriate behavior and time-out for undesirable behavior, Wasik, Senn, Welch, and Cooper (1969) altered the disruptive school behavior of two boys. A detailed analysis of the teacher's behaviors demonstrated their role in altering child behaviors. Similarly, Zimmerman and Zimmerman (1962) used teacher attention for appropriate behavior and withdrawal of attention for inappropriate behavior to control behavior of two "emotionally disturbed" boys. Bizarre academic responses and tantrums were extinguished in both cases.

Meichenbaum, Bowers, and Ross (1968) employed token reinforcement to increase the performance of classroom tasks with institutionalized female adolescent offenders. For attentive behaviors in the afternoon class sessions, the girls received tokens (backed by money). Although this effectively controlled behavior in the afternoons, it made no improvement in the morning class sessions. When contingent reinforcement was extended to include the mornings, behavior changed in the morning sessions as well. By the end of the school year, these girls were not significantly different in inappropriate classroom behaviors from noninstitutionalized girls in a nearby school.

Graubard (1969) used a group-reinforcement contingency to improve academic and appropriate classroom behavior with eight disturbed delinquent boys. In order for the students to receive reinforcement (points redeemable for prizes or money), *each* student had to be performing appropriately when a bell sounded. Also, academic goals were defined individually for reinforcement. Inappropriate behavior was effectively controlled with this regime relative to a period in which reinforcement was delivered independently of behavior.

Tyler (1967) altered the academic performance of a 16-year-old institutionalized delinquent boy. Tokens (exchangeable for comfortable sleeping quarters and the right to wear noninstitutional clothes) were delivered for grades on academic tasks. Over 20 weeks of the study, classroom grades showed a slight improvement in several areas of study. Tyler and Brown (1968) improved the test performance of 15 adolescent boys by giving money for correct answers on tests based on a television newscast. Performance was significantly higher under contingent than noncontingent reinforcement. However, the actual gains in test performance were slight (10%) under contingent reinforcement.

Burchard (1967; experiment I) evaluated reinforcement in a program for institutionalized antisocial adolescents who were mildly retarded. Token reinforcement (exchangeable for a variety of items and privileges) was delivered for in-seat behavior in workshop and classroom settings. In-seat behavior was accelerated with contingent reinforcement, but not with reinforcement delivered independently of performance.

Antisocial behaviors

Behavior modification has been used to alter antisocial behaviors. In general, the populations which consistently perform severe antisocial acts are treated in residential programs or housed in penal institutions. Hence, this group may rapidly leave the realm of school problems, following adjudication of cases. Nevertheless, it is instructive to consider programs for delinquent individuals.

Phillips, Phillips, and their associates (Bailey, Timbers, Phillips, & Wolf, 1971; Bailey, Wolf, & Phillips, 1970; Phillips, 1968; Phillips, Phillips, Fixen, & Wolf, 1971) evaluated operant procedures in a home-style facility for predelinquent boys. The youths had been adjudicated by juvenile court. In the facility, the boys earned tokens for the performance of a variety of behaviors related to their everyday life. The tokens were exchangeable for privileges, snacks, special events, money, and games. Tokens were withdrawn for the performance of undesirable behaviors. In several experiments, aggressive verbal behaviors, use of poor grammar, uncleanliness, tardiness, and speech articulation errors were reduced substantially with the contingent removal of tokens or delivery of tokens for incompatible responses. In one study (Bailey et al., 1970), token reinforcement delivered in the residential facility for behavior at a nearby school controlled disruptive behaviors in the classroom. Aside from careful evaluation of the reinforcement contingencies, these studies have shown that gradually fading reinforcement or punishment can be achieved without loss of behavioral improvements.

Burchard and Tyler (1965) used time-out from reinforcement to control destructive behaviors in an institutionalized male adolescent. The placement of the boy into an isolation room for disruptive acts was combined with reinforcement. Tokens (poker chips exchangeable for consumable items, recreational activities, and privileges) could be earned for each hour he remained out of isolation. The time period for staying out of isolation in order to earn tokens was eventually lengthened to 2 hours. Over 5 months, deviant offenses (e.g., stealing, sniffing glue, fighting) decreased 33%. Moreover, the seriousness of the offenses decreased substantially. Minor infractions (running in the cottage and disruptive classroom behavior) constituted a large portion of the offenses after treatment, rather than the previous more serious behavior; prior to the program, the subject was considered much less amenable to staff control than he was afterward.

Burchard (1967; experiment II) used punishment (withdrawal of tokens plus isolation) to decrease a variety of antisocial behaviors (stealing, lying, cheating, fighting, damaging of property, and physical and verbal assault). This procedure was compared with an experimental phase in which tokens were withdrawn independently of performance of behavior. When the aversive events were administered contingently, the frequency of antisocial behaviors declined.

DISADVANTAGED CHILDREN, UNDERACHIEVERS, AND CHILDREN WITH LEARNING DISABILITIES

The use of behavior modification with children whose performance is below normal for their age has been extensive. While much of the operant work reviewed in this chapter focused extensively on the consequences of behavior related to academic skills, behavior modification also has emphasized the events antecedent to responding in the classroom. Thus, attention has been given to developing instructional materials (Englemann, 1967) and programming academic tasks (Birnbrauer et al., 1965; Homme et al., 1969) to facilitate learning. In several studies reviewed below, special academic materials were used so that learning might proceed systematically and complex responses could be shaped gradually.

Academic skills

Staats and his associates (Staats, 1968; Staats, Minke, Finley, Wolf, & Brooks, 1964; Staats, Staats, Schultz, & Wolf, 1962) devised methods for developing language and reading skills in children in which stimuli materials are presented automatically and responses are reinforced with tokens (exchangeable for a variety of prizes). Individual sessions are used instead of group sessions, and training may last over several months. The particular experimental procedure in several studies has been shown to sustain attentive performance and to develop verbal repertoires in otherwise deficient children. Staats, Minke, Goodwin, and Landeen (1967) exposed 18 underachieving junior high school students to token reinforcement (backed by money) for improvements in oral reading and comprehension. Subprofessionals (high school seniors and adult volunteers) conducted the individual sessions. Subjects participating in the reinforcement program (for a mean of 38.2 hours of training) significantly improved in reading skills relative to controls not exposed to the program. However, no differences between groups were found on standardized tests following the token program. Staats, Minke, and Butts (1970) used token reinforcement to develop reading responses in culturally disadvantaged black ghetto children. The program, lasting from 4 to 5 months, significantly improved reading responses and vocabulary words learned and retained.

McKenzie, Egner, Knight, Perelman, Schneider, and Garvin (1970) reported behavior-modification programs carried out by teachers with three underachieving or slow-learning children. By ignoring inappropriate behaviors and by using praise, feedback on number of correct responses, and grades as reinforcement, performance on academic tasks and attentiveness to lessons were altered. Evans and Oswalt (1968) altered the academic performance of underachieving students in classrooms by making reinforcing consequences for the entire class (early dismissal or storytelling) contingent upon the performance of the underachievers. In four experiments in different classrooms, the weekly test scores in spelling, arithmetic, and comprehension were improved for underachieving students when the contingencies were operative. The remaining students in each of the classes, for whom reinforcing consequences were not contingent, did not improve in these academic areas during treatment. The authors noted the use of peer support for the underachieving students, which developed in two of the classes as a result of this type of contingency. Haring and Hauck (1969) used token reinforcement to improve reading skills in elementary school boys considered disabled readers. Feedback for performance and points (backed by edible rewards and prizes) increased performance on programmed reading materials. Written and oral academic performance under continuous reinforcement was superior to performance under intermittent reinforcement. As a result of this training program, the students increased their frequency of correct reading responses and spent more time working on assignments. Also, gains in reading levels ranged from 1½ to 4 years, following only 5 months of training.

Wolf, Giles, and Hall (1968) also used token reinforcement to improve the academic skills of elementary students who scored at least 2 years below their grade norm on a standardized achievement test. In a remedial classroom after school, students performed reading, arithmetic, and English tasks and received tokens contingent upon their work. Two separate experiments demonstrated that the number of tokens for a task was directly related to performance of that task. Shifts in token earnings to zero for a particular task led to cessation of performance of that task. Perhaps most important, over the course of 2 years, students who participated in the program improved their report-card grades and made a median gain of 1.5 years on a standard achievement test. Control subjects similar to the subjects exposed to the token program gained only .8 years on the achievement test in the same period.

McKenzie, Clark, Wolf, Kothera, and Benson (1968) used classroom grades as tokens to develop academic behaviors of children with learning disabilities. Grades were given weekly for performance on programmed instructional materials. These were taken to the parents, who systematically approved of good grades and mildly disapproved of poor grades. In a subsequent experimental phase, weekly allowances given by parents were made contingent upon grades at school. Eventually, the length of time for receiving grades and back-up reinforcement was extended to resemble the typical school situation. Interestingly, the use of a reinforcement system in which the home provides the back-up reinforcers need not add cost for the program to the school or home. The quantity of reinforcement often does not need to be increased from previously established levels; but the relationship of reinforcement to the behavior must be contingent. Ordinarily this is not the case.

Miller and Schneider (1970) used tokens to reinforce writing responses basic to handwriting in a Head Start program. Tokens presented for correct responses were exchangeable for play privileges and snacks. The students worked at much higher rates during contingent token reinforcement than during noncontingent token reinforcement. At the termination of the study, comparison of a control class with children who received the reinforcement program showed significant gains on a writing achievement test only for the latter group.

Lahey (1971) used modeling without reinforcement to alter the descriptive verbal repertoires of children enrolled in a Head Start program. The experimenters modeled the use of descriptive adjectives; the procedure dramatically altered the use of this response class in the children exposed to the experimenter, but not in control subjects.

Hart and Risley (1968) developed acquisition and usage of adjective-noun combinations with disadvantaged preschool children. Making reinforcement (access to various materials) contingent upon the use of color-noun combinations led to significant gains in such usage and in spontaneous vocabularies of the children. While "traditional" teaching methods resulted in language change, spontaneous verbal behavior was unaffected until the reinforcement contingencies were invoked. Reynolds and Risley (1968) used access to play materials and social reinforcement to increase spontaneous speech in a child from a low-socioeconomic background. The child received the materials after responding to requests by a teacher. The materials, rather than teacher attention, were the controlling reinforcer in increasing spontaneous speech.

Learning disabilities and special education "problems," of course, are not unique to the preschool and elementary school level. A few interesting programs have been reported with older subjects with academic deficits. Broden, Hall, Dunlap, and Clark (1970) used social and token reinforcement to develop appropriate behavior and academic skills in junior high school students who were several years behind in academic work. Students were given tokens if they were performing appropriately when a timer sounded (on the average of every 8 minutes). Behaviors improved under reinforcement but did not generalize to those periods of the day in which the contingencies were not in effect. When these periods were included into the reinforcement contingencies and fines were invoked for disruptive behaviors, control was achieved.

Clark, Lachowicz, and Wolf (1968) developed a token program for school dropouts between the ages of 16 and 21. Ten females who were dropouts working for a neighborhood organization were divided into two groups. One group worked on academic activities for 3½ hours each morning for 5 days per week. Wages for performance during this time were based on number of correct answers on instructional materials. The other group received job placement. At the end of approximately 8 weeks, the group receiving monetary reinforcement for academic performance gained 1.3 years on a standard achievement test, whereas the job group gained only 0.2 years in the same period. Gains for the academic training group were evident in reading, arithmetic, and language skills.

Classroom deportment

Haring, Hayden, and Nolen (1969) evaluated reinforcement in developing appropriate classroom behavior, language responses, and discrimination skills in Head Start children. Behaviors initially reinforced with tokens (exchangeable for minutes in a play area) were eventually maintained with social reinforcement. Time-out was also shown to suppress inappropriate responses. The behaviors were maintained for several children in follow-up reports, even though the children were in settings different from the demonstration class.

Jacobson, Bushell, and Risley (1969) regulated the degree to which Head Start children switched activities in the classroom by requiring them to perform a task (simple matching problem or academic task) before changing activities. In two studies discussed in the paper, excessive switching of activities was reduced by invoking response requirements. These studies exemplify the application of the reciprocal of the Premack principle. In this program, high-probability behavior (switching activities) was decreased by requiring the performance of a low-probability behavior (performing a task).

Mingo, Desper, and Krauss (1970) used teacher attention to reduce the extensive play behaviors of a Head Start boy who played extensively with feminine toys and clothes. Removal of attention for feminine play and attention provided for masculine play behaviors reduced feminine play to levels similar to that of male peers. Selective reinforcement altered what were considered to be signs of putative homosexual tendencies.

Allen, Turner, and Everett (1970) used various procedures to improve the behaviors of two Head Start children. Extinction was used to reduce tantrum and aggressive behaviors. Reinforcement was used to increase play behaviors and motor performance. It was of interest that for one child, social interaction with peers improved after undesirable behaviors were extinguished; these social interactions were not specifically focused upon in training.

AUTISTIC CHILDREN

While some may consider early infantile autism a category of emotional disturbance, recent interest and research in the field (e.g., the new *Journal of Autism and Childhood Schizophrenia)* warrant a separate section. Subsequent to Kanner's description of the syndrome he labeled "early infantile autism," many models have been set forth to explain its etiology and to suggest therapeutic procedures (Ward, 1970). These have included the psychoanalytic model of Bettelheim (1967), the biological-genetic model of Rimland (1964), the perceptual-impairment model of Hermelin (1966), and the operant-learning model of Ferster (Ferster, 1961; Ferster & DeMyer, 1967).

With the exception of the behavioral approach to treatment, the effects of therapeutic endeavors have been disappointing. This is not to advocate that research with other models, particularly the biological-genetic model, should be abandoned. It is entirely possible that some of the behavior disorders of autism may indeed have a physiological basis (see Boullin, Coleman, & O'Brien, 1970; Boullin, Coleman, O'Brien, & Rimland, 1971) and, as with mental retardation associated with phenylketonuria, they may someday be amenable to organic treatment.

However, given the present state of knowledge, treatment based on the learning model appears to be the most effective approach. Perhaps the unique effectiveness of behavior modification stems from the behavioral approach of specifying the disorder in terms of target behaviors and of arranging the child's environment so as to effect a change in those target behaviors.

The most extensive work with autistic behaviors has been conducted by Lovaas and his colleagues at U.C.L.A. A large part of their research efforts has been geared toward establishing effective communication and speech in their subjects. By defining target speech behaviors, breaking down these responses into their components, teaching these components, chaining them into the complete response, and ignoring echolalic speech, Lovaas and company have been able to teach speech, including storytelling, to almost completely echolalic children. In addition to extensive use of modeling, the experimenters found it necessary to use primary positive reinforcement (Lovaas, 1964; Lovaas, Berberich, Perloff, and Schaeffer, 1966; Lovaas, Freitag, Kinder, Rubenstein, Schaeffer, and Simmons, 1966). Wolf, Risley, and Mees (1964) and Risley and Wolf (1967), while engaged in more general training programs, have similarly been able to establish functional speech in autistic children.

Several investigators have employed behavior-modification procedures to increase the self-help skills of children diagnosed as autistic. By use of primary and social reinforcement and shaping procedures, such responses as the wearing of glasses (Wolf et al., 1964), toilet training (Wolf, Risley, Johnston, Harris, & Allen, 1967), hand washing, hair brushing, and bed making (Lovaas, Freitag, Nelson, & Whalen, 1967) have been taught.

Punishment procedures, primarily electric shock and time-out, have been employed to decrease the strength of self-destructive and tantrum behaviors (Wolf et al., 1964), inappropriate autistic behaviors and tantrums (Risley & Wolf, 1967), physical harm to self and other (Wolf et al., 1967), and self-stimulatory and tantrum behavior (Lovaas, Schaeffer, & Simmons, 1965). Risley (1968) found no bad side effects from the use of electric shock to reduce the dangerous climbing behavior of an autistic child; this behavior had been resistant to change by time-out procedures in the home and to extinction and reinforcement of incompatible behaviors in the laboratory. Risley's finding corroborated that of Lovaas: faradic aversive stimuli as a last resort are warranted in some cases, even from a humane standpoint (Lovaas, 1967). The data also replicated the findings of Wolf et al. (1967) that teaching of a incompatible behavior failed to decrease an undesirable behavior; however, Lovaas, Freitag, Gold, and Kassorla (1965) had used the technique successfully with their subjects.

The junior author and his students recently found that a teacher using a token program in a special education class of primarily autistic children was able to modify the children's classroom behaviors. In this study, the contingent use of teacher attention alone was not sufficiently strong to change adequately the students' behavior; when tokens and teacher attention were used concurrently the desired changes occurred. Also, in a clincal case study,[1] parents were trained to use primary and social reinforcement to teach their autistic child appropriate self-help and social skills. While these studies have all the problems of case studies, they at least provide encouraging information regarding alternatives to institutionalizing children labeled autistic.

For the first time since Kanner's description of the behavior disorders called infantile autism, there are treatment procedures that seem to work. As is obvious from this brief review, the applications to date, while effective, have been limited in scope; it is hoped that future research will be extended beyond present limitations.

CHILDREN WITH SPEECH DISORDERS

As with all the behavior disorders discussed in this chapter, appropriate assessment of the disorder — and its antecedent and consequent stimuli — is essential. The treatment procedures that might then be used to decrease stuttering, for example, would be determined by whether stuttering is a result of anticipatory anxiety, in which case systematic desensitization might be in order, or whether it is maintained by attention, in which case some operant punishment or extinction procedure might be the treatment of choice.

Behavior modification has been attempted primarily with the speech problems of stuttering, articulation difficulty, and echolalia. Since echolalia is one of the behaviors commonly associated with early infantile autism, and since consequently most of the research with echolalia has been a part of speech-treatment programs with subjects assessed as autistic, the discussion in this section is limited to the other two disorders.

---

[1] W.E. Craighead, K.D. O'Leary, & J.S. Allen, personal communication, 1972.

While there are many factors including physiological deficiencies that may contribute to these disorders, there are at least three factors of paramount significance in any assessment of speech dysfunction that should be considered in the establishment of a treatment program. The first factor is simply that the subject lacks the appropriate skills necessary to emit the target behavior. The second is that conditioned anxiety may interfere with the emission of the appropriate response, assuming that the response exists within the subject's behavioral repertory. The final factor is that the person may have the skill to emit the target behavior but instead emits the inappropriate response because of the reinforcement he receives (e.g., attention). This third factor may be an influential one, regardless of how the speech disorder developed; what one gets out of a response is, more frequently than not, an important factor in its maintenance.

Stuttering

Although the problem of stuttering would seem a good target behavior for behavioral therapists, it has only recently been conceptualized in those terms (Brady, 1968; Brutten & Shoemaker, 1967; Gray & England, 1969). A great deal of operant research has been conducted, particularly using electric shock, in reducing and eliminating speech disorders. Bandura (1969) and Siegel (1970) provided a comprehensive review of this research; the essence of the findings is that punishment procedures reduce the frequency of stuttering. However, there have been the usual problems of generalization and the question of the recurrence of the response once the shock treatment is terminated (see Daly & Frick, 1970). Time-out has also been used to reduce the frequency of stuttering; however, Adams and Popelka (1971) presented data which questioned the punishment interpretation of this treatment procedure with its usual application in therapy for stuttering.

Brady (1971) recently proposed a promising treatment procedure which could be used in varied special education settings. The method is designed to facilitate generalization or carry-over; and while it is operant in nature, it incorporates a shaping procedure that, except in extreme cases, should be adequate to allow the person to gradually overcome any inhibitory anxiety he may experience. In those cases involving extreme anxiety, the procedures may be augmented by systematic desensitization. Another advantage of Brady's procedure is that it avoids the ethical questions regarding the use of electric shock incorporated into most of the punishment regimes.

Brady outlined a procedure in which stutterers are seen on a weekly basis according to the following treatment phases: In the first phase, the treatment rationale is explained to the subject, and it is demonstrated that he can speak with nearly 100% fluency with the aid of a desk metronome. The subject is instructed to practice at home with a desk metronome for at least 45 minutes per day. The second phase involves the shaping of speech toward a normal rate and cadence. This is done by gradually increasing the rate of the metronome beats and by lengthening the units of speech for each beat. This phase usually lasts 2 to 4 weeks, includes home practice, and continues until the subject is able to speak at a normal rate (100 to 160 words per minute) and has attained a nonfluency rate 20% or less than his initial nonfluency rate.

In the third phase, a switch is made to a miniaturized electronic metronome, worn much like a hearing aid, that can be used in real-life situations; the purpose is maximum generalization from therapy. The subject then ranks the situations he faces in real life according to anticipated speech difficulty (similar to a systematic desensitization hierarchy) and begins to use his metronome in those situations, commencing with the least difficult and gradually moving to the most difficult. The treatment sessions may be spaced further apart (e.g., 3 weeks between sessions). As Brady has indicated, one should be keenly attuned to the possible difficulties encountered in this phase of the treatment.

In the fourth phase, the metronome is gradually and systematically phased out of use. This is done in the same hierarchical fashion as in the third phase. Again, efforts to talk without the metronome begin with the least difficult speech situations and gradually move to the more difficult situations. The final fifth phase is really a follow-up period in which treatment may be reinstated on a periodic basis. The rationale and occasions for the fifth phase of treatment were presented in greater detail by Brady.

Brady has reported 90% success with 23 severe stutterers who have completed the therapy program. While the program seems particularly promising, especially in its innovative attempt at facilitating generalization, it needs further evaluation. These evaluations include questions regarding specific aspects of the procedure, e.g., timing parameters of the metronome (Jones & Azrin, 1969), as well as the overall treatment. If continued support is forthcoming, such procedures should be incorporated into treatment programs, where appropriate, in special education settings.

Articulation

Much of the traditional speech therapy, although it may not have been labeled "behavior therapy," has incorporated many principles of behavior modification. Usually a response, e.g., misarticulated phoneme, is defined for remediation; then it may be modeled by the therapist for the subject to imitate; and the therapist may praise or even give primary reinforcement following a correct response. More recently these principles have been recognized, and efforts have been made to determine how to effectively teach and maintain correct articulations and how to effect generalization or carry-over to the subject's spontaneous speech. Mowrer (1971) provided a comprehensive review of this body of literature, with particular emphasis on generalization. He concluded that methods of articulation therapy, utilizing these principles, have been demonstrably effective in training and maintaining correct responses. This was true in all five stages of articulation therapy that he described. Mowrer concluded that as the techniques of teaching correct articulations have advanced in sophistication (e.g., McLean's multistimulus approach, 1970), the degree of transfer or generalization has been enhanced. He speculated that as these training methods continue to increase in sophistication, there will be less need for extratherapy training such as using parents as trainers, in order to promote generalization. While that may eventually be supported, present research with some of the most contemporary behavioral approaches indicates that there is a greater degree of generalization when training occurs in extratherapy settings (Griffiths & Craighead, 1972.

Data to date indicate that paraprofessionals may be used to enhance this carry-over from articulation therapy. Classroom teachers (Mowrer, 1971), parents (Gray & Fygetakis, 1968; Mowrer, 1971), and peers (Bailey et al., 1971; Mowrer, 1971) have all been used in various ways to facilitate generalization in articulation therapy.

GENERALIZATION

A major concern in using behavior-modification procedures is that children who are exposed to extrinsic reinforcement may become dependent upon the reinforcers and respond only in their presence. It is frequently suggested that once the reinforcers are withdrawn, the behaviors previously reinforced will extinguish. The withdrawal of reinforcement does lead to extinction, and this principle is taken into account when the reduction in undesirable behaviors is a goal. The concern with maintenance of behaviors after the contingency is withdrawn, then, is justified (see Kazdin & Bootzin, 1972; O'Leary & Drabman, 1971). Maintenance of behavior after reinforcement withdrawal is referred to as *resistance to extinction*. This is a small part of a broader issue, namely, the degree to which the target behavior generalizes to other situations in which reinforcement is not forthcoming. This is referred to as *stimulus generalization*, i.e., generalization of responses to other stimuli conditions. These situations include performance *after* reinforcement is withdrawn; and performance of the behavior *during* the period in which reinforcement is delivered but in specific situations in which reinforcement is absent. For example, resistance to extinction occurs if a reinforcement program in a classroom is withdrawn and behaviors are maintained. Stimulus generalization occurs if classroom behaviors are reinforced in the morning sessions and not in the afternoons, but behaviors are nonetheless changed in the afternoons; here the target response is generalized to situations in which the contingencies were different.

In one sense, resistance to extinction is a special case of stimulus generalization. When reinforcement is withdrawn from a situation, this changes the *situation*; if the previously reinforced behavior continues in the new situation, that process can be conceived of as stimulus generalization. Nevertheless, the cessation of reinforcement in a situation is usually described as extinction; stimulus generalization is reserved for discussing a transfer of performance from one set of stimuli or one situation to a different set of stimuli.

Another type of generalization is *response generalization*. This refers to changes of responses in the individual other than those which are specifically reinforced or punished as part of the behavior-modification program. For example, if physically aggressive behaviors are altered through punishment, these responses should decrease. If verbally aggressive behaviors decrease as well, response generalization has occurred.

Although both types of generalization are important to the behavior-change enterprise, stimulus generalization is particularly crucial. Even if behaviors may be readily altered, it is essential that the changes be maintained long after training is terminated. Further, it is essential that the behaviors are performed in settings other than that in which training occurred.

Stimulus generalization

The evidence bearing on stimulus generalization has shown fairly consistently that behavior changes only when and where reinforcement contingencies are in effect. The removal of the contingencies typically results in decrements in the target response. When reinforcers are either removed entirely or delivered noncontingently, target behaviors return to baseline or near baseline levels (Bailey et al., 1970; Birnbrauer et al., 1965; Burchard, 1967; Craig & Holland, 1970; Graubard, 1969; Herman & Tramontana, 1971; Hunt et al., 1968; Hunt & Zimmerman, 1969; Jens & Shores, 1969; Kuypers et al., 1968; Miller & Schneider, 1970; O'Leary, Becker, Evans, & Saudargas, 1969; Phillips, 1968; Phillips et al., 1971; Sulzbacher & Houser, 1968; Tyler & Brown, 1968; Wolf et al., 1968; Zimmerman et al., 1969b; Zimmerman et al., 1969c). There have been only a few exceptions showing that behaviors are maintained when the contingencies are withdrawn (Hewett et al., 1968; Surratt, Ulrich, & Hawkins, 1969).

As mentioned earlier, investigators frequently remove the reinforcement contingency during the evaluation of the program in order to demonstrate that reinforcement is controlling behaviors. This type of design, in effect, depends upon showing a decrement in behavior. As a result, there have been several demonstrations of the failure of responses to be maintained when reinforcement is withdrawn. It should be emphasized that the purpose of most investigations in the literature has been to demonstrate that intractable behaviors can be altered with behavior-modification techniques. Hence, few studies have attempted to develop procedures which will ensure that changes effected with reinforcement will be maintained in extinction (see Kazdin & Bootzin, 1972). There are several procedures, outlined later in the discussion, which can ensure that changes *will* be maintained when the contingencies are withdrawn.

Aside from resistance to extinction, the generalization of behaviors to situations in which reinforcement is absent has been investigated in a few studies. Usually, there has been an examination of generalization of behaviors from a reinforced period of the day to a period of the day in which reinforcement is not delivered. Several studies in school settings showed that reinforcement at one time of the day or in one situation did not generalize to other periods of the day or other situations (Becker, Madsen,

Arnold, & Thomas, 1967; Broden et al., 1970; Kuypers et al., 1968; Meichenbaum et al., 1968; O'Leary et al. 1969). There were several exceptions to this (Hunt & Zimmerman, 1969; Kazdin, 1973c; Schwarz & Hawkins, 1970; Walker, Mattson, & Buckley, 1969). The major conclusion that can be drawn from these studies is that in restricted circumstances, there may be generalization of behaviors across situations. However, these circumstances are not clear at the present time.

Individuals participating in a reinforcement program can usually discriminate when and where the contingencies are in effect. Hence, performance does not generalize across situations. For example, Wahler (1969) found that the control of deviant behaviors of children in the home did not generalize to performance at school. However, when the behaviors at school also were included in the reinforcement contingencies, these behaviors readily improved. Individuals make finer discriminations than gross situational differences in responding to reinforcement. Redd (1969) demonstrated that retarded children will differentially respond with appropriate behaviors to adults who differentially administer reinforcement. An adult who reinforces contingently will evoke appropriate behavior to a greater extent than one who reinforces contingently and noncontingently at different times. In view of these specific response tendencies, generalization is not achieved automatically unless specifically programmed. If behaviors are desired in various situations, those situations should be included into the contingencies.

In studies of punishment, several investigators found little or no recovery of undesirable target responses once the punishment was removed (Hamilton et al., 1967; Luckey et al., 1968; Risley, 1968). However, there have been reports in which responses have recovered after withdrawal of punishment (Sulzbacher & Houser, 1968; Ramp et al., 1971). As for generalization across situations, aversive contingencies often become strongly associated with the specific situation in which they are used. Hence, generalization across situations may not occur unless punishment is extended across several situations (Birnbrauer, 1968; Corte et al., 1971). In addition, the effects of punishment may be specific in the response that is suppressed, with little or no response generalization (Birnbrauer, 1968; Hamilton & Standahl, 1969; Risley, 1968). From the above studies, the major conclusion which can be reached is that generalization across situations and maintenance of responses during extinction are not automatic. If no steps are taken to ensure stimulus generalization, it is unlikely to occur. Thus, the status of stimulus generalization is not at all clear because few studies have made specific efforts to ensure that behaviors are maintained or performed in a variety of situations.

Favorable results have been obtained in those few studies that include provisions for response maintenance in the program. For example, Patterson and Brodsky (1966) treated a child who had multiple problems at home and at school. Aside from focusing on target behaviors in the child, changes were programmed in the child's environment to increase the likelihood that behaviors would be maintained. The child's peers were reinforced for reciprocating desirable social interaction. Moreover, parents were trained to use reinforcement principles at home. In view of the importance of ensuring maintenance of behaviors after the behavior-modification program is withdrawn, a description of several procedures to achieve this end follows, along with a brief discussion of response generalization.

Response generalization

It is readily conceivable that alteration of a particular behavior will effect changes in other behaviors which are related to the target response. Even though the specific goal of a behavior-modification program is to focus on one or a few responses, other responses may change as a result of the program. When particular responses such as obstreperous behaviors are altered, it is likely that others will be as well (Allen et al., 1970). A change in the child may trigger changes in his environment (e.g., social interactions with peers and teachers), which will further affect his behavior.

In spite of the importance of response generalization and its implications, few studies have assessed concomitant changes in behaviors along with the assessment of target responses. Thus, in most studies it is not possible to conclude from the data that favorable behavior changes were made in addition to those of initial focus. There are some exceptions to this. Burchard and Tyler (1965) focused on the frequency of disruptive behaviors by using time-out for these behaviors, and token reinforcement for nondisruptive behaviors. The frequency and severity of behaviors changed. The topographical changes in the response class constituted response generalization. Kubany, Weiss, and Sloggett (1971) used reinforcement and time-out to control the disruptive behavior of a deviant first-grade boy. Although the contingencies were aimed only at modifying disruptive behavior, tardiness decreased as well.

In a token economy for retarded students, Zimmerman et al. (1969c) reported the emergence of cooperative behaviors between students, even though these responses were not included in the reinforcement contingency. Hingtgen, Sanders, & DeMyer (1965) shaped cooperative responses in pairs of schizophrenic children. However, physical contact between the children also increased. In a token program for Head Start children, Miller and Schneider (1970) reported anecdotally that improvements in handwriting (the reinforced responses) were accompanied by an increase in cooperative behaviors, favorable attitudes toward school, and improvements in the children's ability to understand instructions.

From these studies, it is evident that beneficial side effects of a behavior-modification program can occur. Few investigators have attempted to evaluate the effect of the contingencies on any measures other than a specific, circumscribed target response. Additional response measures are needed to assess specific improvements, as well as side effects, which occur with reinforcement and punishment.

Procedures to augment response maintenance

A major concern of educators using behavioral approaches is to ensure maintenance of gains after the initial behavior changes are made and the program is withdrawn. Unfortunately, this area has not been studied extensively in reinforcement practices. An assumption has been made that if desirable behavioral changes are made through extrinsic reinforcement, the changes will be supported naturally (i.e., reinforced) by the environment. Apparently this assumption is not well supported, because the removal of extrinsic reinforcement usually results in decrements in previously reinforced behaviors, as reviewed above. Kazdin and Bootzin (1972) discussed numerous procedures designed to facilitate response maintenance after the reinforcement program is withdrawn. It is useful to review these procedures briefly.

Initially, social reinforcement may be used to maintain behaviors which are developed through token reinforcement or contingency contracting. Although all children may not respond to praise, social approval can be reinforcing by pairing it with something that already is reinforcing, such as tokens (Locke, 1969). Subsequently, praise alone can be used to maintain behavior. Wahler (1968) used token reinforcement (points exchangeable for toys) in the home to develop cooperative behaviors in two children. Praise was paired with the delivery of tokens. When the tokens were withdrawn, behaviors were maintained with social approval. Before the pairing of tokens and social approval, praise was ineffective as a reinforcer. Thus, one way to maintain behavior, if extrinsic reinforcers have been used, is to substitute natural reinforcers, such as praise.

Another procedure for ensuring response maintenance is to develop the target behavior in a variety of stimulus settings so that the responses do not become associated with a restricted set of circumstances. Goocher and Ebner (1968) used stimulus variation to train a deviant child to perform appropriate classroom behavior. Initially, training was carried out only in the presence of the experimenter. Gradually planned distractions were introduced (e.g., television). Training was shifted to the classroom itself in the presence of other children. Throughout training, deviant behavior increased whenever distracting stimuli were introduced, but they quickly extinguished. After training was terminated, appropriate behavior was maintained in the classroom. Similarly, in a residential setting for retardates, Lent (1967, 1968) successfully trained adolescent retardates in household activities which they would have to perform upon discharge. A model home was built on the grounds of the institution in order to simulate the conditions under which the behaviors ultimately had to be performed. This represents one of the few attempts to reinforce behaviors in an institutional setting under stimulus conditions similar to extra-treatment conditions.

Another technique to maintain responses is to train parents or relatives to carry out the contingencies. Several studies have been reported which illustrated the use of this technique. Salzinger, Feldman, and Portnoy (1970) trained parents of brain-damaged children to handle and maintain behaviors in the home. O'Leary, O'Leary, and Becker (1967) reinforced a child for engaging in cooperative behaviors in the home. Eventually, the child's mother was trained to carry out the reinforcement program. Peers have also been used to help maintain behavior changes in hyperactive children (Patterson, 1965b) and the mentally retarded (Kazdin, 1971b).

The parameters of reinforcement can be varied to alter the resistance to extinction of target behaviors (Kimble, 1961). For example, manipulation of the delay of reinforcement can be used to enhance response maintenance. The delay between the response and reinforcement gradually can be lengthened. In the case of token reinforcement, the delay between the receipt of tokens and exchange of tokens for back-up rewards also can be extended. O'Leary and Becker (1967) used points to control instruction-following behavior in elementary school students. The number of times reinforcement was delivered decreased, and the delay between token reinforcement and exchange of tokens increased up to a 4-day delay period. The variation of delay to augment resistance of responses to extinction is desirable, primarily because of the resemblance of delayed reinforcement in a training setting with reinforcement in the natural environment. Rewards in the natural environment (e.g., grades, money) are delayed, and thus it would seem profitable to train children in special education settings to perform behaviors without immediate reward. Research bearing on this technique to facilitate response maintenance is needed.

Other parameters of reinforcement can be varied during acquisition, to maintain behaviors in extinction. Reinforcement schedules have not been studied in behavioral programs in terms of their effect on extinction. Reinforcement can be programmed to become increasingly intermittent, after the target-response rate is high. Thus, initially reinforcement is given for each response; eventually more and more responses are required for reinforcement. For example, Phillips et al. (1971) gradually reduced the number of times when token reinforcement was given to predelinquent boys for performing target behaviors. In the beginning of the program, target behaviors were reinforced frequently until well established. At the termination of the program, reinforcement was given intermittently on few occasions. When behavior was checked (infrequently and unpredictably), the number of tokens given for reinforcement was very large. This procedure maintained behavior at a high level with significantly less frequent reinforcement. Similarly, Kazdin and Polster (1973) reinforced withdrawn adult retardates for interacting socially. The S continuously reinforced for these behaviors showed an immediate extinction of social behaviors when reinforcement was withdrawn. The S who was intermittently reinforced continued high levels of social interaction over several weeks of extinction.

It is unclear at the present time whether the use of intermittent reinforcement will only postpone extinction of the target response or will prevent it entirely. The effects of variations of reinforcement during acquisition have been inconsistent (Haring & Hauck, 1969; Meichenbaum et al., 1968); they warrant more investigation.

There are other techniques which can enhance the maintenance of behavior following removal of reinforcement contingencies (Kazdin & Bootzin, 1972): the amount of reinforcement can be gradually diminished until the response is being performed with no reinforcement; self-reinforcement can be used whereby a child is trained to reinforce himself (Johnson, 1969; Lovitt & Curtiss, 1969). Research is needed concerning techniques to maintain behaviors which will be as powerful as techniques used to effect initial change.

TRAINING STAFF, ATTENDANTS, AND TEACHERS

The training of staff in contact with children in special education settings is crucial to a behavior-modification program. Because of the powerful control that attendants and teachers can exert on children's behavior, investigators have regarded staff training as an essential element for an effective program (Gardner, 1973; Kazdin & Bootzin, 1972; Krasner, 1968; Kuypers et al., 1968; Liberman, 1968; Miron, 1966; O'Leary & Drabman, 1971). No matter how well planned the program, poorly trained personnel can easily vitiate its beneficial effects. Inadvertent punishment or reinforcement can alter or negate the effectiveness of the contingencies. Whenever behavior modification is conducted in the classroom, for example, it is the teacher who ultimately administers reinforcement. The teacher alone is the arranger of the contingencies because she generally works alone. (This led Bijou [1970] to refer to the teacher as the "Lone Arranger.") She arranges classroom contingencies to develop study habits, present materials in a manner that will facilitate learning, and eliminate undesirable behaviors which interfere with academic performance. Similarly, in nonclassroom settings, those who interact most frequently with the children have the greatest opportunity to reinforce, ignore, and punish behaviors. While this is desirable when the contingencies are executed properly, it may have unfortunate consequences when the contingencies support undesirable behaviors. In many instances, attendants and teachers maintain inappropriate behaviors by reinforcing deviant responses (Buehler, Patterson, & Furniss, 1966; Ebner, 1967; Gelfand, Gelfand, & Dobson, 1967). Hence, the concern for adequately training teachers and other persons in staff positions (see Becker, Engelmann, & Thomas, 1971; Buckley & Walker, 1970; Meacham & Wiesen, 1969; Skinner, 1968) seems justified. It should be noted that there have been a few programs in which behavior change is accomplished with minimal training of staff (Kuypers et al., 1968). However, the effects obtained with minimally trained staff may be less than those which could be achieved with well-trained staff (cf. O'Leary & Becker, 1967).

Training staff is a task which ultimately reduces to changing certain staff behaviors. Thus, all the problems of changing the behavior of the children also present themselves when staff training is undertaken. The desirable target behaviors for teachers need to be identified, and some program has to be developed to alter these behaviors. Finally, training has to ensure that the behaviors are maintained. The behaviors required of staff depend upon the specific setting in which the staff member functions, such as an institution, day-care center, public school, and so on. In general, the staff must be trained to reinforce consistently those behaviors which should be increased and to ignore, or minimally punish, those behaviors which need to be suppressed. Of course, most people believe that they perform this way. However, those who are untrained are usually not systematic in their application of the principles outlined earlier in the chapter. In addition, punishments (time-out, mild disapproval, loss of tokens) are usually preceded by reprimands, which do not suppress behavior in the long run (Madsen, Becker, Thomas, Koser, & Plager, 1970; O'Leary, Kaufman, Kass, & Drabman, 1970). Specific conditions must obtain in administering reinforcement to maximize its effect on performance (such as the immediate delivery of reinforcement after appropriate behavior).

Most regimes used to train staff rely on the usual academic procedures of lectures, discussions, readings, and examinations. While such training usually imparts *knowledge* of operant principles, it is unlikely that teachers and attendants can perform appropriately thereafter when dealing with children (Hall & Copeland, 1971). Hence, behavior modifiers have become concerned with methods of training staff to skillfully implement the contingencies. As one might suspect, operant principles have been used in training teachers to become effective behavior modifiers. For example, McNamara (1971) used token reinforcement to train teachers to ignore disruptive classroom behavior and to attend to appropriate behavior of the students. Tokens earned by one teacher were exchanged at the end of the day for beer. Other investigators used time off from work (Watson, Gardner, & Sanders, 1971), special recognition (Roberts & Perry, 1970), and feedback (Cooper, Thomson, & Baer, 1970; Kazdin, 1973a; Panyan, Boozer, & Morris, 1970) to alter staff behavior in behavior-modification programs. Other techniques, such as role-playing and self-paced instruction (Watson et al., 1971), have been used as part of training procedures to develop proficiency in applying operant techniques. Excellent intensive programs for training school personnel have been explicated by Hall and Copeland (1971).

Once behaviors of the staff are developed sufficiently, procedures may be needed to ensure that these behaviors are maintained. Often it is assumed that when teachers and attendants become proficient, skills will be maintained by natural contingencies, i.e., improved behaviors of the students. However, the assumption that staff behaviors are maintained by these consequences remains an assumption. A teacher may not even be responsive to behavior changes in the child (see Loeber, 1971). In fact, other factors are operative that may lead to extinction of desirable teacher behaviors. The natural contingencies often support undesirable teacher behaviors. For example, the effects of administering social approval for appropriate student behaviors are frequently somewhat delayed. On the other hand, punishment, such as shouting reprimands, may be immediately effective. Unfortunately, the immediate effects of punishment may reinforce the teacher for these behaviors, despite their long-term deleterious effects (Madsen et al., 1970; O'Leary et al., 1970). For behavioral skills to be maintained, staff may need to be trained to evaluate their own behavior to ensure that the contingencies are being carefully followed. The issue of maintaining high levels of staff proficiency has not been well investigated at the present time and deserves study. So far, the primary goal has been effecting the initial change in staff behavior.

SUMMARY

This paper has presented an overview of the application of the principles of learning, particularly operant conditioning, to special education settings. Following a general statement of the principles of operant conditioning and guidelines for the establishment of a behavior-modification program, the authors reviewed what has been accomplished by the use of behavior modification in several different special education settings.

Behavior-modification procedures with the mentally retarded have been employed to effectively modify self-help skills; to decrease disruptive and destructive behaviors; and to increase language skills, desired classroom behaviors, work and vocationally oriented behaviors, and appropriate social skills. Specific behaviors which generally cause a child to be labeled "emotionally disturbed" have also been favorably altered. Hyperactive behaviors have been reduced, appropriate social behaviors have been increased, appropriate classroom behaviors have been taught and maintained, and the frequency of certain antisocial behaviors has been reduced. The implications and limitations of these findings were noted.

The next section reviewed the materials and special programs designed to teach disadvantaged students, students with learning disabilities, and underachievers. The integration of the activities of all professionals in special education was cited as particularly important in enhancing future effectiveness in this area. The final problem areas were autism and speech disorders (stuttering and articulation problems); specific treatment programs and their evaluation were discussed.

Two major issues were then described. The first centered around generalization (both stimulus and response). Most studies have not found generalization of behavior to situations in which the contingencies were not in effect. Means to ensure generalization should be included in behavior-modification programs. Several suggestions for enhancing generalization were discussed. The second major issue was staff training and the maintenance of desired staff behavior; staff training was seen as similar to any behavior-modification program, involving the same principles and the same systematic implementation and maintenance.

In summary, behavior-modification procedures, while still limited in the range of their attempted application, have been particularly effective in bringing about desired behavioral changes in several special education settings. The future appears both challenging and promising.

References

Adams, M.R., & Popelka, G. The influence of "time-out" on stutterers and their disfluency. *Behavior Therapy,* 1971, **2**, 334-339.

Allen, K.E., Hart, B., Buell, J.S., Harris, F.R., & Wolf, M.M. Effects of social reinforcement on isolate behavior of a nursery school child. *Child Development,* 1964, **35**, 511-518.

Allen, K.E., Turner, K.D., & Everett, P.M. A behavior modification classroom for Head Start children with problem behaviors. *Exceptional Children,* 1970, **37**, 119-127.

Anderson, D., Morrow, J.E., & Schleisinger, R. The effects of token reinforcers on the behavior problems of institutionalized female retardates. Paper presented at the Western Psychological Association Convention, San Francisco, May 1967.

Ayllon, T., & Azrin, N.H. *The token economy: A motivational system for therapy and rehabilitation.* New York: Appleton-Century-Crofts, 1968.

Azrin, N.H., Bugle, C., & O'Brien, F. Behavioral engineering: Two apparatuses for toilet training retarded children. *Journal of Applied Behavior Analysis,* 1971, **4**, 249-253.

Azrin, N.H., & Foxx, R.M. A rapid method of toilet training the institutionalized retarded. *Journal of Applied Behavior Analysis,* 1971, **4**, 89-99.

Baer, D.M., & Guess, D. Receptive training of adjectival inflections in mental retardates. *Journal of Applied Behavior Analysis,* 1971, **4**, 129-139.

Baer, D.M., Wolf, M.M., & Risley, T.R. Some current dimensions of applied behavior analysis, *Journal of Applied Behavior Analysis,* 1968, **1**, 91-97.

Bailey, J.S., Timbers, G.D., Phillips, E.L., & Wolf, M.M. Modification of articulation errors of pre-delinquents by their peers. *Journal of Applied Behavior Analysis,* 1971, **4**, 265-281.

Bailey, J.S., Wolf, M.M., & Phillips, E.L. Home-based reinforcement and the modification of pre-delinquents' classroom behavior. *Journal of Applied Behavior Analysis,* 1970, **3**, 223-233.

Bandura, A. A social learning interpretation of psychological dysfunctions. In P. London & D. Rosenhan (Eds.), *Foundations of abnormal psychology.* New York: Holt, 1968.

Bandura, A. *Principles of behavior modification.* New York: Holt, 1969.

Barrett, B.H., & Lindsley, O.R. Deficits in acquisition of operant discrimination and differentiation shown by institutionalized retarded children. *American Journal of Mental Deficiency,* 1962, **67**, 424-436.

Barrish, H.H., Saunders, M., & Wolf, M.M. Good behavior game: Effects of individual contingencies for group consequences on disruptive behavior in a classroom. *Journal of Applied Behavior Analysis,* 1969, **2**, 119-124.

Barton, E.S. Inappropriate speech in a severely retarded child: A case study in language conditioning and generalization. *Journal of Applied Behavior Analysis,*

Barton, E.S., Guess, D., Garcia, E., & Baer, D.M. Improvements of retardates' mealtime behaviors by timeout procedures using multiple baseline techniques. *Journal of Applied Behavior Analysis,* 1970, **3**, 77-84.

Baumeister, A.A., & Klosowski, R. An attempt to group toilet train severely retarded patients. *Mental Retardation,* 1965, **3**, 24-26.

Becker, W.C., Englemann, S., & Thomas, D.R. *Teaching: A course in applied psychology.* Chicago: Science Research Associates, 1971.

Becker, W.C., Madsen, C.H., Arnold, C.R., & Thomas, D.R. The contingent use of teacher attention and praise in reducing classroom behavior problems. *Journal of Special Education,* 1967, **1**, 287-307.

Becker, W.C., Thomas, D.R., & Carnine, D. Reducing behavior problems: An operant conditioning guide for teachers. In W.C. Becker (Ed.), *An empirical basis for change in education.* Chicago: Science Research Associates, 1971.

Bensberg, G.J., Colwell, C.N., & Cassel, R.H. Teaching the profoundly retarded self-help activities by shaping behavior techniques. *American Journal of Mental Deficiency,* 1965, **69**, 674-679.

Bettelheim, B. *The empty fortress: Infantile autism and the birth of the self.* New York: The Free Press, 1967.

Bijou, S.W. What psychology has to offer education—now. *Journal of Applied Behavior Analysis,* 1970, **3**, 65-71.

Bijou, S.W., & Baer, D.M. *Child development: A systematic and empirical theory.* Vol. I. New York: Appleton-Century-Crofts, 1961.

Bijou, S.W., Birnbrauer, J.S., Kidder, J.D., & Tague, C.E. Programmed instruction as an approach to teaching of reading, writing, and arithmetic to retarded children. *Psychological Record,* 1966, **16**, 505-522.

Bijou, S.W., Peterson, R.F., Harris, F.R., Allen, K.E., & Johnston, M.S. Methodology for experimental studies of young children in natural settings. *Psychological Record,* 1969, **19**, 177-210.

Birnbrauer, J.S. Generalization of punishment effects—a case study. *Journal of Applied Behavior Analysis,* 1968, **1**, 201-211.

Birnbrauer, J.S., & Lawler, J. Token reinforcement for learning. *Mental Retardation,* 1964, **2**, 275-279.

Birnbrauer, J.S., Wolf, M.M., Kidder, J., & Tague, C.E. Classroom behavior of retarded pupils with token reinforcement. *Journal of Experimental Child Psychology,* 1965, **2**, 219-235.

Bostow, D.E., & Bailey, J.B. Modification of severe disruptive and aggressive behavior using brief time-out and reinforcement procedures. *Journal of Applied Behavior Analysis,* 1969, **2**, 31-37.

Boullin, D.J., Coleman, M., & O'Brien, R.A. Abnormalities in platelet 5-hydroxytryptamine efflux in patients with infantile autism. *Nature,* 1970, **226**, 371-372.

Boullin, D.J., Coleman, M., O'Brien, R.A., & Rimland, B. Laboratory predictions of infantile autism based on 5-hydroxytryptamine efflux from blood platelets and their correlation with the Rimland E-2 score. *Journal of Autism and Childhood Schizophrenia*, 1971, **1**, 63-71.

Bourgeois, T.L. Reinforcement theory in teaching the mentally retarded: A token economy program. *Perspectives in Psychiatric Care*, 1968, **6**.

Brady, J.P. A behavioral approach to the treatment of stuttering. *American Journal of Psychiatry*, 1968, **125**, 843-848.

Brady, J.P. Metronome-conditioned speech retraining for stuttering. *Behavior Therapy*, 1971, **2**, 129-150.

Brierton, G., Garms, R., & Metzger, R. Practical problems encountered in an aide administered token reward cottage program. *Mental Retardation*, 1969, **7**, 40-43.

Broden, M., Hall, R.V., Dunlap, A., & Clark, R. Effects of teacher attention and a token reinforcement system in a junior high school special education class. *Exceptional Children*, 1970, **36**, 341-349.

Brown, L., & Pearce, E. Increasing the production rates of trainable retarded students in a public school simulated workshop. *Education and Training of the Mentally Retarded*, 1970, **5**, 15-22.

Brown, P., & Elliott, R. Control of aggression in a nursery school class. *Journal of Experimental Child Psychology*, 1965, **2**, 103-107.

Brutten, E.J., & Shoemaker, P.J. *The modification of stuttering.* Englewood Cliffs, N.J.: Prentice-Hall, 1967.

Buckley, N.K., & Walker, H.M. *Modifying classroom behavior: A manual of procedure for classroom teachers.* Champaign, Ill.: Research Press, 1970.

Buehler, R.E., Patterson, G.R., & Furniss, J.M. The reinforcement of behavior in institutional settings. *Behaviour Research and Therapy*, 1966, **5**, 157-167.

Burchard, J.D. Systematic socialization: A programmed environment for the habilitation of antisocial retardates. *Psychological Record*, 1967, **17**, 461-476.

Burchard, J.D., & Tyler, V.O. The modification of delinquent behaviour through operant conditioning. *Behaviour Research and Therapy*, 1965, **2**, 245-250.

Cantrell, R.P., Cantrell, M.L., Huddleston, C.M., & Wooldridge, R.L. Contingency contracting with school problems. *Journal of Applied Behavior Analysis*, 1969, **2**, 215-220.

Clark, C.A., & Walberg, H.J. The use of secondary reinforcement in teaching inner-city school children. *Journal of Special Education*, 1969, **3**, 177-185.

Clark, M., Lachowicz, J., & Wolf, M.M. A pilot basic education program for school dropouts incorporating a token reinforcement system. *Behaviour Research and Therapy*, 1968, **8**, 183-188.

Coleman, R. A conditioning technique applicable to elementary school classrooms. *Journal of Applied Behavior Analysis*, 1970, **3**, 293-297.

Cooper, M.L., Thomson, C.L., & Baer, D.M. The experimental modification of teacher attending behavior. *Journal of Applied Behavior Analysis*, 1970, **3**, 153-157.

Corte, H.E., Wolfe, M.M., & Locke, B.J. A comparison of procedures for eliminating self-injurious behavior of retarded adolescents. *Journal of Applied Behavior Analysis*, 1971, **4**, 201-213.

Craig, H.B., & Holland, A.L. Reinforcement of visual attending in classrooms for deaf children. *Journal of Applied Behavior Analysis*, 1970, **3**, 97-109.

Crosson, J.E. A technique for programming sheltered workshop environments for training severely retarded workers. *American Journal of Mental Deficiency*, 1969, **73**, 814-818.

Daly, D.A., & Frick, J.V. The effects of punishing stuttering expectations and stuttering utterances. A comparative study. *Behavior Therapy*, 1970, **1**, 228-239.

Dayan, M. Toilet training retarded children in a state residential institution. *Mental Retardation*, 1964, **2**, 116-117.

Doubros, S.G. Behavior therapy with high level, institutionalized retarded adolescents. *Exceptional Children*, 1966, **33**, 229-233.

Ebner, M. An investigation of the role of the social environment in the generalization and persistence of the effect of a behavior modification program. Unpublished doctoral dissertation, University of Oregon, 1967.

Engelmann, S. Teaching reading to children with low mental ages. *Education and Training of the Mentally Retarded*, 1967, **2**, 193-201.

Evans, G.W., & Oswalt, G.L. Acceleration of academic progress through the manipulation of peer influence. *Behavior Research and Therapy*, 1968, **6**, 189-195.

Evans, G.W., & Spradlin, J.E. Incentives and instructions as controlling variables of productivity. *American Journal of Mental Deficiency*, 1966, **71**, 129-132.

Ferster, C.B. Positive reinforcement and behavioral defects of autistic children. *Child Development*, 1961, **32**, 437-456.

Ferster, C.B., & DeMyer, M.K. A method for the experimental analysis of the behavior of autistic children. In S. Bijou & D.M. Baer (Eds.), *Child development: Readings in experimental analysis.* New York: Appleton-Century-Crofts, 1967.

Gardner, J.M. Differential effectiveness of two methods for teaching behavior modification techniques to institutional attendants. Paper presented at the American Association on Mental Deficiency, Washington, D.C., 1970.

Gardner, J.M. Training the trainers: A review of research on teaching behavior modification. In C.M. Franks & R. Rubin (Eds.), *Progress in behavior therapy, 1971.* New York: Academic Press, 1973.

Gelfand, D.M., Gelfand, S., & Dobson, W.R. Unprogrammed reinforcement of patients' behaviour in a mental hospital. *Behaviour Research and Therapy*, 1967, **5**, 201-207.

Giles, D.K., & Wolf, M.M. Toilet training institutionalized, severe retardates: An application of operant behavior modification techniques. *American Journal of Mental Deficiency*, 1966, **70**, 766-780.

Girardeau, F.L., & Spradlin, J.E. Token rewards in a cottage program. *Mental Retardation,* 1964, **2**, 345-351.

Goocher, B.E., & Ebner, M. A behavior modification approach utilizing sequential response targets in multiple settings. Paper presented at the Midwestern Psychological Association, Chicago, May 1968.

Gorton, C.E., & Hollis, J.H. Redesigning a cottage unit for better programming and research for the severely retarded. *Mental Retardation,* 1965, **3**, 16-21.

Graubard, P.S. Utilizing the group in teaching disturbed delinquents to learn. *Exceptional Children,* 1969, **35**, 267-272.

Gray, B.B., & England, G. (Eds.) *Stuttering and the conditioning therapies.* Monterey, Calif.: The Monterey Institute for Speech and Hearing, 1969.

Gray, B.B., & Fygetakis, L. Mediated language acquisition for dysphasic children. *Behaviour Research and Therapy,* 1968, **6**, 263-280.

Griffiths, H., & Craighead, W.E. Generalization in operant articulation therapy. *Journal of Speech and Hearing Disorders,* 1972, **37**, 485-494.

Guess, D. A functional analysis of receptive and productive speech: Acquisition of the plural morpheme. *Journal of Applied Behavior Analysis,* 1969, **2**, 55-64.

Guess, D., Sailor, W., Rutherford, G., & Baer, D.M. An experimental analysis of linguistic development: The productive use of the plural morpheme. *Journal of Applied Behavior Analysis,* 1968, **1**, 297-306.

Hall, R.V., & Copeland, R.E. The responsive teaching model: A first step in shaping school personnel as behavior modification specialists. Paper presented at the Third Banff International Conference on Behavior Modification, Calgary, Alberta, April 1971.

Hamilton, J.W., & Standahl, J. Suppression of stereotyped screaming behavior in a 24 year old profoundly retarded girl. *Journal of Experimental Child Psychology,* 1969, **7**, 114-121.

Hamilton, J.W., & Stephens, L.Y. Reinstating speech in an emotionally disturbed mentally retarded young woman. *Journal of Speech and Hearing Disorders,* 1967, **32**, 383-389.

Hamilton, J.W., Stephens, L.Y., & Allen, P. Controlling aggressive and destructive behavior in severely retarded institutionalized residents. *American Journal of Mental Deficiency,* 1967, **71**, 852-856.

Haring, N.G., & Hauck, M.A. Improved learning conditions in the establishment of reading skills with disabled readers. *Exceptional Children,* 1969, **35**, 341-352.

Haring, N.G., Hayden, A.H., & Nolen, P.A. Accelerating appropriate behaviors of children in a Head Start program. *Exceptional Children,* 1969, **35**, 773-784.

Hart, B.M., Reynolds, N.J., Baer, D.M., Brawley, E.R., & Harris, F.R. Effect of contingent and non-contingent social reinforcement on the cooperative play of a preschool child. *Journal of Applied Behavior Analysis,* 1968, **1**, 73-76.

Hart, B.M., & Risley, T.R. Establishing use of descriptive adjectives in the spontaneous speech of disadvantaged preschool children. *Journal of Applied Behavior*

Analysis, 1968, **1**, 109-120.

Herman, S., & Tramontana, J. Instructions and group versus individual reinforcement in modifying disruptive group behavior. *Journal of Applied Behavior Analysis,* 1971, **4**, 113-119.

Hermelin, B. Psychological research. In J.K. Wing (Ed.), *Early childhood autism.* London: Pergamon Press, 1966.

Hewett, F.M., Taylor, F.D., & Artuso, A.A. The Santa Monica Project: Evaluation of an engineered classroom design with emotionally disturbed children. *Exceptional Children,* 1968, **35**, 523-529.

Hingtgen, J.N., Sanders, B.J., & DeMyer, M.K. Shaping cooperative responses in early childhood schizophrenics. In L.P. Ullmann & L. Krasner (Eds.), *Case studies in behavior modification.* New York: Holt, 1965.

Homme, L.E., Csanyi, A., Gonzales, M., & Rechs, J. *How to use contingency contracting in the classroom.* Champaign, Ill.: Research Press, 1969.

Homme, L.E., DeBaca, P.C., DeVine, J.V., Steinhorst, R., & Rickert, E.J. Use of the Premack principle in controlling the behavior of nursery school children. *Journal of the Experimental Analysis of Behavior,* 1963, **6**, 544.

Honig, W.K. Introduction. *Operant behavior: Areas of research and application.* New York: Appleton-Century-Crofts, 1966.

Hopkins, B.L. Effects of candy and social reinforcement, instructions, and reinforcement schedule learning on the modification and maintenance of smiling. *Journal of Applied Behavior Analysis,* 1968, **1**, 121-129.

Hundziak, M., Maurer, R.A., & Watson, L.S. Operant conditioning in toilet training severely mentally retarded boys. *American Journal of Mental Deficiency,* 1965, **70**, 120-124.

Hunt, J.G., Fitzhugh, L.C., & Fitzhugh, K.B. Teaching "exit-ward" patients appropriate personal appearance by using reinforcement techniques. *American Journal of Mental Deficiency,* 1968, **73**, 41-45.

Hunt, J.G., & Zimmerman, J. Stimulating productivity in a simulated sheltered workshop setting. *American Journal of Mental Deficiency,* 1969, **74**, 43-49.

Jacobson, J.M., Bushell, D., & Risley, T.R. Switching requirements in a Head Start classroom. *Journal of Applied Behavior Analysis,* 1969, **2**, 43-47.

Jens, K.E., & Shores, R.E. Behavioral graphs as reinforcers for work behavior of mentally retarded adolescents. *Education and Training of the Mentally Retarded,* 1969, **4**, 21-28.

Johnson, S.M. Effects of self-reinforcement and external reinforcement in behavior modification. *Proceedings of the 77th Annual Convention of the American Psychological Association,* 1969, **4**, 535-536.

Jones, R.J., & Azrin, N.H. Behavioral engineering: Stuttering as a function of stimulus duration during speech synchronization. *Journal of Applied Behavior Analysis,* 1969, **2**, 223-229.

Kazdin, A.E. The effect of response cost in suppressing behavior in a prepsychotic retardate. *Journal of Behavior Therapy and Experimental Psychiatry*, 1971, **2**, 137-140. (a)

Kazdin, A.E. Toward a client administered token reinforcement program. *Education and Training of the Mentally Retarded*, 1971, **6**, 52-55. (b)

Kazdin, A.E. The assessment of teacher training in a reinforcement program. *Journal of Teacher Education*, 1973, in press. (a)

Kazdin, A.E. Methodological and assessment considerations in evaluating reinforcement program in applied settings. *Journal of Applied Behavior Analysis*, 1973, in press. (b)

Kazdin, A.E. Role of instructions and reinforcement in behavior changes in token reinforcement programs. *Journal of Educational Psychology*, 1973, in press. (c)

Kazdin, A.E., & Bootzin, R.R. The token economy: An evaluative review. *Journal of Applied Behavior Analysis*, 1972, **5**, 343-372.

Kazdin, A.E., & Polster, R. Intermittent token reinforcement and response maintenance in extinction. *Behavior Therapy*, 1973, in press.

Kerr, N., Meyerson, L., & Michael, J. A procedure for shaping vocalizations in a mute child. In L.P. Ullmann & L. Krasner (Eds.), *Case studies in behavior modification*. New York: Holt, 1965.

Kimble, G.A. *Hilgard and Marquis' conditioning and learning*. New York: Appleton-Century-Crofts, 1961.

Kimbrell, D.L., Luckey, R.E., Barbuto, P., & Love, J.G. Operation dry pants: An intensive habit-training program for severely and profoundly retarded. *Mental Retardation*, 1967, **5**, 32-36.

Kirby, F.D., & Toler, H.C. Modification of preschool isolate behavior: A case study. *Journal of Applied Behavior Analysis*, 1970, **3**, 309-314.

Kircher, A.S., Pear, J.J., & Martin, G.L. Shock as punishment in a picture-naming task with retarded children. *Journal of Applied Behavior Analysis*, 1971, **4**, 227-233.

Krasner, L. Applications of token economy in chronic populations. Paper presented at the American Psychological Association, San Francisco, September 1968.

Kubany, E.S., Weiss, L.E., & Sloggett, B.B. The good behavior clock: A reinforcement/ time out procedure for reducing disruptive classroom behavior. *Journal of Behavior Therapy and Experimental Psychiatry*, 1971, **2**, 173-179.

Kuypers, D.S., Becker, W.C., & O'Leary, K.D. How to make a token system fail. *Exceptional Children*, 1968, **11**, 101-108.

Lahey, B.B. Modification of the frequency of descriptive adjectives in the speech of Head Start children through modeling without reinforcement. *Journal of Applied Behavior Analysis*, 1971, **4**, 19-22.

Lent, J.R. A demonstration program for intensive training of institutionalized mentally retarded girls. Progress report, January 1967, U.S. Department of Health, Education, and Welfare.

Lent, J.R. Mimosa Cottage: Experiment in hope. *Psychology Today*, 1968, **2**(1), 50-58.

Liberman, R. A view of behavior modification projects in California. *Behaviour Research and Therapy*, 1968, **6**, 331-341.

Lindsley, O.R. An analysis of operant discrimination and differentiation in chronic psychotics. Paper presented at the Eastern Psychological Association, Philadelphia, April 1958.

Lindsley, O.R. Direct measurement and prothesis of retarded behavior. *Journal of Education*, 1964, **147**, 62-81.

Locke, B. Verbal conditioning with retarded subjects: Establishment or reinstatement of effective reinforcing consequences. *American Journal of Mental Deficiency*, 1969, **73**, 621-626.

Loeber, R. Engineering the behavioral engineer. *Journal of Applied Behavior Analysis*, 1971, **4**, 321-326.

Logan, D.L., Kinsinger, J., Shelton, G., & Brown, J.M. The use of multiple reinforcers in a rehabilitation setting. *Mental Retardation*, 1971, **9**, 3-5.

Lovaas, O.I. Control of food intake in children by reinforcement of relevant verbal behavior. *Journal of Abnormal and Social Psychology*, 1964, **68**, 672-677.

Lovaas, O.I. A behavior therapy approach to the treatment of childhood schizophrenia. In J.P. Hill (Ed.), *Minnesota symposia on child psychology*. Minneapolis: University of Minnesota Press, 1967.

Lovaas, O.I., Berberich, J.P., Perloff, B.F., & Schaeffer, B. Acquisition of imitative speech in schizophrenic children. *Science*, 1966, **51**, 705-707.

Lovaas, O.I., Freitag, G., Gold, V.J., & Kassorla, I.C. Experimental studies in childhood schizophrenia: Analysis of self-destructive behavior. *Journal of Experimental Child Psychology*, 1965, **2**, 67-84.

Lovaas, O.I., Freitag, G., Kinder, M., Rubenstein, B., Schaeffer, B., & Simmons, J. Establishment of social reinforcers in two schizophrenic children on the basis of food. *Journal of Experimental Child Psychology*, 1966, **4**, 109-125.

Lovaas, O.I., Freitag, L., Nelson, K., & Whalen, C. The establishment of imitation and its use for the development of complex behavior in schizophrenic children. *Behaviour Research and Therapy*, 1967, **5**, 171-181.

Lovaas, O.I., Schaeffer, B., & Simmons, J. Building social behavior in autistic children by use of shock. *Journal of Experimental Research in Personality*, 1965, **1**, 99-109.

Lovaas, O.I., & Simmons, J. Manipulation of self destruction in three retarded children. *Journal of Applied Behavior Analysis*, 1969, **2**, 143-157.

Lovitt, T.C., & Curtiss, K.A. Academic response rate as a function of teacher- and self-imposed contingencies. *Journal of Applied Behavior Analysis*, 1969, **2**, 49-53.

Luckey, R.E., Watston, C.M., & Musick, K. Aversive conditioning as a means of inhibiting vomiting and rumination. *American Journal of Mental Deficiency*, 1968, **73**, 139-142.

MacCubrey, J. Verbal operant conditioning with young institutionalized Down's syndrome children. *American Journal of Mental Deficiency,* 1971, **75**, 696-701.

MacDonald, W.S., Gallimore, R., & MacDonald, G. Contingency counseling by school personnel: An economical model of intervention. *Journal of Applied Behavior Analysis,* 1970, **3**, 175-182.

Madsen, C.M., Becker, W.C., Thomas, D.R., Koser, L., & Plager, E. An analysis of the reinforcing function of "sit down" commands. In R.K. Parker (Ed.), *Readings in educational psychology.* Boston: Allyn & Bacon, 1970.

Mahoney, K., VanWagenen, R.K., & Meyerson, L. Toilet training of normal and retarded children. *Journal of Applied Behavior Analysis,* 1971, **4**, 173-181.

McKenzie, H.S., Clark, M., Wolf, M.M., Kothera, R., & Benson, C. Behavior modification of children with learning disabilities using grades as tokens and allowances as back-up reinforcers. *Exceptional Children,* 1968, **34**, 745-752.

McKenzie, H.S., Egner, A.N., Knight, M.F., Perelman, P.F., Schneider, B.M., & Garvin, J.S. Training consulting teachers to assist elementary teachers in the management and education of handicapped children. *Exceptional Children,* 1970, **37**, 137-143.

McLean, J. Extending stimulus control of phoneme articulation by operant techniques. *American Speech and Hearing Association Monographs,* 1970, **14**, 9-45.

McNamara, J.R. Teacher and students as a source for behavior modification in the classroom. *Behavior Therapy,* 1971, **2**, 205-213.

Meacham, M., & Wiesen, A. *Changing classroom behavior: A manual for precision teaching.* Scranton, Pa.: International Textbook, 1969.

Meichenbaum, D.H., Bowers, K., & Ross, R.R. Modification of classroom behavior of institutionalized female adolescent offenders. *Behaviour Research and Therapy,* 1968, **6**, 343-353.

Miller, L.K., & Schneider, R. The use of a token system in project Head Start. *Journal of Applied Behavior Analysis,* 1970, **3**, 213-220.

Minge, M.R., & Ball, T.S. Teaching of self-help skills to profoundly retarded patients. *American Journal of Mental Deficiency,* 1967, **71**, 864-868.

Mingo, A.R., Desper, G.M., & Krauss, S. Increasing the probability of a Head Start. In G.A. Fargo, C. Behyns, & P. Nolen (Eds.), *Behavior modification in the classroom.* Belmont, Calif.: Wadsworth, 1970.

Miron, N.B. Behavior shaping and group nursing with severely retarded patients. In J. Fisher & R. Harris (Eds.), Reinforcement theory in psychological treatment: A symposium. *California Department of Mental Hygiene Research Monograph,* 1966, No. 8.

Mowrer, D.E. Transfer of training in articulation therapy. *Journal of Speech and Hearing Disorders,* 1971, **36**, 427-446.

Musick, J.K., & Luckey, R.E. A token economy for moderately and severely retarded. *Mental Retardation,* 1970, **8**, 35-36.

O'Leary, K.D., & Becker, W.C. Behavior modification of an adjustment class: A token reinforcement program. *Exceptional Children,* 1967, **9**, 637-642.

O'Leary, K.D., Becker, W.C., Evans, M.B., & Saudargas, R.A. A token reinforcement program in a public school. A replication and systematic analysis. *Journal of Applied Behavior Analysis,* 1969, **2**, 3-13.

O'Leary, K.D., & Drabman, R.S. Token reinforcement programs in the classroom: A review. *Psychological Bulletin,* 1971, **75**, 379-398.

O'Leary, K.D., Kaufman, K.F., Kass, R.E., & Drabman, R.S. The effects of loud and soft reprimands on the behavior of disruptive students. *Exceptional Children,* 1970, **37**, 145-155.

O'Leary, K.D., & O'Leary, S.G. (Eds.) *Classroom management: The successful use of behavior modification.* New York: Pergamon Press, 1972.

O'Leary, K.D., O'Leary, S.G., & Becker, W.C. Modification of a deviant sibling interaction pattern in the home. *Behaviour Research and Therapy,* 1967, **5**, 113-120.

Panyan, M., Boozer, H., & Morris, N. Feedback to attendants as a reinforcer for applying operant techniques. *Journal of Applied Behavior Analysis,* 1970, **3**, 1-4.

Patterson, G.R. An application of conditioning techniques to the control of a hyperactive child. In L.P. Ullmann & L. Krasner (Eds.), *Case studies in behavior modification.* New York: Holt, 1965. (a)

Patterson, G.R. A learning theory approach to the treatment of the school phobic child. In L.P. Ullmann & L. Krasner (Eds.), *Case studies in behavior modification.* New York: Holt, 1965. (b)

Patterson, G.R., & Brodsky, G. A behaviour modification programme for a child with multiple problem behaviours. *Journal of Child Psychology and Psychiatry,* 1966, **7**, 277-295.

Peine, H.A., Gregersen, G.F., & Sloane, H.N. A program to increase vocabulary and spontaneous speech. *Mental Retardation,* 1970, **8**, 38-44.

Perline, I., & Levinsky, D. Controlling maladaptive classroom behavior in the severely retarded. *American Journal of Mental Deficiency,* 1968, **73**, 74-78.

Phillips, E.L. Problems in educating emotionally disturbed children. In N.G. Haring & R.L. Schiefelbusch (Eds.), *Methods in special education.* New York: McGraw-Hill, 1967.

Phillips, E.L. Achievement place: Token reinforcement procedures in a home-style rehabilitation setting for "pre-delinquent" boys. *Journal of Applied Behavior Analysis,* 1968, **1**, 213-223.

Phillips, E.L., Phillips, E.A., Fixen, D.L., & Wolf, M.M. Achievement place: Modification of the behaviors of pre-delinquent boys within a token economy. *Journal of Applied Behavior Analysis,* 1971, **4**, 45-59.

Premack, D. Reinforcement therapy. In D. Levine (Ed.), *Nebraska symposium on motivation: 1965.* Lincoln, Neb.: University of Nebraska Press, 1965.

Ramp, E., Ulrich, R., & Dulaney, S. Delayed timeout as a procedure for reducing disruptive classroom behavior: A case study. *Journal of Applied Behavior Analysis,* 1971, **4**, 235-239.

Ray, E.T., & Shelton, J.T. The use of operant conditioning with disturbed adolescent retarded boys. Paper presented at the 20th Mental Hospital Institute, Washington, D.C., October 1968.

Redd, W.H. Effects of mixed reinforcement contingencies on adults' control of children's behavior. *Journal of Applied Behavior Analysis*, 1969, **2**, 249-254.

Reynolds, G.S. *A primer of operant conditioning*. New York: Scott, Foresman, 1968.

Reynolds, N.J., & Risley, T.R. The role of social and material reinforcers in increasing talking of a disadvantaged preschool child. *Journal of Applied Behavior Analysis*, 1968, **1**, 253-262.

Rimland, B. *Infantile autism: The syndrome and its implications for a neural theory of behavior*. New York: Appleton-Century-Crofts, 1964.

Risley, T.R. The effects and side effects of punishing the autistic behaviors of a deviant child. *Journal of Applied Behavior Analysis*, 1968, **1**, 21-34.

Risley, T.R., & Wolf, M.M. Establishing functional speech in echolalic children. *Behaviour Research and Therapy*, 1967, **5**, 73-88.

Roberts, C.L., & Perry, R.M. A total token economy. *Mental Retardation*, 1970, **8**, 15-18.

Roos, P., & Oliver, M. Evaluation of operant conditioning with institutionalized retarded children. *American Journal of Mental Deficiency*, 1969, **74**, 325-330.

Sailor, W., Guess, D., Rutherford, G., & Baer, D.M. Control of tantrum behavior by operant techniques during experimental verbal training. *Journal of Applied Behavior Analysis*, 1968, **1**, 237-243.

Salzinger, K., Feldman, R.S., & Portnoy, S. Training parents of brain-injured children in the use of operant conditioning procedures. *Behavior Therapy*, 1970, **1**, 4-32.

Schumacher, J., & Sherman, J.A. Training generative verb usage by imitation and reinforcement procedures. *Journal of Applied Behavior Analysis*, 1970, **3**, 273-287.

Schwartz, M.L., & Hawkins, R.P. Application of delayed reinforcement procedures to the behavior of an elementary school child. *Journal of Applied Behavior Analysis*, 1970, **3**, 85-96.

Siegel, G.M. Punishment, stuttering, and disfluency. *Journal of Speech and Hearing Research*, 1970, **13**, 677-714.

Skinner, B.F. *Science and human behavior*. New York: Macmillan, 1953.

Skinner, B.F. *The technology of teaching*. New York: Appleton-Century-Crofts, 1968.

Staats, A.W. A general apparatus for the investigation of complex learning in children. *Behaviour Research and Therapy*, 1968, **6**, 45-50.

Staats, A.W., Minke, K.A., & Butts, P. A token-reinforcement remedial reading program administered by black therapy technicians to problem black children. *Behavior Therapy*, 1970, **1**, 331-353.

Staats, A.W., Minke, K.A., Finley, J.R., Wolf, M.M., & Brooks, L.O. A reinforcer system and experimental procedure for the laboratory study of reading acquisition. *Child Development*, 1964, **35**, 209-231.

Staats, A.W., Minke, K.A., Goodwin, W., & Landeen, J. Cognitive behavior modification: "Motivated learning" reading treatment with subprofessional therapy technicians. *Behaviour Research and Therapy*, 1967, **5**, 283-299.

Staats, A.W., Staats, C.K., Schultz, R.E., & Wolf, M. The conditioning of textual responses using "extrinsic" reinforcers. *Journal of the Experimental Analysis of Behavior*, 1962, **5**, 33-40.

Stuart, R.B. *Trick or treatment: How and when psychotherapy fails.* Champaign, Ill.: Research Press, 1970.

Sulzbacher, S.I., & Houser, J.E. A tactic to eliminate disruptive behaviors in the classroom: Group contingent consequences. *American Journal of Mental Deficiency*, 1968, **73**, 88-90.

Surratt, P.R., Ulrich, R.E., & Hawkins, R.P. An elementary student as a behavioral engineer. *Journal of Applied Behavior Analysis*, 1969, **2**, 85-92.

Tate, B.G., & Baroff, G.S. Aversive control of self-injurious behavior in a psychotic boy. *Behaviour Research and Therapy*, 1966, **4**, 281-287.

Tate, B.G., & Baroff, G.S. Training the mentally retarded in the production of a complex product: A demonstration of work potential. *Exceptional Children*, 1967, **9**, 405-408.

Tharp, R.G., & Wetzel, R.J. *Behavior modification in the natural environment.* New York: Academic Press, 1969.

Thorne, G.L., Tharp, R.G., & Wetzel, R.J. Behavior modification techniques: New tools for probation officers. In W.C. Becker (Ed.), *An empirical basis for change in education.* Chicago: Science Research Associates, 1971.

Tyler, V.O. Application of operant token reinforcement for academic performance of an institutionalized delinquent. *Psychological Reports*, 1967, **21**, 249-260.

Tyler, V.O., & Brown, G.D. Token reinforcement of academic performance with institutionalized delinquent boys. *Journal of Educational Psychology*, 1968, **59**, 164-168.

VanWagenen, R.K., Meyerson, L., Kerr, N., & Mahoney, K. Field trials of a new procedure for toilet training. *Journal of Experimental Child Psychology*, 1969, **8**, 147-159.

Vukelich, R., & Hake, D.F. Reduction of dangerously aggressive behavior in a severely retarded resident through a combination of positive reinforcement procedures. *Journal of Applied Behavior Analysis*, 1971, **4**, 215-225.

Wahler, R.G. Behavior therapy for oppositional children: Love is not enough. Paper presented at the Eastern Psychological Association, Washington, D.C., April 1968.

Wahler, R.G. Oppositional children: A quest for parental reinforcement control. *Journal of Applied Behavior Analysis*, 1969, **2**, 159-170. (a)

Wahler, R.G. Setting generality: Some specific and general effects of child behavior therapy. *Journal of Applied Behavior Analysis*, 1969, **2**, 239-246. (b)

Walker, H.M., Mattson, R.H., & Buckley, N.K. The functional analysis of behavior within an experimental class setting. In A.M. Benson (Ed.), Modifying deviant social behaviors in various classroom settings. *University of Oregon, Department of Special Education Monograph,* 1969, **1**.

Ward, A.I. Early infantile autism: Diagnosis, etiology, and treatment. *Psychological Bulletin,* 1970, **73**, 350-362.

Wasik, B.H., Senn, K., Welch, R.H., & Cooper, B.R. Behavior modification with culturally deprived school children: Two case studies. *Journal of Applied Behavior Analysis,* 1969, **2**, 181-194.

Watson, L.S. Applications of behavior shaping-devices to training severely and profoundly retarded children in an institutional setting. *Mental Retardation,* 1968, **6**, 21-23.

Watson, L.S., Gardner, J.M., & Sanders, C. Shaping and maintaining behavior modification skills in staff members in an MR institution: Columbus State Institute Behavior Modification Program. *Mental Retardation,* 1971, **9**, 39-42.

Wheeler, A.J., & Sulzer, B. Operant training and generalization of a verbal response form in a speech-deficient child. *Journal of Applied Behavior Analysis,* 1970, **3**, 139-147.

White, G.D., Nielsen, G., & Johnson, S.M. Timeout duration and the suppression of deviant behavior in children. *Journal of Applied Behavior Analysis,* 1972, **5**, 111-120.

Whitman, T.L., Mercurio, J.R., & Caponigri, V. Development of social responses in two severely retarded children. *Journal of Applied Behavior Analysis,* 1970, **3**, 133-138.

Wiesen, A.E., & Watson, E. Elimination of attention seeking behavior in a retarded child. *American Journal of Mental Deficiency,* 1967, **72**, 50-52.

Wolf, M.M., Giles, D.K., & Hall, R.V. Experiments with token reinforcement in a remedial classroom. *Behaviour Research and Therapy,* 1968, **6**, 51-64.

Wolf, M.M., Risley, T.R., Johnston, M., Harris, F.R., & Allen, K.E. Application of operant conditioning procedures to the behaviour problems of an autistic child: A follow-up and extension. *Behaviour Research and Therapy,* 1967, **5**, 103-111.

Wolf, M.M., Risley, T.R., & Mees, H. Application of operant conditioning procedures to the behaviour problems of an autistic child. *Behaviour Research and Therapy,* 1964, **1**, 305-312.

Zeilberger, J., Sampen, S.E., & Sloane, H.N. Modification of a child's problem behaviors with the mother as therapist. *Journal of Applied Behavior Analysis,* 1968, **1**, 47-53.

Zimmerman, J., Overpeck, C., Eisenberg, H., & Garlick, B. Operant conditioning in a sheltered workshop. *Rehabilitation Literature,* 1969, **30**, 326-334. (a)

Zimmerman, J., Stuckey, T.E., Garlick, B.J., & Miller, M. Effects of token reinforcement on productivity in multiply handicapped clients in a sheltered workshop. *Rehabilitation Literature,* 1969, **30**, 34-41. (b)

Zimmerman, E.H., & Zimmerman, J. The alteration of behavior in a special classroom situation. *Journal of the Experimental Analysis of Behavior,* 1962, **5**, 59-60.

Zimmerman, E.H., Zimmerman, J., & Russell, C.D. Differential effects of token reinforcement on instruction-following behavior in retarded students instructed as a group. *Journal of Applied Behavior Analysis,* 1969, **2,** 101-112. (c).

INSTRUCTIONAL PROGRAMS FOR TRAINABLE-LEVEL RETARDED STUDENTS

Lou Brown, Ph.D.

University of Wisconsin[1]

THE STUDENTS

Dunn (1973) presented arguments why students formerly called "aments," "idiots," "imbeciles," "trainable," and "severely retarded" should now be labeled students with "moderate and severe general learning disabilities." Kirk (1972), in a recent revision of his survey text, retained the use of the label "trainable mentally retarded." Rosenzweig and Long (1960) used the term "dependent retarded child." Stephens (1971) chose to refer to the same level student as "developmentally young." Bradley, Hundziak, and Patterson (1971) used the phrases "moderately retarded" and "severely retarded," as does the American Association on Mental Deficiency (Heber, 1961). More extensive discussion of presumed correlates of such labels (MA, IQ, estimates of mental growth, comparison with other levels of retardation, learning characteristics, organic impairments) can be found elsewhere (e.g., Dunn, 1973; Goldberg & Rooke, 1967; Kirk, 1972; Stephens, 1971).

There can be little doubt that such terms will, like their predecessors, gradually acquire aversive properties, and that new labels will be generated as a consequence. The real question is whether the students to whom the labels apply will change. Grouping and labeling students may be important for a variety of reasons: research, fund raising, regulating and administering school programs, and so forth. However, unless grouping and labeling contribute to a change in the functioning level of the students, they have little instructional relevance.

On the other hand, it is possible that a label or an assumption might change the manner in which people, at least temporarily, view and react to one another. With this in mind, an attempt is made here to change in some small way the orientation that many people have toward students labeled "imbeciles," "trainables," "moderately and

[1] The writing of this chapter was supported in part by NICHD Grant 5 PO1 HD 03352-02 to the University of Wisconsin Center on Mental Retardation. All royalties that accrue from this chapter have been assigned to the Madison Area Association for Retarded Children.

severely retarded," and the like. This attempt is centered around the locus of the problem. Historically, the locus has been placed within the student; i.e., it is the student who has a severe general learning disability; it is the student who is only trainable; it is the student who is severely retarded, an imbecile, and so on. Recently, many writers (e.g., Bijou, 1966; Lindsley, 1964) have questioned this placement of the locus of the problem and have emphasized experiential and environmental considerations as an alternative locus. This change is endorsed here primarily because there is little that teachers can do about factors such as defective genes, brain damage, or biochemical malfunctioning. There is much that can be done, however, if we attempt to treat the environmental factors that teachers have control over as independent variables. It is hypothesized that systematic manipulation of environmental variables will assist in the development of an instructional technology that effectively teaches these students to engage in response patterns and life styles that have been unavailable to them in the past.

If the locus of the problem is changed from inside to outside the student, then some descriptive term such as "students who present teachers with severe instructional problems" might be considered an alternative to the previously used label. However, since the last thing special education needs is another euphemism, the writer requests that the reader abolish the stimulus trace of the previous sentence. Since most special educators use the term "trainable" for those students who do not function adequately in classes for "educable" students, the label "trainable-level retarded" will be used here (relunctantly). Labels notwithstanding, the important point to be realized is that there are many developmentally crucial skills that can be taught to these students, if we consider the instructional problem ours rather than theirs.

HISTORICAL NOTE

Historically, parents of trainable-level retarded children attempted to provide instruction either by placing them in public or private residential facilities or by tutoring them at home. In the late 1940s and the early 1950s, many parents rejected these alternatives as the only possible ones and worked for community-based instructional programs. The National Association of Retarded Children (NARC) was organized and became the primary force behind the demand for, and realization of, community-based programs.

The development of these programs passed through three phases, not necessarily distinct. First, parents struggled to find space in which to place their children during the day: Private facilities were constructed, school basements and boiler rooms were adapted, and church school rooms were put into use. Second, these local facilities were staffed initially by volunteers, retired school teachers, and parents themselves; subsequently, parents sought specially trained and certified teachers to staff their hard-earned facilities, in the hope that such teachers could generate the necessary behavioral development. Third, parents struggled for effective and relevant instructional programming; in short, they wanted quality education for their handicapped children.

There are still many communities in this country with no local physical facilities for trainable students. There are communities which have provided facilities but lack certified personnel. There are other communities that have facilities and certified personnel but lack effective and relevant instructional programs.

Securing physical facilities and certified teachers are, for the most part, a function of economics; it should be relatively easy in our society to obtain them. Local and federal financial support can be obtained in many ways (tax grants, tuition grants, contributions, and so forth); a facility can be constructed or adapted. State and federal priorities can be established and funded so that teacher training programs at colleges and universities can turn out certified teachers in a relatively short time. However, providing trainable-level retarded students with quality education is another matter. At this point, *no amount of money will provide these students with the skills they are capable of acquiring.* The professional community simply does not have the instructional technology to teach them what they need to know and what they are capable of learning.

In the late 1940s and early 1950s, few trainable-level retarded students in the United States were receiving instructional services from public schools. Although public school programs for such students had been initiated in St. Louis in 1929 and in New York City in 1934, few general educators at the time would have considered it a rational suggestion that the public schools have a responsibility to these students. In the early 1970s, virtually every state in the nation adopted some community provision for services to trainable-level retarded students. According to a report by the President's Committee on Mental Retardation (1967), the number of public school classes for such students rose from approximately 2,500 in 1963 to approximately 8,500 by 1967.

It can be assumed that within the next 5 to 10 years, public school programs for trainable-level retarded students will be in existence in almost every school district in the United States, primarily because there will be (a) continued pressure by the NARC and its local affiliates on legislative bodies and local school boards; (b) litigation and judicial interpretations that make education the legal right of all children in the United States; (c) a shift in federal funding priorities favoring severely and multiply handicapped children; (d) the growing intolerance for large multiple-failure residential institutions, their expense, and their limited space.

When these classes are established, it is doubtful that circumscribed instructional objectives, such as personal safety, personal control, and self-amusement, will be adequate (Goldberg & Rooke, 1967). If a trainable-level retarded student is to be placed in public school programs for 15 years (age 5-20), it is extremely unlikely that such programs can be justified if, at the end of that time, all that can be expected is that he will be maintained at home or placed in a traditional residential facility. Whether trainable-level retarded students should be enrolled in public school programs

(Goldberg & Cruickshank, 1958) or placed in residential institutions is no longer the question. These students will be enrolled in public school programs and will remain in the community in adulthood. Special education is now faced with a new challenge: What are the ultimate objectives of school programs for trainable-level retarded students, and how do we approximate their realization?

LONGITUDINAL OBJECTIVES OF INSTRUCTIONAL PROGRAMS

The primary longitudinal objective of instructional programs for trainable-level retarded students should be to teach the skills necessary for the students to function adequately in a community setting. The curriculum must therefore provide for the development of such skills. Merely delineating the behavioral repertoire necessary for adequate functioning in a community setting is so complex and arbitrary a task that in all probability it could never be considered complete. Even more formidable is the task of teaching this behavioral repertoire to students exhibiting low acquisition rates, stimulus-and-response generalization problems, interpersonal difficulties, sensory anomalies, and so forth. Unfortunately, the developmental and learning difficulties of trainable-level retarded students have frustrated many of the best-intentioned teachers to the point that they have given up and merely distributed materials to make potholders. This initial fatalism can be overcome, however, by reading *Christmas in Purgatory* (Blatt & Kaplan, 1967); visiting or reading a newspaper exposé of several of our large multipurpose residential facilities; talking to the parent of a 35-year-old mongoloid; or playing with a group of warm, happy, loving multiply handicapped preschoolers. It then becomes easier to appreciate the importance and humaneness of developing adequate community living skills.

The teachers' contribution to the development of the necessary skills will depend on the instructional programs to which the students are exposed during their school years. Because the instructional programs for trainable-level retarded students will become increasingly important in the next few years, several words concerning such programs are warranted.

Any instructional program contains at least three major components: what to teach (content or objectives); what instructional aids to use (materials); and how to teach (instructional technology).[2] The major emphasis of school programs in the past has been on what to teach. For example, Lance (1971) stated, "Methodology and materials, however important they are to a successful program, are secondary to the establishment of realistic objectives [p. 39]."

In the view of the writer, a realistic objective is an objective that can be realized. Assume that a teacher decides that her students should be able to follow the

---

[2]Instructional objectives, instructional materials, and instructional technology are artifically delineated in order to focus attention on instructional technology.

instructions on the back of a box containing a cake mix (objective or content), and then assembles all the instructional aids necessary to develop the behaviors of concern (materials). Assume further that the students do not acquire the behaviors necessary to make a cake. Since the objective was not realized, it was unrealistic. What usually happens prior to the preceding situation is that the teacher selects objectives requiring less complex behavioral repertoires such as making potholders, brushing teeth, or folding napkins, until she arrives at a task that the students can perform successfully. By this process an objective becomes realistic by default.

Certainly the scope and sequence of the instructional objectives presented to trainable-level retarded students are crucial to their development, and in no sense does the writer intend to minimize their importance. However, the purpose here is to emphasize the importance of, and the necessity for, an improved instructional technology. As teachers, we could specify our objectives ad infinitum, secure the most advanced and sophisticated materials, and still fail to teach the students. Why? In the writer's view, we do not know *how* to teach the students (a) to perform the responses necessary to attain the objectives or (b) to emit the responses required by the materials.

INSTRUCTIONAL MODEL: BEHAVIORISTIC TASK ANALYSIS

A model, as the term is used here, is an abstract conceptualization of assumptions and principles that serve as a priori foundations of an instructional system. A teacher brings such a model to the instructional situation. This model is often ill-defined and contains many nebulous assumptions concerning the use of materials, rules of learning, and tactics of teaching. But it contains preliminary conceptualizations that have a direct bearing on the organization of the classroom and the activities conducted within it.

A model is valid or invalid depending upon whether or not its implementation solves the problem for which the model was developed. For example, assume a model airplane is generated and then a full-scale airplane is built, based upon the dictates of the model. If the plane flies effectively, the model was valid. If the plane does not fly, then either the model was invalid or it was not properly implemented. We are left with at least three alternatives if the plane does not fly: Reject the model in toto, make revisions that seem logical in the model, or retrace our implementation strategies. Two points should be noted: First, all models involve a priori assumptions, biases, hopes, and so on. Second, the validity of a model when applied to a practical problem can only be established empirically.

The instructional model presented here and recommended for teachers of trainable-level retarded students is referred to as behavioristic task analysis (Brown, Bellamy, & Sontag, 1971). Task analysis typically refers to dividing complex instructional objectives into a sequence of less complex components. Behavioristic task analysis demands the additional requirements (a) that each component be defined in terms of observable motor responses to specified stimuli and (*b*) that a series of instructional tactics be applied systematically, which tactics are designed to teach the student the behavioral components of the sequence.

Principles of task analysis have been applied in educational programs for centuries. Indeed, deciding upon what responses to teach a student and dividing the criterion response into a series of component responses are probably the least difficult demands of the model. Curriculum guides, textbooks, and related literature concerning trainable-level retarded students are characterized by their relatively detailed descriptions of the components of instructional tasks (e.g., Buddenhagen, 1971; D'Amelio, 1971; Frankel, Happ, & Smith, 1966; Kolburne, 1965; Molloy, 1963; Rosenzweig & Long, 1960). The difficulty arises, however, when one attempts to teach the students to perform the responses in the series. Again, *what* to teach is only one of our problems. *How* to teach is the primary one.

INSTRUCTIONAL ASSUMPTIONS

There are at least three crucial instructional assumptions that seem particularly applicable to teachers of trainable-level retarded students: instructional environmentalism, instructional determinism, and instructional empiricism. All three of these assumptions have been delineated before by various educators, philosophers, and psychologists. They are presented and described here to focus attention on the instructional variables that the teacher can manipulate.

Instructional environmentalism

For centuries, people have engaged in sometimes lengthy, sometimes esoteric, sometimes valuable, and sometimes bigoted debates about the differential contributions of biological and environmental variables to the development of human behavior. Some took extreme positions, attributing all behavior to either nature or nurture. Most people now realize the differential and interactive effects of both. Indeed, it is now widely accepted that even such a dichotomized conceptualization (nature-nurture) is artificial.

The purpose here is not to argue the relative effects of either heredity or environment but rather to emphasize environment. In a classroom for trainable-level retarded students, a teacher is likely to encounter students who have many manifestations of genetic anomalies; obvious neurological and orthopedic impairments; degenerative diseases; or vision, hearing, and speech difficulties. Confronted with such obvious indices of organic malstructure and function, it is tempting to attribute instructional failure to biological factors. In fact, however, the failure of the student to acquire certain skills may not be due to biological factors but rather to the teacher's failure to attempt manipulations that neutralize or circumvent what have been perceived as instructional impediments.

The assumption of instructional environmentalism recognizes the potential effects of biological factors on a student's functioning, but recognizes also that a teacher can do little, if anything, about such factors. What a teacher *can* do is manipulate the instructional environment (factors outside of the student's body) and assess the effectiveness of her manipulations on the behavioral development of the student.

Instructional determinism

It is the rare teacher who would suggest that students should have the same behavioral repertoire in June that they had the previous September. Most teachers assume that students acquire behaviors, skills, information, and so forth, during the academic year *because* of manipulations made by the teacher. Indeed, if a student does not develop behaviorally over the academic year because of the teacher's instruction, then human and economic resources will have been wasted. Most students in public schools acquire behaviors incidentally, vicariously, observationally, from casual personal interactions, from television, and so on. Trainable-level retarded students have substantial difficulty acquiring needed behaviors in these ways. Thus, the teacher of trainable-level retarded students, because she cannot rely on her students to acquire needed behaviors indirectly or outside of class, must take a more active role in deciding which specific behaviors her students should develop.

One way to focus the responsibility of student development on the instructional program is for the teacher to make the assumption of instructional determinism. Admittedly, a teacher arrives at instructional objectives in cooperation with the school board, administrative superiors, parents, and so on. Ultimately, however, the final responsibility for crystallizing objectives lies with the teacher. What the teacher is saying when she somewhat arbitrarily specifies a behavioral objective for her class is, "I have decided that my students will acquire these behaviors, and I am going to do *a, b,* and *c* in an attempt to teach them." She then arranges the classroom environment so as to maximize the probability that the desired results will occur. In effect, she determines what behaviors she wants and what manipulations she will make to develop them. If the behaviors she specifies do, in fact, occur because of her environmental manipulations, the instructional program was successful; if they do not occur, the program was unsuccessful.

If a teacher makes the assumption of instructional determinism, then, by definition, she assumes the responsibility for the behavioral development of the students. If this development does not occur, it is more probable that the teacher would attribute the lack of development to her instructional program rather than to factors outside her domain (uncooperative parents, brain damage, genes, and so forth).

Instructional empiricism

A third crucial assumption for teachers of trainable-level retarded students is that of instructional empiricism. When a teacher makes this assumption she is in effect saying, "As a result of my instruction, the students will change in a manner that I can verify." This assumption places great responsibility upon the teacher in that she cannot claim that her showing, telling, explaining, modeling, presenting, and so forth, are instruction. She can claim instruction only when there has been a demonstrated development in the behavioral repertoire of the student. Her actions may or may not effect change in the student. The teacher who makes the assumption of instructional empiricism is in a much better position to evaluate her effectiveness because she continually attempts to measure student development.

Thus, if a teacher makes the three preceding assumptions, she is in effect saying, "I will teach my students to make these responses. My technology of teaching will be based on manipulating environmental variables, and I will measure the observable responses of the students to discern whether my technology allowed me to generate the responses of concern."

Parenthetically, it should be noted that it is becoming popular to say to a teacher, "If the student fails, you have failed." With many student failures this may, in fact, be true. With trainable-level retarded students, however, it must be realized that the technology for effecting *substantial* development is emerging but is currently unavailable to most teachers (Gold, 1972). It is one thing to criticize a teacher for not applying available and effective technology; it is another to criticize her for not developing students when the technology is unavailable.

DIRECT VERSUS INFERENTIAL MEASUREMENT

Much, if not most, educational measurement is based on assumptions of inferential statistics. Because of the difficulty, expense, time, and energy needed to measure every response a teacher has to develop, educators have turned to obtaining measures of behavior samples that are assumed to be representative of the population of behaviors in the students' repertoires. Let us say, for example, that a teacher wishes to measure whether or not her students can add any two numbers that total 10. Instead of measuring a response to every permutation, she typically selects a sample set of problems from the population of problems. If a student responds correctly to the sample, then the teacher infers that the student can respond correctly to other problems requiring the same operations. Similar examples of inferential measurement can be found in almost every content area.

Inferential measurement is an extremely questionable measurement strategy when one is concerned with measuring the effects of instruction on the behavioral development of trainable-level retarded students. If such a student can solve the problems $2 + 5 = $ ___ and $6 + 4 = $___ , or can verbally label the words "mother" and "dog," a teacher cannot infer that the same student can solve the problems $6 + 1 = $___ and $8 + 2 = $___ , or can verbally label the words "father" and "cat." If a teacher is interested in whether or not a trainable mentally retarded student can make a particular response, she must *directly* measure that response; i.e., the teacher must have empirical verification of the existence of the behaviors of concern.

Direct measurement is particularly crucial in attempts to teach cumulative tasks.

If the correct performance of the responses in component *c* of a task are dependent upon the correct performance of the responses in components *a* and *b,* then the teacher must guarantee that *a* and *b* responses are in the behavioral repertoire of the student before she even considers progression to component *c.* Since most developmental skills are in many ways cumulative (mathematics, reading, language, speech, practical arts), teachers of trainable-level retarded students must be prepared to spend relatively long periods of time and considerable effort developing basic behavioral repertoires.

Few, if any, teachers have the time, resources, or inclination to measure directly each response each student makes in each instructional setting. Therefore, the teacher must decide which behaviors are so important to the development of the student that she should expend the time and energy to verify their existence. Very little attention is given in this chapter to specific direct-measurement techniques that have practical value for classroom teachers. However, most of the instructional programs presented in later sections of this chapter involve the use of such techniques; the reader is referred to the primary sources.

ESSENTIAL COMPONENTS OF BEHAVIORISTIC TASK ANALYSIS

Many of the components of behavioristic task analysis presented below have been delineated elsewhere (e.g., Mager, 1962). However, one rarely encounters such components in literature concerned with trainable-level retarded students. The components described here are essentially those delineated by Brown, Bellamy, and Sontag (1971). They considered the following as tentative basic components of behavioristic task analysis:

First, the teacher must specify terminal objectives in behavioristic terms. That is, she must convert the required criterion performance into observable responses.

Second, the teacher must analyze the criterion responses and divide them into a series of less complex responses.

Third, the teacher must arrange the responses she decides are necessary for completion of the terminal response into a series.

Fourth, the teacher must teach or verify the existence of the student's ability to perform each response in the series.

Fifth, the teacher must teach the students to perform each response in the series in *serial* order.

Sixth, in an attempt to delineate successes and failures, the teacher must record student performance during each training phase so that adjustments can be made during the teacher process [p. 3].

Each of the above six requirements should be met in each instructional program. However, they may not occur in the order listed above, or two or more requirements may be met simultaneously.

INSTRUCTIONAL TECHNOLOGY

The remaining portion of the chapter will be concerned with delineating an emerging instructional technology that seems particularly applicable to teaching

111

trainable-level retarded students. Instructional technology, as the term is used here, refers to the use of some form of behavioristic task analysis and the systematic application of empirically derived principles of learning the instructional problems of teachers of trainable-level retarded students. (For a detailed description of the principles of concern, the reader is referred to the many texts concerned with elucidating elementary principles of behavior or applied behavior analysis. The works of Bandura, 1969, and Whaley and Malott, 1969, are excellent examples.) The purpose here is to show that imitation training, contingent reinforcement, graduated modeling, stimulus fading, stimulus control, response differentiation, and response priming can be incorporated into instructional programs to generate developmentally crucial behavioral repertoires in trainable-level retarded students.

Teaching trainable-level retarded students to imitate

Imitation, as the term is used here, refers to an observer matching the behavior of a model *because* the model emitted the behavior (Peterson, 1968). The ability to imitate has historically been recognized as one of the most crucial prerequisites to the development of complex behavioral repertoires (Itard, 1962; Seguin, 1866). Apparently, most children develop rather complex and effective imitative as well as other observational learning skills prior to the time they enter school. That is, most children use language patterns similar to those used by their parents and play the games their peers play; e.g., boys imitate the behavior patterns of adolescent and adult males, while girls imitate the behavior patterns of adolescent and adult females. When children enter school, a teacher can say, "Watch me and do what I do," or "Listen, children, and say what I say," with a reasonable expectation that the students will match many of the behaviors modeled. If a student does not or cannot imitate the teacher, or, for that matter, imitate his parents, peers, or siblings, then he must acquire crucial developmental skills by less efficient methods, e.g., trial and error or successive approximations (Bandura, 1965).

One of the most crucial behavioral deficits of trainable-level retarded students is their general inability to imitate complex response patterns such as speech, language, play, and social and motor responses. Teachers of these students, therefore, cannot say, "Do what I do," "Say what I say," or "Watch the TV and do what the children on TV are doing," and expect their students to match the behaviors modeled. In this case the teacher has at least two alternatives: She can attempt to teach her students without relying upon imitative skills, or she can teach her students to imitate. In the view of the writer, the latter is the more developmentally sound alternative. If she chooses it, she is then forced to consider *how* she can teach imitation; or whether there is a procedural sequence to follow that will result in the students' learning it. At this point it appears that the answer to her second consideration has to be a qualified *no* for several reasons. First, procedures that will result in all children learning to imitate are probably unavailable. Second, most of the successful systematic attempts at teaching basic imitative skills have been conducted in research settings involving one-to-one teacher-student (researcher-subject) ratios, a large number of training trials, and long periods of training time. On the other hand, a rudimentary technology of teaching basic imitation skills to nonimitative or poorly imitative children has been developed. The following paragraphs delineate several basic imitation-training procedures that were systematized primarily by research psychologists but used in applied settings by instructional personnel (Lovaas, Berberich, Perloff, & Schaeffer, 1966; Metz, 1965; Peterson, 1968; Risley & Wolf, 1967; for a more technical and precise description of these procedures, the reader is referred to the primary sources). In addition, Larsen and Bricker (1968) have organized an instructional manual for parents and teachers of severely and profoundly retarded children. This manual contains a readable, practical presentation of basic imitative-training procedures; it is a highly recommended instructional resource for those concerned with instructing retarded students.

The results of the research just cited strongly suggest that many trainable-level retarded students can be taught to imitate. However, before these procedures can be used in classrooms, they must be adapted for group application, since classroom teachers can rarely afford the luxury of a one-to-one ratio over long periods of time. York, Brown, Yoder, and Scheerenberger (1972) adapted the procedures described by Risley and Wolf (1967) and Larsen and Bricker (1968) for institutional ward aides in a group instructional setting involving severely and profoundly retarded institutionalized children. An example of one of their instructional sequences follows:

Once the four students (S_1, S_2, S_3, S_4) were taught to sit in their seats and look at the teacher (establish and maintain eye contact), the following sequence was followed in an attempt to teach the students to imitate:

1. The teacher (T) confronted S_1 and said "Do this," and raised both her hands above her head. If S_1 matched the behavior the teacher modeled, the teacher immediately smiled, said "Good," and put a piece of cereal in his mouth.

2. If S_1 did not raise his hands above his head, T again said "Do this," and modeled the correct response. If S_1 still did not emit the correct response, T then primed the correct response. That is, she physically guided his hands to the correct position. When the hands of S_1 reached the correct position, T smiled, said "Good boy," and put a piece of cereal in his mouth.

3. T then confronted S_2, said "Do this," and clapped her hands. If S_2 did not clap his hands, T again said "Do this," and modeled the correct response. If S_2 still did not emit the correct response, T then primed the correct movements, smiled, said "Good boy," and put a piece of cereal in his mouth. T then confronted S_3, said "Do this," and patted both her knees with her hands. If S_3 matched the behavior she modeled, T smiled, etc. (Step 1). If S_3 did not match the correct response, T primed him (Step 2). Exactly the same procedure was followed with S_4, except that a different gross motor response was modeled. Subsequently the responses modeled were rotated so that an S received gross exposure to four different modeled responses in every four trials.

4. After each S was primed through each of the four responses on approximately ten occasions, prime-fading was initiated. That is, the intensity of the prime was attenuated. For example, if the modeled response was hand clapping, T gradually reduced the pressure exerted on S's wrist until she was merely making contact with his skin. Subsequently T merely touched S's hands with her fingers. Finally, T would say "Do this," clap her hands, and S would clap his hands.

When each student matched the four different behaviors modeled by the teacher, they were imitating. That is, they matched the behavior of the teacher because the teacher modeled it. Stated another way, the teacher was a stimulus that controlled the responses made by the students (stimulus control). Once the students could imitate these and other gross motor movements, they were then asked to imitate less discrete motor movements (touch eye, touch ear, make mouth movements). Subsequently, the students were taught to imitate speech sounds (oo, ah, ba, ma, pa, tee, and so forth) and finally words.[3]

Teaching a group of students to imitate a teacher has in itself little functional value unless, of course, the instructional objective is to make the student echolalic and echopraxic. Thus, in any instructional program involving imitation training, the teacher must be constantly concerned with the stimuli that control the students' responses. Returning to the preceding example, once imitation of words was developed, transfer of the stimulus control of these verbalizations, from imitation of the teacher's voice to naming the objects these words represented, was crucial to the development of appropriate speech. This transfer of stimulus control was accomplished by first presenting the appropriate object to the child, along with the verbal model of the name of that object. Next, the object was presented first and followed by the verbal model. Gradually the period between presentation of the object and the model was extended, resulting in the students anticipating the model and eventually naming the object upon its presentation alone.

Once a student is imitating, the instructional concern becomes the decision as to what response the teacher wants the student to imitate. The teacher might choose to model such self-help behaviors as dressing, toileting, grooming, and feeding; such manipulative responses as assembling puzzles, tracing, and making lines with pencils; or such verbal behaviors as speaking in sentences or using plural morphemes and verb forms (Brown & Klemme, 1971; Guess, Sailor, Rutherford, & Baer, 1968; Schumaker & Sherman, 1970; Sherman, 1971.)[4]

The following are two examples of how imitation training can be combined with other instructional procedures to establish developmentally crucial behaviors. The first example relates to teaching trainable-level retarded students to follow verbal directions or, stated another way, to establish verbal control over motor responses. As any classroom teacher knows, it is imperative to establish some degree of verbal control of student behavior. The teacher must be able to say, "Put on your coat," "Pass the milk," "Line up at the door," "Write your name," "Open your book to page 210," and so forth, and the students must be able to respond appropriately. A teacher simply cannot be at every student's side, physically priming or modeling the hundreds of

---

[3]For a more detailed description of the specific mouth movements required to make various speech sounds, the reader is referred to Larsen and Bricker [1968, p. 62].

[4]When teaching students to imitate, teachers must be careful not to inadvertently model behaviors they do not want the students to imitate (facial expressions, scratching, use of selected phrases). Students often do not discriminate between the behaviors a teacher models and the behaviors the teacher wants the students to match.

responses the students must make during the school day. Verbal control leads to a more efficient, manageable class.

Since teachers and parents have had difficulty establishing verbal control over their students and children, techniques for establishing this control are crucial components of the instructional repertoires. One such technique, using many principles of imitation training, was described and empirically verified in a classroom setting by Brown, Bellamy, Tang, and Klemme (1971). The objective of the program was to teach two groups of trainable-level retarded students (M CA = 18.0 and 18.6; M IQ = 38 and 32.4) to respond appropriately to five one-component verbal directions (e.g., "Pick up the paper from the floor"); five two-component verbal directions (e.g., "Pick up the paper from the floor and close the door"); and five three-component verbal directions (e.g., "Pick up the paper from the floor, close the door, and bring me the scissors"). The program consisted, first, of obtaining measures of how each group responded to the three sets of directions. The specific instructional procedures used to teach correct responses were as follows:

When a group was seated around the table, T said: "I am going to give each of you some directions to follow. Sometimes I will ask you to do one thing, sometimes I will ask you to do two things and sometimes I will ask you to do three things. When I tell you to do two things, you should do the first thing I say and then do the second thing. When I tell you to do three things you should do the first thing first, the second thing second and the third thing third." T then looked at one student and said, "Mary, pick up that paper from the floor." Each student was given 5 seconds to start reacting to the direction. If a student did not start reacting to the direction, or if he made the wrong response, an error was recorded. If a student responded correctly to a direction the teacher simply said, "Thank you," and gave a different direction to a different student. When each student had been given an opportunity to respond to the 5 one-component directions, the procedure was repeated with the two-component and then the three-component directions.

T gave the first direction in a set to a student (e.g., "Open the door."). If the student responded correctly, T recorded the response and made such presumably reinforcing remarks as "Good," "Fine," "Let's clap for him, class," and "That's right." If a student made an incorrect response, T recorded the response and repeated the direction. If the desired response did not ensue, another student in the group was asked to model the correct response. On the few occasions that a student still could not emit the correct response, T gave the direction, physically guided (primed) the student through the correct response and then reissued the direction. No student failed to respond correctly after priming was employed.

The procedure was then repeated with the remaining students in a group, except that the same direction was never given to successive students.

When the group responded correctly to the one-component directions, the same procedures were used to teach the two- and three-component directions. The only notable departure from procedures occurred when it did not appear that several students would reach criterion on the three-component directions. At this point edibles (cereal or candy) were introduced as additional consequences for correct responding [pp. 3-4].

A modification of a multiple-baseline design was used to measure the effectiveness of the teaching procedures. The results indicated that one group learned to follow the one-, two-, and three-component directions, and the second group learned to follow the one- and two-component directions.

Teachers often provide trainable-level retarded students with environmental stimuli in the anticipation that they will acquire information contained in those stimuli. It is a tenuous assumption that information will be acquired through mere exposure (Brown & Foshee, 1970). Not only do trainable-level retarded students have difficulty attending to and acquiring information about environmental stimuli, but also they have difficulty communicating the substance of those stimuli. Another example of how basic imitation-training procedures can be used to establish crucial developmental repertoires in trainable-level retarded students is an ongoing language-development program being conducted in a public classroom by Brown, Huppler, Pierce, Johnson, and Sontag (1972). In this program the instructional objective is to teach young (M CA = 7) trainable-level retarded students to provide a verbal report of recently viewed behavioral events.

In the first part of the program, the teacher performed five single-component behavioral events, e.g., combing hair, painting a balloon, cutting paper, clapping hands, squeezing a balloon. In the second part of the program, the teacher performed five two-component behavioral events, e.g., combing hair and painting a balloon. While the content and sequence represented extremely rudimentary language skills, the purpose was to delineate the specific instructional procedures used to teach the students to report the events. The specific steps of the procedure were as follows:

1. When the five students involved were seated around a table facing the teacher, the teacher modeled a behavioral event (e.g., the teacher cut a piece of paper with a scissors).
2. After the teacher modeled the behavioral event, she looked at one of the students and said, "What happened?" If the student provided the subject, verb, and object (e.g., teacher combed hair), the subject and verb (teacher combed), or the verb and object (combed hair), the teacher clapped, said "Good boy (girl)" and presented him (her) with a penny, which later would be exchanged for candy, toys, lunch, etc.
3. If the student did not make a correct response, the teacher again said, "What happened?" If a correct response ensued, the student was reinforced. If a correct response did not occur, the teacher modeled it by saying, "Laura combed hair."
4. After the teacher modeled the correct response, she then said, "Now watch," and modeled the behavioral event.
5. The teacher asked the question "What happened?" If the correct response was provided, the student was reinforced.
6. If the correct response was not provided, the teacher modeled it and the teacher said, "Now say it." If the student matched the verbal model, reinforcement was delivered.
7. If a correct response was not provided, the teacher modeled it again and said, "Now say it." If the student matched the verbal responses the teacher modeled, reinforcement was delivered [p. 5].

After very few trials, the students started to provide the correct response the first time the question "What happened?" was asked. When each student could accurately describe each of the five single-component behavioral events, the same procedures were used to teach verbal reporting of five two-component behavioral events.

Reading

Nigel Hunt, who manifests Down's syndrome, wrote a book (Hunt, 1967). If he could do this, he probably could read well enough to survive in a community. There are those who would emphasize that Nigel Hunt was not so genetically impaired as other mongoloids and therefore could learn to perform such complex intellectual behaviors. Those making environmentalist assumptions, of course, would emphasize that Nigel Hunt learned to read and write because of the environmental manipulations of others, and that the difference between Mr. Hunt and thousands of other mongoloid persons is that his parents (not school personnel, incidentally) were sufficiently ingenious, dedicated, and uninhibited by "professional" opinions and expectancies to teach him. If, in fact, much of the difference between Nigel Hunt and other mongoloid persons is due to the training provided by parents, it should be possible for *certified* teachers to teach other mongoloids to read at least as well.

Gray, Baker, and Stancyk (1969), after reviewing literature concerning the general area of teaching reading to children of many levels of intellectual functioning, concluded:

Anyone familiar with reading is aware of the enormous volume of literature on the subject. The wide unevenness in quality of information and the appearance of conflicting results contribute to a very hazy, disorganized and confused situation. . . . From the mass of evidence presented in the literature it is quite possible to substantiate a variety of positions based upon selectively choosing the appropriate references. Thus, from a larger perspective it would appear that the general findings from much of the research data are inconclusive [p. 255].

Reading as it relates to trainable-level retarded students seems at least as confusing in that the same arguments applicable to teaching reading to any child are also applicable to trainable-level retarded students. In addition, teachers of these students have to contend with the "why bother" hypothesis; i.e., there are those who think that teaching trainable-level retarded students to read is an impossible task and that any such attempts will therefore result in wasted time, effort, and expense. There are also those who have suggested that reading instruction for trainable-level retarded students should be confined to concerns over differential responding to safety or caution words (Goldberg & Rooke, 1967). Finally, it appears that most nonretarded children can learn to read regardless of the instructional procedures employed or the theoretical assumptions underlying those procedures, and that trainable-level retarded students have failed to learn to read regardless of procedures or theoretical assumptions. Consequently, the potential of the latter for effective community functioning has been severely depressed.

If it is a tenable assumption that basic reading skills are crucial to survival in a community setting, then there are at least three instructional issues that must be confronted. First, are trainable-level retarded students intellectually capable of learning to read to such an extent that they can function in a community setting? Second, what specific reading content should be taught? Third, *how* should reading be taught?

In the view of the writer, most trainable-level retarded students are intellectually capable of meeting the reading requirements necessary to function effectively in many social and vocational community settings. The problem, however, is that the professional community has not yet delineated and empirically verified the instructional procedures to teach the necessary skills. Furthermore, until such procedures are available, concerns over what to teach are academic rather than instructional.

Examples of two divergent views on how trainable-level retarded students might be taught to read are found in the writings of Kolburne (1965) and MacAulay (1968). When discussing a phonic approach to teaching reading, Kolburne made the remarkably definitive statement:

Do not attempt to teach trainable children to read by means of phonics. It is a waste of time and effort. The concept and application of phonics require a greater amount of intellectual capacity than these youngsters possess. It is entirely too abstract for them to grasp. One might as well try to teach them the theory of numbers. It can't be done [p. 107].

Instead of a phonetic approach, Kolburne recommended a form of the "whole word" approach.

MacAulay, on the other hand, not only recommended a phonetic approach but also provided some empirical support for its efficacy. Her program consisted of teaching individual sounds, sound blends, a naming vocabulary, and, when appropriate, word phrases. While her procedures were quite similar to those described in this chapter's section on imitation, they are presented here in some detail to show how the systematic application of basic learning principles and behavioristic task analysis can result in demonstrable progress toward the development of a technology of reading instruction for trainable-level retarded students.

MacAulay's first instructional objective was to teach 11 students to produce sounds (CA range = 9-15, IQ range = 27-92; several of the students were nonverbal). The procedures used to accomplish this are described below:

In starting training, the teacher pointed to a letter or color symbol on an easel in front of the child, and said the sound with his mouth hidden (an auditory S^D). If the child produced a crude approximation of the sound, the teacher instantly placed a token in a dish in front of the child and verbally praised him. The giving of tokens was always paired with verbal, social approval. After successful attempts, better approximations were required for reinforcement. In other words, the criteria for reinforcement were made more strict. This procedure was continued until a close-to-perfect approximation was produced. If no acceptable approximation was made after 10 trials, a visual S^D was added (mouth observation). If no acceptable approximation was made after 10 additional trials, a hand cue was added.

A hand on the throat indicated a voiced sound, and a hand in front of the mouth indicated a voiceless, plosive, or fricative sound. One of the child's thumbs was placed in front of the teacher's mouth with the other four fingers on the teacher's throat. The child's other hand was placed in a similar fashion in front of his own mouth and against his throat [p. 105].

The second instructional objective was to teach the students to reproduce verbally 31 sounds in response to graphic symbols. The procedures used to accomplish this are described below:

The sounds (m) and (b) were taught first. After each sound had been produced correctly or with an acceptable approximation 10 times in response to the symbols (Procedure 1), the child was drilled on the two sounds. The two symbols were on an easel in front of the child. The teacher pointed to one symbol and the child responded with the accepted production. He then was reinforced with a token paired with social approval. If the sound was incorrect, he was given an auditory S^D. If the response was still unacceptable, a visual S^D (mouth observation) was given. If the first two prompts did not work, a hand cue was added. For the first two sounds about 60 to 70 presentations were made [p. 106].

After a student learned to label the 31 symbols, flash cards were used to teach sound blending. The procedures used to teach blending are described below:

The teacher and child said the sounds simultaneously while the teacher held the card under his mouth and slowly moved his finger along under the sounds as they were produced. The teacher and child slowly mouthed the sound combinations together. The hand cue of moving the open palm slowly indicated blending. Most of the children needed very little prompting on blending, and it was not found necessary to teach blending more directly [p. 108].

Subsequently, utilizing essentially these same procedures, several students were taught to (a) identify whole words, (b) identify the picture or object the words represented, and (c) match a printed word with an object or a picture.

MacAulay's program was reasonably successful. (For a more detailed presentation of the results, the reader is referred to the original manuscript.) Suffice it here to present a few examples: An 11-year-old mongoloid boy with an IQ of 56 learned to read nine words and subsequently was placed in a programmed reading series; an 11-year-old boy with an IQ of 43, described as "autistic," was taught to speak three words clearly and match those words with pictures or objects; a 9-year-old boy with an IQ of 28 was taught to speak seven words and to match six of them with the appropriate written word or picture. MacAulay's efforts were part of a research study. Unfortunately, information is not available as to whether the programs were continued and expanded when the study was completed. Nevertheless, the success of her programs suggested that a phonetic approach to teaching trainable-level retarded students to read may have instructional merit and is worthy of further empirical investigation.

During the past 2 years, the author and his colleagues developed several teaching programs designed to teach trainable-level retarded students to read. All of the programs were conducted in public school classrooms by teachers and university students. In addition, all of the programs except one involved teaching more than one student at a time. It was assumed either that the students had the necessary auditory and visual discrimination, articulation, and imitation skills to be successful in the programs, or that such skills would be acquired as the programs progressed.

The objectives of the first two programs (Brown, Hermanson, Klemme, Haubrich, & Ora, 1970) were (a) to verify the effectiveness of a standard sight-word drill; (b) to arrange the instructional arrangement so as to foster the development of a sight-word-acquisition learning set; and (c) to demonstrate that the sight-word drill used to teach word labeling in an individual instructional setting (one to one) could be adapted to a group instructional setting (six to one) without loss of instructional efficiency.

In the first program, the words from a basic programmed reading book were printed on flash cards, and a trainable-level retarded student (CA = 12; IQ = 47) was asked to identify them. The words the student labeled correctly were removed, and the remaining words were arranged in 17 three-word sets in the order in which they appeared in the book. The following sight-word drill was used to teach the student to label the words in the sets:

The first word of a set was presented, and the TA (teacher aide) said: "Do you see this word?" (the TA pointed to the card and did not remove his finger until Hope looked at the card) "This word says_____. What does this word say?" When Hope matched the label, TA immediately smiled and made such statements as "Good," "Fine," "Great job," "I am proud of you," and "You're learning to read." The TA then presented the second and third cards in the set and followed exactly the same modeling and reinforcement procedures as were used for the first word in the set.

When Hope had the opportunity to match the label of each word in the set, the TA presented the first word again and said, "What does this word say?" If Hope correctly labeled the word, the TA displayed approval and presented the next card in the set. If Hope did not label the word correctly, the TA modeled the correct label, asked Hope to match the modeled label, displayed approval when she did so, and presented the next word in the set. This procedure was followed until Hope correctly labeled the three words in the set on three consecutive presentations without the modeling cues. When she reached criterion on a set, the teacher colored the bar graph to reflect her progress and congratulated her in the presence of her classmates. The same procedure was used with all 17 sets [p. 122].

The results suggested that the student developed a sight-word-acquisition learning set. That is, she tended to make fewer errors as she progressed through the 17 sets, before she reached criterion. If it can be demonstrated that other trainable-level retarded students can be taught to "learn to learn" by classroom teachers, and that such skills are generalizable across academic tasks, it seems reasonable that these children will be able to progress through academic content much faster than has previously been supposed.

In the second program, six students (CA range = 12-14; IQ range = 36-49) were taught to label two sets of five sight words. One set of words was taught individually using the procedure described above, and the second set of words was taught in a group setting. The group training procedures were identical to the individual training procedures, with the exception that the opportunity to respond was rotated among the six students. While both sets of words were learned, those words taught in the group setting were learned in fewer trials. Subsequently, two of the six students were taught to use the teacher's procedures to teach each other and to conduct sight-word review sessions with other students in their class (Brown, Fenrick, & Klemme, 1971).

Thus far the cited programs required word calling, which is a component of, but cannot be called, reading. Most people would agree that before a series of responses can be called reading, the student must in some way grasp the concept the words represent, abstract meaning from the words, comprehend the message of the author, and so forth. MacAulay (1968) suggested that one way to measure whether a student "understands" a word is to have him match a word with a picture or an object. Brown and Perlmutter (1971) used the term "functional reading" in an attempt to operationalize reading as it might be applicable for trainable-level retarded students. They considered reading as requiring at least two sets of responses. First, reading requires that a student verbally label a printed stimulus or series of stimuli. Second, a student must respond differentially to the printed stimulus or stimuli. For example, if a student is presented with a flash card upon which the word "dog" is written, the student must make at least two responses: He must verbally label the word, and he must respond in some way (e.g., point to a picture of a dog) that indicates he understands the word. Admittedly, this definition of reading is inappropriate for many students, many less literal levels of reading, many verb conjugations, and so forth. However, it provides a reasonable starting point toward developing a technology of teaching reading to trainable-level retarded students, primarily because it converts the often nebulous term "reading" into a series of discrete motor responses made to clearly delineated stimuli. By using these two criteria for functional reading as guides, attempts have been made to demonstrate that trainable-level retarded students can be taught to read nouns, adjectives, unconjugated verbs, and complete sentences.

Brown, Jones, Troccolo, Heiser, and Bellamy (1972), utilizing the sight-word drill described, taught two 5-year-old mongoloid students (MA = 2.4 and 2.9; IQ = 49 and 49) to label 12 different objects (e.g., milk, crayon, straw) and the corresponding 12 written words. Subsequently, the 12 objects were displayed in a row on a table. The teacher presented one of the 12 word cards and asked a student to label the word and then touch the object. The two students reached criterion on this task in 13 trials. In accordance with the definition of functional reading, the students could now read 12 nouns. Once the two students could read the 12 nouns, the teacher then taught them to read 12 adjective-noun phrases. That is, the students were taught to label white milk and chocolate milk, red crayon and blue crayon, and so on, instead of just milk and crayon. They were then taught to label 12 flash cards containing the 12 adjective-noun phrases. Finally, they were taught to label the phrases on the cards and touch the objects the words represented.

Brown, Huppler, Pierce, York, & Sontag (1972) devised a six-step program designed to teach three trainable-level retarded students (M IQ = 42; M CA = 8) to read five unconjugated action verbs. Teaching the reading of verbs presented different instructional problems from teaching nouns and adjectives, in that overt movement seemed a necessary ingredient of meaning. Thus, the program was divided into the following phases:

1. It was verified that the students could perform five different physical actions in response to the verbal directions of the teacher (walk, run, sit, touch, color).
2. The students were taught to verbally label five pictures depicting the five different actions.
3. The students were taught to touch each of the five action pictures in response to a verbal cue provided by the teacher.
4. The students were taught to label five verb flash cards.
5. The students were taught to label the flash cards and then touch the appropriate action pictures.
6. The students were taught to label the five verb flash cards and perform the action indicated by each [p. 2].

The procedures to verify that the students could respond correctly to verbal directions (Phase 1) were essentially those used in the direction-following program previously described (Brown, Bellamy, Tang, & Klemme, 1971). The procedures to teach the responses required in Phases 2, 3, 4, 5, and 6 were essentially those used to teach the reading of nouns and adjective-noun phrases.

Thus far, it has been demonstrated that trainable-level retarded students can be taught to read (at least according to the already stated definition of reading) nouns, adjectives, and unconjugated verbs. A logical next step would be to teach the reading of sentences. This was accomplished in a program reported by Brown and Perlmutter (1971). In this program, utilizing essentially the same procedures described in the previous reading programs, seven trainable-level retarded students (M CA = 16; M IQ = 44) were taught to functionally read nine different sentences: The penny is (in, on top of, on the bottom of, in front of, in back of, over, under, on the right side of, on the left side of) the box. The program was divided into the following phases:

1. The students were taught to label the 17 different words.
2. The students were taught to label the words in the order in which they occurred in the sentences (label from left to right).
3. The students were taught to point to the location of the penny referred to, when the teacher labeled the words in a sentence.
4. The students were taught to label the words in sentence order and respond differentially by touching the penny referred to in the sentence they labeled.
5. The students were taught to listen to the teacher label words in the sentences and then respond differentially.

The whole-word approach to teaching reading to trainable-level retarded students, as it has been described, has obvious practical implications. Through this method, many students might be taught to acquire valuable skills (filling work orders, cooking from the order slip of a waitress, cooking from a recipe, traveling about a community, and so forth), as well as engage in socially and psychologically important activities that require a rudimentary reading repertoire. For example, Brown, Van Deventer, Johnson, and Sontag (1972) taught four adolescent females (M CA = 14.9; M IQ = 44) to read a restaurant menu. Their program consisted of the following five phases:

1. The students were taught to label 15 pictures of common foods and drinks (root beer, barbecue, hamburger, fried eggs, bacon, hot dogs, etc.).
2. The students were taught to label the printed words representing the 15 foods and drinks.
3. The students were taught to label the printed words and then touch the picture of the food or drink the words represented.
4. The students were taught to label the words as they appeared on a food menu.
5. The students were brought to a restaurant, ordered, and ate the food of their choice (the money used to pay for the food was earned by the students during the teaching phases) [p. 2].

In these seven programs conducted by Brown and his colleagues, a whole-word approach was used with some success. However, it is questionable whether the exclusive use of the whole-word approach can teach these children to read all the words necessary to function effectively in a community environment. At some point, the development of an adequate reading repertoire would be facilitated if they were taught basic phonetics, spelling, the use of contextual cues, and other word-attack skills. At this point it is conjecture whether such skills should be taught before, during, or after a student has acquired a rudimentary whole-word sight vocabulary. However, it appears that such skills are necessary for substantial increases in reading achievement.

There have been several limited attempts to teach trainable-level retarded students basic word-attack skills. MacAulay (1968) provided a reasonable example of how a phonetic approach might be used. The following is a report of a program developed by Brown, Bellamy, Bancroft, and Sontag (1972) designed to teach three mongoloid students (*M* CA = 12.0; *M* IQ = 38) to spell. The program was divided into the following five phases:

1. The students were required to imitate the teacher as she made the sound of each letter in the alphabet.
2. A match-to-sample task was used to verify that each student could visually discriminate between the different letters.
3. A flash-card drill was used to teach the students to label letters they could not label on a pretest.
4. The students were taught to point to letters when the teacher pronounced the letter sound.
5. The students were taught to label letters as they occurred in words.

The instructional objectives of the program were realized in that the three students correctly labeled the letters in the following words: vase, box, pencil, zebra, ghost, yellow, desk, queen. Logical extensions of this program, of course, would include teaching the students to label the words after they had labeled the letters and teaching the student to ask such questions as "Teacher (mother), what does_____spell?"

This section was concerned with selected issues related to teaching trainable-level retarded students to read. The cited programs exemplified *how* these students may be taught. While the programs were encouraging and suggestive of further research, they were nevertheless propaedeutic. For example, MacAulay's (1968) programs were effective as far as they went, but it is obvious that we are a long way from providing the students with the full range of needed skills. The programs reported by Brown and his colleagues were cross-sectional rather than longitudinal, and we are forced to ask whether one group of students can be taught to make all the responses made by the many different groups. Nevertheless, despite the inadequacies of evidence and the extreme complexities of the instructional task, it appears (at least to the writer) that the issue is no longer *whether* trainable-level retarded students are capable of reading but rather *how* we can go about developing their reading skills. We now realize that functioning effectively in a community setting is dependent upon a minimal reading repertoire; it can be hoped that applied research over the next few years will provide more effective instructional procedures.

Mathematics

If trainable-level retarded students are to function effectively in a community setting, they must also be able to comprehend and use basic mathematical concepts and operations. The student must be able to use money, tell time, function within a time schedule, read recipes involving fractions, function in vocational settings requiring quantitative production quotas, and so on. Given that basic mathematical skills are essential components of any student's development, two problems immediately arise: the sequence through which a student should progress and the technology of teaching the student to perform the responses required in each step of the sequence.

Perhaps, under ideal conditions, specific mathematical skills could be delineated and arranged in a series. The students could then enter the community with enough basic knowledge of mathematics to adapt to situations requiring such skills. Unfortunately, it does not appear that we have available a valid sequence or technology of teaching the components in the sequence. On the other hand, we are closer to approximating a tenable sequence of mathematics skills than an effective technology of teaching those skills. For a more detailed consideration of the developmental sequencing of mathematical skills and concepts, the reader is referred to Bereiter (1968) and Becker (1971). The purpose here is to emphasize that even if we knew the language skills prerequisite to mathematical development (Hargis, 1971) – e.g., if we knew whether concepts such as large or small, more or less, and whole or part should precede rote and rational counting, or vice versa – we would still have to arrive at instructional procedures which would result in the student acquiring the necessary skills and concepts.

As might be predicted, there is meager information to which a teacher of trainable-level retarded students can turn for help on how to teach basic mathematical skills (Bradley et al., 1971). The available information is incomplete, unsystematic, cross-sectional, and, for the most part, lacking in empirical verification (see Bellamy & Brown, 1972, Brown, Bellamy, & Gadberry, 1971; Brown, Bellamy, Gadberry, & Sontag, 1971; Coleman, 1970; Kolburne, 1965; McCarthy & Scheerenberger, 1966).

Nevertheless, many basic mathematical skills can be taught to trainable-level retarded students. Bellamy and Brown[2] (1972) reported instructional procedures, extensions of those utilized by Brown, Bellamy, Gadberry, and Sontag (1971), that resulted in a group of trainable-level retarded students acquiring the skills necessary to add any two numbers that totaled 10 or less. In the Bellamy and Brown program, it was arbitrarily decided that adding any two numbers totaling 10 or less would be facilitated if the students could perform at least the following responses:

1. label printed numerals (1-10)
2. write numerals from a verbal cue

[2]Cited with permission from *Training School Bulletin,* 1972, The Training School Unit of the American Institute for Mental Studies, Vineland, N.J.

3. count quantities of lines and report the total verbally
4. draw quantities of lines corresponding to printed numerals
5. count quantities of lines and write the total
6. complete two pre-addition exercises involving stimulus fading

The instructional procedures used to teach the students to perform the responses required in each step of the sequence were well delineated and are presented in detail. The following procedure was used to teach the students to label the printed numerals:

When the students were seated at a table in the classroom, the teacher (T) presented the student with a numeral and asked him to provide the verbal label. If the student responded appropriately, he was complimented and given an edible.

When an incorrect response occurred, T recorded the error and modeled the correct response, "This is a (3)." The initial instruction was presented again: "What is this numeral?" One repetition of the modeling procedure was sufficient to produce the correct response on the few occasions that T's first model did not suffice. Praise and applause were given when the correct response occurred, but edibles were provided only when S responded correctly to the initial presentation of the Numeral Card [p. 4].

This procedure was followed until each student could verbally label each of the 10 numeral cards.

Teaching the students to write numerals from a verbal cue was accomplished as follows: The student was instructed to write a numeral. If she responded appropriately, she was praised and given an edible.

When an incorrect response was recorded, T first said, "No, that is not a (4). Try again." If the correct response was still not emitted, T modeled the response, i.e., wrote "4" on a sheet of paper so the S could observe both T's writing and the written numeral, and then repeated the initial direction: "Write the numeral (4)." On the occasions that the desired response still was not emitted, T repeated the instruction and then guided S's hand as necessary for him to write the numeral. As soon as the correct response occurred, S was praised and applauded, but edibles were not given [p. 5].

Teaching the students to count quantities of lines and verbally report the total was accomplished in the following manner: T placed a card with a quantity of lines from 1 to 10 in front of S and asked, "How many are there?" If the S responded correctly, T dispensed praise, and so forth.

When an incorrect response occurred, T first instructed S to "Try again. Count these lines and tell me how many there are." If the ensuing response was incorrect, T modeled the desired behaviors and then repeated his instruction. If the correct response still did not occur, T physically guided S's hand as S pointed to each line in turn and voiced the appropriate numeral. Praise and applause followed the correct response, but edibles were given only when S responded correctly to the initial presentation of the Quantity Card [p. 5].

Teaching students to draw quantities of lines corresponding to printed numerals was taught in the following manner: A student was given a slip of paper with a numeral on it and instructed to draw the "right number of lines under the numeral." If the student responded correctly, he was praised, and so forth.

When an incorrect response occurred, T said, "No, that is not the right number of lines. How many lines were you supposed to draw?" When S correctly labeled the numeral on the slip, T gave S a duplicate slip and asked him to "Try again. Draw the right number of lines under the numeral." If the correct response did not occur, T then modeled the response (i.e., drew the appropriate number of lines), gave S another duplicate slip, and repeated his instruction. If the correct response still did not occur, S was physically guided as necessary to perform the required behaviors. S received praise and applause when he emitted the correct response [p. 6].

Essentially, the same procedures were used to teach the students to count quantities of lines and write the total.

In the first pre-addition exercise, a student was given a sheet of paper with an addition problem and the correct quantities of lines drawn under *both* numerals. The student was instructed to "count all these lines [teacher pointed to the lines under *both* numerals] and write the total here [teacher pointed to the horizontal line provided for the answer to the additional problem]." If the student responded incorrectly, S was given a duplicate slip and asked to:

"Try again. Count all the lines [pointing to the lines under both numerals] and write the total here [pointing to the horizontal line provided for the answer to the addition problem]." If the correct response did not then occur, T modeled the behaviors involved and then repeated his instruction. The desired response consistently followed this procedure. Praise and applause followed the correct response [p. 7].

The second pre-addition exercise differed from the first in that the quantities of lines were provided only under the first numeral on the mimeographed slip (stimulus fading). The student was then instructed to:

"Draw the right number of lines under this numeral [pointing to the second numeral]; then count all the lines, and write the total." When an incorrect response occurred, T gave S a duplicate problem and instructed him to "Try again. Draw this many lines [pointing to the second numeral]; then count all the lines and write the total." If the correct response still did not occur, T's modeling of the behaviors involved was sufficient to produce the correct response. Praise and applause followed the correct response [p. 7].

In the final task (addition), the student was presented with a sheet of problems and instructed to:

"Draw the right number of lines under *both* numerals, then count the lines, and write the total." When the initial response was incorrect, T gave S a duplicate problem and instructed him to "Try again. Draw the right number of lines under *both* numerals, then count all the lines, and write the total." Verbal instructions were sufficient in every case to produce the correct response. Praise and applause were given when the correct response occurred [p. 8].

At the end of the 268 instructional trials, the four students (M CA = 16.6; M IQ = 39) correctly solved the problems. That is, the students could now add any numbers totaling 10 or less.

The Bellamy and Brown program has been described in detail because it is a reasonable example of how behavioristic task analysis and the systematic application of basic learning principles might be used to develop rudimentary arithmetic skills. Certainly there is more to teaching mathematics than was encompassed by this program; and certainly there is a substantial discrepancy between adding two numbers totaling 10 and performing the mathematical skills necessary to function effectively in a community environment. On the other hand, the students in the program had been enrolled in public school programs for trainable-level retarded students from 2 to 11 years (M = 5.5). It is the opinion of the writer that if those students had been programmed from age 5, or even sooner, their mathematical repertoire would have been far more advanced at age 16.

Space does not permit a more comprehensive presentation of other instructional procedures that have been used to teach basic arithmetical skills to trainable-level retarded students, or to conjecture as to how procedures used to teach students of different intellectual abilities might be adapted. It is hoped that the model and the discussion thus far will assist the reader who is concerned with such an endeavor.

Prevocational behaviors

If trainable-level retarded students are to function effectively in a community, they must have marketable vocational-behavioral repertoires. That is, they must have work skills which will yield a profit for their employer and a reasonable wage for their work. There is no more poignant testimony to the failure of public school programs than 18-year-old trainable-level retarded students leaving school. When we inquire whether they are prepared to function in a community, whether they have been taught to shop, travel, work, engage in satisfying leisure activities, relate to others of a different intellectual status, and function within a complex legal structure, the answer is *no*. Confronting such failures forces us to realize how far we must go before we can say that we have provided these children with what they need.

Enabling a trainable-level retarded student to function in a complex community vocational setting requires more than a public school program can provide. The status of the national economy, parental expectancies, employer attitudes, and acceptance by nonretarded peers are only a few of the nonschool factors relevant to successful vocational placement. While such factors must be considered, the objectives of school programs should be to develop the physical, social, and academic skills necessary to function effectively in a vocational environment. In the recent past, progress has been made toward the delineation of a technology for teaching trainable-level retarded students to perform successfully on vocational tasks involving discrete motor responses. However, most of these tasks have been extremely simple and required little intelligence and training (Gold, 1968), e.g., stuffing envelopes, collating, sorting sandpaper, making decorative bows with colored ribbon. This focus reflects the assumption held until recently that trainable-level retarded students were incapable of performing effectively on any remunerative vocational task. However, it is becoming increasingly apparent that as the technology of teaching improves, increasingly complex behaviors can be taught (Gold, 1969; for a more detailed discussion of literature related to the vocational training of trainable-level retarded students, the reader is referred to Gold, 1972). The purpose here is to show how behavioristic task analysis and the systematic application of basic learning principles have resulted in the acquisition of functional vocational repertoires by trainable-level retarded students.

An excellent example of how trainable-level retarded students can be systematically taught to perform functional vocational behaviors is provided by Crosson (1969). His objective was to teach seven males (M IQ = 27) to operate a drill press which produced manufactured wooden pencil holders. The task was divided into the following components:

1. Assume position facing drill press.
2. Adjust position, moving right shoulder in line with drill.
3. Extend left hand to stack of precut blanks.
4. Remove blank from stack.
5. Transfer blank to drilling jig.
6. Align and position in alignment block well (black).
7. Remove left hand; close 2nd, 3rd, and 4th fingers against palm.
8. With palm down, place exposed surface of 2nd finger against lower edge of blank.
9. Place thumb against near edge, index finger against far edge of blank; grasp firmly.
10. Extend right hand to drill press lever.
11. Open and lift hand, palm facing lever.
12. Extend thumb, forming V with index finger.
13. Bring palm in contact with tip of lever with shaft intersecting V.
14. *Slowly* rotate forearm downward (minimum interval 5 seconds) allowing shaft to rotate through V.
15. At point lever ceases to rotate, extend forearm directly toward rear of machine, allowing lever to rest at base of thumb.
16. At point lever ceases to rotate, release and allow to return to initial position [p. 815].

Once the task had been divided into components and arranged in a sequence, the instructional problem was to teach the worker to perform each component in the correct sequence. Crosson's instructional procedure was as follows:

1. A trainer modeled (demonstrated) the first component of the sequence and instructed or gestured the trainee to match the behavior modeled.

2. If the trainee matched the behavior modeled, he was reinforced immediately.

3. If the trainee did not match the behavior modeled, the trainer then primed (physically guided) the movements necessary for a correct response.

4. The trainer then faded the prime and then faded his instruction and gestures until the stimulus properties of the task were sufficient to control the correct response.

5. Once the first component in the behavioral sequence was occurring consistently, reinforcement was withheld until the second component was taught. When the first and second components were occurring in succession, reinforcement was then delivered.

These procedures were followed until each of the 16 behavioral components in the chain occurred in the correct order. When the trainee demonstrated that he could consistently perform the entire sequence correctly, the reinforcement schedule was attenuated until it represented other more "natural" workshop incentive systems.

One of the few systematic attempts to teach trainable-level retarded students to perform relatively complex vocational tasks was reported by Gold (1969). Using training procedures derived from basic psychological research in visual-discrimination learning (Gold & Scott, 1971), he taught 64 trainable-level individuals to assemble 15- and 24-piece bicycle brakes. Half of the trainees were taught to assemble the 15-component brake as it came from the factory. The remaining half of the trainees worked on the same task, except that the components they worked with were color-coded; if the components were assembled correctly, the color cues on each component could be seen by the trainees. Subsequently, both groups were taught to assemble the 24-component brake. The group that was taught to assemble the 15-component brake with the color cues learned the task in half the number of trials required by the groups which did not have color-coded materials. In addition, most of the trainees learned to assemble the 24-piece brake significantly faster than the 15-piece brake.

Of particular interest here is how the task was divided into components requiring discrete and cumulative motor responses, and how the trainees were taught to perform the responses. For illustrative purposes, the 15-component brake is described below. Each of the components was placed in a separate compartment of a 15-compartment tray. The trainee was required to remove components from left to right and assemble them. The task was divided in the following manner [Gold & Scott, 1971, p. 15]:

Part	Manipulation	Verbal Cue
1. (axle)	Pick up.	–
2. (expander)	Turn wrong, right.	"Try another way." "Good."
	Thread to 1 inch.	"Stop."
3. (bearing)	Push on.	–
4. (cap)	Put on.	–
5. (arm)	Put on wrong, right.	"Try another way." "Good."
	Hold down.	
6. (nut)	Thread on.	"Make it tight."
	Turn assembly over.	"Turn it over."
7. (sub.)	Put on wrong, right.	"Try another way." "Good."
8. (hub)	Put on wrong, right.	"Try another way." "Good."
	(Be sure to look through it.)	
9. (bearing)	Put on.	–
10. (drive)	Put on.	–
11. (bearing)	Put on.	–
12. (cone)	Thread part way on.	"Stop."
	Turn over.	"Turn it over."
13. (shoe)	Put it in.	–
14. (shoe)	Put it in.	–
	Lift.	"Lift."
	Turn, shake, etc. (seat)	–
	Grasp, turn over.	"Turn it over."
	Finish cone.	–
15. (nut)	Thread on.	"Good."

The instructional procedures consisted of the following:

The S was seated at a table on which the tray was placed, with four disassembled brakes in the compartments. The E was seated beside him. Before the S's first trial on the training task, and before the *S*'s first trial on the transfer task, the entire procedure was demonstrated once by *E*. The demonstration consisted of the *E* bringing one of each part forward, in front of the compartment divider, so that one set of parts was in position, then assembling the unit. Errors were made, according to a standardized demonstration format, and verbal cues that would be given when the *S* made an error were used. The most frequently used cue was, "Try another way." The purpose of the demonstration was to show the subject how to respond to the few verbal cues used, and not to teach the task [p. 14].

If trainable-level retarded students can be taught such complex tasks as assembling bicycle brakes, at least two issues arise: First, it is likely that as our instructional technology improves, it will be possible to teach such student workers to perform even more complex vocational tasks. (No doubt there already are vocational training programs around the country that have taught more complex tasks.) Second, it seems that once workers have been taught to complete a work task accurately, the problem of production rates must then be attacked (Brown, Huppler, Perlmutter, Bellamy, & Sontag, 1971; Brown, Johnson, Gadberry, & Fenrick, 1971; Brown & Pearce, 1970; Brown, Van Deventer, Perlmutter, Jones, & Sontag, 1972), as well as such requirements as maintaining high rates of accurate production under typical vocational incentive systems (Brown, Bellamy, Perlmutter, Sackowitz, & Sontag, 1972). Performing complex tasks at high rates for long periods of time is incompatible with many of the performance problems typically encountered in vocational settings, e.g., inability to delay gratification, distractibility, inappropriate social interactions. However, such crucial and complex noninstructional factors (unions, contracts, employer attitudes, and travel) have yet to be dealt with effectively.

Language

Many persons concerned with instructional programs for trainable-level retarded students are rapidly coming to realize the importance of language and language behavior. Broadly considered, language deficits are probably the most pervasive and crucial cognitive-behavioral deficits presented by these students. However, this area is beyond the scope of the present chapter. (The reader interested in an overview of language as it relates to mental retardation is referred to McLean, Yoder, & Schiefelbusch, 1972. For the development of basic language concepts in trainable-level retarded students, see Larsen & Bricker, 1968; Chalfant & Silikovitz, 1970; and Tawney & Hipsher, 1970.)

There is little doubt that in the next few years the language development of trainable-level retarded students will receive increasing attention. It is hoped that at least some of this attention will focus on the delineation of a sequence of language development that is relevant to trainable-level retarded students and on procedures that classroom teachers can use to teach the responses required in the sequence.

The future

Primarily owing to parental efforts, there has been a slight but important departure from the way our society has historically treated trainable-level retarded students. In the past, the primary treatment approaches have been their segregation in inadequate, ineffectual, and often inhumane residential facilities, or isolation at home because of systematic exclusion from many community services available to their age peers. Currently, we are in the process of shifting to more community-based and relevant service-delivery systems (Barker, 1971). There is little doubt that the students, their parents, and the community at large will benefit in numerous ways from this shift. As the momentum of the shift accelerates, many new economic, social, and educational demands will be placed on existing community resources, e.g., space in crowded schools, teacher allocations, subsidized vocational settings, and tolerance for variations in appearance and behavior. There is a distinct possibility that placement in large residential custodial facilities might be superseded by placement in small community-based facilities.

In this chapter, the writer has emphasized the need for the development of an empirically verified instructional technology because the behavioral repertoire of trainable-level retarded students needs substantial enhancement. It is incumbent upon the professional community to generate the technological vehicles to effect behavioral enhancement because the need for it is so pervasive. The emphases expressed here are not intended to minimize the importance of improvement in other areas related to the development of trainable-level retarded students. The legal rights of retarded persons, relevant instructional content, preschool education, teacher training, parent training and counseling, prenatal diagnosis, abortion, sterilization, subsidized vocational programs, community attitudes, and instructional materials all must receive careful scrutiny if the life style of trainable-level retarded students is to be changed substantially in the near future.

Finally, it should be realized that the model, as well as the sample programs presented here, represent the professional bias of the writer. No doubt there are many professionals with different points of view who have generated effective and exciting instructional programs for similar students. As the number of trainable-level retarded students enrolled in public school programs increases, others will become involved in their destiny, leading to (one hopes) services superior to those of the past.

References

Bandura, A. Behavioral modification through modeling procedures. In L. Krasner & L. Ullman (Eds.), *Research in behavior modification.* New York: Holt, 1965.

Bandura, A. *Principles of behavior modification.* New York: Holt, 1969.

Barker, E. Current and significant: ENCOR — A community's alternative to institutionalization. *Education and Training of the Mentally Retarded,* 1971, **6,** 185-190.

Becker, W.C. Teaching concepts and operations — or how to make kids smart. In L.A. Hamerlynck & F.W. Clark (Eds.), *Behavior modification for exceptional children and youth.* Calgary, Alberta: John D. McAra, 1971.

Bellamy, T., & Brown, L. A sequential procedure for teaching addition skills to trainable retarded students. *Training School Bulletin,* 1972, **69**(1), 31-44.

Bereiter, C. *Arithmetic and mathematics.* San Rafael, Calif.: Dimensions, 1968.

Bijou, S.W. A functional analysis of retarded development. In N.R. Ellis (Ed.), *International review of research in mental retardation.* New York: Academic Press, 1966.

Blatt, B., & Kaplan, F. *Christmas in purgatory.* Boston: Allyn & Bacon, 1967.

Bradley, B.H., Hundziak, M., & Patterson, R.M. *Teaching moderately and severely retarded children.* Springfield, Ill.: Charles C Thomas, 1971.

Brown, L., Bellamy, T., Bancroft, J., & Sontag, E. Development of selected pre-reading skills in young trainable students. Paper presented at the meeting of the Wisconsin-American Association of Mental Deficiency Convention, Racine, May 1972.

Brown, L., Bellamy, T., & Gadberry, E. A procedure for the development and measurement of rudimentary quantitative concepts in low functioning trainable students. *Training School Bulletin,* 1971, **68,** 178-185.

Brown, L., Bellamy, T., Gadberry, E., & Sontag, E. Teaching addition to young trainable students: A sequential procedure. Paper presented at the meeting of the State Convention of the Wisconsin Association of Retarded Children, Rhinelander, Wisconsin, May 1971.

Brown, L., Bellamy, T., Perlmutter, L., Sackowitz, P., & Sontag, E. The development of quality, quantity, and durability in the work performance of retarded students in a public school prevocational workshop. *Training School Bulletin,* 1972, **69**(2), 58-69.

Brown, L., Bellamy, T., & Sontag, E. The development and implementation of a public school prevocational training program for trainable retarded and severely emotionally disturbed children. Madison, Wis.: Madison Public Schools, 1971.

Brown, L., Bellamy, T., Tang, P., & Klemme, H. A procedure for teaching trainable students to follow verbal directions. Unpublished manuscript, University of Wisconsin, 1971.

Brown, L., Fenrick, N., & Klemme, H. Trainable level retarded students teach trainable level retarded students. *Teaching Exceptional Children*, 1971, **4**(1).

Brown, L., & Foshee, J. A comparison of techniques for increasing attending to visual stimuli in classrooms for retarded students. *Education and Training of the Mentally Retarded*, 1970, **6**, 4-11.

Brown, L., Hermanson, J., Klemme, H., Haubrich, P., & Ora, J. Using behavior modification principles to teach sight vocabulary. *Teaching Exceptional Children*, 1970, **2**(3), 120-128.

Brown, L., Huppler, B., Perlmutter, L., Bellamy, T., & Sontag, E. Effects of contingent charting and money on the production rates of trainable level retarded students. Unpublished manuscript, University of Wisconsin, 1971.

Brown, L., Huppler, B., Pierce, L., Johnson, N., & Sontag, E. Teaching young trainable level retarded students to report behavioral events. Unpublished manuscript, University of Wisconsin, 1972.

Brown, L., Huppler, B., Pierce, L., York, B. & Sontag, E. Teaching trainable level retarded students to read unconjugated action verbs. *Journal of Special Education*, 1973, in press.

Brown, L., Johnson, S., Gadberry, E., & Fenrick, N. Increasing individual and assembly line production rates of retarded students. *Training School Bulletin*, 1971, **67**, 206-212.

Brown, L., Jones, S., Troccolo, E., Heiser, C., & Bellamy, T. Teaching functional reading to young trainable students: Toward longitudinal objectives. *Journal of Special Education*, 1972, **6**, 237-246.

Brown, L., & Klemme, H. Teaching trainable level retarded children to speak in sentences. Paper presented at the meeting of the Madison Area Association of Retarded Children, In-Service Training Project, Madison, Wisconsin, June 1971.

Brown, L., & Pearce, E. Increasing the production rates of trainable retarded students in a public school simulated workshop. *Education and Training of the Mentally Retarded*, 1970, **5**, 15-22.

Brown, L., & Perlmutter, L. Teaching functional reading to trainable level retarded students. *Education and Training of the Mentally Retarded*, 1971, **6**, 74-84.

Brown, L., Van Deventer, P., Johnson, P., & Sontag, E. Teaching adolescent trainable level retarded students to read a restaurant menu. Unpublished manuscript, University of Wisconsin, 1972.

Brown, L., Van Deventer, P., Perlmutter, L., Jones, S., & Sontag, E. Effects of consequences on production rates of trainable retarded and severely emotionally disturbed students in a public school workshop. *Education and Training of the Mentally Retarded*, 1972, **7**(2), 74-81.

Buddenhagen, R.G. *Establishing vocal verbalizations in mute mongoloid children.* Champaign, Ill.: Research Press, 1971.

Chalfant, J.C., & Silikovitz, R.G. *Systematic instruction for retarded children: The Illinois program. (Experimental ed.) Part I, Teacher-Parent Guide.* Washington,

D.C.: U.S. Department of Health, Education, and Welfare, 1970.

Coleman, R. A pilot demonstration of the utility of reinforcement techniques in trainable programs. *Education and Training of the Mentally Retarded*, 1970, 5, 68-70.

Crosson, J.E. A technique for programming sheltered workshop environments for training severely retarded workers. *American Journal of Mental Deficiency*, 1969, 73, 814-818.

D'Amelio, D. *Severely retarded children: Wider horizons.* Columbus, O.: Charles E. Merrill, 1971.

Dunn, L. *Exceptional children in the schools.* (2nd ed.) New York: Holt, 1973.

Frankel, M.G., Happ, F.W., & Smith, M.P. *Functional teaching of the mentally retarded.* Springfield, Ill.: Charles C Thomas, 1966.

Gold, M.W. Preworkshop skills for the trainable: A sequential technique. *Education and Training of the Mentally Retarded*, 1968, 3, 31-37.

Gold, M.W. *The acquisition of a complex assembly task by retarded adolescents.* Urbana, Ill.: University of Illinois, Children's Research Center, 1969.

Gold, M.W. Research on the vocational habilitation of the retarded: The present, the future. In M.R. Ellis (Ed.), *International view of research in mental retardation.* New York: Academic Press, 1972.

Gold, M.W., & Scott, K.G. Discrimination learning. In B. Stephens (Ed.), *Training the developmentally young.* New York: John Day, 1971.

Goldberg, I.I., & Cruickshank, W.M. The trainable but noneducable: Whose responsibility? *National Education Association Journal*, 1958, 47, 622-623.

Goldberg, I.I., & Rooke, M.L. Research and educational practices with mentally deficient children. In N.G. Haring & R.L. Schiefelbusch (Eds.), *Methods in special education.* New York: McGraw-Hill, 1967.

Gray, B.B., Baker, R.D., & Stancyk, S.E. Performance determined instruction for training in remedial reading. *Journal of Applied Behavior Analysis*, 1969, 2, 255-263.

Guess, D., Sailor, W., Rutherford, G., & Baer, D.M. An experimental analysis of linguistic development: The productive use of the plural morpheme. *Journal of Applied Behavior Analysis*, 1968, 1(4), 297-306.

Hargis, C.H. The significance of the grammar of one-to-one correspondence in teaching counting to the retarded. *Education and Training of the Mentally Retarded*, 1971, 6, 170-171.

Heber, R. A manual on terminology and classification in mental retardation. *American Journal of Mental Deficiency.* Monograph Supplement (2nd ed.), 1961.

Hunt, N. *The world of Nigel Hunt: The diary of a mongoloid youth.* New York: Garrett, 1967.

Itard, J.M.G. *The wild boy of Aveyron.* New York: Appleton-Century-Crofts, 1962.

Kirk, S.A. *Educating exceptional children.* (2nd ed.) Boston: Houghton Mifflin, 1972.

Kolburne, L.L. *Effective education for the mentally retarded child.* New York: Vantage Press, 1965.

Lance, W.D. Introduction. In B. Stephens (Ed.), *Training the developmentally young.* New York: John Day, 1971.

Larsen, L.A., & Bricker, W.A. *A manual for parents and teachers of severely and moderately retarded children.* Nashville, Tenn.: George Peabody College, 1968.

Lindsley, O.R. Direct measurement and prosthesis of retarded behavior. *Journal of Education,* 1964, **147,** 62-81.

Lovaas, O.I., Berberich, J.P., Perloff, B.F., & Schaeffer, B. Acquisition of imitative speech by schizophrenic children. *Science,* February 1966, 705-707.

MacAulay, B.D. A program for teaching speech and beginning reading to nonverbal retardates. In H.N. Sloane, Jr., & B.D. MacAulay (Eds.), *Operant procedures in remedial speech and language training.* Boston: Houghton Mifflin, 1968.

Mager, R.F. *Preparing instructional objectives.* Palo Alto, Calif: Fearon, 1962.

McCarthy, J.J., & Scheerenberger, R.C. A decade of research on the education of the mentally retarded. *Mental Retardation Abstracts,* 1966, 3(4), 481-501.

McLean, J.E., Yoder, D.E., & Schiefelbusch, R.L. *Language intervention with the retarded: Developing strategies.* Baltimore: University Park Press, 1972.

Metz, J.R. Conditioning generalized imitation in autistic children. *Journal of Experimental Child Psychology,* 1965, **2,** 389-399.

Molloy, J.S. *Trainable children: Curriculum and procedures.* New York: John Day, 1963.

Peterson, R. Imitation: A basic behavioral mechanism. In H.N. Sloane, Jr., & B.D. MacAulay (Eds.), *Operant procedures in remedial speech and language training.* Boston: Houghton Mifflin, 1968.

The President's Committee on Mental Retardation. *MR67: A first report to the President.* Washington, D.C.: The Superintendent of Documents, 1967.

Risley, T., & Wolf, M. Establishing functional speech in echolalic children. *Behavioural Research and Therapy,* 1967, **5,** 73-88.

Rosenzweig, L.E., & Long, J. *Understanding and teaching the dependent retarded child.* Darien, Conn.: Educational Publishing, 1960.

Schumaker, J., & Sherman, J.A. Training generative verb usage by imitation and reinforcement procedures. *Journal of Applied Behavior Analysis,* 1970, **3,** 273-287.

Seguin, E. *Idiocy: Its treatment by the physiological method.* New York: William Wood, 1866.

Sherman, J.A. Teaching generative behavioral repertoires to retarded children: Imitation and language. In L.A. Hamerlynck & F.W. Clark (Eds.), *Behavior modification for exceptional children and youth.* Calgary, Alberta: John D. McAra, 1971.

Stephens, B. (Ed.) *Training the developmentally young.* New York: John Day, 1971.

Tawney, J.W., & Hipsher, L.W. *Systematic instruction for retarded children: The Illinois program. (Experimental ed.) Part II, Systematic Language Instruction.* Washington, D.C.: U.S. Department of Health, Education, and Welfare, 1970.

Whaley, D.L., & Malott, R.W. *Elementary principles of behavior.* (3rd ed.) Kalamazoo, Mich.: Behaviordelia, 1969.

York, R.T., Brown, L., Yoder, D., & Scheerenberger, R.C. Development of prelanguage and language skills in severely and profoundly retarded institutionalized retarded children. Paper presented at the meeting of the AAMD International Convention, Minneapolis, May 1972.

CONTEMPORARY ISSUES IN THE EDUCATION OF THE BEHAVIORALLY DISORDERED

Albert H. Fink, Ph.D.
Raymond M. Glass, Ph.D.

Indiana University

TOWARD A DEFINITION OF THE PROBLEM

The report of the Joint Commission on Mental Health of Children (1970) documented a staggering social problem that confronts the United States. Millions of citizens suffer emotional problems severe enough to require specialized services; the collective social response to this need is nothing short of inadequate. Of these millions, one can count large numbers of school-age children who experience behavior problems and who lack needed assistance. The indictment of a society which countenances, unwittingly or not, lack of fulfillment among so many of its younger citizens must be harsh indeed. Blatt (1971), in his review of the Commission's work, suggested that our society may not, in fact, be committed to its young, and that we may be a "self-centered" rather than a "child-centered" society. Discomfiting support for this point of view came from Bakan (1971), who in scholarly, emotive, and even macabre terms considered the specific questions of child abuse – its primeval, instinctual origins and its meaning in the life of modern man. Support came also from the pages of *Exodus from Pandemonium* (1970), Blatt's personal and human embrace of the tragedy of institutional care.

If the origins of these failures are unclear to us, it may nevertheless be possible to consider prescriptive responses to the needs of the behaviorally disordered. Blatt's statement to the Joint Commission that "hardly anywhere is responsibility assigned to a profession [p. 279]" for rectifying the state of affairs is both an admonition and a challenge, no less to the professional educational community than to the world at large. What indeed is the responsibility that rests upon the educational structure, both as an independent organism and in conjoint arrangements with other institutional forces, to deal with the pressures of youthful energy? And what are the particularized responsibilities of the special educator within the context?

The historical response of education to the behaviorally disordered has been marked by the presumption that other agents – child guidance clinics, private medical practitioners, social welfare, and so forth – had an inherent responsibility for creating the conditions of change. The tacit belief of the public school system was that such external responsibility came from what Benne (1970) called "the authority of expertise" in contrast to "the authority of rules." And such disclaimers by the public school system to the assumption of hegemony over the direct treatment of the behaviorally disordered were long unchallenged. The deference of the educator to the "expert other" was an understandable posture. On the one hand, large numbers of problem children, parents, and teachers pressed for solutions. On the other hand, eager professionals in the community at large offered a panacea. No one doubted that current public school expertise was hardly adequate. The dependency system which emerged was thus not a forced marriage. A comfortable and mutually beneficial arrangement was entered into between the public schools and the medical-psychological-sociological support complex.

It would be difficult to state precisely when the relatively one-sided nature of the bargain became evident; for clearly both internal and external pressures upon the schools were not reduced appreciably, if at all, by increased referrals of problem children and youth to outside agencies (Cowen, Gardner, & Zax, 1967). Nevertheless, perceptible changes in attitude and practice within the public school sector became evident. One important stimulus was the simple fact of the unresolved problem; another was educational and psychological theory which advanced the view that solutions to the problems of the behaviorally disordered within the context of the public schools have theoretical as well as practical validity (Bower & Hollister, 1967; Hewett, 1968; Morse, 1971b). This is not to say that the educator's traditional relationship to other professionals have been without redeeming features; on the contrary. There have been, in fact, salutary effects, the most significant of which may have been, and may continue to be, recognition of the contribution that all "helping professions" can make to the welfare of children. This perception has become manifest in psychoeducational team structures found within the school system and between agencies of which the school is a part (Long, Morse, & Newman, 1971).

A further demand for attitude change came from the report of the Joint Commission. Included in its comprehensive recommendations for meeting the crisis in mental health was the imperative: "Special education programs must be an integral part of the continuum of services to be provided [p. 40]." The Commission noted that within this context, appropriate programming should include preschool home-training programs, regular and special nursery programs, regular public school classes (under certain conditions), special classes within regular schools, and special schools. The Commission, in short, recognized both the need for service and the alternative patterns by which that service may be provided to best meet individual differences.

This challenge to the public school system would be difficult to accept and deal with at the best of times; coming, as it does, when assumptions of long standing about our educational structure and its proper place and purpose in society are under careful but insistent scrutiny (Illich, 1968; Lurie, 1970; Sarason, 1971; Silberman, 1970; Stretch, 1970; Toffler, 1970), the task is confounded. In the midst of this confluence, Sherman (1970) provided a reasoned statement of the issue's central element:

Schools have lost touch with the times. They appear to have become increasingly dysfunctional and out of harmony with the shifting values and trends of the environment that surrounds them and the institutions they overlap. Intimate associations between school and society . . . have broken down, and the relationship that once was symbiotic, and that did not develop by accident, no longer serves mutual advantage [p. 1].

He asserted that until educators exhume and examine the bases for their assumptions, embrace and not avoid "value controversy," and integrate belief systems with action systems, no solutions are possible.

It is apparent that even greater uncertainty, responsibility, and challenge may be the inheritance of the professional community as it has (a) come to recognize its potential responsibility for dealing constructively with the problems of the socially and emotionally handicapped and has (b) begun to provide programs in support of that perception.

A crisis of identity

If, as Erikson (1968) suggested, an identity crisis means in part the loss of "a sense of historical continuity," then one may safely say that special education confronts such an issue. A rash of unexpected concerns faces a field heretofore sanguine and secure in its belief in the essential rightness of its purpose.

The break in the movement toward even fuller conceptual support for a steadily increasing array of specialized services for children was perhaps marked most dramatically by Dunn's memorable criticism (1968). His attack on a belief system which fostered uncritical acceptance, both by regular and special educators, of the special class system as naturally beneficent for educable mentally handicapped children induced strident and articulate debate; it is doubtful whether all its repercussions have yet been felt. Not the least of the effects have been significant commentaries by special educators who apparently required only this stimulus to crystallize their own views. The willingness of special educators to search their own assumptions and engage in critical self-analysis can only be regarded as a healthy sign. It remains to be seen whether special education, as currently known, can survive such internal assault in the context of an environment which only grudgingly supported it when ranks were more united.

Dunn's most serious criticism was that one cannot, on the basis of available evidence, justify much special class programming for the mildly handicapped. While his arguments were directed toward programming for the educable mentally handicapped, it is clear that the issue has immediacy for children who are behaviorally disordered. The central issue is whether, in fact, the special class has any demonstrable effect on children placed there. Does the special class, in other words, make a difference in the lives of the children it it? And if it does make a difference, is it sufficiently great to justify the allocation of resources to support it?

In dealing with the question of whether special class placement makes a difference, Christoplos and Renz (1969) suggested that considerable evidence does not support the argument in favor of the special class: "Research findings have consistently indicated no differences in performance between those placed in special classes and those placed in regular classes [p. 371]."

The authors recognized and attached importance to the confounding problem of "identifying appropriate educational goals" in a complex world, implying that different goals for children placed in special classes, and thus different performance measures for these children, make "straightforward" comparisons suspect.

In an incisive analysis, MacMillan (1971) expanded the analytical possibilities of the question. He expressed dissatisfaction with conclusions that research on special classes proves them ineffective, since he contended that such research frequently contained problems in sampling and measurement instruments and in inadequate control of preplacement procedures. Thus, according to MacMillan, much of the evidence against special class placement is of doubtful validity. MacMillan also raised the important problem of the "teacher variable," which tends not to be controlled and which contributes further to the inadequacy of special class evaluation procedures. In this connection, MacMillan made an important point: "A given administrative arrangement is neither good nor bad – what really counts is what is done with the group once it is established [p. 2]."

A second and critical issue deals with the negative effects of labeling. Opponents of special class placement argue that the mere act of identifying a child for a special class characterizes that child as having socially undesirable traits, and that the resulting stigma which attaches to that child has deleterious effects. These, it is presumed, outweigh whatever advantages might obtain from the special class (Rist, 1970; Rosenthal & Jacobson, 1968).

A related concern within the general problem area of identification (apart from epistemological questions and those of negative impact upon the child) is that of the "expectancy phenomenon." Categorizing a child as different may, conceivably, mean a number of things. It may mean that a teacher will strive to provide a match between actual ability, however demonstrated, and curriculum. It may also mean a belief that the child cannot succeed in the same way as other children. This belief may result, as Rosenthal and Jacobson (1968) suggested, in greater achievement on the part of children *believed* to be superior even if, in fact, they do not differ intellectually from others. Their work was widely cited to support the notion that the identification of children as intellectually or emotionally deviant intensifies that deviance through the mechanism of a "self-fulfilling prophecy." Thus, runs the argument, children classed as deviant will remain deviant, in some large measure as a function of the teacher's expectations. If only teachers did not *know* that they were that way!

In general, it is difficult to refute the hypothesis that expectancy, or set, is a likely contributor to student success or failure. Gozali and Meyen (1970), while unable to replicate Rosenthal and Jacobson's work, recognized the partial contribution of teacher set to pupil achievement. They pointed out, though, that "to believe that changing expectations will resolve our educational problems is erroneous[p. 424]."

Rist (1970) emphasized the role of teacher expectancy as it interacts with student social class and the resulting differential student achievement; he also confirmed that the problem cannot be handled simply by manipulation of the teacher-expectancy variable. There is indeed a complex set of variables embedded in the question. Teacher set is, of course, a critical feature; but it is seen by Rist as, at the very least, cumulative, i.e., a communication network among teachers which reinforces a negative set of beliefs about socially and economically inferior children and which establishes a pattern of school response that maintains and even widens attainment differences between deprived and not so deprived and between those believed to be better and those believed to be worse. Rist argued that this pattern of interaction between teacher and students within the central city did not reflect teachers who "could not or would not teach their students [p. 447]." In his view, teachers taught well, but the level of teaching was not available equally, i.e., qualitatively, to all students:

For the students of high socio-economic background who were perceived by the teachers as possessing desirable behavioral and attitudinal characteristics, the classroom experience was one where the teachers displayed interest in them, spent a large proportion of teaching time with them, directed little control-oriented behavior towards them, held them as models – and continually reinforced statements that they were "special" students [p. 447].

The arguments opposing labeling practices express concern over such issues as the "self-fulfilling prophecy" and have strong emotional appeal and a certain logic; one might be tempted to assert that if one simply did not label and/or if one did not have "expectations," i.e., if one did not make predictions, there would then be, ipso facto, no problems. However, it is not likely that such an argument would hold up long, if for no other reason than its logical fallacy that problems exist only if identified.

But labels can be used with less-than-desirable clarity and discrimination. Labels can be affixed carelessly, improperly, and without sufficient regard for individual differences. Labels can come to be, as Menninger (1967) suggested, "restrictive and obstructive"; but yet, he continued, "this does not mean the discarding of useful terminology ... [p. 33]." He argued that there is an important distinction between naming a person as, for example, "having schizophrenia" (restrictive), in contrast to characterizing the person as one who displays schizophrenic behaviors (flexible). In the one instance, a static "medical model" diagnosis is implicit with all that it suggests in terms of the person "possessing a disease." In the other instance, the person is viewed as *exhibiting* a nonstatic behavior pattern. In Menninger's view, the behavior pattern may appropriately be identified as conforming to a given syndrome which is *subject to change*. That is, any given behavior pattern displayed on one occasion may alter significantly on the next. The label, when attached to the person as "thing," cannot characterize the person as the dynamic organism he is.

For special educators of the behaviorally disordered, the distinction drawn by Menninger has great significance and applicability. It goes beyond the issues raised by

Trippe (1966), i.e., that educators must consider and apply their own demarcations, identifications, and solutions to the problems of the behaviorally disordered, and that in order to do so traditional dependence upon "other directed" labeling systems must be foresworn. It reaches to the core of the matter, which is how best to characterize the behavior problem with which one must deal. And it asks, too, whether dissatisfaction with the labels of others means no labels at all! Lourie and Lourie (1971) suggested that there is much that needs to be done:

We still parcel out children to institutions essentially on the basis of social, legal and sometimes diagnostic labels that neither describe the child nor offer a sound prescriptive base for treatment [p. 597].

But there is another issue here. The attack on labeling seems to include the judgment that the label and its negative impact result from special class placement. Following MacMillan (1971), can one really agree with the position that labeling begins only when the special class process begins? Does the behavior-problem child find himself stigmatized only at the point of his interface with special education? Or does it occur as part of a larger and longer context? If the latter is the case, then special programming enters into the stigmatizing process much more obliquely and with less distinctive and definitive effect than believed. Undoubtedly, special programming may "confirm" a problem for many children; but such an identification may also serve as a means of structuring the issue, removing ambivalence, and permitting reconstructive efforts to take place. For many of the emotionally handicapped, special services, including the special class, may present opportunities for revitalization rather than psychological fettering. At least one cannot discount that possibility.

The attack on current models of special education has also come about on grounds of "racism." By this it is meant that the special educational establishment differs little, if at all, from the broader educational institution or from society at large and enforces its prejudices through oppressive practices. Johnson (1969), in a vigorous commentary, asked: "If special education placement, as currently operating, is questionable for white children, what makes it any more valid for blacks? [p. 244]."

What indeed? There is considerable support for this concern that the public educational system will continue to repress black Americans through arbitrary labeling and selection practices (Clark, 1968; Coleman, Campbell, Hobson, McPartland, Mood, Weinfield, & York, 1966; Kerner, 1968). Johnson believes that what is needed is a reformulation of educational practices within the context of the unique cultural and historical experience of black Americans. This position was supported by Baratz and Baratz (1971):

Research on the Negro has been guided by an ethnocentric liberal ideology which denies cultural differences and thus acts against the best interests of the people it wishes to understand and eventually help [p. 253].

Baratz and Baratz argued further that the norm of the white middle-class American is improperly imposed upon all Americans with the belief that the principle of equality for all citizens is thereby advanced:

The application of this misinterpreted egalitarian principle to social science data has often left the investigator with the unwelcome task of describing Negro behavior not as it is, but rather as it deviates from the normative system defined by the white middle class [p. 254].

In this view, the assimilation hypotheses so common among American historians are rejected and replaced by the contention that individual differences in culture and tradition (i.e., not only biological and psychological differences) are important and must be allowed to flourish. It may be so, as Miller (1964) suggested, that "education is the escape route from poverty [p. 15]"; but the paths may be very different indeed.

Another principal argument advanced in opposition to special class placement for the mildly handicapped is that regular educational programs are now more capable of meeting individual differences than in the past (Deno, 1971; Dunn, 1968). It is difficult to know whether this is a pious hope or whether there is, in fact, a realistic base for such an assertion. There is certainly no shortage of advocacy for such a position. Harshman (1969) argued that an emphasis upon individual differences and an appropriate curriculum geared to these differences should enable many children to return to and/or remain in the mainstream of education; and that what this requires is more attention to the identification of those behaviors which are appropriate for the regular classroom. Lord (1971) also argued the importance of individualization of instruction but noted that "no principle of instruction has had such universal support at the theoretical level and . . . such limited genuine application [p. 23]."

He advanced the view that more integration of special children into regular classes can meaningfully occur of *training* of teachers, both regular and special, is modified. This newer training model would focus upon competencies, in dealing with the variables that influence learning. Morse (1971a) commented:

If teachers are to make a place for more of our special pulils, their greatest need is a clear model for the new-style classroom. One of its primary constituents should be accommodation to broad variability [p. 65].

More emphasized the compexity of the issue, correctly pointing out that the teacher is not so expert as to be able to handle, *by herself,* all the educational needs of all the children in the classroom. It is clear that "accommodation to broad variability" is a function of all the significant elements in the school complex – specialists, consultants, principals, other teachers – who work in conjunction with the regular classroom teacher. And she is likely to be a more skillful model than is customary.

This approach received little encouragement from Rubin and Balow (1971), who undertook a study of the incidence of children presenting educational or behavioral problems in the normal school setting. In the longitudinal-study population of 967 normal children in kindergarten through third grade, it was found that 41% of the children was identified by teachers as having problems and classified in one or more of the following categories: special class placement, retention, receipt of special services, and problems of behavior and attitude. Special placement or special services had actually been provided for 24.3% of the children in the study. Rubin and Balow concluded:

The large proportion of children identified by teachers as needing special educational services raises serious questions about the ability of our educational system, as presently organized and conducted, to accommodate the broad range of differences found within the typical school population [p. 299].

In sum, those concerned with the education of the behaviorally disordered may rightly stand confused. At the same time that demands for services are increasing, calls abound for reappraisal of theories, concepts, and operations. This paradox may be more apparent than real, however. What appears to be occurring is a fundamental examination of the proper role of special education. This shift in posture might be characterized in a number of ways; it is suggested that one useful manner of considering the question is in terms of a movement away from a "reactive advocacy" which generously and relatively uncritically accepts the undesirables of the regular educational program into various specialized support services. Special education appears to be much more willing, both conceptually and operationally, to view itself as an "active advocacy." This means a greater willingness, based upon a perceived obligation, to tackle the broader and more intensive issues of the larger educational process. Questions of individualization of instruction, integration into the regular classroom (or, one could suppose with reason, integration into the special classroom!), and patterns of support services thus take on different meaning when examined within such a framework.

Within this context of change, there are evident efforts to deal with the problem of understanding and describing the behaviorally disordered and how to act upon that understanding and description. It has been suggested that Menninger drew an important basic distinction between a label which identifies a thing and a label which identifies a more fluid behavioral pattern. This idea found an important elaboration and transformation in Reynolds (1971), who argued the need for educational relevance of data used in decision making for children. His position is that a distinction must be drawn between *source* and *decision* variables as they apply to the problems of children. "The difference between *source* and *decision* variables is that the first are the basis of identifying the problem and the second are the basis of making the educational decisions [p. 53]."

The use of a decision-variables approach in programming for behaviorally disordered children would, on the one hand, permit more appropriate use of traditional diagnostic data and, on the other hand, allow greater appreciation of and attention to specific educational competency needs.

PUBLIC SCHOOL INTERVENTION APPROACHES
FOR THE BEHAVIORALLY DISORDERED

At present there is no clearly agreed-upon set of objectives and strategies for teaching difficult children (Weiner, 1969). Although most educators would agree that common objectives are mastery of basic academic skills, successful interaction with peers, and establishing control over impulses that may lead to disruptive behavior, marked differences in philosophical and theoretical conceptualizations of the learner often lead to diverse goals and teaching-learning strategies.

Differences in intervention goals and strategies and resulting arguments among some practitioners as to which techniques are more "appropriate" are related to a major philosophical debate occurring within the broader context of education regarding how the teaching-learning process is conceptualized. "Third force" or humanistic psychology (Maslow, 1968) brought into focus a reconceptualization of the teacher-learning process that stands in sharp contrast to the prevailing behavioristic theories of learning. A growing body of literature on humanistic education stresses the importance of fulfilling basic needs of safety, esteem, and self-actualization (Glasser, 1969; Maslow, 1968); developing self-directed learners (Rogers, 1969); enhancing interpersonal sensitivity (Brown, 1971; Jones, 1968; Weinstein & Fantini, 1970); and increasing independence and control over one's life (Glasser, 1969). Each of these writers advocated a shift towards greater student involvement in decision making regarding his learning experiences, integration of affective learning experiences into the school curriculum, and greater mutuality in teacher-pupil relationships. Disruptive and disturbed classroom behavior is often viewed as a reaction to frustrated needs for esteem, self-worth, and independence.

In contrast to a humanistic view of education is the position that learning occurs most efficiently through the systematic manipulation of tasks and rewards (Skinner, 1954). The development of computer-assisted instruction (CAI), programmed learning devices, and (recently) performance contracting, with its emphasis on providing incentives to students for accomplishing predetermined academic tasks, represent the broadest application of behavioristic principles to education. Learner involvement and decision making regarding educational tasks appear to be minimized. Disruptive and "disturbed" classroom behavior is often viewed as stemming from inappropriate models (Bandura & Walters, 1963), inconsistent reinforcement, or the rewarding of inappropriate behaviors (Hewett, 1968), with classroom teaching goals usually focusing on increasing task attention, academic performance, and decreasing disruptive classroom behaviors (Hewett, Taylor, & Artuso, 1969; O'Leary & Becker, 1967).

Thus, the larger humanistic-behavioristic debate appears in microcosm with regard to goals and strategies for behaviorally disordered children. Moreover, complexity is added when a psychodynamic stance is taken — a position which holds that learning for the behaviorally disordered should focus on the resolution of conflict between instinctual drives and social demands. Despite the apparent discrepancies in learning objectives and strategies generated by these diverse educational philosophies, the differences may not be mutually exclusive. Rather, the development of basic attending behaviors, enhancement of academic skills, and the decrease in certain inappropriate classroom behaviors may open the way for, or directly contribute to, the development of esteem, interpersonel competence, and independent (Bower & Hollister, 1967). Perhaps the more critical issues may be (a) whether specific techniques designed to achieve short-range objectives of behavior control and academic-skill development include the learner's involvement and commitment (Glasser, 1969) and are therefore congruent with broader humanistic objectives; (*b*) whether these objectives are implemented once behavior control has been established.

In short, there is a need for an integrated framework for teaching difficult children, rather than for the highlighting of differences in educational goals and strategies. The complex interactions between learners, teachers, schools, personal values, parents, and community values render any single approach to the education of difficult children only minimally effective. The following overview of recent contributions and trends regarding the education of emotionally disturbed children is presented in the context of an integrated framework. Although specific interventions stem from diverse conceptualizations of the learner, each contributes to the goals outlined above.

Core conditions of teacher-pupil relationships

The growth-enhancing potential of teacher-pupil relationships assumes high priority among educators concerned with pupil self-esteem and independence (Moustakas, 1966; Rogers, 1969). While research on the impact of specific teacher personality characteristics has generated contradictory and sometimes discouraging results (Getzels & Jackson, 1963), the counseling literature has isolated a core of relationship conditions central to client growth (Carkhuff & Berenson, 1967; Rogers, 1969) and potentially related to student growth (Aspy, 1965; Rogers, 1969; Scheuer, 1971). Counselors who exhibit high levels of empathic understanding, authenticity, and positive regard in their counseling interchanges appear to generate more constructive client growth than counselors who exhibit lower levels of these conditions, regardless of the particular theoretical persuasions of either (Carkhuff & Berenson, 1967; Fiedler, 1950).

More recently, Rogers (1969) suggested that these core conditions may also be critical in educational settings and cited exploratory research to support this contention (Aspy, 1965). Rogers's main thesis was that the classroom teacher exerts a potent influence on children's feelings of self-worth by the learning experiences he provides and by the messages conveyed through teacher-pupil interactions. The extent to which the teacher attempts to facilitate significant learning that stems from expressed or emplied pupil concerns – and the dgree to which the teacher conveys acceptance, authenticity, and empathic understanding in her interchanges with students – are critical variables in the teaching-learning process. Translating his counselor-client core conditions to teacher-learner conditions, these qualities are:

Realness in the facilitation of learning: When the facilitator is a real person ... entering into a relationship with the learner without presenting a front or a façade, he is much more likely to be effective. He is a person to his students and not a faceless embodiment of a curricular requirement nor a sterile tube though which knowledge is passed ... [pp. 106-107].

Prizing, acceptance, trust: A caring for the learner, but a non-possessive caring. It is an acceptance of the other individual as a separate person, having worth in his own right. Such a teacher can accept the student's occasional apathy, his erratic desires.... He can accept personal feelings which both disturb and promote learning. The facilitator's acceptance of the learner is an operational statement of his essential confidence and trust in the capacity of the human organism [pp. 109-111].

Empathic understanding: When the teacher has the ability to understand the student's reactions from the inside . . . the reaction in the learner follows something of this pattern, "At last someone understands how it feels and seems to me without wanting to analyze me or judge me . . . . Now I can blossom and grow and learn" [pp. 111-112].

Although the specific role of these relationship conditions in the education of difficult children has been speculative (Knoblock & Garcea, 1968), Scheuer (1971) found a positive but weak correlation between academic gains of emotionally disturbed adolescents and the degree to which they perceived their teachers as exhibiting empathy, genuineness, and positive regard. These results suggest the need for additional investigation of the impact of these and related relationship conditions on children's academic and social-emotional growth. Of particular interest for research and teacher-training purposes is the contextual nature of Rogers's core conditions. In addition to having potential as therapeutic variables in themselves, these conditions may also help to establish teachers as an influential force in the child's life, thus enhancing the effectiveness of more direct teacher-influence techniques. Strong (1968), for example, suggested that high levels of Rogers's conditions may serve to effect greater trust in the teacher-therapist, an increased willingness to identify and discuss problems, and a stronger commitment to try out alternative behavior patterns. Thus, these core relationship conditions may be as vital to the "behavior modifier" as to those who use less direct intervention approaches.

Affective curriculum experience

The recent appearance of exemplary teaching programs designed to enhance pupil self-esteem, expand awareness of human emotions, and develop interpersonal communication skills represents another contribution that has potential value, both in terms of fostering positive mental health for all school children and of serving as specific learning experiences for children who exhibit behavioral problems. For example, Bessell and Palomares' (1967) Human Development Curriculum presented a series of discussion activities designed to enhance children's communication skills, increase intra- and interpersonal sensitivity, and generate realistic awareness of personal competencies. Weinstein and Fantini (1970) presented a prototype curriculum and sample activities designed to enhance pupil esteem and autonomy and increase awareness of the "connectedness" of people. Brown (1971) demonstrated the application of awareness-training activities and group-discussion activities to enhance trust among students and to expand empathic awareness of human emotions. Glasser's (1969) description of classroom meetings demonstrated a potential teacher resource for enhancing pupil esteem, attraction to school, and problem-solving skills by involving students in decision-making processes regarding classroom learning experience, behavioral interpersonal problems, and general human relations problems.

Each of these programs stemmed from a common criticism that traditional classroom practices fail to provide learning experiences that focus on developmental concerns central to the lives of children. Among these concerns are: What about me is like and different from others? How competent am I? Can I exercise control over aspects of my life? In many ways, these questions serve as concrete examples of Rogers's (1969) "significant learning" and may also help to increase teacher genuineness, positive regard, and empathic understanding, insofar as they orient the teacher to constructively focus on children's perceptions, feelings, and interpersonal behavior. It is largely speculative whether these programs can make a clear contribution towards the prevention of school-based emotional problems or, indeed, can be directly utilized with children who demonstrate behavior problems. However, the establishment of these and related programs should clear the way for a number of controlled investigations and may bring forth a potentially exciting and innovative resource for all teachers.

Learners as teachers

Reversing the traditionally passive role of the learner and placing him in a position of limited authority and responsibility through teaching others has been described as a potentially effective means for increasing self-esteem, attraction to school, and academic achievement (Gartner, Kohler, & Reissman, 1971; Lippitt & Lohman, 1965). Exemplary cross-age teaching programs have been established in public schools (Fleming, 1969; Wright, 1969) and as part of community-involvement programs (Cloward, 1967; Melaragno & Newmark, 1970). While comparatively few studies have been reported in the special education literature (concerning behavior-problem children specifically employed as tutors), several reports demonstrated the potential efficacy of this strategy. For example, Cloward (1967) reported dramatic gains (3.4 years) in reading achievement for black and Puerto Rican adolescents who tutored third- and fourth-grade children 4 hours a week over a 6-month period. Adolescents who only completed the pre- and postreading tests demonstrated a gain of 1.7 years of reading achievement in the same time period. Benefits also accrued for the younger children who demonstrated a gain of 6 months of reading achievement in comparison to a gain of 3.5 months for nontutored controls. As a part of the treatment program, the tutors received pay and also participated in regular in-service training sessions. In another less dramatic but equally illustrative study, results were reported for ninth-grade boys with behavior problems who "counseled" younger boys three times a week and participated in weekly supervisory sessions with an adult counselor (Jones, 1969). When compared to a no-treatment "control group," nonsignificant but positive gains in grade-point average, school attendance, and teacher ratings of classroom conduct occurred in favor of the peer counselors. Significant improvement in teacher ratings of classroom conduct also occurred for the younger boys, although no control groups were established for comparative purposes.

Although the above-mentioned studies can be criticized from a methodological point of view, each suggested the potential value of directly involving students in the teaching-learning process. Thus, although further research may be needed, it would appear that cross-age teaching is a valuable classroom strategy. Open questions are the extent to which this procedure can be used and whether or not it is equally appropriate at all age levels and for different interpersonal coping styles.

Behavior-modification approaches

The appearance of an entire issue of *Exceptional Children* (October, 1970), a number of research reviews (Axelrod, 1971; Hanley, 1970; Lipe & Jung, 1971) and research reports (Glavin, Quay, & Werry, 1971; Haring, Hayden, & Nolen, 1969; Hewett, Taylor, & Artuso, 1969) have attested to the continuing popularity of behavior-modification programs in special and regular classes settings. It is also apparent from a recent national study of exemplary programs for the emotionally disturbed (Cook, Cort, Flocco, & Sanford, 1971).

These studies and reviews clearly demonstrated that task attention and academic productivity can be increased, while specific inappropriate classroom behavior can be decreased, by differential reinforcement and contingency management. They established that behavior modification is a useful intervention technique for teachers of difficult children.

Increasing learner involvement in behavior-modification programs

Although behavior-modification techniques have received criticism on the basis that such procedures can inappropriately be applied to reduce student autonomy and increase the arbitrary use of teacher authority (Wood, 1968), some recent applications have begun to dispel this criticism. For example, Graubard (1969) reported a procedure in which students established minimal behavioral standards for themselves, with individual rewards contingent upon group performance. In an earlier study, Minuchin, Chamberlain, and Graubard (1967) made use of peers as classroom observers, recorders of specific behavior of peers, and dispensers of rewards; they found that they (peers) were more effective than authority figures.

Cook,[1] has reported on a school intervention project conducted by Cobb, Ray, and Patterson in which the objective of the intervention was to effect an increase in the child's rate of reinforcement for appropriate behavior by involving him in a contingency program which enabled him to earn reinforcers for the entire class. The reinforcers were points toward a class reward (party, extra recess) and praise. This group contingency has been found to be more powerful than an individual contingency.

Csapo (1971) reported a project where teams of three children served as helpers for each other. One "well behaving" child served as a model, another as an observer, while a third "behavior problem" child was asked to model specific appropriate classroom behaviors of the well-behaving child. The observer noted instances of modeling and rewarded the child for demonstrating the appropriate behaviors.

[1]C. Cook, personal communication, 1971.

Significant improvements in classroom behavior occurred and were maintained during nonreward periods. Cobb (1970) demonstrated, in an interesting study of prediction of academic achievement, that children who talked about academic material to peers as well as attending to task were more likely to achieve than children who attended to task without peer interaction. He suggested that there are important implications for social-learning theorists concerned with engineering the classroom environment, and concluded:

If a child were taught to attend and talk to his peers about academic material at higher levels than baseline, he has more chance of significantly increasing his achievement level than if his self-concept alone is altered [p. 11].

The possibility has also been suggested that children establish their own learning goals, activities, and reward systems (Lovitt, 1970). Should these eventualities occur, behavior-modification strategies are likely to become more attractive to those concerned with the potentially restrictive elements of earlier behavior-modification programs. As a matter of speculation, it is not inconceivable that such programs could significantly enhance pupil self-esteem and control over their learning activities. Whether such programs would lose their identity as traditional and rigorous behavior-modification programs, and hence generate confusion as to which specific elements of the intervention program contribute most to change, are relevant issues and empirical questions. An interesting clinical report of such a program was reported by Weinstein (1971), where children established required amounts of work time that would occur each school day and also established individual learning goals and activities.

Related behavior-modification approaches

Other behavior-modification strategies are beginning to be applied to school-based problems. The use of behavior-rehearsal procedures (systematic role playing) has been offered as a useful technique for helping to resolve specific social and interpersonal difficulties (Lazarus, 1966). Succinctly, behavior rehearsal is a procedure whereby desirable social or interpersonal behaviors are practiced or rehearsed under simulated conditions prior to attempting the actual behaviors in natural situations. Although few experimental studies have been conducted, several clinical reports seemed to forecast the efficacy of behavior-rehearsal procedures. Gittleman (1965) described a program where "emotionally disturbed children" rehearsed appropriate nonaggressive responses to specific interpersonal situations that typically resulted in aggressive outbursts, while Lazarus (1966) established behavior rehearsal as a more productive technique than direct advice or nondirective therapy for adults with specific interpersonal problems.

Modeling procedures (Bandura & Walters, 1963) also stand as potentially useful interventions for establishing specific prosocial behaviors. For example, O'Connor (1969) employed a procedure whereby withdrawn preschoolers watched films of other children making successively more intensive contacts with other children with positive consequences ensuing, while a soundtrack highlighted the appropriate behaviors emitted by the models. Posttest observations of classroom behavior, as well as follow-up teacher ratings, revealed that children who watched the models made significantly more social interactions than control children.

Increase in the autonomy of students is also promoted by strategies that attempt directly to improve the self-management skills of learners. A well-documented and developed example of this objective is employed by Haring at the Experimental Education Unit, Seattle (Cook & Flocco, 1971). In this program, which focuses upon the remediation of inappropriate academic and social behaviors in moderately and severely disturbed children aged 6-18, heavy reliance is placed upon continuous measurement techniques to provide feedback to pupils on their progress and to teachers on the progress of their intervention strategies. Within the system applied at the Experimental Education Unit, specific intervention techniques include:

1. Individualized academic programming
2. Differential reinforcement for specific behaviors
3. Systematic manipulation of academic programming and reinforcement conditions
4. Precision measurement of academic and social behaviors [p. ii]

Rate of student response – and its measurement – is a key element in the program and is considered to have theoretical significance and important implications for behavioral scientists (Cohen, Gentry, Hulten, & Martin, 1972).

Parents as intervention agents

An important development in work with behaviorally disordered children is an increasing utilization of parents as agents of intervention. Klaus and Gray (1968), for example, noted the beneficial effects of assisting parents of preschool children to offer specific cognitive experiences to their children. An extensive and successful project, aimed at utilizing parents in the treatment of young emotionally disturbed children, was carried out at the League School for Seriously Disturbed Children in Brooklyn, New York. The impetus for the program was an extensive waiting list for admission to the school, with a concurrent shortage of guidance and treatment facilities. In order to provide some service to the children, the League School initiated a limited, part-time intervention program in 1966. It was directed toward parent and child and aimed at training parents to become better teachers of their own children. Following a brief trial on an after-school basis, a weekly 3-day home training program was begun. Briefly, the program operated as follows: In weekly 1-hour individual teaching sessions during the school year, the mother sat in the room as a nonparticipating observer of the teacher-child interaction. Bi-weekly parent discussion groups were arranged, during which a small number of parents met with the social worker and training director. Results from the first 3 years of the program's operation (Doernberg, Rosen, & Walker, 1969) indicated that while neither the experimental nor control groups showed differences in intelligence, the experimental group showed a significant increase in level of social maturity and in six of the seven subscales of the Vineland.

The control group showed significant increases in two of the subscales. The experimental group also showed significantly greater improvement in activity level, speech level, and comprehension of language.

Another interesting program was reported by Patterson, Cobb, and Ray (1973). Their interest was in the development of a social-engineering technology for reprogramming the social environment of hyperaggressive boys. Financed initially in 1966 through a National Institutes of Mental Health grant, the focus of the project was on teaching social-learning theory and behavior-modification techniques to parents and working out with them and their children specific contingency programs to be applied at home. One therapist was assigned to work with the family on an intensive basis (several visits to the home and daily telephone contact) for 1 to 3 months.

A principal feature of the social-learning project was a reliance upon naturalistic observation to pinpoint the behaviors which were most in need of change and to monitor the progress of the family in meeting their goals for change. Specially trained observers visited the home every 2 weeks and collected frequency data on the occurrence of 29 social behaviors. These data were graphed, fed back to the family, and used as a basis for revising contingency programs. The investigators found this program quite effective and reported a 46% reduction in behaviors targeted for change.

Another program that utilizes parents as well as nonprofessional community personnel as helping agents is the Primary Mental Health Project, Rochester, New York (Cowen, 1971). This project emphasizes early detection of "maladapting" primary grade children, with intervention agents (selected for warmth, interpersonal competence, and concern for and interest in children) providing direct assistance. This is generally in the form of twice-a-week individual interviews between adult and child. Although final results of the project are not available, there is sufficient evidence to suggest that this may be an important breakthrough in primary mental health programming.

An innovative program was reported by Regal and Elliot (1971), who found that "emotionally disturbed children" who received academic tutoring from their parents made significant academic gains when compared to untutored children. The children's classroom teachers met with parents, gave specific lesson guides and reinforcement guidelines, and then met with parents at selected times to discuss progress and problems. While there have not been many studies reported which would permit generalizations about the impact of parent intervention programs, the available evidence suggests that it is possible to secure unity of purpose between parents, teachers, and children and that parents can play a larger role in intervention than has been thought possible.

To recapitulate, it is apparent that teachers are capable of providing effective assistance to the behaviorally disordered, in conjunction with professional personnel (psychologists, counselors, remediation experts, and specialized consultants) and nonprofessionals (parents and aides).

Traditional psychological theories have served as schemes for characterizing the pattern and type of intervention applied. Typically, this has meant an interventionist stance couched in terms of one or another of the major belief systems: psychoanalytic, psychodynamic or psychoeducational, behaviorist, or an emergent "humanism." These major systems provided a useful framework for considering the problems manifested by the behaviorally disordered. When applied rigorously, they have tended to be limiting in scope; when applied more flexibly, they have lost some measure of integrity.

It is suggested that an integrative framework be considered; such a model would view the development of social and personal competencies as major goals. Within that context, the development of basic attending behaviors, enhancement of academic skills, and the reduction of inappropriate classroom behaviors are viewed as key contributing factors; and these, further, are considered within the context of the complex nature of interactions which occur among learners, teachers, schools, parents, and community and individual values.

IMPLICATIONS AND CONCLUSIONS

Criticism against the practice of placing difficult children into segregated educational facilities raises a major issue for all educators apart from its challenge to the traditional identity of those specifically concerned with "emotionally disturbed" children. How can special services and skills be offered to children and classroom teachers without removing children from the mainstream of education and without creating or perpetuating a parallel school system? This is an extremely complex issue and depends heavily on the larger school system's willingness and ability to tolerate greater pupil diversity. It would appear that, at the very least, the focus of school programs for difficult children must shift emphasis from a concern over *settings* (i.e., special classes, part-time special classes, and so forth) to specific *services* that can be established for children and teachers. To move towards a service-oriented model necessitates at least the elimination of nosological or "disease oriented" procedures for identifying children which hold few if any relevant implications for children's specific academic and social-emotional learning needs. Rather, educationally relevant charac-terizations of children need to be developed and implemented, with these characteriza-tions tied to specific intervention needs and services. Particular needs of difficult children may be more appropriately viewed within the context of individualizing pupil instruction and broadening the scope of learning experiences offered by the school, rather than as a specific problem for "special educators" operating out of closed-door settings.

Specially trained teachers provide, in partnership with professionals and nonprofessionals alike, at least the following important services for children and/or classroom teachers. Each of these techniques or strategies may be delivered directly within the regular classroom, or by removing children from the regular classroom for relatively short periods of time:

1. Assessment of children's academic needs and learning styles.

2. Assessment of the types of classroom structure and reward systems the child best responds to.

3. Provision of specific diagnostic teaching services for children and/or assistance to classroom teachers in synthesizing diagnostic information into individualized programs for selected children.

4. Assistance in incorporating "better-adjusted peers" as helpers in specific behavior management programs designed for individual children in regular classrooms.

5. Facilitation in the adoption of specific esteem-building activities for children, such as programs in cross-age teaching and cross-age counseling.

6. Provision of specific social-learning experiences such as participating more effectively in a group discussion or simply learning how to share materials with others, play games in small groups, or offer help to other students.

7. Provision, through classroom teachers, of affectively oriented learning experiences that help children and teachers better understand human emotions and how emotions influence behavior Included here would be aid to the classroom teacher in adopting curricular programs or strategies that focus on the entire class participating in problem-solving sessions regarding interpersonal difficulties and broader human relations problems.

8. Assistance to classroom teachers in the development of specific management strategies or programs regarding specific children.

9. Provision of emotional support and/or problem-solving-oriented discussion experience for children who are momentarily "in crisis."

10. Establishment of more links between parents and school by interpreting specific service goals to parents and/or by establishing specific programs that use parents as tutors.

For teacher-training institutions, the implications of new modes of thinking about the behaviorally disordered and the provision of appropriate service to them are at once clear and complex. On the one hand, it is evident that traditional training models are rapidly becoming obsolete (Tompkins & Saettler, 1970). There is less reliance upon clinical emphases and greater interest in and movement toward the view that behavioral problems are pragmatic issues of primary educational relevance.

This emergent view has attendant complexities. It requires that training programs clearly define the goals which are laid out for trainees; this, in turn, requires a clear conceptualization and specification of teaching objectives for children (Fink, 1972). As was evident at the 1971 meeting of Training Program Directors in Minneapolis, an emphasis upon educationally relevant characteristics of children, when considered in competency-based terms as opposed to clinical and categorical distinctions, does not by itself offer a training panacea. A danger is that one offers old wine in new bottles; another is that competency quantity may be mistaken for quality. On the other hand, a clear advantage accrues from a competency model which (a) requires the establishment of objectives within a wide but integrated spectrum of educational objectives and (*b*) permits both trainers and trainees the opportunity for continuous feedback and evaluation of progress. If such training objectives are considered in the light of developing concepts of the proper role of the special education complex and its primary functionary, the "special" teacher, then the capacity of the entire educational system to meet the needs of children with behavior disorders can be expected to increase markedly.

References

Aspy, D. A study of three facilitative conditions and their relationship to the achievement of third grade students. Unpublished doctoral dissertation, University of Kentucky, 1965.

Axelrod, S. Token reinforcement programs in special classes. *Exceptional Children,* 1971, **37**, 371-379.

Bakan, D. *Slaughter of the innocents.* San Francisco: Jossey-Bass, 1971.

Bandura, A., & Walters, R.H. *Social learning and personality development.* New York: Holt, 1963.

Baratz, S.S., & Baratz, J.C. Early childhood intervention: The social science base of institutional racism. In S. Chess & A. Thomas (Eds.), *Annual progress in child psychiatry and child development.* New York: Brunner/Mazel, 1971.

Benne, K.D. Authority in education. *Harvard Educational Review.* 1970, **40**, 385-410.

Bessell, H., & Palomares, U. *Methods in human development.* San Diego, Calif.: Human Development Training Institute, 1967.

Blatt, B. *Exodus from pandemonium.* Boston: Allyn & Bacon, 1970.

Blatt, B. Review of "Crisis in child mental health: Challenge for the 1970s. Report of Joint Commission on Mental Health of Children." *Exceptional Children,* 1971, **38**, 277-280.

Bower, E.M., & Hollister, W.G. *Behavioral science frontiers in education.* New York: Wiley, 1967.

Brown, G. *Human teaching for human learning.* New York: McGraw-Hill, 1971.

Carkhuff, R.R., & Berenson, B.G. *Beyond counseling and therapy.* New York: Holt, 1967.

Christoplos, F., & Renz, P. A critical examination of special education programs. *Journal of Special Education,* 1969, **3**, 371-378.

Clark, K.B. The Negro and the urban crisis. In K. Gordon (Ed.), *Agenda for the nation.* Garden City, N.Y.: Doubleday, 1968.

Cloward, R. Studies in tutoring. *Journal of Experimental Education,* 1967, **36**(1), 14-25.

Cobb, J.A. The relationship of discrete classroom behaviors to fourth-grade academic achievement. *Oregon Research Institute Research Bulletin,* 1970, **10**(10).

Cohen, M.A., Gentry, N.D., Hulten, W.J., & Martin, G.L. Measures of classroom performance. In N.G. Haring & A.G. Hayden (Eds.), *The improvement of instruction.* Seattle: Special Child Publications, 1972.

Coleman, J.S., Campbell, E.Q., Hobson, C.F., McPartland, J., Mood, A.M., Weinfeld, F.D., & York, R.L. *Equality of educational opportunity.* Washington, D.C.: United States Government Printing Office, 1966.

Cook, C., Cort, H.R., Flocco, E., & Sanford, J. A study of exemplary programs for emotionally disturbed children. Final report, 1971, Educational Services Division, General Learning Corporation, New York, N.Y., Contract No. OEC-0-70-4922, U.S. Office of Education.

Cook, C., & Flocco, E. "A" and "B" classes at the Experimental Education Unit. Site visit report, 1971, Educational Services Division, General Learning Corporation, New York, N.Y., Contract No. OEC-0-70-4922, U.S. Office of Education.

Cowen, E.L. Emergent directions in school mental health. *American Scientist,* 1971, **59**, 723-733.

Cowen, E.L., Gardner, E.A., & Zax, M. *Emergent approaches to mental health problems.* New York: Appleton-Century-Crofts, 1967.

Csapo, M. *Utilization of normal peers as behavior change agents for reducing the inappropriate behavior of emotionally disturbed children in regular classroom environments.* (Doctoral dissertation, University of Kansas) Ann Arbor, Mich.: University Microfilms, 1971, No. 71-27, 137.

Deno, E.N. Strategies for improvement of educational opportunities for handicapped children: Suggestions for exploitation of EPDA potential. In M.C. Reynolds & M.D. Davis (Eds.), *Exceptional children in regular classrooms.* Minneapolis: University of Minnesota, Department of Audio-Visual Instruction, 1971.

Doernberg, N.L., Rosen, B., & Walker, T.T. A home training program for young mentally ill children, 1969. (ED 047 456)

Dunn, L.M. Special education for the mildly retarded — Is much of it justifiable? *Exceptional Children,* 1968, **35**, 5-22.

Erikson, E.H. *Identity, youth and crisis.* New York: Norton, 1968.

Exceptional Children, 1970, **37**(2).

Fiedler, F. The concept of an ideal therapeutic relationship. *Journal of Consulting Psychology,* 1950, **14**, 239-245.

Fink, A.H. Teacher-pupil interaction in classes for the emotionally handicapped. *Exceptional Children,* 1972, **38**, 469-474.

Fleming, C. Pupil tutors and tutees learn together. *Today's Education,* 1969, **58**, 22-24.

Gartner, A., Kohler, M., & Riessman, F. *Children teach children: Learning by teaching.* New York: Harper, 1971.

Getzels, J.W., & Jackson, P.W. The teacher's personality and characteristics. In N.L. Gage (Ed.), *Handbook of research on teaching.* Chicago: Rand McNally, 1963.

Gittleman, M. Behavior rehearsal as a technique in child treatment. *Journal of Child Psychology and Psychiatry,* 1965, **6**, 251-255.

Glasser, W.H. *Schools without failure.* New York: Harper, 1969.

Glavin, J.P., Quay, H.C., & Werry, J.S. Behavioral and academic gains of conduct problem children in different classroom settings. *Exceptional Children,* 1971, **37**, 441-446.

Gozali, J., & Meyen, E.L. Academic performance of educable mentally retarded pupils in special classes. *Journal of Special Education,* 1970, **4**, 417-424.

Graubard, P.S. Utilizing the group in teaching disturbed delinquents to learn. *Exceptional Children,* 1969, **36**, 267-272.

Hanley, E.M. Review of research involving applied behavior in the classroom. *Review of Educational Research,* 1970, **40**, 597-625.

Haring, N.C. Hayden, A., & Nolen, P. Accelerating appropriate behaviors of children in a Head Start program. *Exceptional Children,* 1969, **35**, 773-784.

Harshman, H. Toward a differential treatment of curriculum. *Journal of Special Education,* 1969, **3**, 385-387.

Hewett, F.M. *The emotionally disturbed child in the classroom.* Boston: Allyn & Bacon, 1968.

Hewett, F.M., Taylor, F.D., & Artuso, A.A. The Santa Monica project: Evaluation of an engineered classroom design with emotionally disturbed children. *Exceptional Children,* 1969, **35**, 523-529.

Illich, I.D. The futility of schooling in Latin America. *Saturday Review,* 1968, **51**(16), 57-59, 74-75.

Johnson, J.L. Special education and the inner city: A challenge for the future or another means for cooling the mark out? *Journal of Special Education,* 1969, **3**, 241-251.

Joint Commission on Mental Health of Children. *Crisis in child mental health: Challenge for the 1970's.* New York: Harper, 1970.

Jones, D.W., II. *The treatment of deviant behavior by youth involvement in public school.* (Doctoral dissertation, University of Oregon) Ann Arbor, Mich.: University Microfilms, 1969, No. 69-12, 616.

Jones, R. *Fantasy and feeling in education.* New York: Harper, 1968.

Kerner, O. (Chm.) *Report of the National Advisory Commission on Civil Disorders.* New York: Bantam, 1968.

Klaus, R., & Gray, S. The early training project for disadvantaged children – a report after five years. *Society for Research in Child Development Monograph,* 1968, **4**(33).

Knoblock, P., & Garcea, R. Teacher-child relationships in psychoeducational pro-graming for emotionally disturbed children. In J. Hellmuth (Ed.), *Educational therapy.* Vol. 2. Seattle: Special Child Publications, 1968.

Lazarus, A. Behavior rehearsal vs. non-directive therapy vs. advice in affecting behavior change. *Behavior Research and Therapy,* 1966, **4**, 209-212.

Lipe, D., & Jung, S.M. Manipulating incentives to enhance school learning. *Review of Educational Research,* 1971, **41**, 249-280.

Lippitt, P., & Lohman, J. Cross-age relationships – an educational resource. *Children,* 1965, **12**, 113-117.

Long, N.J., Morse, W.C., & Newman, R.G. *Conflict in the classroom: The education of children with problems.* (2nd ed.) Belmont, Calif.: Wadsworth, 1971.

Lord, F.E. Complete individualization of instruction: An unrealized goal of the past century. In M.C. Reynolds & M.D. Davis (Eds.), *Exceptional children in regular classrooms.* Minneapolis: University of Minnesota, Department of Audio-Visual Instruction, 1971.

Lourie, N.V., & Lourie, B.P. A noncategorical approach to treatment programs for children and youth. In S. Chess & A. Thomas (Eds.), *Annual progress in child psychiatry and child development.* New York: Brunner/Mazel, 1971.

Lovitt, T. Behavior modification: Where do we go from here? *Exceptional Children*, 1970, **37**, 157-167.

Lurie, E. *How to change the schools: A parents' action handbook on how to fight the system.* New York: Random House, 1970.

MacMillan, D.L. Special education for the mildly retarded: Servant or savant. *Focus on Exceptional Children*, 1971, 2(9), 1-11.

Maslow, A.H. Some educational implications of the humanistic psychologies. *Harvard Educational Review*, 1968, **38**, 685-696.

Melaragno, R., & Newmark, J. *Tutorial community project: Report of the second year, July 1969 – August 1970.* Santa Monica, Calif.: System Development Corporation, 1970.

Menninger, K. *The vital balance: The life process in mental health and illness.* New York: Viking, 1967.

Miller, S.M. Poverty and inequality in America. In F. Riessman, J. Cohen, & A. Pearl (Eds.), *Mental health of the poor.* New York: The Free Press, 1964.

Minuchin, S., Chamberlain, P., & Graubard, P. A project to teach learning skills to disturbed delinquent children. *American Journal of Orthopsychiatry*, 1967, **37**, 555-567.

Morse, W.C. *Classroom disturbance: The principal's dilemma.* Arlington, Va.: The Council for Exceptional Children, 1971. (a)

Morse, W.C. Problems of accommodation. In M.C. Reynolds & M.D. Davis (Eds.), *Exceptional children in regular classrooms.* Minneapolis: University of Minnesota, Department of Audio-Visual Instruction, 1971. (b)

Moustakas, C. *The authentic teacher.* Cambridge, Mass.: Howard E. Doyle, 1966.

O'Connor, R.D. Modification of social withdrawal through symbolic modeling. *Journal of Applied Behavior Analysis*, 1969, **2**, 15-22.

O'Leary, K.D., & Becker, W.C. Behavior modification of an adjustment class: A token reinforcement program. *Exceptional Children*, 1967, **33**, 637-642.

Patterson, G.R., Cobb, J.A., & Ray, R.S. A social engineering technology for retraining the families of agressive boys. In H. Adam & L. Unikel (Eds.), *Issues and trends in behavior therapy.* Springfield, Ill.: Charles C. Thomas, 1973, in press.

Regal, J.M., & Elliot, R.N., Jr. A special program for special education. *Exceptional Children*, 1971, **38**, 67-68.

Reynolds, M.C. Categories and variables in special education. In M.C. Reynolds & M.D. Davis (Eds.), *Exceptional children in regular classrooms.* Minneapolis: University of Minnesota, Department of Audio-Visual Instruction, 1971.

Rist, R.C. Student social class and teacher expectations: The self-fulfilling prophecy in ghetto education. *Harvard Educational Review*, 1970, **40**, 411-451.

Rogers, C.R. *Freedom to learn.* Columbus, O.: Charles E. Merrill, 1969.

Rosenthal, R., & Jacobson, L. *Pygmalion in the classroom.* New York: Holt, 1968.

Rubin, R., & Balow, B. Learning and behavior disorders: A longitudinal study. *Exceptional Children*, 1971, **38**, 293-299.

Sarason, S. *The culture of the school and the problem of change.* Boston: Allyn & Bacon, 1971.

Scheuer, A.L. The relationship between personal attributes and effectiveness in teachers of the emotionally disturbed. *Exceptional Children,* 1971, 37, 723-731.

Sherman, V.S. Two contrasting educational models: Applications and policy implications. Educational Policy Research Center. Research memorandum EPRC-6747-9 SRI Project 6747, Stanford Research Institute, Menlo Park, Calif.: 1970.

Silberman, C. *Crisis in the classroom: The remaking of American education.* New York: Random House, 1970.

Skinner, B.F. The science of learning and the art of teaching. *Harvard Educational Review,* 1954, 24, 86-97.

Stretch, B.B. The rise of the free school. *Saturday Review,* 1970, 53, 76-79, 90-93.

Strong, S. Counseling: An interpersonal influence process. *Journal of Counseling Psychology,* 1968, 15, 215-224.

Toffler, A. *Future shock.* New York: Random House, 1970.

Tompkins, J.R., & Saettler, H.L. Planning research on education of emotionally disturbed children and on training teachers of emotionally disturbed children. Keynote address presented at the Special Study Institute, George Peabody College, Nashville, 1970.

Trippe, M.J. Educational therapy. In J. Hellmuth (Ed.), *Educational therapy.* Vol. 1. Seattle: Special Child Publications, 1966.

Weinstein, G., & Fantini, M. *Toward a humanistic education: A curriculum of affect.* New York: Praeger, 1970.

Weinstein, L. The zoomer class: Initial results. *Exceptional Children,* 1971, 38, 58-65.

Weiner, B. Goals of teaching. In P.S. Graubard (Ed.), *Children against schools.* Chicago: Follett, 1969.

Wood, F. Behavior modification techniques in context. *Council for Children with Behavior Disorders Newsletter,* 1968, 5, 12-15.

Wright, E. Upper-graders learn by teaching. *The Instructor,* 1969, 78(2), 102-103.

INTELLIGENCE TESTING OF ETHNIC MINORITY-GROUP AND CULTURALLY DISADVANTAGED CHILDREN[1]

Jerome M. Sattler, Ph.D.

California State University, San Diego

This review considers the factors involved in administering an intelligence test, standardized on a white population, to children who are members of ethnic minority groups or of culturally disadvantaged groups. Pertinent theoretical views and sociocultural material are also included. The review does not consider material related to racial- and ethnic-group differences in intelligence; this topic recently has received considerable attention (Bereiter, 1969; Cronbach, 1969; Crow, 1969; Dreger & Miller, 1968; Elkind, 1969; Hirsch, 1970; Hudson, 1971; Hunt, 1969; Jensen, 1969; Kagan, 1969). The chapter, therefore, is limited to the issues concerning the administration, interpretation, and applicability of intelligence tests when they are given to ethnic minority-group children and to culturally disadvantaged children.

Intelligence tests can no longer be thought of simply as useful, objective educational tools. The accumulation of evidence — indicating that test results are the interactional end product of complex examinee, examiner, and situational variables — has necessitated a reevaluation of the objectivity of individual intelligence tests (Donahue & Sattler, 1971; Sattler, 1969; Sattler, Hillix, & Neher, 1970; Sattler & Martin, 1971; Sattler & Theye, 1967; Sattler & Winget, 1970; Sattler, Winget, & Roth, 1969). Although intelligence testing still constitutes one of the important links in the educational chain, some believe it must be discarded because it supposedly has become a tool of the white majority — a tool that is being used to suppress the rights of ethnic minority children and, in particular, of Negro children (Davis, 1971; Williams, 1970a). The issues concerning intelligence testing of ethnic minority-group children and of

[1]The preparation of this review was partly supported by Department of Health, Education, and Welfare, Social and Rehabilitation Service Grant 15-P-55277/9-02, "Intelligence Test Modifications on Handicapped and Nonhandicapped Children." The author is grateful to Charles F. Dicken, Ralph Mason Dreger, William A. Hillix, Edward A. Jacobson, Arthur R. Jensen, and Virginia R. Sattler for their valuable criticism and suggestions.

culturally disadvantaged children are complex, for they are woven into the very fabric of society. Test results, as Brim (1965) pointed out, have an impact on the individual's self-esteem, influence his life chances, and engage his deepest political and social attitudes.

Ethnic minority-group children and culturally disadvantaged children represent heterogeneous groups of children, so that it becomes difficult to know what group or groups of children should be so classified. Valentine (1971), for example, found in one single urban community 14 different Afro-American subgroups, each with more or less distinct cultures. It is important, too, to distinguish between ethnic minority-group children and culturally disadvantaged children. This distinction is not usually made, and the label "culturally handicapped" or "culturally disadvantaged" has been used to designate individuals whose values, customs, patterns of thought, language, or even interests are significantly different from the prevailing pattern of the society in which they live (Liddle, 1967). The groups from which culturally handicapped children come include Negroes; Mexicans; Indians; Appalachian whites; Puerto Ricans; foreign-born; migrant farm workers; and unskilled laborers. The terms "culturally handicapped" and "culturally disadvantaged" are relative ones that are applied to children from a variety of groups with diverse values.

The use of the labels "handicapped" and "disadvantaged" to designate ethnic minority-group children (and perhaps other groups of children as well) has been unfortunate, because these terms have value implications. No one has the right to degrade a subculture that does not conform to the patterns of the majority group. Certain behaviors in lower-status groups may be both healthy and justified, on the basis of life conditions differing markedly from those of the dominant culture (Barnes, 1971). The extent to which a group is handicapped may lie only in the eyes of the beholder. This review uses the labeling designations of the cited authors; however, it is hoped that more appropriate, nonpejorative designations will soon be adopted.

A variety of reports is cited in the review, including research and nonresearch studies. While the focus is primarily on individual intelligence tests, studies using group intelligence tests or achievement tests are also cited. Most attention is given to the Negro and Mexican-American ethnic minority groups. Many of the criticisms leveled at the use of intelligence tests with Negroes have also been made with reference to other minorities. Thus, there is a certain amount of overlap in the reviews for each minority group. The review, which spans a 58-year period, brings together the opinions, findings, and recommendations relevant to ethnic and nonethnic subcultural variables and intelligence testing.

BIAS OF INTELLIGENCE TESTS AND TESTING

Arguments against the use of standard intelligence tests with ethnic minority-group children and culturally disadvantaged children have been offered by many writers (Anastasi, 1967; Berdie, 1965; Clark, 1967; Halpern, 1971; Johnson &

Medinnus, 1965; Kagan, 1971; Leland, 1971; Levine, 1966; Masland, Sarason, & Gladwin, 1958; Mundy & Maxwell, 1958; Palmer, 1970; Riessman, 1962; Sarason & Doris, 1969; Schmideberg, 1970; Schubert, 1967; R.L. Williams, 1970a, b, c, 1971; Zigler & Butterfield, 1968). (Material specifically related to the use of intelligence tests with Mexican-American children and with North American Indian children appears in other sections of the review.) These authors contended that standard intelligence tests have a strong white, Anglo-Saxon, middle-class bias, and that ethnic minority-group children and culturally disadvantaged children are handicapped in taking tests because of deficiencies in motivation, test practice, and reading. In addition, rapport problems are postulated, especially when the examinee is black and the examiner is white. Intelligence tests, too, are said to be more related to the nonschool problem-solving experiences of middle-class children than those of lower-class children (Masland et al., 1958; Sarason & Doris, 1969). Palmer (1970) indicated that Western culture emphasizes achievement and problem solving, and that in this culture it is necessary for a child to recognize and to accept intellectual challenge by the time he begins school. However, culturally deprived children may fail to comprehend and to accept the achievement aspects of the test situation. They may view it as an enjoyable child-adult encounter, rather than as a time to achieve; or, if the problem-solving aspects of the situation are recognized, they may be ignored or be responded to on an associative level.

Zigler and Butterfield (1968) presented a variety of reasons which might account for the poor performance of culturally deprived children on standardized intelligence tests. While the children may have an adequate storage and retrieval system to answer questions correctly, they may fail in practice, because they have not been exposed to the material. For example, to the question "What is a gown?" which appears on the Stanford-Binet, they may respond incorrectly because they have never heard the word "gown." Motivational factors may affect the performance of some culturally deprived children; they know what a gown is, but respond with "I don't know" in order to terminate as quickly as possible the unpleasantness of interacting with a strange and demanding adult. Thus, when changes occur in IQ test performances, they may be due to modifications in test content or in motivational factors, neither of which has much to do with the children's thinking abilities.

Zigler and Butterfield cited a series of studies which suggested that culturally deprived children, in comparison with middle-class children, are more wary of adults, more motivated toward securing adults' attention and praise, less motivated to be correct for the sake of correctness alone, and willing to settle for lower levels of achievement success. The results of their own investigation suggested that culturally deprived children (Negro and white) suffer from emotional and motivational deficits which decrease their usual intellectual performance.

Leland (1971) believes that formal testing procedures identify individuals who cannot compete in our technologically oriented culture. Tests therefore become major instruments for casting out the sick, the uneducated, and those with special personal problems. It is the poor, as a group, who are the most vulnerable, and it is *poverty* that is the main characteristic of the disadvantaged. The adaptive strategies of the poor are not always conducive to good test performance. Leland hypothesized that they cope poorly with external pressures and experience failure — even in areas where they have cognitive strengths — because they feel that things often happen to them in spite of themselves and without their participation. Testing situations may arouse tension and feelings of suspicion in the poor child. He may react with aggression or with nonparticipating resistance, but simultaneously feel that it is important to establish a friendly relationship with the examiner. A heightened preoccupation with his relationship with the examiner may, in turn, reduce the saliency of the test questions. Such strategies leave the poor child ill equipped to cope with tests. Leland made the telling observation that when a child who performs adequately in his own environment is given a label as a result of testing, the label makes him visible to others. Testing thereby makes an otherwise invisible person visible and begins to create social problems where previously none had existed.

The Association of Black Psychologists also maintained that current standardized tests should not be used to test black children (Williams, 1970a):

The Association of Black Psychologists fully supports those parents who have chosen to defend their rights by refusing to allow their children and themselves to be subjected to achievement, intelligence, aptitude and performance tests which have been and are being used to — A. Label Black people as uneducable. B. Place Black children in 'special' classes and schools. C. Perpetuate inferior education in Blacks. D. Assign Black children to educational tracts [sic]. E. Deny Black students higher educational opportunities. F. Destroy positive growth and development of Black people [p. 5].

Williams maintained that conventional intelligence and ability tests are unfair to black children. Tests endanger the future of black children in many ways, one of which is to place them in slow tracks in school. The teachers, led to believe that the low test scores of black children mean that they are slow, treat them with an expectancy of "slow performance," thereby producing a self-fulfilling prophecy. The evidence to support Williams's claim of teacher expectancy and self-fulfilling prophecy, however, is by no means conclusive. The pitfalls of Rosenthal and Jacobsen's (1968) study have been pointed out by Snow (1969) and Thorndike (1968), and other studies have failed to document the expectancy effect (Claiborn, 1969; Fleming & Anttonen, 1971; Gozali & Meyen, 1970).

Williams (1970b) also argued that black children develop unique verbal skills that are neither measured by conventional tests nor accepted in the middle-class-oriented classroom. In another article, R.L. Williams (1971) argued that traditional ability tests violate the ethnic minority child's civil and constitutional rights under the provisions of the Fourteenth Amendment for equal protection under the law. He cited court cases to illustrate issues related to the use of psychological tests in testing minority groups in the schools, placement of minority-group children in special classes, and selection of children for the track system.

The following exemplifies Williams's (1970c) position concerning the cultural bias of intelligence tests. According to Williams, responses to the Stanford-Binet question "What's the thing for you to do if another boy hits you without meaning to do it?" are dependent on the child's type of neighborhood. In many black communities, the response "Walk away" would mean suicide. Children in black communities are taught to hit back as a means of survival. However, "Hit him back" receives zero credit on the Stanford-Binet. Williams used this and other examples to support his contention that neither test items nor much of the school's curriculum is relevant to the black experience. The poor performance of Negro children on conventional intelligence tests is attributed to the biased content of the tests, i.e., the test material is drawn from outside the black culture.

Hewitt and Massey (1969) agreed with Williams that psychometric tests are used in a biased manner with black children and that this is especially evident when questionable responses are given a score of zero. They pointed out that during a test the examiner-examinee relationship is fraught with communication problems. When a middle-class white examiner tests a black ghetto child, the examiner's enunciation of words may not be clear to the examinee; the examinee, in turn, may use words that cannot be understood by the examiner. Phrases used by black ghetto children may have special meaning, although superficially the phrases are awkward or incorrect or appear to be invented. The test stimuli, too, are vulnerable to cultural bias. Test stimuli that may appear to be *incomplete* to the child who is *not* from an impoverished environment (e.g., items on the Mutilated Pictures test at year level 6 of the Stanford-Binet or items on the Picture Completion test of the Wechsler Intelligence Scale for Children [WISC]) may appear to be *complete* to the ghetto child.

To illustrate the bias of test stimuli, Hewitt and Massey gave an example of a WISC picture-completion item which requires the identification of a tooth missing from a comb. The ghetto child seldom sees a complete comb. To him, a comb is useful even when teeth are missing, to be replaced when it is no longer of any use; i.e., a toothless comb is a commonplace, not a rarity. The ghetto child may respond by saying "hair" or "brush" or "hand." "Additionally, the physical aspects of Negro hair make it difficult to comb and the kinkiness often breaks off teeth more readily than does straight hair. Both economics and physiology influence this question [p. 36]."

Hewitt and Massey held that standard IQ tests are based, in large part, on skills and information acquired in the school. Such tests, therefore, unfairly assess the intellectual skills of the ghetto child who views the school negatively. They concluded that standard intelligence tests will become diagnostic of mental ability only when the educational process is made applicable to the Negro student's life and learning style.

Hewitt and Massey's study lacked adequate item-analysis data; until more data are obtained, their illustrations stand as interesting speculations, rather than as a demonstration of the cultural bias of the WISC. Their statement concerning the relationship between IQ tests and information acquired in the schools is not supported with data, nor do they provide data concerning: (*a*) whether negative attitudes toward school affect learning, (*b*) whether poor learning promotes negative attitudes toward school, or (*c*) whether poor learning is some combination of (*a*) and (*b*). While phonetic variation studies have shown that middle-class white speakers were able to communicate effectively with Negro children (Eisenberg, Berlin, Dill, & Frank, 1968; Peisach, 1965; Quay, 1971; Weener, 1969), less is known about the extent to which white examiners or middle-class black examiners are able to understand the communications of poor black children. Dreger[2] observed that a common complaint in desegregated schools now is "I just can't understand them [poor black children]." Yet these same children communicate exceedingly well with their peers. Dreger also suggested that the black in the South, and to a lesser degree in the North, has spent 350 years perfecting a communication system that will exclude whites and, incidentally, white-oriented blacks. It is no wonder "I can't understand them."

A work group of the Society for the Psychological Study of Social Issues (Division 9 of the American Psychological Association) presented a sound discussion of some of the issues involved in the use of current standardized tests with disadvantaged minority groups (Deutsch, Fishman, Kogan, North, & Whiteman, 1964). The following material is a condensation of their presentation. The three critical issues in testing disadvantaged children involve whether tests (*a*) reliably differentiate among members of minority groups, (*b*) have predictive validity, and (*c*) are interpreted adequately.

Reliability data for specific minority groups are not presented in test manuals, including the manuals for the Stanford-Binet and WISC. Such data are badly needed, especially by institutions that test minority groups. The following trends emerge from studies investigating the characteristics of minority-group children that affect their test performance and test results:

It may be hypothesized that in contrast to the middle-class child the lower-class child will tend to be less verbal, more fearful of strangers, less self-confident, less motivated toward scholastic and academic achievement, less competitive in the intellectual realm, more "irritable," less conforming to middle-class norms of behavior and conduct, more apt to be bilingual, less exposed to intellectually stimulating materials in the home, less varied in recreational outlets, less knowledgeable about the world outside his immediate neighborhood, and more likely to attend inferior schools [Deutsch et al., 1964, p. 132].

The examiner has the responsibility, whenever there is a doubt about test reliability for the sample of children that he is testing, for presenting the results in a cautious manner. Critical decisions should not be made on the basis of "face value" results. Careful study of individual responses will help in determining the extent to which the overall performance is representative of the child's ability.

With regard to predictive validity, the work group pointed out that minority-group status is not a crucial consideration when an examinee is being compared to a specific norm group. However, the examinee's minority-group status *is* important when his scores are explained, or when they are used to make long-range predictions:

[2]R.M. Dreger, personal communication, March 1972.

For example, no inequity is necessarily involved if a culturally disadvantaged child is simply reported to have an IQ of 84 and a percentile rank of 16 on the national norms for a certain intelligence test. However, if this is interpreted as meaning that the child ranks or will rank no higher in learning ability than does a middle-class, native born American child of the same IQ, the interpretation might well be erroneous [Deutsch et al., 1964, p. 134].

The final issue discussed by the work group concerned the interpretation of test results. Errors in test interpretation stem from several sources. For example, responses deviating from the norm of the majority culture may be typical of a minority group and hence not deviant at all (cf. Ellenberger, 1960). Test performance should always be interpreted in light of the child's life experiences. Another source of error relates to construct and content validity. The content of a test may, for some groups, tap motivation as well as the trait purportedly being measured. In addition, the test procedures, which include ways in which questions are asked and responses given, may affect the child's performance. By becoming familiar with the cultural and social background of minority-group children, the examiner may avoid misevaluating test performance.

Mercer (1971) reported data which seemed to support Berdie's (1965) observation that tests may actually lead to and encourage discriminatory practices. Mercer studied the relationship between membership in ethnic minority groups and placement in classes for the mentally retarded in public schools in Riverside, California. While the percentage of children in ethnic groups tested by psychologists closely approximated the ethnic distribution of the entire school population, there was a disproportionate number of Mexican-American and Negro children obtaining IQs below 80. In addition, there were disproportionately more Mexican-American children, but not Negro children, recommended for placement (and finally placed) in classes for the mentally retarded than Anglo-Americans.

Mercer concluded that persons from low socioeconomic levels and ethnic minority groups are more vulnerable to being labeled mentally retarded than persons of other socioeconomic levels and ethnic majority groups. She believed that a "defect hypothesis" (i.e., that mental retardates suffer from specific physiological and cognitive defects over and above their slower rate of development) or a genetic hypothesis could not account for her findings. Instead, she proposed an alternate hypothesis: children from low socioeconomic groups or from ethnic minority groups are more vulnerable to being labeled mentally retarded, because clinical measures (primarily intelligence tests) are interpreted from a culture-bound perspective.

An important article by Cole and Bruner (1971) challenged many prevalent views concerning the psychological processes operating in individuals designated as "culturally deprived." Using material from such diverse fields as anthropology, sociology, linguistics, and psychology, Cole and Bruner marshaled an impressive set of arguments to refute the notion that individuals from certain subcultural groups have cognitive deficits. Labov's (1970) work, in particular, played a crucial role in their analysis. Labov pointed out that in an assessment situation, the only thing controlled is the superficial form of the stimulus — the test question. The examinee's interpretation of the stimulus and the response he believes is appropriate are completely uncontrolled. Therefore, studies on the verbal capacities of children, which often are included in investigations of subcultural differences in cognitive capacity, cannot be valid if the crucial intervening variables of *interpretation* and *motivation* are uncontrolled. Labov also noted that the traditional assessment situation elicits deliberately defensive behavior from Negro examinees. Because the Negro child expects that talking openly will expose him to insult and harm, he may not try to answer the questions. The linguistically deficient child in the assessment situation may demonstrate powerful reasoning and debating skills in his own environment.

Cole and Bruner argued:

Those groups ordinarily diagnosed as culturally deprived have the same underlying competence as those in the mainstream of the dominant culture, *the differences in performance being accounted for by the situations and contexts in which the competence is expressed* [p. 870].

However, they also recognized that a ghetto inhabitant's language training may make him unfit for jobs in the middle-class culture. The assumptions that situational factors are often important determinants of psychological performance and that different cultural groups are likely to respond differently to any given situation led Cole and Bruner to propose a change in traditional ways of psychological experimentation by incorporating "representative design" (Brunswik, 1958) and an analysis of the "ecological significance" of stimulation.

Cole and Bruner indicated that the assessment of competence requires a determination of "first, whether a competence is expressed in a particular situation and, second, what the significance of that situation is for the person's ability to cope with life in his own milieu [p. 874]." The label "cultural *deprivation*," Cole and Bruner maintained, "represents a special case of cultural *difference* that arises when an individual is faced with demands to perform in a manner inconsistent with his past (cultural) experience [p. 874]."

Valentine (1971) suggested that neither the deficit model (cf. Zigler & Butterfield, 1968) nor the difference formulation (cf. Baratz & Baratz, 1970) is adequate in accounting for Afro-American behavior. Instead, he argued for a biculturation model. According to Valentine, biculturation is the

key concept for making sense out of ethnicity and related matters: the collective behavior and social life of the Black community is bicultural in the sense that each Afro-American ethnic segment draws upon both a distinctive repertoire of standardized Afro-American group behavior and, simultaneously, patterns derived from the mainstream cultural system of Euro-American deviation [p. 143].

Afro-Americans are bicultural and bidialectical, and, far from being either deficient or merely different in culture, often have a richer repertoire of life styles than middle-class whites.

NEGRO EXAMINEES AND EXAMINERS' RACE

The examiner's race, as a variable which may affect Negro examinees' performance, has been considered an important variable in the field of intelligence testing, almost from the beginning of the testing movement. Many writers maintained that differences in racial membership affect the examiner-examinee relationship (Anastasi, 1958; Anastasi & Foley, 1949; Barnes, 1969; Blackwood, 1927; Brown, 1944; Deutsch et al., 1964; Garth, 1922; Hilgard, 1957; Klineberg, 1935, 1944; Pettigrew, 1964; Pressey & Teter, 1919; Riessman, 1962; Strong, 1913). Testing Negro children in the South may present a special problem for the white examiner, because the children may have an attitude of fear and suspicion that can interfere with their performance (Klineberg, 1935). According to the above writers, Negro examinees, when tested by white examiners, may display behaviors that reflect their discomfort in the test situation. They may show fear and suspicion, verbal constriction, strained and unnatural reactions, and a façade of stupidity to avoid appearing "uppity." They may also score low to avoid personal threat. The test situation, too, may be viewed by Negroes as a means for white persons, not blacks, to get ahead in society (Pettigrew, 1964). While many of these behaviors, patterns, and perceptions are likely to exist and are important phenomena in their own right, there is no way of knowing to what extent they affect the examinees' scores (Sattler, 1970).

When research studies are reviewed, the results suggest that the examiner's race does not usually affect the performance of Negro and/or white subjects on individual or group-administered intelligence tests. Thus, studies using standard intelligence tests have usually reported that the examiner-race variable was not significant (Caldwell & Knight, 1970; Costello, 1970; Lipsitz, 1969; Miller & Phillips, 1966; Pelosi, 1968), although one study reported a significant examiner-race variable (Forrester & Klaus, 1964), and two studies reported that the examiner-race variable was both significant and nonsignificant (Abramson, 1969; Canady, 1936, as analyzed by Sattler, 1966). Shuey (1966), from her review of literature, concluded that white examiners do not adversely affect the IQ scores of Negro examinees. Such studies are still too few in number to arrive at firm generalizations concerning the effect of the examiner's race on children's performance on intelligence tests. In addition, the small number of examiners used in many studies confounds individual differences and race differences among examiners. Until very recently, cross-examiner studies have been virtually nil.

CULTURE-FAIR TESTS

Attempts to develop culture-free and culture-fair tests have not been successful, as Wesman (1968) maintained, because of the failure to recognize that intelligence is, in part, the summation of the learning experiences of an individual. Therefore, intelligence tests cannot be created without differential exposure to learning having an influence on scores. If the intent is to predict the individual's ability to learn the content of the more general culture, tests designed for the subculture will be less relevant than those which sample from the general culture. The acquisition of conventional verbal abilities will be needed to progress in the general educational system and in the general culture. Vernon (1965) noted that no test can be regarded as culture-fair. Subcultures may develop different kinds of intelligence from that of the predominant culture. Anastasi (1961) stated that so-called culture-fair tests are not free of all cultural influences. Bennett (1970) pointed out that it will be difficult to develop a new type of test which will both predict socially useful criteria and not be influenced by skills valued in the dominant culture.

Cohen (1969) pointed out that nonverbal tests are not culture-free, because they depend upon the ability to reason logically — an ability which is bound to middle-class ways of thinking, i.e., to analytic ways of thinking. The analytic and relational ways of thinking are two basic cognitive styles. Cognitive styles are methods by which individuals select and process information. They are independent of native ability and definable without reference to specific substantive content. The analytic cognitive style consists of (*a*) abstracting salient information from a stimulus or a situation, (*b*) a stimulus-centered orientation to reality, and (*c*) a focusing on specific parts. The relational cognitive style consists of (*a*) a descriptive mode of abstraction, (*b*) a self-centered orientation to reality, and (*c*) a focusing on the global characteristics of a stimulus.

For Negro children, nonverbal tests (or sections of tests) have been found to be as difficult or more difficult than verbal tests. These data do not permit one to determine the extent to which nonverbal tests are culture-bound; they simply indicate that Negro children obtain different scores on verbal and nonverbal tests. For example, Teahan and Drews (1962) found that the Performance scale of the WISC was more difficult than the Verbal scale for Negro junior high school students from the South. In the North, however, Negro children obtained similar scores on the two scales. Caldwell and Smith (1968) found that Southern Negro children obtained higher WISC Verbal than Performance scale IQs. Hughes and Lessler (1965) reported that both normal and mentally retarded Southern Negro children scored lower on the Performance scale than on the Verbal scale of the WISC. Atchison (1955) found that mentally retarded Negro children obtained higher WISC Verbal than Performance scale IQs. Willard (1968) reported that Cattell's Culture Fair Intelligence Test had no advantage over the Stanford-Binet in testing Negro disadvantaged children. Higgins and Sivers (1958) administered the Stanford-Binet, Form L (primarily verbal), and Raven's Progressive Matrices (nonverbal) to low-SES Negro and white children between the ages of 7 and 9. The results showed that Stanford-Binet scores were similar for the two ethnic groups, while, in contrast, Progressive Matrices scores were significantly lower for the Negro than for the white children. Thus, the Stanford-Binet was said to have less ethnic bias than the Progressive Matrices. It is possible, that the Progressive Matrices provides a better estimate of *g* (Spearman's general capacity for abstract reasoning) than the Stanford-Binet.

Costello and Dickie (1970) reported that Negro preschoolers obtained higher Stanford-Binet IQs than Leiter IQs. The highly verbal administration of the Stanford-Binet was somewhat more reassuring to lower-class children and to young children than the procedures used with the Leiter. Stablein, Willey, and Thomson (1961) administered the Davis-Eells Test of General Intelligence on Problem Solving Ability (Davis & Eells, 1953), together with other measures of ability, to Anglo-American and Mexican-American children in grades 2 through 5. The results indicated that the Davis-Eells test was as influenced by cultural factors as were the other measures of intelligence and achievement. Barclay and Yater (1969) compared the Stanford-Binet, Form L-M, with the Wechsler Preschool and Primary Scale of Intelligence (WPPSI) in a sample of culturally disadvantaged Negro and white 5-year-olds, Stanford-Binet IQs were significantly higher than WPPSI IQs; the investigators concluded that the two instruments were not comparable for culturally disadvantaged children and that the WPPSI seemed to be a more difficult test. There were no significant differences between the two ethnic groups on any of the IQ measures.

Jensen (1970a) indicated that the tests on the Stanford-Binet and Wechsler scales which apparently have little status bias include Digit Span, Block Design, and Mazes. The Stanford-Binet may be less status-fair than the Wechsler scales because tests of the same content (e.g., Vocabulary and Digit Span) do not appear at every year level of the scale. Therefore, year levels may differ in their status-fair properties. It is theoretically possible that the discontinuance procedures might prevent some children from taking tests that are potentially less status-biased at a higher year level. This assumes that the higher year level is less biased than the lower year level. The point-scale format of the Wechsler scales does not have such problems. It is not known to what extent the year-level format of the Stanford-Binet produces status bias; it is a question for further investigation.

Jensen listed three ways to judge the status fairness of a test. First, the predictive validity of a test can be studied for different groups in the population. If different predictive validities are found and if the differences cannot be attributed to differences in variance on the test or the criterion, then the test is probably biased in favor of some groups. Second, tests having many culturally loaded items are less likely to be status-fair than tests with few culturally loaded items. Third, tests that are highly resistant to practice gains may be more a measure of internally regulated developmental processes than of environmental influences.

Jensen proposed that "a test is status fair to the degree that its correlation with 'Intelligence A' [genotypic form, related to the innate capacity of the individual] in the population in which the test is used approaches unity [p. 80]." This means that the higher the correlation between phenotype (test) and genotype (Intelligence A), the higher the fairness of the test. The Stanford-Binet, Jensen stated, has a phenotype-genotype correlation of approximately .90 in the normative Caucasian population, a figure which is the square root of the heritability of intelligence test scores. The average value of estimates of heritability is about .80, "which means that about 80

171

per cent of the true score variance on intelligence tests is attributable to genetic factors and about 20 per cent is attributable to nongenetic factors [p. 80]." However, Jensen also indicated that, at present, there are not adequate data to estimate the index of heritability of intelligence test scores in the American Negro population.

In concluding this section, it is important to recognize, as Jensen[3] has noted, that such statements as "No test can be regarded as culture-fair" or "Culture-fair tests are not free of all cultural influences" *and* "There is no line which is perfectly straight" are comparable. Culture fairness is not either-or but a dimension (or number of dimensions) along which various tests can range. The fact that no test lies at either of the end points of this continuum does not invalidate the continuum or the differences in culture loading between tests lying at various points along the continuum.

MODIFYING TEST PROCEDURES

A number of investigations have been designed to evaluate whether changes in test procedures would lead to higher scores on intelligence tests. Zigler and Butterfield (1968) reported that culturally deprived preschool children (Negro and white) obtained higher scores on the Stanford-Binet when a test-administration procedure allowed them to obtain a maximum number of successes early in the testing experience than when the standard procedure was used. Ali and Costello (1971) also reported that modifying the Peabody Picture Vocabulary Test (PPVT) by randomizing the difficulty level, by using detailed instructions, and by using verbal reinforcements led to higher scores than those obtained under standard procedures in a group of preschool Negro disadvantaged children attending a Head Start program. It would be interesting to learn what effects procedures of this type would have with middle-class children.

Quay (1971) reported that changes in test procedures designed to increase motivation (praise or candy) and to facilitate language comprehension (standard English or Negro dialect) did not affect significantly the Stanford-Binet scores of 4-year-old Negro children. Interestingly, the speech of the children was predominantly in dialect in both language conditions of test administration, while comprehension of standard English and dialect was equal.

Sperling (1970) administered a group test of arithmetic to seventh-grade disadvantaged and nondisadvantaged children. In the disadvantaged group, a majority were Negro, followed by white and Puerto Rican; in the nondisadvantaged group, 95% of the students were white. Two conditions of tape-recorded instructions were used. In the "affective-toned" condition, the instructions were elaborate; the children were given reasons for taking the tests and told that their scores would not affect their

---

[3] A.R. Jensen, personal communication, February 1972.

grades. In the "nonaffective-toned" condition, the instructions were perfunctory and insensitive. The results indicated that higher scores were obtained in the affective than in the nonaffective condition, primarily by the nonwhite disadvantaged children.

The difference between scores obtained on individually administered tests and group-administered tests is of interest. Low-SES children may be more distracted in a classroom testing situation than when they are tested individually. Jensen (1970a) suggested that results of studies which indicated that there is a greater discrepancy between group and individual test scores for low socioeconomic children than for middle-class children might have been due to the extrinsic factors in the group-testing situation – e.g., test procedures, instructions, and forms – which might have interfered with the children's performance.

MEXICAN-AMERICAN AND SPANISH-SPEAKING CHILDREN

Five million Mexican-Americans are concentrated in five states – California, Texas, Arizona, Colorado, and New Mexico. The use of Spanish is declining among native-born Mexican-Americans, being used less frequently in large cities in California than in small cities in Texas. The decline in use is most prominent among middle-class Mexican-Americans (Moore, 1970).

There is no easy way to characterize the culture or values of Mexican-Americans. Although Kluckhohn and Strodtbeck (1961) reported that Mexican-Americans are more present-oriented than future-oriented, see man as subjugated to rather than master over nature, and prefer the "being" to the "doing" orientation, these values may well have been adaptive ones for Mexican-American communities (Moore, 1970). Patterns of assimilation are varied. Assimilation is frequent in large cities; yet large Mexican enclaves still exist in some cities in Colorado, New Mexico, and Texas. The varied cultural patterns among Mexican-Americans create dilemmas for Mexican immigrants. It is the poor Mexican-American who tends to follow village patterns of values, even after moving to the cities (Moore, 1970). The middle-class Mexican-American, in contrast, expresses almost identical values to those of middle-class Anglos. The vast majority of Mexican-Americans are culturally heterogeneous; i.e., they are simultaneously users of both Mexican and American cultures in varying quantities (Holland, 1960).

Heffernan (1955) cited a number of cultural problems facing Mexican-American students. Mexican-American youths have a low level of aspiration which results in a failure to achieve commensurate with their ability. Their parents, having limited aspirations for their children and failing to view education as an avenue of social and vocational mobility, do not support educational efforts. Other problems include economic insecurity, inadequate facility in the use of the English language, clashes between their cultural values and those of Anglo-Americans, and low community standards. Heller (1966) suggested that Mexican-American children are not prepared at home for school experiences, and the schools, in turn, are not prepared or equipped to

173

receive and teach them. Nava (1970) noted that no other ethnic minority group of comparable size produces so few high school graduates.

Manuel (1965) indicated that the relatively low achievement of Mexican-American children on intelligence and achievement tests can be accounted for by the following facts: These children, in comparison to Anglo-American children, are more likely (a) to come from culturally disadvantaged homes, (b) to be unable to speak English when they enter school, and (c) to come from families having limited educational aspirations. Heller (1966) essentially agreed with Manuel. He suggested that IQ scores of Mexican-Americans are products of distinct social and cultural circumstances and indicate deficiency in schooling. The skills of Mexican-American children for effective functioning in urban society, he believed, are more limited than those of Anglo-American children.

Research studies on sociocultural factors

Research studies concerned with evaluating the sociocultural patterns and attitudes of Mexican-American children appear to support some of the observations presented in the previous section. Ramirez, Taylor, and Petersen (1971) compared the attitudes of Mexican-American adolescents with those of Anglo-American adolescents on a number of different issues. Both groups were from the lower socioeconomic classes. Mexican-American adolescents were found (a) to have less positive views toward education, (b) to view interpersonal relationships more frequently as the attempt of one person to control another, (c) to have a greater need to escape or to avoid people or situations, and (d) to have a more limited need to achieve. The two groups did not differ on need for affiliation. LaBelle (1970), however, found that Anglo- and Mexican-American fifth graders perceived school-related concepts more similarly than differently.

Linton (1971) studied the sociocultural characteristics of Mexican-American and Anglo-American sixth graders. Mexican-Americans were found to have a more dependent relationship with their relatives, to be more isolated from the school environment, and to be more likely to consider impersonal forces as important factors in their school achievement. Overall, however, the results led Linton to conclude that ethnicity accounts for less variation in sociocultural characteristics than does socioeconomic level. Low-socioeconomic-level Anglo- and Mexican-Americans appear to be part of a larger culture of poverty. Both ethnicity and socioeconomic level contribute to alienation from school.

Peck and Galliani (1962) studied the sociometric choices of Mexican- and Anglo-American adolescents. The Mexican-American students failed, for the most part, to nominate other Mexican-American youths. These findings suggested to the authors that Mexican-American children participate in the process of prejudicially downgrading or ignoring youth of their own ethnic extraction, thereby apparently mirroring their parents' pattern of noninvolvement in political and civic affairs. Mason (1967, 1969), in comparing the California Personality Inventory scores of junior high school students from American Indian, Mexican, and Caucasian ethnic backgrounds, was generally unable to find consistent differences among the groups. The small N in Mason's studies, however, precludes placing high confidence in her results.

Cross-cultural studies of cooperative behavior, using Mexican-American children and children from other groups, have revealed interesting trends. Madsen and Shapira (1970) studied cooperative and competitive behavior of urban Afro-American, Anglo-American, Mexican-American, and Mexican village children between the ages of 7 and 9. While there was a tendency for Mexican-American boys to be less competitive than Mexican-American girls and Afro- and Anglo-Americans of both sexes, the primary findings were that American children in all three ethnic groups behaved in a highly competitive and nonadaptive manner, while the village children in Mexico behaved cooperatively. These results were essentially confirmed in another investigation by Kagan and Madsen (1971); they reported that cooperative behavior was similar in samples of 4- to 5-year-old Anglo-American and Mexican-American children (the only two groups studied at these ages), whereas in a 7-to-9-year-old group, Mexican children were found to be most cooperative, Mexican-Americans next, and Anglo-Americans least.

Hertzig and Birch (1971) reported that failure to cooperate on the Stanford-Binet at the age of 3 years had prognostic significance for Puerto Rican working-class children but not for middle-class white children. On retesting at the age of 6, the white children who were uncooperative at the age of 3 obtained scores which were similar to those obtained by the cooperative white children. However, the Puerto Rican children who were uncooperative at the age of 3 obtained scores on retest that were significantly lower than those obtained by the initially cooperative Puerto Rican children. The investigators suggested that the uncooperative Puerto Rican 3-year-old might have been displaying a pattern of functioning that is antithetical to the subsequent development of effective problem-solving skills. This conclusion may be justified, but another is possible: cooperative Puerto Rican children may be more advanced and thus more cooperative. Finally, it was suggested that intervention programs may be particularly suitable in modifying behavior style for the uncooperative children.

Bilingualism

Manuel (1965) noted that Mexican-American children usually have to learn English as a second language and then are required to use this second language in their school work. Spanish, however, is the language they use outside of school. It is spoken at home and in the community, but seldom used in reading. Because of this form of bilingualism, many children fail to develop a sufficient mastery of either language, and learning is more difficult under such conditions.

Whether or not bilingualism constitutes a handicap depends upon the way in which the two languages have been learned (Anastasi & Cordova, 1953). The child who learns one language at home and another at school may be limited in his mastery of both languages, whereas the child who learns to express himself in at least one language in all types of situations will have minimal, if any, handicaps.

Language differences may also play a role in the adjustment of Mexican-American children to school. Nava (1970) observed that when the young Mexican-American child enters school, he is suddenly forced to socialize and to compete with other children who speak a foreign language. His failure to speak English is grounds for many of his classmates to regard him negatively. He then may fall behind and stay in school only until he can drop out voluntarily. The language gap aggravates and compounds the problems of the Mexican-American child. Classroom experiences become a painful ordeal. His accent is perhaps one of his most immediate handicaps.

Manuel (1965) described the Mexican-American child's initial school experience in a similar way. On entering an Anglo school, the Mexican-American child at the age of 5 or 6 may encounter a strange and alien situation. School is a new experience, with an adult in command with whom he cannot communicate; it is a confusing, fearful, and insecure situation. Those from a low-SES family may come to accept inferiority as a permanent state, developing an attitude of dependency. The feeling of futility is not hard to imagine when poverty is accompanied by language difficulties, little success in school, and rejection by others. Nava's and Manuel's observations, while confined to Mexican-American children, may also be applicable to the educational experience of Southern black children (and perhaps other ethnic minority children).

Speech difficulties

Because Mexican-American children often speak Spanish as their primary language, the Anglo-American examiner may have difficulty communicating with the Mexican-American examinee. The patterns of speech inculcated by use of the primary language, Spanish, can interfere with the correct speaking of English (Beberfall, 1958; Chavez, 1956; Perales, 1965). Speech patterns of bilingual Mexican-American children often are a complex mixture of both English and Spanish, and the children may never become proficient in speaking either language (Holland, 1960).

Chavez (1956) noted that language barriers arise from (a) the different sound that the same letters have in Spanish and English (e.g., i in "hit" or "miss" may be pronounced as ee as in "meet"), and (b) the variations in concepts that exist between the two cultures (e.g., "nose" in some Spanish localities is plural, so that a child may say, "I hit *them* against the door").

Perales (1965) enumerated three types of difficulties encountered by Spanish-speaking children when they speak their own language. First, because their Spanish vocabulary is limited, they may borrow from a limited English vocabulary to complete expressions begun in Spanish. Students may use such expressions as *"yo le dije que* I wouldn't do it" (I said to him that I wouldn't do it) and *"El fue,* but I stayed in *la casa"* (He went, but I stayed in the house). Second, they may give English words Spanish pronunciations and meanings (called *pochismos*). For example, a Spanish speaker may use the word *huachar* (from the English verb "to watch") instead of the correct Spanish verb *mirar,* or the word *chuzar* (from the English verb "to choose") instead of the correct Spanish word *escoger.* Third, they may have difficulties in pronunciation and enunciation. They may say, for example, *"Nos juimos con eos"* for *"Nos fuimos con ellos"* (We went with them).

Rapport

Stereotypes held by either the Anglo examiner toward the Mexican-American examinee or by the Mexican-American examinee toward the Anglo examiner may interfere with rapport. The two ethnic groups are keenly aware of the differences that divide them, and feelings of resentment – stemming from a mutual lack of understanding – are prominent (Madsen, 1964). Anglos generally know little about Mexican-American customs and values (Clark, 1959), nor are they knowledgeable about the conditions that exist in the *barrio* (section of a town in which Mexican-Americans live) (Burma, 1954). The examinee's language may serve as a reduced cue for group identification and, like skin color, it may influence the examiner-examinee relationship in a similar manner (Anastasi & Cordova, 1953).

Anglo-Americans are said to hold distorted images about Mexican-Americans. Mexican-Americans are characterized, according to Simmons (1961), as being unclean, prone to drunkenness, criminal, deceitful, and of low morality. More favorably, they are stereotyped as being musical and romantic, with a love for flowers. Most of the Mexican-Americans' images of the Anglo are formed on the basis of the Anglos' attitude toward them. Anglos are viewed as stolid, phlegmatic, cold-hearted, and distant and are said to be braggarts, conceited, inconstant, and insincere. The favorable views are that Anglos have initiative, ambition, and industriousness.

Simmons indicated that some of the stereotypes have no discernible basis in fact, while others may have at least a kernel of truth. Few if any of the stereotypes are valid and none is demonstrably true of all individuals. The negative images on the part of the Mexican-Americans about Anglo-Americans are primarily defensive rather than justificatory. The Anglo-American stereotypes of the Mexican-American as being childlike and irresponsible support the prejudiced notion that Mexican-Americans are capable only of subordinate status. Saunders (1954) suggested that Anglo stereotypes provide an easy rationalization for maintaining the status quo, thus making unnecessary any attempts to improve conditions for Mexican-Americans.

Inappropriateness of intelligence tests

Arguments against the validity of standardized intelligence tests in the assessment of Mexican-American children center around the personal, social, and cultural differences between Mexican-American children and the normative groups. Sanchez (1934) recognized over 35 years ago the necessity to consider the characteristics of the normative group and the examinee population: "A test is valid only to the extent that the items of the test are as common to each child tested as they were to the children upon whom the norms were based [p. 766]." He found that the 1916 Stanford-Binet presents vocabulary difficulties for Spanish-speaking children.

Many words were used in the 1916 Stanford-Binet, either in the specific directions or in specific responses required by the tests, that are not in the standard vocabulary of Spanish-speaking children. Shotwell (1945) reported that mentally retarded Mexican-American children performed better on the Arthur Performance Scale (Arthur, 1943) than Anglos of comparable age and intelligence. This led her to conclude that standard intelligence tests are not valid for the assessment of Mexican-Americans and other racial groups. However, this conclusion is questionable because the sample was from a limited segment of the IQ distribution, and no other ethnic groups were studied.

Cook and Arthur (1951) also reported that Mexican-American children between the ages of 6 and 16 obtained significantly lower scores on the Stanford-Binet (form not indicated) than on the Arthur Performance Scale. The results were attributed to limited language facility and to cultural differences between the Mexican-American children and the normative group. Kidd (1962) studied the Stanford-Binet (Form L) performance of Mexican-American children from both the upper and lower socio-economic classes. The results suggested that the Stanford-Binet provides a valid measure of the intellectual level of upper-class but not of lower-class Mexican-American children. Only three tests in the scale were found to be culturally fair: Paper Cutting at year levels 9 and 11 and Memory for Designs at year level 9.

Ramirez and Gonzalez (1971) noted that intelligence tests fail to measure adequately the intelligence of Mexican-American children because the language and content of the tests are inappropriate, the group is not represented in the norms, and the testing situation is atypical. An additional criticism, which may stimulate the development of new tests, is that standard tests are not suitable for Mexican-American children because their cognitive style may be primarily relational, while the test requires an analytic mode. However, the authors failed to provide conclusive evidence indicating that Mexican-Americans are more relational than analytic in their cognitive style. (See section on culture-fair tests for a discussion of cognitive style.)

Translating a test

Spanish has been used, either in the test directions only or in the complete test, to administer standardized intelligence tests to Spanish-speaking children. Keston and Jimenez (1954) were interested in determining the effects of translating the Stanford-Binet into Spanish. Form M of the Stanford-Binet was first administered in English to Mexican-American bilingual fourth-grade pupils. Four weeks later, Form L of the Stanford-Binet was administered in Spanish. On Form M, the mean IQ was 86; on Form L, the mean IQ was 72. Scores on the English version were thus significantly higher than scores on the Spanish version. Students who performed better on the Spanish version than on the English version were usually low-ability students. The authors theorized that the sample had a higher level of development in the English language than in the Spanish language. The Spanish translation is not suited to bilingual Mexican-American children because the Spanish spoken by the children contains archaisms, contaminations, and Anglicisms. The investigators contended that the development of proficiency in the Spanish language usually ceases when Mexican-American children enter grade school and begin their formal education in the English language. They concluded that while the English version of the Stanford-Binet does not give an accurate measure of the intelligence of bilingual Mexican-American children, it gives a fairer and more accurate result than the Spanish version.

Roca (1955) pointed out that there are numerous problems involved in translating an entire test. Working in Puerto Rico, he translated and adapted the WISC and Stanford-Binet (Form L). Some items were found to be too difficult, while others were too easy. On the WISC Vocabulary subtest, for example, words such as "spade," "mantis," "spangle," and "belfry" were either too easy when translated into Spanish, or else they had additional meanings. Items within subtests were also found to be of a different level of difficulty from the standard version. Thus, even after translation, a test may not be valid for Spanish-speaking children. As Sanchez (1934) noted, translating a test may be of no value if the items have not been experienced by the child.

Chandler and Plakos (1969) set out to evaluate whether Mexican-American children in classes for the educable mentally retarded might have been placed incorrectly, on the basis of scores obtained on the English version of WISC. They used the Spanish version of the WISC, Escala de Inteligencia Wechsler para Niños, which was standardized in Puerto Rico and published by The Psychological Corporation. However, the investigators modified the Spanish version of the WISC because some of the items are apparently not applicable for Mexican-American children. The Puerto Rican norms, however, were still used. In order to make the test applicable to Mexican-Americans, whose native tongue is a Spanish idiomatic to various regions in Mexico, some words were changed, such as *bola* to *pelota* and *concreto* to *cemento;* acceptable answers were expanded, so that to the question "Where is Chile?" credit was given to "in a can" or "in a field" or "in a store." Using the modified Spanish version of the WISC, the children obtained an increase of 12.45 points over their scores on the English version of the WISC. The investigators concluded that many Mexican-American children may have been placed in educable mentally retarded classes solely on the basis of performance on an invalid test (i.e., the English version of the WISC). Their procedure, however, warranted no such conclusion. Not only were standard procedures violated in administering the Spanish version of the WISC, thereby making use of the Puerto Rican norms inappropriate, but, in addition, validity data for the scores obtained on the Spanish version of the WISC by the Mexican-American children were not presented.

The Sweetwater Union High School District of Southern California agrees with Chandler and Plakos in stating that the Puerto Rican version of the WISC presents problems for use with Mexican-American children.[4] A number of examples point out

[4]M. Grossman and H. Teller, personal communication, July 1971.

needed modifications. On the Information subtest, the question concerning the distance between New York and Puerto Rico is inappropriate for Mexican-American children. A suggested substitution is the distance between Mexico D.F. and Monterey for children educated in Mexico, or the distance between New York and Chicago for those educated in the United States. A substitute for the number of pounds in a ton might be the number of meters in a kilometer. On the Arithmetic subtest, *bolitas de vidrio* could be replaced with *canicas* for the word "marbles." These and other examples indicate that the Puerto Rican version of the WISC should not be used without modification in the testing of Mexican-American children. Modifications, however, are not the final answer until questions of reliability and validity are answered.

Galvan (1968) administered the WISC in English and in Spanish to bilingual and culturally deprived Mexican-American children who were in grades 3, 4, and 5. Giving the WISC in Spanish was found to facilitate performance, primarily on the Verbal scale. However, the validity of the two-language versions was equal, as noted by the .46 correlation between the California Achievement Test and the WISC given in Spanish, and the .52 correlation between the California Achievement Test and the WISC given in English. The correlation between the two verbal scales was .53, while the correlation between the two performance scales was .97.

Holland (1960) sought to determine the effects of bilingual administration of the WISC Verbal scale in a sample of Mexican-American children in grades 1 through 5 who had been recommended for testing because of academic or emotional problems. The bilingual administration consisted of (a) giving the subtest instructions in English first, followed by repeating the instructions in Spanish if the instructions were not understood or only partially understood; and (b) giving credit to a correct answer given in either language. The test questions, however, were presented in English. The children obtained a mean bilingual Verbal scale IQ of 85, a mean English Verbal scale IQ of 81, and a mean Performance scale IQ of 91. Differences between the two Verbal scale IQs decreased from the first grade to the fifth grade. Holland suggested that the English Verbal scale IQ can be considered to represent the present level of functioning in English language skills. The bilingual Verbal scale IQ may represent the future potential for verbal skills, when the examinee's knowledge of English is approximately equal to that of Spanish. Again, this conclusion is particularly questionable in view of the fact that *neither* language is adequate, and it is very doubtful that "future potential" is adequately assessed by even the bilingual administration.

Other studies which investigated the effects of English and Spanish instructions on intelligence test scores have reported that the language in which the instructions were administered was either a significant factor or a nonsignificant factor. Mitchell (1937) and Mahakian (1939) both found that on a nonlanguage group intelligence test (Otis Classification Test) administered to Mexican-American children in grades 1 through 3, Spanish instructions resulted in higher scores than English instructions. However, in Mitchell's study, the teacher who read the instructions in Spanish was himself Spanish, while regular class teachers (apparently Anglo-Americans) gave the English language instructions. Thus, his study confounded language of instruction and ethnic membership of the tester. Anastasi and Cordova (1953) studied the effects of using Spanish and English instructions to administer Cattell's Culture Fair Intelligence Test to Puerto Rican children in grades 6 through 8. Language of instruction had no significant effect upon performance.

Mahakian (1939) administered a reading-comprehension test in English and in Spanish to bilingual Mexican-American children in grades 4 through 7. On the section of the test measuring comprehension of paragraphs, scores were higher on the English version than on the Spanish version in the fifth grade and beyond. However, on the section of the test measuring knowledge of words, the children in all the grades were able to define more Spanish than English words. Mahakian's findings, then, were equivocal concerning comparative language proficiency in bilingual Mexican-American children.

Studies which investigated the effects of translating test content or test instructions from English into Spanish indicated that such procedures are fraught with hazards. Translation of a test makes it a hybrid of neither culture. The need is for construction of tests in the native language, with native cultural norms, administered by native psychologists.

Performance on the WISC

Hewitt and Massey (1969) made several observations concerning the performance of Mexican-American children on the WISC. Their passivity, or unwillingness to engage in competition, may cause them to do poorly on all WISC timed subtests, especially on the Block Design. For Mexican-American children, the Coding subtest, however, may be the least culturally biased of the WISC subtests, in spite of its being a timed subtest; the Information and Comprehension subtests may be the most culturally biased. Mexican-American children, too, are said to have difficulty with abstractions, in seeing alternatives, and in changing their problem-solving techniques. Finally, they reported that many psychologists have noted that upon retest 3 to 5 years after initial testing, WISC Verbal scale scores remained depressed while Performance scale scores improved. Hewitt and Massey's observations remain as plausible but unconfirmed speculations until empirical support is presented.

Altus (1953) compared the WISC scores of bilingual Mexican-American children with those of monolingual Anglo-American children. The sample consisted of 11-year-old children who had been referred for screening for special classes for the mentally retarded. The Anglo children obtained significantly higher scores than the Mexican-American children on the full scale and on the Verbal scale, and on the Information, Comprehension, Similarities, Vocabulary, and Picture Completion subtests. However, the two groups did not obtain significantly different scores on the Performance scale. Altus concluded that the retardation of bilingual Mexican-American children appears to be a linguistic one.

Talerico and Brown (1963) described the WISC scores obtained by Puerto Rican children divided into three age groups (6-8, 9-11, 12-15); they had been attending a child psychiatric clinic. In all three groups, the Performance scale IQ was higher than the Verbal scale IQ by about 6 to 12 points. The largest differences between the IQs on the two scales were in the two youngest age groups. In the total group, the three easiest subtests were Picture Completion, Block Design, and Object Assembly, while the three hardest tests were Arithmetic, Information, and Vocabulary.

Christiansen and Livermore (1970) investigated the effects of both social class and ethnic origin as variables related to the WISC scores of adolescent male and female Anglo-Americans and Mexican-Americans from the middle and lower socioeconomic classes. The results indicated that social class was a more important factor in differentiating among children than ethnic origin. On all the WISC measures studied, lower-class children obtained significantly lower scores than middle-class children. However, Mexican-American children also obtained significantly lower scores than Anglo-American children on combinations of WISC subtests measuring general intelligence, retention of verbal knowledge, and ability to use verbal skills in new situations. The investigators suggested that the bilingual nature of the Mexican-American home makes it difficult for the children to acquire verbal skills needed in an Anglo culture.

Killian (1971) studied the WISC performance (together with performance on the Illinois Test of Psycholinguistic Abilities and Bender-Gestalt) of male and female Anglo-American, Mexican-American monolingual children, and Mexican-American bilingual children, who were matched on school achievement and were attending kindergarten or first grade. The school achievement scores were slightly above average. The full-scale and Performance scale IQs of the Anglo-American children ($M = 98$ and 97) were significantly higher than those of the Mexican-American bilingual children ($M = 88$ and 90), but not significantly higher than those of the Mexican-American monolingual children ($M = 92$ and 93). The Anglo-American children also obtained a significantly higher Verbal scale IQ ($M = 100$) than both Mexican-American groups (monolingual $M = 92$, bilingual $M = 88$).

Anglo-American children were significantly higher on the Comprehension and Picture Arrangement subtests than the two Mexican-American groups. In addition, at the kindergarten level, but not at the first-grade level, Anglo-American children were significantly higher on the Information subtest than the Mexican-American children. Scores on the Arithmetic, Vocabulary, Block Design, Object Assembly, and Coding subtests were not significantly different among the groups. Bilingualism did not generally play a significant role in distinguishing the performance of the two Mexican-American groups.

The WISC results, together with findings on the other two tests, suggested to Killian that the Mexican-American children did not have a profile indicating severe and early restriction of experience at home. Rather, their major difficulty seemed to be in the area of input, namely, problems with interpreting meaningful words and pictures that were presented in sequence. The results concerning the differential performance of the Anglo- and Mexican-American groups on the Information and Comprehension subtests were interpreted to mean that during the first grade the school is able, apparently, to increase the Mexican-American child's general information knowledge, but is not as successful in enhancing his understanding of social skills and values.

In Killian's study there would be little reason to expect that the Mexican-American children would have restricted experiences at home, because they were matched with Anglo-American children on achievement scores that were above average. An interesting way to interpret the results is to say that Mexican-American children with lower IQs (measured) do as well (achievement scores) as Anglo-American children with higher IQs.

NORTH AMERICAN INDIAN CHILDREN

The appropriateness of using tests standardized on white children with North American Indian children has also been questioned. Turner and Penfold (1952) described some of the handicaps of North American Indian children that interfere with their educational morale, which, in turn, are likely to affect their test performance. The children are said to lack confidence because of a long history of social failure, the absence of distinguished members, discrimination by whites, and failure of some members who have left the reservation. Additional handicaps include a lack of tradition of education, low socioeconomic level, reduced attendance in school, language deficiencies in the home, an inadequate school system, and reduced test motivation.

Other difficulties were described by McDiarmid (1971). Communication is difficult because of the many different dialects that are found among North American Indian tribes. Motivational problems arise because of differences between middle-class white children and Indian children. Middle-class white children, it is assumed, are testwise and have culturally conditioned achievement motivation. These assumptions mean that they desire to do well, are able to attend carefully to directions, and have a sense of time and competition. Indian children, in contrast, are handicapped in these areas. Slowly changing seasons may be as important to them as clock time, and competitive individualism is punished. The examiner, too, may encounter difficulty in administering the test and in interpreting test results when he meets such behaviors as infrequent speech, limited responses to test questions, and speaking softly. In the comparative study of ethnic groups, McDiarmid favors the approach of Lesser, Fifer, and Clark (1965), which focuses on patterns of differences among ethnic groups rather than on the absolute amounts of differences.

There is some evidence indicating that Indian children are more successful on the WISC Performance scale than on the WISC Verbal scale. Turner and Penfold (1952) reported that a sample of Indian children between 7 and 14 obtained a Performance scale IQ that was 11 points higher than their Verbal scale IQ. Observations of test behavior indicated that there were few errors made on the Coding subtest, while much time was taken to answer the Verbal scale items. Generally the Indian children appeared to be in greater fear of making a mistake than has been observed in white children.

Cundick (1970) studied the performance of Southwestern American Indian children in prekindergarten through sixth grade on four intelligence tests. On the WPPSI and WISC, available from prekindergarten through third grade, Verbal scale IQs were significantly lower than those for the normative groups (obtained from the test manuals) in all of the grades tested. Performance scale IQs, on the other hand, were significantly lower than the normative groups only at the prekindergarten level. Schooling thus did not seem to raise Verbal scale IQs for these children during their first 4 years of education. The mean Draw-a-Man IQs, available for all of the grades studied, were very close to the expected mean IQ of 100 after the second grade. The PPVT, also available for all grades studied, showed, in sharp contrast, a narrow range of mean IQs (53 to 69), with IQs dropping lower after the third grade. The results of Cundick's study demonstrated the need to select tests carefully in the assessment of ethnic groups, and to determine for each specific population the degree to which different tests are comparable.

JENSEN'S ASSOCIATIVE-ABILITY AND COGNITIVE-ABILITY THEORY

Jensen (1970b) developed a theory of mental functioning which seems to explain the results of numerous investigations which have studied cognitive processes of culturally disadvantaged children. He postulated the existence of two types of abilities: Level 1, or associative ability, and Level 2, or cognitive ability. The two types of abilities are viewed as having underlying genetic processes that are essentially different. While the abilities may be correlated, they also may have different developmental rates. Level 2 functions are partly dependent on Level 1 functions, but the reverse does not hold. Current behavioral tests are likely to measure both levels, but different tests measure the abilities to different degrees. Examples of Level 1 abilities are digit-span memory, free recall, serial learning, and paired-associate learning. Level 2 abilities include conceptual- and abstract-reasoning tasks.

Standard intelligence tests are usually a mixture of Level 1 and Level 2 functions, but most measure Level 2 ability. Spearman's g factor — a capacity for abstract reasoning — is a major factor in most intelligence tests. In the WISC, Digit Span forward and Digit Symbol subtests are relatively pure measures of Level 1 abilities. The Vocabulary subtest and Information subtest contain items which depend upon previous learning. Level 1 abilities are involved in these two subtests (and others), especially for the easier, more concrete words and simple factual-content questions. The Arithmetic reasoning problems, especially the more difficult ones, the Similarities items, and the Block Design items likely reflect Level 2 abilities. Jensen classified the Porteus Maze Test as being more a measure of Level 1 than of Level 2 processes. Tests of immediate memory span are good measures of Level 1 processes.

Jensen noted that Levels 1 and 2 are essentially orthogonal (uncorrelated) to Cattell's (1963) fluid and crystallized general intelligence. Fluid intelligence is a basic capacity for learning and problem solving, independent of education and experience. Crystallized intelligence is the result of the interaction of the individual's fluid intelligence and his culture; it consists of learned knowledge and skills. Digit-span tests measure fluid intelligence *and* Level 1 abilities, while the Progressive Matrices test and Cattell's Culture Fair Intelligence Test measure fluid intelligence *and* Level 2 abilities.

Socioeconomic status is postulated to be largely independent of Level 1 abilities but correlated with Level 2 abilities. Hypothetical growth curves for Level 1 and Level 2 abilities in middle and low socioeconomic classes suggest that in both classes, Level 1 abilities are nearly equal throughout the developmental period, while Level 2 abilities are not. Level 2 abilities show a progressively widening cleavage in development, in favor of the middle and upper socioeconomic classes.

The hypothetical growth curves can help to explain the finding that low socioeconomic children do progressively poorer in school ("cumulative deficit" theory). The school's curriculum becomes increasingly abstract and conceptual (Level 2 abilities) with advancing grades, and children with below-average Level 2 ability, regardless of their Level 1 standing, will therefore be at an increasing disadvantage. Jensen proposed that the educational process for low socioeconomic children with below-average Level 2 ability be revitalized by having instruction in the basic school subjects more in accord with Level 1 processes than with the Level 2 processes currently employed.

Jensen suggested that memory span is a more adequate measure of general intelligence than is generally believed. However, memory span is not a unitary ability. Digit Span forward appears to be an almost pure measure of Level 1 abilities, while Digit Span reversed, a task calling for a transformation of input, involves some Level 2 ability. Digit Span has a substantial correlation with IQ in the normative population of the Wechsler and Stanford-Binet tests, but in the low socioeconomic classes the correlation is negligible. Jensen attributed this finding to a deficiency in Level 2 mechanisms in the low socioeconomic classes. Digit-span tests and general IQ tests, therefore, appear to measure different mental abilities.

In severe grades of mental retardation, Levels 1 and 2 are both markedly deficient. It is in the area of the milder forms of mental retardation, especially those termed "familial," where Jensen's theory takes on importance. He proposed that *primary retardation* be the term used to refer to deficiency in Level 1 abilities, and *secondary retardation,* the term for deficiency in Level 2 abilities. Individuals who achieve IQs on conventional tests in the range between -1 and -2 *SD*s below the mean (i.e., IQs of 70 to 85) are largely from groups called "culturally disadvantaged." It is unfortunate that these individuals are labeled "retarded," because many of them are average in Level 1 abilities. Further, once they leave school they are not perceived as being retarded. Jensen maintained that these children are, in actuality, neither "slow learners" nor possessors of a pattern of abilities that is the result of cultural deprivation. Jensen marshaled an impressive array of evidence to support his theory. While his theory is not without criticism (e.g., Humphreys & Dachler, 1969; Voyat, 1970), he has given the fields of psychology and education a stimulus for action and has shown how intelligence tests can aid not only in the understanding of mental ability but also in the application of teaching methods.

VALUE AND VALIDITY OF INTELLIGENCE TESTS

Value of intelligence tests

Intelligence tests still have their adherents. Despite the frequent criticisms leveled against the IQ, a child's IQ, obtained in a standard situation, has more behavioral correlates than any other psychological measure (Kohlberg & Zigler, 1967). Tests permit the measurement of change, provide information about the individual's initial status, and help in understanding the nature of intelligence and the effects of environmental variables (Anastasi, 1967). Test scores of underprivileged minority children are useful indices of immediate or present functioning (McNemar, 1964).

In related areas of testing, Ebel (1964) and Messick and Anderson (1970) expressed concern about the social consequences of *not* testing. If educational tests are abandoned, it will become more difficult to encourage and reward individual efforts to learn. Programs will be difficult to evaluate, and educational opportunities might be based more on ancestry and influence and less on aptitude and merit. Decisions on curriculum would be based less on evidence and more on prejudice and caprice. Thus, the consequences of not testing might be to increase bias and discrimination.

Lorge (1966) noted that tests point out differences among groups. Because tests may reveal the inequalities of opportunity available to various groups, they may also provide the stimulus for social inventions to facilitate the maximum development of each individual's potentialities. Thus, knowing that differences exist may lead to the gradual disappearance of some kinds of bias. Brim (1965) suggested that minority groups should be favorably inclined toward use of ability tests because tests constitute a universal standard of competence and potential. Other selection methods may decrease the opportunities of minority-group members. While tests actually have many of these advantages, the material covered in the present review shows how diligently safeguards must be applied to the administration, scoring, and interpretation of tests, if they are to have value.

The Stanford-Binet, which was standardized on an American-born white population, can be considered as the representative of standard intelligence tests. Since this test bears the brunt of criticism directed against all intelligence tests, it is reassuring to find that studies have usually reported that culturally disadvantaged children and children of ethnic minority groups prefer the Stanford-Binet to other instruments (e.g., WPPSI) and obtain higher scores on the Binet than on other intelligence tests (see validity subsection and culture-fair section). The explanation of Fagan, Broughton, Allen, Clark, and Emerson (1969) appears to be a reasonable one for accounting for certain of the findings that concern the Stanford-Binet test:

The lower-class child is frequently shy, nonverbal, activity-oriented, and sensitive to failure. The frequent switching of materials, the briefer verbal demands, and the less apparent failure experiences made the Binet more appropriate [than the WPPSI] [p. 609].

Validity of intelligence tests

Studies investigating the validity of standardized intelligence tests with populations of ethnic minority groups usually report validity coefficients which are similar to those obtained with white populations. An extensive investigation of the Stanford-Binet (Form L-M) by Kennedy, Van de Riet, and White (1963), with a sample of 1,800 Negro elementary school children between the ages of 5 and 16 who were living in the southeastern United States, indicated that there was a .69 correlation between the Stanford-Binet MA and scores on the California Achievement Test. The Binet also correlated significantly with teachers' ratings and with grades in academic areas. Bruininks and Feldman (1970) reported that the Stanford-Binet (Form L-M) correlated significantly (r = .67) with the Metropolitan Achievement Test in a sample of disadvantaged children, 80% of whom were Negro, between the ages of 9 and 11. Olivier and Barclay (1967) reported that in a sample of Negro and white children between the ages of 4 and 6 enrolled in a Head Start program, Stanford-Binet tests were found to have generally the same level of difficulty that they have in the normative population.

Johnson and Johnson (1971) found that the Stanford-Binet (Form L-M) and the Slosson Intelligence Test, a test similar to the Stanford-Binet, yielded higher scores than either the PPVT or the Draw-a-Man test, with a sample of 5-year-old Negro and Mexican-American children in Head Start programs. Hall (1970) found that PPVT scores were related significantly to reading achievement scores in a sample of culturally disadvantaged Negro first graders.

There have been at least two reports indicating that the WISC, as well as other intelligence tests, may not be appropriate for Negro children. Young and Bright (1954) noted that WISC scores were not valid for their sample of Southern Negro children between the ages of 10 and 13 because the children seemed to be functioning effectively in their own environment, even though they had obtained low scores. Cooper, York, Daston, and Adams (1967) found that of four tests (WISC, Revised Beta Examination, Ammons Full Range Picture Vocabulary Test, and Porteus Maze Test), the Porteus Maze Test was the only one capable of differentiating Southern Negro adolescents who were behaviorally retarded from those who were not behaviorally retarded.

The position taken by some writers — that IQs are not valid for some persons because they are functioning effectively in their own environment — does not do justice to the concept of the validity of intelligence tests. Effective functioning in one's own environment is not the criterion by which the validity of the IQ is determined. The effectiveness of a person's functioning is in large part dependent upon his particular milieu. What is effect in one setting may be ineffective in another.

Intelligence tests are intended to measure factors that pertain to the culture as a whole; therefore, their validity rests on criteria derived from the general culture and not from any specific subcultural group.

RECOMMENDATIONS

Many different recommendations have appeared concerning the assessment of ethnic minority children and culturally disadvantaged children. Some have favored a moratorium on testing (Davis, 1971; Williams, 1970a), while others advocated ways in which testing can become a more useful tool in the educational process. Anastasi (1961), Davis (1971), and Jensen (1970a) all agreed that a wide range of mental tasks should be given when testing ethnic minority groups. Anastasi noted that neither a single test score nor any small number of scores can provide an adequate picture of the intellectual abilities of a group. The sampling of cognitive abilities, according to Jensen, is especially important in order to discover the strengths and weaknesses of children from educationally disadvantaged backgrounds, since there may be more variability in their pattern of abilities than in children who are not disadvantaged. Jensen advocated the use of tests of g that are free from obvious cultural content for the assessment of educationally disadvantaged children, in order to select children with potentially strong academic aptitude. Examples of such tests are the Progressive Matrices (Raven, 1952), Culture Fair Intelligence Test (Cattell, 1959), and Domino Test (Gough & Domino, 1963).

Mercer (1971) suggested that correcting the culture-bound perspective of current intelligence tests would require the establishment of separate norms for various sociocultural groups. A person's score on an intelligence test would then be interpreted with reference to both standard norms and his own sociocultural group norms. The former comparison would reflect how the person stands in relationship to the general population of the United States, while the latter comparison would reflect the amount of knowledge the person has acquired about the culture of the dominant society compared with others who have had comparable opportunities to learn. A score interpreted with reference to the standard norms might indicate how far the person has to go in order to participate in the dominant culture, while a score interpreted with reference to the sociocultural norms might indicate the probability that the person might reach a particular level in the dominant culture, if given adequate educational experiences.

Clark (1960) noted that there is a need for the development of tests which will better reflect the potential intelligence of children from culturally disadvantaged groups and a need to make intelligent and accurate interpretations of results, particularly when the results are used as a basis for making school judgments and class assignments of children that will affect their future lives. Newland (1970) indicated that present and future tests are needed to evaluate the psychological processes by which children learn; tests should not be used solely to sample what has been learned and to infer capacity to learn from their scores. Milgram (1970) advocated changing the curriculum and teaching approaches for black children, rather than devising new tests. Abolishing tests will not remove the adverse conditions which black children find in the community and in the schools.

The assessment of Mexican-American children will improve when changes are made both in the educational system and in some of the children's attitudes, perceptions, and behaviors, according to Ramirez et al. (1971). These authors, along with Holland (1960), suggested that bilingual education may prove to be valuable, since it may lead to greater facility in both English and Spanish. Ramirez et al. want to involve the parents in the educational process by helping them learn ways of reinforcing their children's achievements. In working with Mexican-American children (as well as with children from other groups), it is important to understand the examinee's culture and community. The examiner who is able to help Mexican-American children feel pride in their native language and culture and to learn Spanish himself will be making important strides in facilitating the educational process (Nava, 1970).

Alternatives to the standard goals of classification in the assessment process are being offered. E.B. Williams (1971) indicated that the proper task of testing is to discover ways to help the individual; it is not to exclude individuals from entering courses of study or occupations. Education should change from focusing on the selection of individuals to gaining more knowledge about individuals and ways in which they can be served. Who is to determine the standard, and for whose benefit has the standard been defined? asked Williams. Holtzman (1971) pointed out that the need for educational reform has led to the development, in many fields of learning, of individualized instruction involving self-paced learning. The curriculum consists of units of instruction or modules which are linked together. Testing consists of evaluating the extent to which the individual has met the training objectives (e.g., the learning of modules), rather than normative testing for measuring individual differences.

Cole and Bruner (1971) suggested that the classroom teacher involved with educating children from "disadvantaged" cultural groups (a) should recognize that educational difficulties displayed by the children represent a difference rather than a special kind of intellectual difficulty; and (b) should concentrate on how to get the child to transfer skills he already possesses to the tasks at hand, rather than attempt to create new intellectual structures. Barnes (1971) would like to see the modal approach to the study of lower-status children (and, in particular, black children) replaced by a social-systems approach. The modal approach focuses on the individual or his family and emphasizes mental health, treatment, and pathology. The social-systems approach emphasizes the interdependence of child and family with other levels of society, the heterogeneity of blacks (and other oppressed groups), the recognition of the black community as a complex social system, and the shift of focus from behaviors of individuals to recurrent interchanges between people. It will be necessary to recognize explicitly the minority child's community, group, and culture in order to break his familiar cycle of educational failure.

Deutsch et al. (1964) pointed out that the handicaps of minority-group children are often so great that their test scores may have meanings different from those of nonminority-group children, even when the scores are numerically the same. Test scores should not be accepted as fixed levels of either performance or potential; instead, they may be used to determine the magnitude of the deprivation which is to be overcome by a planned program of remedial activities. Scores can also be used to compare disadvantaged children with one another. Still another way in which scores can be useful is to compare the child's current test performance with his previous test performance. In the last analysis, the examiner and other test users must accept the responsibilities involved in interpreting and in using educational and psychological tests.

Many comparisons depend upon tests, but they also depend upon *our* intelligence, our good will, and our sense of responsibility to make the proper comparison at the proper time and to undertake proper remedial and compensatory action as a result. The misuse of tests with minority group children, or in any situation, is a serious breach of professional ethics. Their proper use is a sign of professional and personal maturity [p. 144].

CONCLUSION

There may be no answer to the question of whether or not current standardized intelligence tests should be used in the assessment of ethnic minority-group children and culturally disadvantaged children because the question is not properly phrased. The better question is, When and how should they be used? Another question: What are the tasks to be done if assessment is to be better? Obviously, when children differ markedly from the normative group or when they cannot speak English, standard tests should not be used in decision-making situations. Some evidence indicates that intelligence tests have acceptable levels of concurrent validity for ethnic minority children and culturally disadvantaged children, although for some groups less acceptable validity coefficients appear. However, the type of validity in question must always be considered. Little is known about the long-range predictive validity of intelligence tests for ethnic minority-group children and for culturally disadvantaged children. Additional research is sorely needed. Objections to intelligence tests may be overcome if tests are used as measures of outcomes of education and not as screening devices (cf. Thorndike, 1971).

The lack of supporting data for the statements of many writers concerning the effects of the examiner's race on the examinee's performance does not mean that the examiner can be indifferent to the examinee's race. He must be extremely careful when testing examinees of races or cultures other than his own. He should be alert to any nuances in his or the examinee's performance which suggest that an unreliable performance is in the making. Every attempt must be made to elicit the examinee's best performance without, in the process, modifying standard procedures. A competent examiner should have the resources to *administer* an individual test of intelligence to examinees of different races and cultures. Cultural gaps between the examiner and examinee can create communication problems that affect not only rapport but also the examinee's ability to understand and to respond to the test questions according to the intent of the test constructors. Testing examinees from cultures different from that of the examiner is a demanding task; there are no simple solutions. The problem, of course, is exaggerated when the examinee belongs to a culture different from that of the standardization group. However, transcending the examiner-examinee relationship in affecting test performance are problems of test standardization, cultural deprivation, and cultural milieu.

If there is a need to evaluate ethnic minority-group children and culturally disadvantaged children, which test or tests can be used? There are no generally accepted tools that can be used to evaluate children from ethnic minority groups, culturally disadvantaged backgrounds, and other "different" groups. All current tests can be criticized on some grounds. Although educators and psychologists must be responsive to the needs of minority-group children and acknowledge the pleas of individuals like R.L. Williams, they will likely need to use tests in their educational programs. The shortcomings and hazards of using standardized intelligence tests with minority-group and culturally disadvantaged children have been documented in this review. In addition, excellent recommendations have appeared which may pave the way for more appropriate uses of tests. The writer supports the position presented by the work group of the Society for the Psychological Study of Social Issues (Deutsch et al., 1964). Standardized intelligence tests may be used, but only if their shortcomings and difficulties are recognized when applied to the evaluation of children coming from ethnic minority and culturally disadvantaged groups. Tests should never be used if they do not contribute to the development of the child or to the body of knowledge of a field of study. Obviously, no tests should be used in ways, or under conditions, that would physically or emotionally harm any child. However, it is difficult to spell out convincingly how tests *do* contribute, especially if the audience represents ethnic minority-group members. Finally, tests are needed which can evaluate the thought processes, modes of perceiving, and modes of expression for different cultures and which also accord some recognition to the differing contents in different cultures.

References

Abramson, T. The influence of examiner race on first-grade and kindergarten subjects' Peabody Picture Vocabulary Test scores. *Journal of Educational Measurement,* 1969, **6**, 241-246.

Ali, F., & Costello, J. Modification of the Peabody Picture Vocabulary Test. *Developmental Psychology,* 1971, **5**, 86-91.

Altus, G.T. WISC patterns of a selective sample of bilingual school children. *Journal of Genetic Psychology,* 1953, **83**, 241-248.

Anastasi, A. *Differential psychology.* (3rd ed.) New York: Macmillan, 1958.

Anastasi, A. Psychological tests: Uses and abuses. *Teachers College Record,* 1961, **62**, 389-393.

Anastasi, A. Psychology, psychologists, and psychological testing. *American Psychologist,* 1967, **22**, 297-306.

Anastasi, A., & Cordova, F.A. Some effects of bilingualism upon the intelligence test performance of Puerto Rican children in New York City. *Journal of Educational Psychology,* 1953, **44**, 1-19.

Anastasi, A., & Foley, J.P., Jr. *Differential psychology.* (2nd ed.) New York: Macmillan, 1949.

Arthur, G. *A point scale of performance tests. Vol. I. Clinical manual.* (2nd ed.) New York: Commonwealth Fund, 1943.

Atchison, C.O. Use of the Wechsler Intelligence Scale for Children with eighty mentally defective Negro children. *American Journal of Mental Deficiency,* 1965, **60**, 378-379.

Baratz, S.S., & Baratz, J.C. Early childhood intervention: The social science base of institutional racism. *Harvard Educational Review,* 1970, **40**, 29-50.

Barclay, A., & Yater, A.C. Comparative study of the Wechsler Preschool and Primary scale of Intelligence and the Stanford-Binet Intelligence Scale, Form L-M, among culturally deprived children. *Journal of Consulting and Clinical Psychology,* 1969, **33**, 257.

Barnes, E.J. Cultural retardation or shortcomings of assessment techniques. In *47th Annual International Convention. Denver, Colorado, April 1969.* Washington, D.C.: Council for Exceptional Children, 1969.

Barnes, E.J. The utilization of behavioral and social sciences in minority group education: Some critical implications. In W.R. Rhine (Chm.), Ethnic minority issues on the utilization of behavioral and social science in a pluralistic society. Symposium presented at the American Psychological Association, Washington, D.C., September 1971.

Beberfall, L. Some linguistic problems of the Spanish-speaking people of Texas. *Modern Language Journal,* 1958, **42**, 87-90.

Bennett, G.K. Response to Robert Williams. *Counseling Psychologist,* 1970, **2**(2), 88-89.

Berdie, R.F. The Ad Hoc Committee on Social Impact of Psychological Assessment. *American Psychologist,* 1965, **20**, 143-146.

Bereiter, C. The future of individual differences. *Harvard Educational Review,* 1969, **39**, 310-318.

Blackwood, B. A study of testing in relation to anthropology. *Mental Measurements Monographs,* 1927, **4**, 1-119.

Brim, L.G. American attitudes toward intelligence tests. *American Psychologist,* 1965, **20**, 125-130.

Brown, F. An experimental and critical study of the intelligence of Negro and white kindergarten children. *Journal of Genetic Psychology,* 1944, **65**, 161-175.

Bruininks, R.H., & Feldman, D.H. Creativity, intelligence, and achievement among disadvantaged children. *Psychology in the Schools,* 1970, **7**, 260-264.

Brunswik, E. *Representative design in the planning of psychological research.* Berkeley, Calif.: University of California Press, 1958.

Burma, J.H. *Spanish-speaking groups in the United States.* Durham, N.C.: Duke University Press, 1954.

Caldwell, M.B., & Knight, D. The effect of Negro and white examiners on Negro intelligence test performance. *Journal of Negro Education,* 1970, **39**, 177-179.

Caldwell, M.B., & Smith, T.A. Intellectual structure of southern Negro children. *Psychological Reports,* 1968, **23**, 63-71.

Canady, H.G. The effect of "rapport" on the I.Q.: A new approach to the problem of racial psychology. *Journal of Negro Education,* 1936, **5**, 209-219.

Cattell, R.B. *Handbook for the Culture Fair Intelligence Test: A measure of "g."* Champaign, Ill.: Institute for Personality and Ability Testing, 1959.

Cattell, R.B. Theory of fluid and crystalized intelligence: A critical experiment. *Journal of Educational Psychology,* 1963, **54**, 1-22.

Chandler, J.T., & Plakos, J. Spanish-speaking pupils classified as educable mentally retarded. *Integrated Education,* 1969, **7**(6), 28-33.

Chavez, S.J. Preserve their language heritage. *Childhood Education,* 1956, **33**, 165, 185.

Christiansen, T., & Livermore, G. A comparison of Anglo-American and Spanish-American children on the WISC. *Journal of Social Psychology,* 1970, **81**, 9-14.

Claiborn, W.L. Expectancy effects in the classroom: A failure to replicate. *Journal of Educational Psychology,* 1969, **60**, 377-383.

Clark, K.B. Psychodynamic implications of prejudice toward children from a minority group. In M.G. Gottsegen & G.B. Gottsegen (Eds.), *Professional school psychology.* Vol. 1. New York: Grune & Stratton, 1960.

Clark, K.B. *Dark ghetto.* New York: Harper, 1967.

Clark, M. *Health in the Mexican American culture.* Los Angeles: University of California Press, 1959.

Cohen, R.A. Conceptual styles, culture conflict, and nonverbal tests of intelligence. *American Anthropologist,* 1969, **71**, 828-856.

Cole, M., & Bruner, J.S. Cultural differences and inferences about psychological processes. *American Psychologist,* 1971, **26**, 867-876.

Cook, J.M., & Arthur, G. Intelligence ratings for 97 Mexican children in St. Paul, Minn. *Journal of Exceptional Children,* 1951, **18**, 14-15, 31.

Cooper, G.D., York, M.W., Daston, P.G., & Adams, H.B. The Porteus Test and various measures of intelligence with Southern Negro adolescents. *American Journal of Mental Deficiency,* 1967, **71**, 787-792.

Costello, J. Effects of pretesting and examiner characteristics on test performance of young disadvantaged children. *Proceedings of the 78th Annual Convention of the American Psychological Association,* 1970, **5**, 309-310.

Costello, J., & Dickie, J. Leiter and Stanford-Binet IQ's of preschool disadvantaged children. *Developmental Psychology,* 1970, **2**, 314.

Cronbach, L.J. Heredity, environment, and educational policy. *Harvard Educational Review,* 1969, **39**, 338-347.

Crow, J.F. Genetic theories and influences: Comments on the value of diversity. *Harvard Educational Review,* 1969, **39**, 301-309.

Cundick, B.P. Measures of intelligence on Southwest Indian students. *Journal of Social Psychology,* 1970, **81**, 151-156.

Davis, A., & Eells, K. *Manual for the Davis-Eells Test of General Intelligence on Problem Solving Ability.* Yonkers, N.Y.: World Book, 1953.

Davis, W.M., Jr. Are there solutions to the problems of testing black Americans? In M.M. Meier (Chm.), Some answers to ethnic concerns about psychological testing in the schools. Symposium presented at the American Psychological Association, Washington, D.C., September 1971.

Deutsch, M., Fishman, J.A., Kogan, L., North, R., & Whiteman, M. Guidelines for testing minority group children. *Journal of Social Issues,* 1964, **20**, 129-145.

Donahue, D., & Sattler, J.M. Personality variables affecting WAIS scores. *Journal of Consulting and Clinical Psychology,* 1971, **36**, 441.

Dreger, R.M., & Miller, K.S. Comparative psychological studies of Negroes and whites in the United States: 1959-1965. *Psychological Bulletin,* 1968, **70** (3, Pt. 2).

Ebel, R.L. The social consequences of educational testing. *School and Society,* 1964, **92**, 331-334.

Eisenberg, L., Berlin, C.I., Dill, A., & Frank, S. Class and race effects on the intelligibility of monosyllables. *Child Development,* 1968, **39**, 1077-1089.

Elkind, D. Piagetian and psychometric conceptions of intelligence. *Harvard Educational Review,* 1969, **39**, 319-337.

Ellenberger, H. Cultural aspects of mental illness. *American Journal of Psychotherapy,* 1960, **16**, 158-173.

Fagan, J., Broughton, E., Allen, M., Clark, B., & Emerson, P. Comparison of the Binet and WPPSI with lower-class five-year-olds. *Journal of Consulting and Clinical Psychology,* 1969, **33**, 607-609.

Fleming, E.S., & Anttonen, R.G. Teacher expectancy or My Fair Lady. *American Educational Research Journal*, 1971, **8**, 241-252.

Forrester, B.J., & Klaus, R.A. The effect of race of the examiner on intelligence test scores of Negro kindergarten children. *Peabody Papers in Human Development*, 1964, **2**, 1-7.

Galvan, R.R. *Bilingualism as it relates to intelligence test scores and school achievement among culturally deprived Spanish-American children.* (Doctoral dissertation, East Texas State University) Ann Arbor, Mich.: University Microfilms, 1968, No. 68-1131.

Garth, T.R. The problem of racial psychology. *Journal of Abnormal and Social Psychology*, 1922, **17**, 215-219.

Gough, H.G., & Domino, G. The D 48 Test as a measure of general ability among grade school children. *Journal of Consulting Psychology*, 1963, **27**, 344-349.

Gozali, J., & Meyen, E.L. The influence of the teacher expectancy phenomenon on the academic performances of educable mentally retarded pupils in special classes. *Journal of Special Education*, 1970, **4**, 417-424.

Hall, J.C. *A comparative study of selected measures of intelligence as predictors of first-grade reading achievement in a culturally disadvantaged population.* (Doctoral dissertation, Temple University) Ann Arbor, Mich.: University Microfilms, 1970, No. 70-16, 669.

Halpern, F.C. Clinicians must listen! *School Psychologist Newsletter*, 1971, **25**(2), 15-17.

Heffernan, H. Some solutions to problems of students of Mexican descent. *Bulletin of the National Association of Secondary School Principals*, 1955, **39**(209), 43-53.

Heller, C.S. *Mexican American youth: Forgotten youth at the crossroads.* New York: Random House, 1966.

Hertzig, M.E., & Birch, H.G. Longitudinal course of measured intelligence in preschool children of different social and ethnic backgrounds. *American Journal of Orthopsychiatry*, 1971, **41**, 416-426.

Hewitt, P., & Massey, J.O. *Clinical clues from the WISC.* Palo Alto, Calif.: Consulting Psychologists Press, 1969.

Higgins, C., & Sivers, C.H. A comparison of Stanford-Binet and colored Raven Progressive Matrices IQs for children with low socioeconomic status. *Journal of Consulting Psychology*, 1958, **22**, 465-468.

Hilgard, E.R. *Introduction to psychology.* (2nd ed.) New York: Harcourt Brace Jovanovich, 1957.

Hirsch, J. Behavior-genetic analysis and its biosocial consequences. *Seminars in Psychiatry*, 1970, **2**(1), 89-105.

Holland, W.R. Language barrier as an educational problem of Spanish-speaking children. *Exceptional Children*, 1960, **27**, 42-50.

Holtzman, W.H. The changing world of mental measurement and its social significance. *American Psychologist*, 1971, **26**, 546-553.

Hudson, L. Intelligence, race, and the selection of data. *Race,* 1971, **12**, 283-292.

Hughes, R.B., & Lessler, K. A comparison of WISC and Peabody scores of Negro and white rural school children. *American Journal of Mental Deficiency,* 1965, **69**, 877-880.

Humphreys, L.G., & Dachler, H.P. Jensen's theory of intelligence: A rebuttal. *Journal of Educational Psychology,* 1969, **60**, 432-433.

Hunt, J. McV. Has compensatory education failed? Has it been attempted? *Harvard Educational Review,* 1969, **39**, 278-300.

Jensen, A.R. How much can we boost IQ and scholastic achievement? *Harvard Educational Review,* 1969, **39**, 1-123.

Jensen, A.R. Another look at culture-fair testing. In J. Hellmuth (Ed.), *Disadvantaged child.* Vol. 3. New York: Brunner/Mazel, 1970. (a)

Jensen, A.R. A theory of primary and secondary familial mental retardation. In N.R. Ellis (Ed.), *International review of research in mental retardation.* Vol. 4. New York: Academic Press, 1970. (b)

Johnson, D.L., & Johnson, C.A. Comparison of four intelligence tests used with culturally disadvantaged children. *Psychological Reports,* 1971, **28**, 209-210.

Johnson, R.C., & Medinnus, G.R. *Child psychology: Behavior and development.* New York: Wiley, 1965.

Kagan J.S. *Understanding children.* New York: Harcourt Brace Jovanovich, 1971.

Kagan, J.S. Inadequate evidence and illogical conclusions. *Harvard Educational Review,* 1969, **39**, 274-277.

Kagan, S., & Madsen, M.C. Cooperation and competition of Mexican, Mexican-American, and Anglo-American children of two ages under four instructional sets. *Developmental Psychology,* 1971, **5**, 32-39.

Kennedy, W.A., Van de Riet, V., & White, J.C., Jr. Use of the Terman-Merrill abbreviated scale on the 1960 Stanford-Binet Form L-M on Negro elementary school children of the southeastern United States. *Journal of Consulting Psychology,* 1963, **27**, 456-457.

Keston, M.J., & Jimenez, C. A study of the performance on English and Spanish editions of the Stanford-Binet Intelligence Test by Spanish American children. *Journal of Genetic Psychology,* 1954, **85**, 262-269.

Kidd, A.H. The culture-fair aspects of Cattell's test of g: Culture-free. *Journal of Genetic Psychology,* 1962, **101**, 343-364.

Killian, L.R. WISC, Illinois Test of Psycholinguistic Abilities, and Bender Visual Motor Gestalt Test performance of Spanish-American kindergarten and first-grade school children. *Journal of Consulting and Clinical Psychology,* 1971, **37**, 38-43.

Klineberg, O. *Race differences.* New York: Harper, 1935.

Klineberg, O. Tests of Negro intelligence. In O. Klineberg (Ed.), *Characteristics of the American Negro.* New York: Harper, 1944.

Kluckhohn, F.R., & Strodtbeck, F.L. *Variations in value orientations.* Evanston, Ill.: Row, Peterson, 1961.

Kohlberg, L., & Zigler, E. The impact of cognitive maturity on the development of sex-role attitude in the years 4 to 8. *Genetic Psychology Monographs*, 1967, **75**, 89-165.

LaBelle, T.J. *Attitudes and academic achievement among male and female Anglo and Spanish American fifth grade students.* (Doctoral dissertation, University of New Mexico) Ann Arbor, Mich.: University Microfilms, 1970, No. 70-17, 287.

Labov, W. The logic of nonstandard English. In F. Williams (Ed.), *Language and poverty.* Chicago: Markham, 1970.

Leland, H. Testing the disadvantaged. In W.C. Rhodes (Chm.), Use and misuse of standardized intelligence tests in psychological and educational research and practice. Symposium presented at the American Psychological Association, Washington, D.C., September 1971.

Lesser, G.S., Fifer, G., & Clark, D.H. Mental abilities of children from different social-class and cultural groups. *Child Development Monographs,* 1965, **30**(4, Whole No. 102).

Levine, M. Psychological testing of children. In M.L. Hoffman & L.W. Hoffman (Eds.), *Review of child development research.* Vol. 2. New York: Russell Sage Foundation, 1966.

Liddle, G.P. The school psychologist's role with the culturally handicapped. In J.F. Magary (Ed.), *School psychological services.* Englewood Cliffs, N.J.: Prentice-Hall, 1967.

Linton, T.H. *Sociocultural characteristics, alienation from school, and achievement among Mexican-American and Anglo sixth grade students.* (Doctoral dissertation, New Mexico State University) Ann Arbor, Mich.: University Microfilms, 1971, No. 71-2872.

Lipsitz, S. Effect of the race of the examiner on results of intelligence test performance of Negro and white children. Unpublished master's thesis, Long Island University, 1969.

Lorge, I. Difference or bias in tests of intelligence. In A. Anastasi (Ed.), *Testing problems in perspective: 25th anniversary volume of topical readings from the Invitational Conference on Testing Problems.* Washington, D.C.: American Council on Education, 1966.

Madsen, M.C., & Shapira, A. Cooperative and competitive behavior of urban Afro-American, Anglo-American, Mexican-American, and Mexican village children. *Developmental Psychology,* 1970, **3**, 16-20.

Madsen, W. *Mexican Americans of South Texas,* New York: Holt, 1964.

Mahakian, C. Measuring intelligence and reading capacity of Spanish-speaking children. *Elementary School Journal,* 1939, **39**, 760-768.

Manuel, H.T. *Spanish-speaking children of the Southwest: Their education and the public welfare.* Austin: University of Texas Press, 1965.

Masland, R.L., Sarason, S.B., & Gladwin, T. *Mental subnormality,* New York: Basic Books, 1958.

Mason, E.P. Comparison of personality characteristics of junior high students from American Indian, Mexican, and Caucasian ethnic backgrounds. *Journal of Social Psychology,* 1967, **73**, 145-155.

Mason, E.P. Cross-validation study of personality characteristics of junior high students from American Indian, Mexican, and Caucasian ethnic backgrounds. *Journal of Social Psychology,* 1969, **77**, 15-24.

McDiarmid, G.L. The hazards of testing Indian children. In F.L. Denmark (Chm.), Implications of minority group testing for more effective learning. Symposium presented at the American Psychological Association, Washington, D.C., September 1971.

McNemar, Q. Lost: Our intelligence? Why? *American Psychologist,* 1964, **19**, 871-882.

Mercer, J.R. Sociocultural factors in labeling mental retardates. *Peabody Journal of Education,* 1971, **48**, 188-203.

Messick, S., & Anderson, S. Educational testing, individual development, and social responsibility. *Counseling Psychologist,* 1970, **2**(2), 80-88.

Milgram, N.A. Danger: Chauvinism, scapegoatism, and euphemism. *Clinical Child Psychology Newsletter,* 1970, **9**(3), 2-3.

Miller, J.O., & Phillips, J. A preliminary evaluation of the Head Start and other metropolitan Nashville kindergartens. Unpublished manuscript, Demonstration and Research Center for Early Education, George Peabody College for Teachers, Nashville, 1966.

Mitchell, A.J. The effect of bilingualism in the measurement of intelligence. *Elementary School Journal,* 1937, **38**, 29-37.

Moore, J.W. *Mexican Americans.* Englewood Cliffs, N.J.: Prentice-Hall, 1970.

Mundy, L., & Maxwell, A.E. Assessment of the feebleminded. *British Journal of Medical Psychology,* 1958, **31**, 201-210.

Nava, J. Cultural backgrounds and barriers that affect learning by Spanish-speaking children. In J.H. Burma (Ed.), *Mexican-Americans in the United States: A reader.* Cambridge, Mass.: Schenkman, 1970.

Newland, T.E. Testing minority group children. *Clinical Child Psychology Newsletter,* 1970, **9**(3), 5.

Olivier, K., & Barclay, A. Stanford-Binet and Goodenough-Harris Test performances of Head Start children. *Psychological Reports,* 1967, **20**, 1175-1179.

Palmer, J.O. *The psychological assessment of children.* New York: Wiley, 1970.

Peck, R.F., & Galliani, C. Intelligence, ethnicity, and social roles in adolescent society. *Sociometry,* 1962, **25**, 64-72.

Peisach, E.C. Children's comprehension of teacher and peer speech. *Child Development,* 1965, **36**, 467-480.

Pelosi, J.W. *A study of the effects of examiner race, sex, and style on test responses of Negro examinees.* (Doctoral dissertation, Syracuse University) Ann Arbor, Mich.: University Microfilms, 1968, No. 69-8642.

Perales, A.M. The audio-lingual approach and the Spanish-speaking student. *Hispania,* 1965, **48**, 99-102.

Pettigrew, T.F. *A profile of the Negro American,* Princeton, N.J.: Van Nostrand, 1964.

Pressey, S.L., & Teter, G.F. A comparison of colored and white children by means of a group scale of intelligence. *Journal of Applied Psychology,* 1919, **3**, 277-282.

Quay, L.C. Language dialect, reinforcement, and the intelligence-test performance of Negro children. *Child Development,* 1971, **42**, 5-15.

Ramirez, M., III, & Gonzalez, A. Mexican-Americans and intelligence testing: Racism in the schools. Unpublished manuscript. University of California, Riverside, 1971.

Ramirez, M., III, Taylor, C., & Petersen, B. Mexican-American cultural membership and adjustment to school. *Developmental Psychology,* 1971, **4**, 141-148.

Raven, J.C. *Guide to using Progressive Matrices.* London: Lewis, 1952.

Riessman, F. *The culturally deprived child.* New York: Harper, 1962.

Roca, P. Problems of adapting intelligence scales from one culture to another. *High School Journal,* 1955, **38**, 124-131.

Rosenthal, R., & Jacobson, L. *Pygmalion in the classroom.* New York: Holt, 1968.

Sanchez, G.I. Bilingualism and mental measures. *Journal of Applied Psychology,* 1934, **18**, 765-772.

Sarason, S.B., & Doris, J. *Psychological problems in mental deficiency.* (4th ed.) New York: Harper, 1969.

Sattler, J.M. Statistical reanalysis of Canady's "The effect of 'rapport' on the I.Q.: A new approach to the problem of racial psychology." *Psychological Reports,* 1966, **19**, 1203-1206.

Sattler, J.M. Effects of cues and examiner influence on two Wechsler subtests. *Journal of Consulting and Clinical Psychology,* 1969, **33**, 716-721.

Sattler, J.M. Racial "experimenter effects" in experimentation, testing, interviewing, and psychotherapy. *Psychological Bulletin,* 1970, **73**, 137-160.

Sattler, J.M., Hillix, W.A., & Neher, L.A. Halo effect in examiner scoring of intelligence test responses. *Journal of Consulting and Clinical Psychology,* 1970, **34**, 172-176.

Sattler, J.M., & Martin, S. Anxious and nonanxious examiner roles on two WISC subtests. *Psychology in the Schools,* 1971, **4**, 347-349. 197

Sattler, J.M., & Theye, F. Procedural, situational, and interpersonal variables in individual intelligence testing. *Psychological Bulletin,* 1967, **68**, 347-360.

Sattler, J.M., & Winget, B.M. Intelligence testing procedures as affected by expectancy and IQ. *Journal of Clinical Psychology,* 1970, **26**, 446-448.

Sattler, J.M., Winget, B.M., & Roth, R.J. Scoring difficulty of WAIS and WISC Comprehension, Similarities, and Vocabulary responses. *Journal of Clinical Psychology,* 1969, **25**, 175-177.

Saunders, L. *Cultural difference and medical care: The case of the Spanish-speaking people of the Southwest.* New York: Russell Sage Foundation, 1954.

Schmideberg, M. The socio-psychological impact of IQ tests. *International Journal of Offender Therapy*, 1970, **14**, 91-97.

Schubert, J. Effect of training on the performance of the W.I.S.C. 'Block Design' subtest. *British Journal of Social and Clinical Psychology*, 1967, **6**, 144-149.

Shotwell, A.M. Arthur performance ratings of Mexican and American highgrade mental defectives. *American Journal of Mental Deficiency*, 1945, **49**, 445-449.

Shuey, A. *The testing of Negro intelligence.* (2nd ed.) New York: Social Science Press, 1966.

Simmons, O.G. The mutual images and expectations of Anglo Americans and Mexican Americans. *Daedalus*, 1961, **90**, 286-299.

Snow, R. Review of R. Rosenthal and L. Jacobson, Pygmalion in the classroom. *Contemporary Psychology*, 1969, **14**, 197-199.

Sperling, L. *The effect of differential test environment on group testing scores of disadvantaged students.* (Doctoral dissertation, University of Connecticut) Ann Arbor, Mich.: University Microfilms, 1970, No. 70-15, 555.

Stablein, J.E., Willey, D.S., & Thomson, C.W. An evaluation of the Davis-Eells (Culture-Fair) Test using Spanish and Anglo-American children. *Journal of Educational Sociology*, 1961, **35**, 73-78.

Strong, A.C. Three hundred fifty white and colored children measured by the Binet-Simon Measuring Scale of Intelligence: A comparative study. *Pedagogical Seminary*, 1913, **20**, 485-515.

Talerico, M., & Brown, F. Intelligence test patterns of Puerto Rican children seen in child psychiatry. *Journal of Social Psychology*, 1963, **61**, 57-66.

Teahan, J.E., & Drews, E.M. A comparison of northern and southern Negro children on the WISC. *Journal of Consulting Psychology*, 1962, **26**, 292.

Thorndike, R.L. Review of R. Rosenthal and L. Jacobson, "Pygmalion in the classroom." *American Educational Research Journal*, 1968, **5**, 708-711.

Thorndike, R.L. Educational measurement for the seventies. In R.L. Thorndike (Ed.), *Educational measurement.* (2nd ed.) Washington, D.C.: Council on Education, 1971.

Turner, G.H., & Penfold, D.J. The scholastic aptitude of the Indian children of the Caradoc Reserve. *Canadian Journal of Psychology*, 1952, **6**, 31-44.

Valentine, C.A. Deficit, difference & bicultural models for Afro-American behavior. *Harvard Educational Review*, 1971, **41**, 137-157.

Vernon, P.E. Ability factors and environmental influences. *American Psychologist*, 1965, **20**, 723-733.

Voyat, G. IQ: God-given or man-made? In J. Hellmuth (Ed.), *Disadvantaged child.* Vol. 3. New York: Brunner/Mazel, 1970.

Weener, P.D. Social dialect differences and the recall of verbal messages. *Journal of Educational Psychology*, 1969, **60**, 194-199.

Wesman, A.G. Intelligent testing. *American Psychologist*, 1968, **23**, 267-274.

Willard, L.S. A comparison of Culture Fair Test scores with group and individual intelligence test scores of disadvantaged Negro children. *Journal of Learning Disabilities,* 1968, **1**, 584-589.

Williams, E.B. Testing of the disadvantaged: New opportunities. In F.W. Wright (Chm.), Uses and abuses of psychology: A program for constructive action. Symposium presented at the American Psychological Association, Washington, D.C., September 1971.

Williams, R.L. Danger: Testing and dehumanizing black children. *Clinical Child Psychology Newsletter,* 1970, **9**(1), 5-6. (a)

Williams, R.L. From dehumanization to black intellectual genocide: A rejoinder. *Clinical Child Psychology Newsletter,* 1970, **9**(3), 6-7. (b)

Williams, R.L. Black pride, academic relevance and individual achievement. *Counseling Psychologist,* 1970, **2**, 18-22. (c)

Williams, R.L. Abuses and misuses in testing black children. *Counseling Psychologist,* 1971, **2**, 62-73.

Young, F.M., & Bright, H.A. Results of testing 81 Negro rural juveniles with the Wechsler Intelligence Scale for Children. *Journal of Social Psychology,* 1954, **39**, 219-226.

Zigler, E., & Butterfield, E.C. Motivational aspects of changes in IQ test performance of culturally deprived nursery school children. *Child Development,* 1968, **39**, 1-14.

THE IMPACT (OR LACK OF IT) OF EDUCATIONAL RESEARCH ON CHANGES IN EDUCATIONAL PRACTICE

M. Stephen Lilly, Ed.D.

University of Minnesota, Duluth

This chapter concerns educational research and its relationship to changes in educational practice. The theme is developed that the depiction of the linear relationship between these two activities, by several models of educational innovation, is neither sound nor based in reality. The change process in education appears to be politically based, as opposed to research-based, and draws on research findings on a random basis at best. In the final sections, implications for educational researchers are explored.

The task of relating educational research to educational change cannot be undertaken for the field of special education alone, but should also include general education. There are two reasons for this position: First, special education as a field is relatively young, and its major effort thus far has been in program development and implementation. While research in special education has not been lacking (see any recent issue of the *American Journal of Mental Deficiency*), the field has been so occupied with other issues that research has been neglected. Second, there is little or no difference between general and special education with regard to the relationship between research and practice. Thus, the more inclusive literature of the larger field of general education can and should be brought to bear on the problems of special education.

The focus on this chapter is on research in education, and the conclusions drawn are equally applicable to general and special education. In reviewing the literature, the emphasis is on tapping both research-oriented and practitioner-oriented journals. The data on factors relating to educational change are sparse and inconclusive, but representative studies are included. For the most part, the review of literature covers the past 2 to 3 years, though in a few cases older references are cited.

A case is made for the importance of research in the change process in education, though evidence and opinions to the contrary are also presented. Conclusions are drawn for the educational researcher who wishes to adjust to changing needs in the field of education in general, and special education in particular.

Defining educational research and change

What is meant by educational research and educational change? In defining educational research, one begins with the conviction that a scientific approach to education is both rational and desirable. Roscoe (1969), in calling for a behavioral-science approach to education, defined science as a discipline whose "essential task. . . is to provide an objective, factual, and useful account of the universe [p. 83]." According to Roscoe, the two basic assumptions underlying a scientific approach are: (*a*) "The behavior of the universe is orderly; it is not capricious, chaotic, or spontaneous." (*b*) "Every natural event has an explanation that may eventually be discovered by intelligent and diligent men [p. 83]."

The three domains in science are scientific knowledge, which differs from other knowledge in that it is subject to verification by systematic, objective observation of natural phenomena; scientific theory, which is systematic integration of scientific knowledge; and scientific research. Roscoe defined scientific research as the systematic and empirical study of relationships among variables and stated that "the techniques of statistical analysis enable the researcher to study imperfect relationships and draw definite conclusions [p. 85]."

Dalin (1970) cited three types of educational change: change in curriculum and educational technology; change in decision-making structures which alter the distribution of power and responsibility in the system; and changes in educational structures and administrative arrangements. Dalin pointed out that the first and third types of change are often amenable to the systematic approach characteristic of educational research, while the second type is often heavily influenced by what can best be characterized as political crises. In this chapter, the term "educational change" refers to any or all of the types of change listed above, and is used interchangeably with the term "educational innovation."

Havelock (1969) cited four major orientations to change in education and characterized each of them as follows:

1. The problem-solver model, popular with practitioners, starts with a stated, implied, or assumed need of the client, which is then articulated as a problem. A search for solutions is then accomplished, a solution is chosen and implemented, and, hopefully, need reduction ensues. Havelock stated that "this is a viewpoint that is very consonant with our individualistic and humanistic tradition and it finds its expression in such terms as 'client-centered therapy' and 'student-centered teaching'."

2. The research, development, and diffusion-process model is "represented by those who start from research and the products of research and delineate a path toward the consumer." This model will be examined in some detail below, and thus will not be presented in full at this point.

3. The social-interaction model emphasizes "the measurement of the movement of messages from person to person and system to system." Persons who espouse this model "see the society as a network of roles and channels of communication with

organizational and formal and informal associations forming barriers and overlapping connections." Studies using this model focus on such factors as opinion leadership, personal contact, and social integration.

4. The linkage model, promulgated by Havelock, attempts to glean the necessary elements from the three models just cited and synthesize them into a single model. This model stresses the user as a problem solver who must enter into a reciprocal relationship with an outside resource system, in order to find a problem solution. The resource person must then establish linkage with specialists even more remote from the client, and so on, until the problem is solved. According to Havelock, the process involves "linkage to more and more remote resource persons, and ultimately these overlapping linkages form an extended series which we have sometimes described as a 'chain of knowledge utilization' connecting the most remote sources of expert knowledge in the university with the most remote consumers of knowledge."

A research-based model for change in education

The model of educational change most often espoused by educational researchers is that of research, development, and diffusion, cited above. Guba (1968), representative of this preference, stipulated four steps in the change process: research, development, diffusion, and adoption. Research "has as its basic objective the advancement of knowledge," and "the researcher is not to be concerned with practical applications of his ideas [p. 136]." Development, the second step in the process, "has as its basic objective the identification of operating problems and the formulation of solutions to those problems [p. 137]." Development involves "production, engineering, packaging, and testing a proposed problem, solution and invention [p. 137]." The third step is diffusion, the purpose of which is "to create awareness and provide opportunities for the assessment of invention [p. 137]." The fourth step of the change process, after the invention is available and understandable to practitioners, is its adaptation to the local situation and implementation (adoption). "The adoption process. . . establishes the invention as part of the ongoing program and, in time, converts it into a 'non-innovation' [p. 138]."

In this four-step model of educational change, the steps are seen as more or less sequential, in that a step cannot be completed optimally without drawing on information derived from the prior step. Rubin (1968), while admitting that the four phases of change are not independent of each other in actual practice, implied that they *should* be when he stated:

In the current press for school reform, we have not yet achieved a systematic procedure through which research, development, dissemination, and installation are assigned to the most appropriate agencies and through which an efficient transition from one phase to the next occurs [p. 157].

In summary, the educational researcher's view of educational change adheres to the view that rationality is basic to scientific endeavor (Roscoe, 1969).

THE IMPORTANCE OF EDUCATIONAL RESEARCH

Such a view of educational change, of course, places the highest premium on research, since a solid research base should underlie all subsequent steps in the change process. Robert Hochstein (1971), Director of Public Information of the National Center for Educational Research and Development, summarized this point:

Perhaps the most important aspect of the Office of Education's research effort is that it has created a climate of opinion which recognizes that the attainment of educational progress is inextricably linked to soundly conceived research and development activities [p. 378].

Hochstein continued: "The payoff from the investment in educational research and development can no longer be questioned. It is a fact of life in today's schools [p. 378]." Watson (1971), reinforcing this view, stated that "a major reason that 'mindlessness' continues to characterize school systems is that they fail to recognize the critical need for research [p. 349]."

In establishing the case for the importance of educational research, a great deal of attention is given to research products which either have made or could make "a difference" in educational practice. King (1970) cited 13 "messages" from educational research for practitioners. ranging from the statement that schools should review all curricula to determine their relevance, to the admonition that "children must be challenged." While it is not at all clear how all of these "messages" have derived from educational research, the assumption is made that were it not for research, these "facts" would not have been discovered. Williams (1969) contended that aspects of the learning situation which could be affected by research findings include structure of subject matter (methods), pacing, accommodation of learners' responses, and responsiveness of learners' behaviors. Singer (1970), in discussing reading instruction, cited the 10 most widely influential reading studies as evidence that research *has* made a difference in reading instruction, and given this assumption, reviewed a series of studies which should have − but didn't − make a difference.

An emphasis on research as the basis for change in education has led many researchers to conclude that the education establishment is underinvesting in research and development. For example, the Research and Policy Committee of the Committee for Economic Development (1968), in calling for wider recognition of the importance of educational research, pointed out that the percentage of total education funds in the United States going to research, development, and evaluation is "a small fraction of one per cent of the total investment in education [p. 29]." The Committee compared this with the electrical and communications equipment industry's expenditure of company funds for research and development totaling 3.4% of net sales in 1966. Likewise, International Business Machines invests approximately 5% of its revenue annually in research and development, according to the Committee.

Concern for educational research has led to published debate and argument in the research community, with regard to training of researchers to fill the manpower void. Hopkins (1969) called for self-contained, self-instructional training units to be used for in-service training in field settings; Glass (1969) counseled that research training should remain where it is – in graduate training programs. As Glass pointed out, "unfortunately, it is not that simple to produce competent educational researchers [p. 48]"; in effect, he recommended a deliberate approach to solving the manpower problem.

The trend to applied research and development

While educational researchers have been insistent about the need for educational research activities, there has been an increasing concern within the research community for closer coordination of these activities with the everyday concerns of educational practitioners. Wynne (1970) stated that the schools regard research products as inconsequential at best, and a threat to their operations at worst. King (1970), after citing his 13 "messages" from researchers, admitted that "it is indeed unfortunate that our researchers cannot be of more assistance to the practitioner [p. 58]." Dershimer (1971), executive officer of the American Educational Research Association (AERA), recognized this problem and called upon AERA members to initiate systematic exchanges of information between researchers and policy makers through committees, publications, and the hiring of a communications specialist on the AERA staff.

The overall response of the educational research community to the ever-present and widening gulf between research and practice has been a swing of the pendulum from an emphasis on "basic research" to an emphasis on product-oriented development activities. Hochstein (1971) felt that the skeptics from the 1950s and early 1960s were right in charging that educational research and development had little pay-off, but maintained that the status quo has changed drastically. As evidence of this, Hochstein mentioned such "products" as *Sesame Street,* computer-assisted instruction, individually prescribed instruction, the Patterns in Arithmetic Series from the Wisconsin Research and Development Center in Cognitive Learning, the Intermediate Science Curriculum Study, and the minicourses from the Far West Regional Education Laboratory. Popham (1971), in testifying before Congress for additional educational research and development funds, cited the emergence of a mission orientation in educational research:

Now the educational researcher has been made aware of a desperate need to improve the educational enterprise, and the message is getting through. Whereas a decade ago the bulk of investigations being reported in educational research journals and at professional meetings could be characterized, kindly, as somewhat esoteric, the current drive is for practical relevance [p. 3].

Chase (1970) stated that "existing R&D organizations have set themselves to provide educational agencies with carefully designed and tested products, processes, and systems appropriate to their goals and functions [p. 299]."

Not everyone, of course, is convinced of either the soundness or the effectiveness of this "practicalization" of educational research. Basic researchers such as Wall (1970) were concerned that the merits of a scientific approach to education would be lost:

The tendency to demand that research shall produce immediate practical and policy oriented results, natural enough when considerable public funds are involved and urgent decisions have to be made, must not be allowed to get out of hand. Without progress in the basic sciences, research in education will lack both the instrumentation and the conceptual constructs necessary to its advance [p. 498].

From the practitioner's point of view, on the other hand, the question is not whether education research *should* become more product-oriented, but whether it has fulfilled or can fulfill this mission. In the next section, practitioners' views of educational research are presented, and alternatives to the research-based model for change in education are discussed. Weaknesses of the research-based model for change are pointed out, and an alternate change model is briefly sketched.

AN OPPOSING VIEW ON THE IMPORTANCE OF EDUCATIONAL RESEARCH

Weaknesses in the research and development model for educational change

While educational researchers have recently devoted much time and effort to building (and selling) the case for the indispensability of research for educational progress, not all practitioners are convinced. Neither, for that matter, are all researchers. First, there is serious doubt among many responsible professionals as to the adequacy of the research-and-development change model. Hendrik D. Gideonse (1970), Director of Program Planning and Evaluation for the National Center for Educational Research and Development, pointed out that in an evaluation of educational research and development in the United States, the Organization for Economic Cooperation and Development found an overdependence on linear-deductive change models such as Guba's. Gideonse concluded that the research and development community must examine more closely the process by which change takes place in education.

The linear change model for education was also attacked by Hilgard (1969), who stated:

The greatest fallacy is that there is a linear flow from basic research to development. . . that is, the boys in development do not sit around waiting for the new ideas to come from basic research and then make use of them in designing products. . . . Can we say that the parole system is a technical development of sociological science, the nursery school a consequence of child psychology, the junior high an answer to what we have learned about adolescence. . . [p. 41]?

Hilgard pointed out that service rests only loosely upon science, if at all. Guba's linear change model for education was also attacked by Erlandson and House (1971) and House (1971), who pointed out that the model falsely assumes that persons at each stage of the process place a high value on the eventual successful transfer of their efforts to the next phase. As House stated, "The point is that [the] linear change model assumes pursuit of a common goal by collectives of people, when in fact this does not happen [p. 35]." The researcher sees more importance in satisfying his colleagues than in contributing to the development stage; the developer's success is tied more to the number of products than to their dissemination value; the disseminator is more concerned with numbers than with quality of contacts with users. Finally, the user often makes a decision not on the basis of how well something works, but how easily it is assimilated into his organization and the larger social context (House, 1971). Erlandson and House (1971) stated, "The simple truth is that the most powerful forces in shaping the values and behavior of an individual in an organization will almost certainly be independent of stated organizational objectives [p. 74]." They called for new models of educational change, stating that new models (*a*) should concentrate on what happens, as opposed to what should happen or is logical; and (*b*) should take into consideration relevant political and sociological factors. In other words, these authors maintained that educational change is not as simple or straight-forward in its genesis and maintenance as represented in linear change models based on research and development functioning.

Is present research applied, or can it be?

In addition to this lack of faith in the research-and-development change model for education, there is considerable skepticism with regard to the usefulness of the natural science research model in the social sciences in general, and education in particular. Harris (1971) stated that "methods in the natural sciences still consist largely of processes calling for formulating hypotheses, testing them in controlled experiments, rejecting or accepting them, and the building of a general theory applicable to whole systems"; and that while this approach is appealing to the social scientist, "the prospect of discovering a set of fundamental laws governing the processes of education. . . is illusory [p. 215]." Harris further stated that:

It is not only a question of the difficulties involved in verification and controlled experimentation in the socio-ethical sciences, but a substantive difference in the interrelationships among theory, meaning, and pertinence in the socio-ethical sciences as contrasted with the natural sciences [p. 215].

On a more practical level, Goodlad (1969) said:

We are not likely to have invention in educational practice. . . if we demand research regarding the effects of an invention as a prerequisite to its creation. . . . The researcher cannot go on with his stable research – his conventional criteria, his timeworn measures – and expect to contribute to the advancement of educational practice and science [p. 97].

Just as the appropriateness of using research models can be called into serious question, so can the responsiveness of educational researchers to needs and priorities at the practitioner level. As was pointed out, a case has lately been made that educational research is becoming much more practical, with an increased emphasis on applied research and development (Hochstein, 1971; Popham, 1971). This movement is undoubtedly in response to the growing body of literature concerning the widening schism between educational researchers and practitioners. This schism, already referred to in statements by Wynne (1970) and King (1970), has been even more clearly explicated:

If the object of [educational] research is the development of coherent and workable theories, researchers are nearly as far from that goal today as they are from controlling the weather. If the goal of educational research is significant improvement in the daily functioning of educational programs, I know of little evidence that researchers have made discernible strides in that direction. . . . Research in education will have to venture forth from the safe and sterile surrounding[s] of the traditional laboratory and address itself to that most threatening of settings for the educational researcher, the classroom or its carefully created equivalent [Schulman, 1970, p. 371].

We have spawned a generation of professionals committed to developing new information – however esoteric, limited, and questionable its significance – rather than to implementing solutions to critical problems whose preconditions are reasonably well understood. . . . It is much easier for politicians to provide the small budgets needed for continued research on such variables as modern versus traditional philosophies of education than to face the more serious budgetary shifts that would be required in order to give all children access to the tools of education [Wallach, 1971, p. 542].

Nor, for that matter, has research in the field of special education escaped the sure sword of accountability. Simches (1970) said:

Yes, there has been more money for research and demonstration, but what has been the nature of the research and demonstration project? Has it been relevant to the problem of educating the handicapped child? Of the millions of dollars spent on research projects, can we find ten which have had an impact on the education of the handicapped, or have contributed a body of knowledge which uses education to maximize opportunities for children [p. 8]?

There is, indeed, ample reason to question statements that educational research is becoming more applied in nature. While Popham (1971) was telling Congress that "the current drive [in educational research] is for practical relevance [p. 3]," the *American Educational Research Journal* was preparing to publish an issue one month later containing articles with the following titles: "Student Influence on Teacher Behavior"; "A Multidimensional Analysis of School Satisfaction"; "Student Ratings of Teacher Effectiveness: Validity Studies"; "An Instrument for Assessing Instructional Climate Through Low-Influence Student Judgments"; "An Autotelic Teaching Experiment with Ancillary Casework Services"; "Map Understanding as a Possible Crystallizer of Cognitive Structures"; "Classroom Cheating: Consistent Attitude, Perceptions, and Behavior"; "The Effects of a Tracking System on Student Satisfaction and Achievement"; "Regions of Significant Criterion Differences in Aptitude-Treatment-Interaction Research"; "Multiple Comparisons of Means." While this is an interesting collection of research articles, it can safely be generalized that nearly all of the information contained in that issue was collected *for the sake of increasing knowledge* in a given area of study, *as opposed to creating change in schools and classrooms.*

To discover that the same situation exists in the field of special education, one need only examine any recent issue of the *American Journal of Mental Deficiency,* the closest approximation to a "hard" research journal in the field. Nearly all of the studies reported are of limited interest or use to the practitioner and are addressed primarily to other researchers, in terms of both format and language. The same can be said of research articles in *Exceptional Children, Journal of Learning Disabilities, Journal of Special Education,* and other journals in the field.

The author believes that educational research is not presently in a position to make a major difference in educational practice, owing to inadequacies in the linear research-and-development model for educational change, as well as to the seeming reluctance of many researchers to abandon the "knowledge for knowledge's sake" approach to problem formulation, data collection, and reporting of results. Where, then, do we go from here? What are possible avenues of change? The first step is to design a more adequate model to depict the process of educational change, one solidly based in the needs of practitioners and the social structures in which educators operate. A complete model for change in education will *not* be developed here, but writings of educational practitioners on the change process will be examined and synthesized into a single statement concerning the process of educational change.

A PRACTICAL LOOK AT THE PROCESS OF EDUCATIONAL CHANGE

Characteristics of the educational-change process

What does the process of change in education look like, and what forces are brought to bear in it? A first premise is that the technical soundness of an innovation, as demonstrated by educational research, is seldom necessary and never sufficient to guarantee adoption of that innovation by educational practitioners. Indeed, this appears to be the state of affairs in all of the social sciences; Taylor (1970) stated:

It is rare for an innovation to become popular solely because its utility is demonstrated. In fact, if one thinks of the last 60 years in psychology, fad and faith seem to have been more important than validity. Any major innovation is likely to take on the character of a social movement in which small cohesive groups with novel perspectives influence the social scene. This was true of psychoanalysis, of Darwinism, and of Newtonian world views. . . . Innovation is a sociological and psychological phenomenon. It is important therefore to analyze the way in which social inventions come to be adopted, apart from and irrespective of their presumed scientific merit [p. 77].

This line of reasoning can be applied directly to the field of education by considering the succession of educational innovations in the last 10 years, some proving successful (*Sesame Street*) and others apparently dying on the vine (performance contracting). To go further into history and at the same time bring the point closer to home, what were the bases upon which public school special classes for exceptional children of all types were begun? Were these classes started on the basis of a sound body of research literature on the merits of small class size and homogeneous grouping? Hardly. Several factors contributed to this movement, none having anything to do with educational research; in Taylor's (1970) words, special education quickly took on the characteristics of a "social movement" – a movement which has grown to sizable proportions.

What, then, are the characteristics of the educational-change process? Adams (1969) listed three steps in bringing about change: (*a*) identifying desirable changes; (*b*) discovering processes and resources necessary to develop a locally conceived education program; and (*c*) determining how principals, teachers, parents, community representatives, and pupils can participate in planning the educational program. With

211

more specific reference to the process of change, Mangione (1970) listed four steps: need identification and assessment, establishment of priorities for ideas, search for solutions, and implementation of chosen programs. This list is expanded in the article "What Is Innovation" (1969) to include six steps as follows: assessing needs, defining the problem, developing alternative solutions, implementing chosen solutions, evaluating outcomes, and disseminating relevant information.

Studies of educational change

While the foregoing statements regarding educational change may have face validity, little systematic information is available concerning the educational-change process. As Goodlad (1971) stated:

The processes of change have been haphazard and, insofar as knowledge about change is concerned, virtually noncumulative. We are only slightly better off today with respect to knowing how change is wrought and how to spend our human and dollar resources wisely to effect change than we were twenty years ago [p. 157].

In searching for empirical studies of the change process in education, remarkably little information of a recent nature was found. Bishop (1970) conducted a study testing the hypothesis that "the more highly bureaucratized the organizational structure of a school system, the less likely it was that the system would accommodate educational innovation and change [p. 306]." Innovation was measured on two dimensions: (a) rate of adoption of innovations in school districts, and (b) degree to which several selected innovations were adopted. To the investigator's surprise, extent of bureaucracy in school systems was positively correlated with rate and extent of innovation. Change was more likely in large, urban school systems, as well as in systems with relatively high turnover rates for superintendents. Thus, a number of factors probably interacted in producing greater change in highly bureaucratic school systems.

Hilfiker (1969) studied the relationship between innovativeness in school systems and interpersonal relationships within school systems at three levels: (a) principals as perceived by teachers, (b) interpersonal process norms of professional staff, and (c) interpersonal process norms perceived to exist in professional-staff meetings. This study, designed to investigate personal factors (which will be posited later as a major factor in educational change), demonstrated the following factors to be positively related to innovativeness in school settings: (a) social support provided by the principal as perceived by the professional staff, (b) the perceived adequacy of the staff meetings in terms of problem-solving activities, (c) satisfaction with the amount of time devoted to problem solving in staff meetings, and (d) perceived power of faculty and administrative council meetings combined as a single force. Thus, it appeared that perceived staff influence on the decision-making process was an important variable in producing and maintaining changes in educational systems.

In a study of the use of information in change situations, Murray (1970) contacted both university and junior high school faculty members and asked the two groups what sources of information they considered to be most valuable in making a decision concerning adoption of an educational innovation. The eight choices of information sources are listed in Table 1, along with the rankings of the sources for both groups.

Table 1

Preferences of Types of Information Most Valued by Teachers in Deciding Whether to Adopt an Educational Innovation

Type of information	Preference rank[a]	
	College faculty	Junior high school faculty
Standardized tests	1	6
Logical reasons	2	3
Personal observation	3	2
Teacher questionnaire of users	4	1
School grades	5	5
Endorsement of good friends	6	7
Respected educator's endorsement	7	4
Principal questionnaire	8	8

[a]1 = most preferred; 8 = least preferred.

These rankings show that junior high faculty members were more willing to emphasize logic and peer ratings in adopting an innovation, while discounting the importance of objective, standardized tests, the latter being the first choice of university faculty.

Kohl (1969) asked 58 superintendents in Oregon to indicate their levels of involvement with each of seven innovations, and to judge each innovation with regard to five characteristics. The five levels of innovation were awareness, interest, evaluation, trial, and adoption. At each of these stages, the superintendents were asked to rate the relative importance of the following characteristics of innovations: (a) perceived relative advantage; (b) communicability, or ease of explanation; (c) complexity, or difficulty in understanding and use; (d) divisibility, or degree to which the innovation may be tried on a limited basis; and (e) compatibility, or the consistency of the innovation with existing values and past experience of the adopter. The findings indicated that relative advantage and compatibility were most important at the adoption stage, while communicability, complexity, and divisibility were mentioned most often at the interest stage. With regard to the importance of the various stages of adoption, Kohl stated:

Based on the frequency of superintendents' perceptions of characteristics, the interest stage appears to be the most critical of the stages, followed by the adoption stage, and then the awareness stage. The evaluation stage appears to be the least critical, and the trial stage next least important [p. 128].

With regard to the characteristics of innovation, compatibility was mentioned most often, followed by relative advantage, divisibility, complexity, and communicability.

These research studies, while certainly not conclusive, indicated that the following generalizations may be valid with regard to the educational change process:

1. Change is more likely to occur in larger, more complex school systems.

2. Change is more likely to occur in systems in which the doers (e.g., the teachers) perceive themselves to be significant forces in the decision-making process.

3. University faculty and on-line teachers place different weightings on information sources for change, with university personnel looking for objective evidence of value (e.g., standardized tests) and classroom teachers placing a relatively greater emphasis on face validity and peer ratings.

4. Apparently no one has great respect for opinions of school principals regarding the value of an educational innovation.

5. The two most important stages in the change process, according to school superintendents, are the initial-interest stage and the point of actual adoption of the change at the level of the practitioner.

6. The information of most importance to superintendents in deciding whether or not to accept an educational innovation is the degree to which the innovation is consistent with existing values and past experience of the adopter. Of secondary importance is the perceived relative advantage of the innovation over present practices.

Personal and political factors in educational change

The studies of educational change reviewed above point to two important factors which must be considered in examining the dynamics of innovation but which are completely ignored in the research-and-development linear-change models. These factors are (a) personal characteristics of the initiators and, most important, of the instructional personnel involved in conceiving and carrying out the innovation; and (b) the political situation in, and surrounding, the system in which the change is to be made. While these two factors threaten to make the change process in education unsusceptible to rational analysis, they are of major importance. Precisely because they tend to be the most important factors in determining the nature and stability of educational change, they must be reckoned with. To ignore them is to ignore reality.

With regard to attitudes towards change, and particularly teacher attitudes, it seems to be generally accepted — among nonresearchers, at least — that the personal dimension constitutes a cornerstone upon which change must be built. Miller (1970), on the basis of an informal study of ESEA Title III projects in Michigan, concluded:

The commonly held notion that *materials, equipment,* and *organizational patterns* are the key factors in program development is dispelled. While *time for planning* the operation of new programs is of some importance, from the data available it is apparent that teachers and administrators who are involved in ESEA Title III projects look upon *human factors* as more crucial to curriculum change than non-human or material factors. *Humans* are both the most commonly cited *obstacles to* and *facilitators of* educational change. Working effectively with *people* appears to be the key to successful innovation and change, particularly when the "unknown" is involved [p. 339].

This data-based conclusion is echoed by many educational policy makers and students of the educational-change process. Buchan (1971) cited educational innovations which failed, and emphasized the importance of proper attitudinal preparation for educational innovation among students, teachers, and parents, particularly those who will be most directly affected by the change. In a like vein, Voelz (1969) stated that teacher involvement is the most important factor in successful change: "The implementation of a desired innovation can be effective only when the change has gained teacher allegiance [p. 78]." Klopf (1970) stressed the need for personal change to accompany institutional change and described four levels of personal interaction needed in bringing about personal change – consultation, dialogue, encounter, and confrontation. In short, there is scattered evidence and a great deal of logic to suggest that personal involvement and personal change are indispensable factors, if educational innovations are to have a chance to succeed.

Political factors are also conspicuous by their absence from the research-and-development linear model. The primary responsibility for change in education is at the local level. Murphy (1971), in analyzing the impact of Title I of ESEA, addressed the question of priorities and concluded that, as a rule, local schools are fairly free to meet their own priorities. He concluded that the impetus for change, or lack of it, is at the local level, pointing out that in some cases this even meant that the Title I money was used for other than the poor, because of local priorities.

If the primary impetus for, and control of, change in education are in fact at the local level (and, according to Goodlad [1971], rest in the local school administrators), then the political factors in innovation become evident. Indeed, if a local school administrator approaches the task of educational innovation from a purely technical point of view, without regard to politics, he is likely to encounter insurmountable problems. As Kirst and Walker (1971) pointed out in the *Review of Educational Research:*

The determination of the public school curriculum is not just influenced by political events; it is a political process in important ways. . . . Throughout curriculum policy-making, political conflict is generated by the existence of competing values concerning the proper basis for deciding what to teach. . . . Yet when professional educators write about or study the curriculum, they rarely conceive of their subject in political terms. . . . Consistently followed, this (apolitical) image leads the investigator to search for some sort of mechanism for deciding "scientifically" what children should study in school. . . . It holds out the promise of resolving competing claims at the level of principle [pp. 480-481].

This political view of the educational-change process has been reinforced by numerous other authors (Heger, 1971; Scribner, 1970), and its validity is not likely to be challenged by anyone who is familiar with educational decision making at the local level.

Recognition of the substantial political factors involved in initiating and maintaining educational innovation leads to behaviors which are not necessarily consistent with the principle of utilizing research as the basis for change. As Hamilton (1970) said, "Instructional leaders are encouraged to become students of the society which schools serve [p. 342]." More often than not, this leads to a broadening of the power base for change, as described above. Gerhardt (1969), as a part of an effort to "break down the myth that public education is apolitical" and to initiate change in a local school district, began by forming student groups, lay committees, and teacher task forces to determine areas of change and directions for new programs. Decentralized decision making was stressed heavily by Adams (1969), who described a change-oriented project involving 18 schools in Los Angeles:

Within the guidelines established by the state and the Los Angeles Board of Education, it is my intent that principals, teachers, and community personnel at the local school level plan the program of education for their particular school which best meets the needs of the pupils and the needs of the community. The educational program of any given school may be different from that of a neighboring school or a school in another part of the city [p. 122].

Thus, the politics involved in educational innovation can be a potential barrier to use of a research-based model for change. To proceed as though the political influences do not exist, however — simply because decisions made on a political basis are not always "rational," or based on deductive logic and empirical accounts of technical adequacy — seems in itself irrational.

THE CHANGE PROCESS: IMPLICATIONS FOR RESEARCHERS

On the basis of the foregoing discussion of the process of educational change, the following conclusions are drawn:

1. The linear change model proposed by Guba (1968) and Rubin (1968) does not adequately describe the steps by which educational innovation is introduced in the schools.

2. The primary responsibility for change in the schools rests with local school administrators, who may share this responsibility with others in order to enhance the probability of success of an innovation.

3. Changes in education come about only rarely because of objective evidence indicating that one approach to education is clearly superior to available alternative approaches, in terms of its educational outcomes.

4. In choosing innovative programs for implementation, a variety of sources is likely to be brought in on the planning, making the decision basically political rather than technical.

5. Technical assistance is likely to be sought *after* a decision has been made to implement a specific educational innovation, rather than *before*.

6. The key personnel in insuring the success of an innovation are the instructional agents (e.g., teachers) whose job it is to carry it out, implying that substantial prior training and in-program incentives must be provided for them.

This view of educational change can be made clear if one pictures the educational-change agent (innovator) as a sculptor. In the research-and-development linear model, the assumption is made that this sculptor starts with a picture in his mind of what the final product will look like and, through expeditious use of his talents and tools, proceeds logically through a series of steps to reach the final product. The dynamic-political process of educational change, on the other hand, depicts the innovator/sculptor as sitting before a statue already shaped (albeit vaguely), waiting for a crack to appear so that he can quickly wedge his chisel into it. If he manages to do this, he rushes off to his benefactors to inquire as to the type of final product they wish, hoping that by the time he returns, the crack will still be there.

Let us suppose that a dynamic-political model for educational change were accepted by the educational research community. What are its implications for the future behavior of researchers? At least three alternatives exist: First, a researcher can continue traditional educational research, aimed at formulation and testing of specific hypotheses generated either from educational theory or from previously completed research studies. From these studies, further models can be built requiring further experimental verification. No denigration of this type of research activity is intended, for experimental research has a legitimate place in the development of educational theory. The point is that this type of research activity has very little to do with educational practice, and researchers engaged in experimental studies should not attempt to convince themselves or others of the imminent practical value of their experimentation. Their contribution is at a level other than the practical, and should be recognized as such.

What further alternatives, then, are available to members of the educational research community who wish to have an impact on school practice? The second and third alternatives *both involve tempering the educational researcher's traditional commitment to experimental design and deductive reasoning.* At one level, the researcher can become involved in program evaluation. As stated earlier, while program administrators do not generally demand data prior to choosing to implement an educational innovation, they need information after program implementation concerning the effects of the innovation and ways of improving it.

Third, researchers wishing to have a direct impact on educational practice can carry out program packaging and dissemination. This step, which comes after program development and demonstration, is the vital link between applied educational research and practice; it has received scant attention from all sectors of the educational community.

EDUCATIONAL PROGRAM EVALUATION

In concluding that educational experimentation (research) bears little relationship to educational practice, it does not necessarily follow that data collection on ongoing educational programs is of no value. Rather, the argument is made that this data collection should take some form other than controlled experimentation. It is from this logic that the field of educational evaluation has grown, along with rather sharp differentiation between research and evaluation. Trachtman (1970) echoed the statements of many educators by declaring that research cannot answer educational problems in its present form, and by expressing the hope that school psychologists will turn to educational evaluation activities, as opposed to basic research.

Guba (1969) contended that researchers should not bring their skills to bear on evaluation efforts, since researchers are interested in control of variables, while evaluators attend to "invited interference." Guba pointed out that an evaluator's task is to be of service to practitioners interested in solving a number of burdensome problems simultaneously, as well as in refining and adjusting solutions continuously:

Thus, an evaluation paradigm that emphasizes control when invited interference is needed; that prevents attention to more than one problem at a time, no matter how pressing other problems may be; that provides only terminal data; and that renders impossible the crucial requirements for continuous adjustment and refinement, simply cannot be judged very useful, but in fact crippling to [the evaluator's] . . . purposes. . . . What is needed now, as quickly as possible, is a divorce. Research and evaluation have little in common, and a continuing relationship would be hurtful to both. Both are legitimate forms of inquiry and both must be guided by a conceptual paradigm. But the research paradigm is not the paradigm of evaluation, nor can it ever be. Now this is not to say that persons who think of themselves as researchers ought not to engage in evaluative inquiry, but rather that when they do, they must divest themselves of their classic methodologies and devise new ones appropriate to the needs of evaluation [pp. 4-5].

Morgan (1971) listed 10 specific differences between research and evaluation, including purpose, design, data collection, and reporting procedures.

As a practical example of the need for differentiation between research and evaluation, Light and Smith (1970) presented an analysis of the Westinghouse evaluation of Head Start programs. They pointed out that the purpose of the post hoc experimental approach in this evaluation study was to estimate the average effect of experimental programs and compare it with the average effect of nonexperimental programs. A major conclusion was that on the average, the effect of Head Start programs on children's development was not significant. Light and Smith, however, pointed out that a better inquiry would have been: Which of the program centers worked well for reasons which are known to us, and which can be reestablished in any future program centers? The latter, and more appropriate, question could hardly have been approached through experimental research procedures.

Early efforts in the area of program evaluation focused on development of models for evaluation, resulting in a plethora of such models containing slight to relatively major variations on a theme (e.g., Atkinson, 1967; Carter, 1969; Crane & Abt, 1969; EPIC, 1968; Fogel, 1971; Foley, 1970; Scriven, 1967; Stake, 1967; Stufflebeam, 1967). A detailed analysis of each of these evaluation models (which are only samples of those available) is not presented here, since the purpose of this section is to present a rationale for involvement of researchers in evaluation activities, as opposed to a technical basis for conducting program evaluation. The most common emphasis in program-evaluation models is the specification of objectives, processes, and outcomes and the determination of relationships between these three elements. While these are the basic elements, if one wants to have five elements rather than three, or emphasize process over output (or vice versa), he can surely find an evaluation model to fit his needs. Specialized evaluation models based on such concepts as systems analysis (Carter, 1969) and cost-effectiveness analysis (Crane & Abt, 1969) are also available, if one wants to expand beyond the basic model.

A model exists for nearly every purpose that one can imagine in education and, in short, *no further work on model building is needed.* Proger (1971), in calling for more formal evaluation of learning-disabilities programs to lead to "informed decisions" concerning service functions, stated that program evaluation has risen to its "level of functional incompetence" — there are numerous model builders but no one implementing the models. Evaluation needs less theorizing and more action.

In approaching evaluation from a functional point of view, it is crucial to attend to the basic purpose of evaluation: to provide decision makers with data which have a direct bearing on decisions they must make. Thus, unlike the researcher, the evaluator has a client. More often than not, the first step for a program evaluator is to assist program personnel in specifying the objectives of the program, since it is impossible to measure progress without having a clear idea of goals. Once objectives are specified, one must attend to the purposes of the evaluation and the uses to be made of evaluation data. *These are decisions to be made by program personnel,* with the assistance of the evaluator.

Once objectives of the program and purposes of the evaluation are set, the evaluator's task is to come up with means of collecting the needed data. This involves the very difficult steps of specifying dependent variables and locating (or developing) acceptable criterion measures. At this point, the evaluator has an opportunity for the kind of creative planning not usually demanded in research activities. As pointed out earlier, the teacher or practitioner who must do the work is an important factor in educational innovation; nothing discourages a teacher more quickly than complicated data-collection systems which take away an inordinate amount of time from instructional periods. Thus, the task of an evaluator at this point is to collect the necessary information, without disrupting the classroom situation or discouraging the direct instructional agents. To accomplish this, we had best leave our research orientation behind!

Once the data are collected, the evaluator's role is to organize the information to meet the needs of the program personnel. Again, the emphasis is on the needs of the client, as opposed to the building of knowledge or theory. When the information is assembled in a manner acceptable to both the evaluator and his client, the evaluator's job is done.

In summary, a case has been made for differentiation between research and evaluation, and for an emphasis on practical application of already-developed evaluation models. What is needed at the present time is not further evaluation models, but rather specific evaluation plans to apply existing models to specific projects. It can be expected that no two evaluation plans will be exactly the same, since an evaluator is unlikely to encounter identical political and personal situations in different projects, even if located in the same setting. The present need is for evaluation practitioners;

educational researchers have some unique qualifications for this role, providing that the experimental approach of asking and answering questions can be left behind, or at least temporarily put aside.

PROGRAM PACKAGING AND DISSEMINATION

An area of major concern to the educational research community is improvement of communications between researchers and practitioners. As stated earlier, Richard Dershimer (1971), executive officer of AERA, proposed an AERA program for exchange of information between researchers and policy makers, including establishment of a communications specialist in the AERA central office. Recognition of this problem leads directly to the second suggested alternative course of action for researchers wishing to have an impact on school practice: program packaging and dissemination.

According to at least one study of the educational-change process (Kohl, 1969), the most critical stage is that of initial interest, when the impetus for change is present and the school personnel responsible for initiating change are considering possible courses of action. It is at this point that information on a number of program alternatives would be most helpful to educational-change agents.

One of the first major attempts at dissemination of educational information was the Educational Resources Information Center (ERIC) network, a series of centers geared to storage and retrieval of published reports and journal articles relevant to education. ERIC stores titles and abstracts of reports and articles; professionals in the field may request search and retrieval of information pertaining to specific descriptor terms, as well as print or microfiche copies of reports in the ERIC system. In addition, ERIC centers distribute annotated bibliographies on specific areas of education and publish *Research in Education,* a monthly abstract and index journal. Between 1965 and the present time, 19 ERIC clearinghouses have been established in varying subject areas, including a clearinghouse on exceptional children housed at the Council for Exceptional Children (CEC). ERIC-CEC is responsible for publication of *Exceptional Child Education Abstracts,* among other activities.

While the ERIC network is a potentially valuable source of information for educational researchers, students, and other professionals interested in gathering basic information, it is of limited use to educational practitioners engaged in change of educational programs. Such practitioners need information that is not generally included in journal articles and other published project reports, e.g., information on items such as program costs, extent of teacher training required, and scheduling of student activities. In short, searching for program alternatives at the "interest" level of the educational-change process, educational practitioners need clear, concise, and practical program descriptions.

The relative lack of practical information is a major problem in education. In the words of Lilly and McDonald (1972):

Dissemination of information on instructional programs is an area of educational research and development which has received scant attention, in which the need for further development work is great. The impetus for change in instructional programs, particularly in the area of special education, is strong within local school districts. Detailed information on instructional programming alternatives is generally not available to local school administrators who bear the major brunt of program decision-making in the schools. Unlike specific instructional materials, which can generally be obtained for detailed inspection prior to purchase, instructional programs cannot be easily examined. Instructional programs are more pervasive in nature, and cannot be touched, listened to, sniffed, dropped on the floor, or measured with a ruler. Instructional programs involve teacher training, in-class teaching activities, administrative arrangements, and a myriad of other teacher, student and administrator behaviors which tend to elude precise description. In short, the administrator who is deciding to implement an instructional program involving the elements cited above has a uniquely difficult task, and to this point, the information available to help in such decision-making activities has been limited in both quantity and format [p. 1].

While information packaging has not been an area of high priority in educational research and development, some examples can be found. Woodward (1971) reported on a Project Information Exchange (PIE) used in the Philadelphia schools to alert teachers and others in the school system to innovative projects. PIE provides an annual catalog containing descriptions of innovative projects, a book of free materials which can be ordered from the catalog, an information telephone service for 24-hour order of the free materials, and a regular information-update column in the Philadelphia school district monthly newsletter.

At the federal level, information packaging and dissemination are the responsibility of the National Center for Educational Communication (NCEC) in the U.S. Office of Education. According to Lee Burchinal (1971), director of NCEC, "the National Center for Educational Communication provides a locus, budget, array of skilled communications specialists, and commitment for delivering information about exemplary practices and validated materials to those who need it [p. 7]." One objective of NCEC is to disseminate summarized and interpreted information on priority educational topics, through the Targeted Communications Program. This program solicits proposals for interpretive summaries of current knowledge and practice on priority topics, published in the PREP (Putting Research into Educational Practice) series of interpretive reports on "educational research and development directed at solutions to problems faced by the nation's schools."

A final example of program packaging and dissemination emphasizes a mediated presentation of instructional programs, presented from a practical point of view. This approach to program packaging, called the Total Information Package (TIP), was developed at the Northwest Regional Special Education Instructional Materials Center at the University of Oregon. The following excerpt from a project report describes the general concept of TIP, as well as its specific application to a single instructional program — in this case the product of a research and development project (Lilly & McDonald, 1972):

The Total Information Package is a multi-media kit making use of cassette tapes, film strips, and printed materials to convey basic information concerning a given instructional program. The following assumptions have been made in developing the TIP concept:

1. The printed word is inadequate, in and of itself, for conveying information on innovative instructional programs to practitioners.

2. In areas in which the printed word is used as a communication device, professional reports tend to be a sterile and non-productive medium for bringing about educational change.

3. Alternatives to written reports in professional journals and convention meetings must be found, if we hope to effect the adoption of innovative instructional programs in school settings.

4. Key decision makers with regard to planning specific changes in educational programming are generally educational administrators at the local level (as opposed to state administrators and local teachers).

5. Information on new programs must be brought to the attention of these administrators in forms that (1) command and keep their attention and interest, and (2) provide them with all the relevant information needed to make a preliminary decision concerning the value of the program.

6. The information provided in such packages as outlined in (5) must provide the administrator an opportunity to (a) proceed through the program in a logical fashion, (b) make a preliminary decision concerning the value of the program, (c) answer procedural questions concerning implementation of the program, (d) confront problems and special considerations to be taken into account in implementing the program, and (e) systematically present information concerning the program to other interested parties, e.g., teachers, superintendents, school board members, federal project coordinators, parents, etc.

In short, the TIP is designed to assist local school administrators in making a decision regarding the appropriateness of implementing a specific instructional program in their schools or school districts.

Total Information Package #1

The first Total Information Package which has been developed describes the Engineered Learning Project (ELP)... the result of a programmatic research study at the University of Oregon that has focused on three primary areas: (1) development of procedures and instruments for identifying deviant children in the classroom setting; (2) development and evaluation of a treatment model that is both efficient and effective in remediating behavioral and academic deficits; and (3) investigation of strategies that will facilitate the generalization and maintenance of treatment gains back to the regular classroom. During the four-year period from 1966 to 1970, a treatment model was developed and evaluated that is very effective in modifying the behavior of acting-out, deviant children in the classroom. The model was implemented in an experimental classroom setting and has three major components. These are token reinforcement, social reinforcement, and time-out procedures. These treatment variables were implemented simultaneously along with a rigorous academic program in the basic skill areas of reading, language, and arithmetic. Children who were assigned to the experimental classroom averaged a mean gain of one year in both arithmetic and reading achievement. Strategies were designed and implemented for programming generalization and maintenance of these gains back to the regular classroom.

The Total Information Package on ELP contains as its basic element a series of five cassette-filmstrip units describing various facets of the ELP program.

The five units consist of eight sections which vary between 8 and 15 minutes in length and which are titled:

Unit I	What is ELP?
Unit II	Why it works (A)
	Why it works (B)
Unit III	Where it works best (A)
	Where it works best (B)
Unit IV	How to make it work (A)
	How to make it work (B)
Unit V	What happens when it works

Users of the TIP are encouraged to spread their viewing of the cassette-filmstrip units over 2 – 4 sittings since the arrangement of units is facilitative in this regard.

In addition to the cassette-filmstrip units, TIP #1 contains response cards to be returned to the NRSEIMC by each viewer, a brochure describing and illustrating the Engineered Learning Project, an exemplary cost analysis for ELP on an annual basis, ELP resource materials and equipment, and a tabular summary of the contents of TIP #1. A 20-page, illustrated and pictorial booklet describing other relevant information about ELP is also included in the package [pp. 2-4].

TIP #1 was developed in prototype form, field-tested with local school administrators, revised, produced, and distributed throughout the Special Education Instructional Materials Center/Regional Media Center Network. Evaluation data on the use and impact of ELP #1 have been collected; further evaluation is being conducted at the present time.

Obviously, not all educational researchers will be inclined to or suited for information packaging and dissemination; it requires a high degree of sensitivity to problems faced by educational practitioners, as well as a working knowledge of educational media in many cases. The demands made by information packaging and dissemination activities, however, are justified by the importance of the resulting products.

AND WHAT ABOUT SPECIAL EDUCATION?

This chapter has examined the process of educational change, particularly as it relates to educational research, and suggested alternative activities for researchers wishing to have a more direct impact on educational practice. It was stated early in the chapter that the task of relating educational research to educational change could not be undertaken for the field of special education alone, and that the more inclusive literature of the larger field of general education can and should be brought to bear on the problems of special education.

Special education is presently encountering forces for change at least as powerful as in any other area of education; the author believes that we can and should profit from the experience and knowledge of our colleagues in general education in attempting to grasp and, ultimately, maximize the process of change. We must not put blind faith in research efforts. The special education research community is not substantially different from the larger educational research community, in terms of its output and its effects on educational practice.

The two alternatives to experimental research activities offered in this chapter – program evaluation and information packaging and dissemination – may be especially appropriate for special education researchers, who, on the whole, seem more attuned to practical needs and constraints than their regular education peers. These two areas represent crucial needs in the field of special education.

All facets of education are presently under close scrutiny, and educational research cannot expect to escape the limelight indefinitely. For this reason, as well as for professional satisfaction, the author urges colleagues and readers to build relevance into their professional activities.

References

Adams, E.B. Project eighteen: A catalyst for change. *Education,* 1969, **90,** 122-125.

Atkinson, G. Evaluation of educational programs: An exploration. In W.H. Strenell (Ed.), *Rationale of education evaluation.* Pearland, Tex.: Interdisciplinary Committee on Education Evaluation, Gulf Schools Supplementary Education Center, 1967.

Bishop, L.K. Bureaucracy and educational change. *Clearing House,* 1970, **44,** 305-309.

Buchan, W.J. Design for introducing educational change. *Education,* 1971, **91,** 298-300.

Burchinal, L.G. Program of the National Center for Educational Communication. *Educational Researcher,* 1971, **22,** 7-9.

Carter, L.F. The systems approach to education: Mystique and reality. *Educational Technology,* 1969, **9,** 22-31.

Chase, F.S. R&D in the remodeling of education. *Phi Delta Kappan,* 1970, **51,** 299-304.

Committee for Economic Development. *Innovation in education: New directions for the American school.* New York: Author, 1968.

Crane, P., & Abt, C.C. A model for curriculum evaluation. *Educational Technology,* 1969, **9,** 17-25.

Dalin, P. Planning for change in education: Qualitative aspects of educational planning. *International Review of Education,* 1970, **16**(4), 436-450.

Dershimer, R.A. 1971 report to the members. *Educational Researcher,* 1971, **22,** 6-7.

EPIC: Generalized scheme for evaluation of innovations. In *The EPIC forum.* Tucson, Ariz.: Educational Programs for Innovative Curriculums, 1968.

Erlandson, D.A., & House, E.R. Theory and practice: Why nothing seems to work. *National Association of Secondary School Principals Bulletin,* 1971, **55,** 69-75.

Fogel, R.L. An approach for program evaluation. *Educational Technology,* 1971, **11,** 39-42.

Foley, W.J. Future of administrative and educational evaluation. *Educational Technology,* 1970, **10,** 20-25.

Gerhardt, F. Strategies for instructional leaders. *Educational Leadership,* 1969, **26,** 359-362.

Gideonse, H.D. The OECD policy review of U.S. educational R&D. *Educational Researcher,* 1970, **21,** 5-8.

Glass, G.V. Research notes (reply to John E. Hopkins). *Phi Delta Kappan,* 1969, **51,** 48.

Goodlad, J.I. Thought, invention, and research in the advancement of education. In *The schools and the challenge of innovation.* New York: Committee for Economic Development, 1969.

Goodlad, J.I. Educational change: A strategy for study and action. *Journal of Secondary Education,* 1971, **46,** 156-166.

Guba, E.G. The process of educational innovation. In R.R. Goulet (Ed.), *Educational change: The reality and the promise.* New York: Citation Press, 1968.

Guba, E.G. Significant differences. *Educational Researcher,* 1969, **20**(3), 4-5.

Hamilton, N.K. Sensing and timing in change. *Educational Leadership,* 1970, **27,** 341-342.

Harris, J.B. Meaning and pertinence of educational theory. *School and Society,* 1971, **99,** 214-217.

Havelock, R.G. Planning for innovation through dissemination and utilization of knowledge. Final report, July, 1969, University of Michigan, Center for Research on Utilization of Scientific Knowledge, Contract No. OEC-3-7-070028-2143, U.S. Office of Education.

Heger, H.K. Educational change and pedagogical validity. *Clearing House,* 1971, **45,** 563-567.

Hilfiker, L.R. Interpersonal characteristics and innovativeness in school systems. *Journal of Applied Behavioral Science,* 1969, **5,** 441-445.

Hilgard, E.R. The problem of R&D within behavioral sciences. *Journal of Research and Development in Education,* 1969, **3**(4), 37-48.

Hochstein, R. Payoff from educational R&D. *Phi Delta Kappan,* 1971, **52,** 376-378.

Hopkins, J.E. Educational R, D, and D: Manpower projections and a proposal. *Phi Delta Kappan,* 1969, **50,** 584-586.

House, E.R. A critique of linear change models in education. *Educational Technology,* 1971, **11,** 35.

King, J.C. What behavioral research has meant to the practitioner. *National Elementary Principal,* 1970, **49,** 55-58.

Kirst, M.W., & Walker, D.F. An analysis of curriculum policymaking. *Review of Educational Research,* 1971, **41,** 479-509.

Klopf, G.J. Interaction processes and change. *Educational Leadership,* 1970, **27,** 334-338.

Kohl, J.W. Adoption, adoption stages, and perceptions of the characteristics of innovations. *California Journal of Educational Research,* 1969, **20,** 120-131.

Light, R.J., & Smith, P.V. Choosing a future: Strategies for designing and evaluating new programs. *Harvard Educational Review,* 1970, **40,** 1-28.

Lilly, M.S. & McDonald, J.E. Total information package: An approach to disseminating information on instructional programs. Final report, 1972, University of Oregon, Northwest Regional Special Education Instructional Materials Center, Grant No. OEG-0-71-4774, U.S. Office of Education.

Mangione, S. Bringing perspective to the change situation. *Educational Leadership,* 1970, **27,** 359-362.

Miller, P.L. Innovation and change in education. *Educational Leadership,* 1970, **27,** 339-340.

Morgan, D.L. Evaluation: A semantic dilemma. *Educational Technology,* 1971, **11,** 46-48.

Murphy, J.T. Title I of ESEA: The politics of implementing federal education reform. *Harvard Educational Review,* 1971, **41,** 35-63.

Murray, F.B. Creditability of information for educational innovation. *Journal of Educational Research,* 1970, **64,** 17-20.

Popham, W.J. AERA members testifying in D.C. (Excerpt from statement presented to the Appropriations Committee, U.S. House of Representatives, March 10, 1971). *Educational Researcher,* 1971, **3,** 10.

Proger, B.B. Program evaluation: The model-building game. *Journal of Learning Disabilities,* 1971, **4,** 292-306.

Randall, R.S. An operational application of the CIPP model for evaluation. *Educational Technology,* 1969, **9,** 40-44.

Roscoe, J.T. Toward a behavioral science approach to education. *Education,* 1969, **90,** 83-86.

Rubin, L.J. Installing an innovation. In R.R. Goulet (Ed.), *Educational change: The reality and the promise.* New York: Citation Press, 1968.

Schulman, L.S. Reconstruction of educational research. *Review of Educational Research.* 1970, **40,** 371-396.

Scribner, J.D. Politics of educational reform: Analyses of political demand. *Urban Education,* 1970, **4,** 348-374.

Scriven, M. The methodology of evaluation. In R.W. Tyler, R.M. Gagné, & M. Scriven (Eds.), *Perspectives in curriculum evaluation.* Chicago: Rand McNally, 1967.

Simches, R.F. Inside outsiders. *Exceptional Children,* 1970, **37,** 5-15.

Singer, H. Research that should have made a difference. *Elementary English,* 1970, **47,** 27-34.

Stake, R.E. The countenance of educational evaluation. *Teachers College Record,* 1967, **68,** 523-540.

Stufflebeam, D.L. The use and abuse of evaluation in Title III. *Theory into Practice,* 1967, **6,** 126-133.

Taylor, J.B. Introducing social innovation. *Journal of Applied Behavioral Science,* 1970, **6,** 69-77.

Trachtman, G.M. Evils of educational research. *Phi Delta Kappan,* 1970, **52,** 123-125.

Voelz, S.J. Changing teachers' attitudes toward change. *Educational Technology,* 1969, **9,** 75-78.

Wall, W.D. Research and educational action. *International Review of Education,* 1970, **16**(4), 484-501.

Wallach, M.A. The humble things we know – and ignore – about quality in elementary education. *Harvard Educational Review,* 1971, **41,** 542-549.

Watson, B.C. Rebuilding the system: Practical goal or impossible dream? *Phi Delta Kappan,* 1971, **52,** 349-353.

What is innovation? *Educational Technology,* 1969, **9,** 35-36.

Williams, J.D. Instructional agents as transmitters of research findings. *International Review of Education*, 1969, **15**(4), 460-476.

Woodward, S.L. Project information exchange for Philadelphia. *Phi Delta Kappan*, 1971, **52**, 348.

Wynne, E. Education research: A profession in search of a constituency. *Phi Delta Kappan*, 1970, **52**, 245-247.

RESEARCH AND THEORY IN
SPECIAL EDUCATION ADMINISTRATION

Leonard C. Burrello, Ed.D.[1]

University of Michigan

In the area of special education administration, little research has been reported in the literature. Voelker and Mullen's (1963) review reported limited research on program development, administration, and the supervisory behavior of special educators; Willenberg (1966) noted that:

The paucity of specific research may be due to three problem areas: (1) There is still lacking a clear theoretical basis for this area of study; (2) the need and responsibility for this type of research has been given a low priority; and (3) there is a shortage of trained research personnel to accomplish the task [p. 145].

In the period between 1966 and 1969, the Council for Exceptional Children published a set of abstracts and a major review concerning administration in special education. In the first publication (1966), four pages were devoted to this topic. In the second reference, which contained 81 abstracts, none was related to preparation or description of role responsibilities.

Reynolds (1969) indicated that program development in special education had either doubled or tripled in the last 20 years, yet no space was devoted to the area of administration. In the following year, Meisgeier and Sloat (1970) devoted a chapter to a review of administration in the first textbook on the process of administration of special education. The majority of studies cited dealt with surveys or studies of the preparation of administrators, the tasks which they perform, and the skills necessary for special education administrators. These studies described the perception of administrators of special education either as a group or in comparison with the perceptions of others outside the area, such as general education administrators, special class teachers, or ancillary personnel. The Special Education Administration Consortium, a group composed of university professors of special education

[1]The author acknowledges the assistance of Daniel D. Sage, Ed.D., associate professor of special education, Syracuse University, and Laurence Callen, Ph.D., program director for administration, Institute for the Study of Mental Retardation and Related Disabilities, University of Michigan.

229

administration, supported a collection of 101 dissertations on the topic, which were either completed or in progress in 1971. Between 1959 and 1965, only seven of these were completed, possibly a consequence of the levels of federal support available for the development of training programs in the area of administration of special education. The focus of these dissertation topics reveals an interesting profile.

Analysis of the dissertations brings to light a significant theme that has appeared in the literature, first with Connor (1963), then Willenberg (1966), and most recently, Willower (1970) and Kohl and Marro (1971). All of these later writers reiterated the concern which Connor first articulated:

Views of the administrative field which stress only specific elements, vaguely related activities and "practical" matters, must be replaced by consideration in the *context of theories* that describe, explain, predict, economize and assist decisions [p. 435].

Approximately 10% of the cited studies dealt with the preparation of administrators at the state and local levels and the relationship between training and administrative style; 20% of the studies focused on the organization of programs for exceptional children within local programs, or at the local, county, and state level; 30% of the dissertations related directly to administrative or supervisory behavior; and the remaining 40% of the studies dealt with a variety of topics with little or no relationship to the organization, administration, and supervision of special education. This collection of studies only serves to underscore Willower's (1970) observation that Connor's (1963) article has had but little "notable impact [p. 591]."

This chapter deals with a review of 20 dissertations which, Rucker (1971) reported, were completed between 1967 and 1971. Other articles and dissertations which dealt principally with the administration and supervision of special education, and which have been published within the same time period, are also discussed. Considerations for a conceptualization of a theory of special education administration will be presented which will focus on what Willower (1970) suggested as fruitful areas of inquiry. He stated:

The nature of various types of organizations, their characteristics as social systems or as small societies, and their relationships with and adaptation to the larger environment will serve as the basis of new conceptualization of special education [p. 592].

Finally, a set of research questions will be posed, on the basis of a theory of administration which conceptualizes administration as a social process. They are presented in an attempt to foster development of research efforts which will lead to operational criteria within the area of special education administration.

REVIEW OF RESEARCH ON ADMINISTRATION AND SUPERVISION
OF SPECIAL EDUCATION

The administrative references collected by Rucker (1971) and selected for review have a number of characteristics in common. They have been grouped into four areas: (*a*) *within-group studies:* surveys of special education administration with regard to perception of a task or attitudes toward some area of concern; (*b*) *between-group studies:* surveys of attitudes of special education administrators as compared with other groups, such as superintendents of schools, generally based upon perceptions of task or function and skill analysis needed to perform outlined functions; (*c*) *organizational climate studies:* associated with directors of special education within intermediate or regional school districts; (*d*) *descriptive studies:* description of factors which influence the development of special education programs and services. All four groups of studies were primarily descriptive and almost exclusively obtained by means of questionnaires. Few studies were based upon any theoretical or conceptual base.

As any new field of study develops, it tends to pass through several distinct stages. Getzels, Lipham, and Campbell (1968) described the process through which research evolves. They indicated that:

First comes more or less random description of phenomena. Then elements of the phenomena are classified into sensible categories; taxonomies are constructed. Efforts are made to understand the relationships among the elements and between classes. Theoretical frameworks are conceived. Generalizations about the functioning of the parts in the whole are advanced and the prediction about future events ... tested; systematic models capable of dealing not only with existing structure, but with change in the structures are formed [p. 150].

Research in special education administration has been primarily of the first order. Recently, descriptive classifications of phenomena into logical categories and taxonomies have been suggested, in order to organize findings into generalizable categories. Some studies of this type, therefore, have been included in the following review. Where results were in disagreement with previous studies, they will be noted.

Research group 1: Within-group studies

Taylor (1967) surveyed 78 special education administrators in unified school districts in California, in order to determine their perceptions of their present role of administrator of special classes, and what their role might be under ideal conditions.

The respondents were subdivided into three classifications by size of district: small, medium, and large. The results were reported in terms of percentages. Among all subjects, 60% held a general supervisory certificate and recommended it as a prerequisite; no respondent from the small- or medium-sized districts indicated a need for a special education supervisory credential. One-half of all subjects for all districts recommended that a line-staff relationship should exist between themselves and certified personnel in the special education program. Kohl and Marro, in a similar study (1971), found that of 1,145 administrators of special education studied, 40% held general education administrative credentials, and 33% held a special education credential.

Taylor also found that 75% of all subjects indicated that they interviewed and selected teachers, and 95+% indicated that they should continue this practice. Among all subjects, 50% formally evaluated special education teachers, and 80+% indicated that they should continue in this practice. Subjects involved in budget preparation totaled 70%; 90+% desired to continue this practice.

With regard to administrator training, Taylor recommended that preservice training programs for special education administrators should be grounded primarily in educational administration, with a minor in special education, in order to be eligible to obtain a general or standard educational administrative credential.

A second study was undertaken by Newman (1968) to determine if special education administrators actually performed certain tasks, whether they ideally should perform these tasks, and the relative importance of these tasks. Gulick and Urwick's (1937) historical conceptualization of seven functional areas of administrative activities was utilized in the questionnaire. Gulick and Urwick's theory includes the areas of planning, organizing, staffing, directing, coordinating, reporting, and budgeting. Newman found that there were no significant differences between what the administrators actually performed and the tasks they felt they ideally should perform. Functional tasks, ranked in order of importance, were planning, organizing, directing, and coordinating. When administrators were compared on the basis of their training, it was found that 82% had formal special education courses and experiences, while 22% had no such training. The most outstanding difference in task rating between these two groups was that those personnel with special education training ranked the directing function as most often performed.

Newman's study revealed that research was not being used as a basis for improvement and clarification of special education programs; further, that there appeared to be a direct relationship between teaching and the performance of administrative tasks – particularly planning, development, and evaluation of teachers. There also appeared to be a direct relationship between training in the education of exceptional children and the performance of administrative tasks in planning and directing of in-service activities.

Newman suggested that there should be more direct observational research concerning tasks involved in the administration of special education programs. Research centered upon the position of the special education administrator is also needed, both from the point of view of the position of the role in the hierarchy within school districts, and from the point of view of attitudinal acceptance. She would like to see studies to establish whether experience in special education teaching is necessary in the preparation of administrators of special education. Finally, she encouraged personnel in graduate training programs for administration of special education to work in programs for educational administration and supervision and to develop special education administration training programs.

Downey (1971) reported on relationships between selected situational and leadership variables of special education administration and the leadership dimensions of initiating structure and consideration described by Halpin and Croft (1963). A semantic-differential questionnaire requiring judgments on administrative behavior in terms of initiating structure and consideration elicited responses from 53 special education administrators. The questionnaire also included a personal data form. On the basis of this survey, it was found that the variables typically prescribed for special education administrators lacked predictive validity with the leadership dimensions of initiating structure and consideration. Only two predictor sets were found to indicate a significant interaction. These were the interaction between the academic-degree level and size of student population within a school district, and the organizational structure in the employing district. The interactional analysis indicated that the director of special education in larger, more complex administrative districts tended to provide higher scores on initiating structure. If the leadership-behavior dimension of consideration were to be viewed as an important aspect of the behavior of the special education administrative leader, the size and complexity of special education administrative units must be carefully controlled.

A fourth study of this type conducted by Burrello (1969). The purpose was to develop and validate an instrument to measure the need values of special education administrators, based upon Rotter's (1954) social-learning theory. The five need categories defined in professional situations were recognition-status; protection-dependence, or deference to others; dominance; independence; and love and affection within professional situations. In order to test the validity of the instrument, the author hypothesized that there would be no relationship between administrator's scores on the behavior-preference inventory and scores made by their respective instructional staff on eight simulated situations depicting the administrator's need preferences. Fifty directors of special education, 25 from local school districts and 25 from intermediate school districts, met the predesigned criteria and agreed to participate. The administrators took the instrument twice over a 2-week period, and a random sample of each administrator's instructional staff reacted to situations describing administrator preferences. A significant relationship was found between an administrator's need preferences and his respective staff's ranking of administrative need preferences. It was concluded that the Behavior Preference Inventory (BPI) apparently described the need values of special education administrators in approximately the same fashion as their instructional subordinates perceived them. A normative test sample was also randomly selected from 341 members of the Council of Administration of Special Education (CASE), and 125 directors and supervisors returned the BPI, personal data sheet, and personnel résumé. These formed the foundation for computed norms.

Comparisons were also made to determine the relationship between administrative need scores, differentiated on the basis of certain demographic variables on both test samples. Seven comparisons were found to be significant. In the experimental sample composed of 50 administrators, age and the organizational variable (local school district or intermediate school district) were found to be significant in relationship to recognition-status, protection-dependence or deference to others, and independence. In the normative sample, sex, age, and size of program were found to be significant in relationship to the need categories of independence, protection-dependence, and love and affection.

Research group 2: Between-group studies

This group of research articles deals with the role of the special education administrator as perceived by himself and others. Courtnage (1967) studied the differences of opinions and attitudes between public school superintendents and special education administrators on educating handicapped children and children with special needs, and on the assignment of administrative responsibilities for programs within public schools with different pupil enrollments. Questionnaires were distributed to 129 superintendents and 123 special education administrators from 15 Western and midwestern states. He found that there was strong agreement between the two respondent groups regarding most responsibilities and issues of special education administration. Size of district was not a significant factor in determining differences between these two groups on any one issue. The only interesting difference was that special education administrators felt that programs for culturally and/or educationally disadvantaged youngsters should be the responsibility of special education, while superintendents argued that such programs should be in another school department, e.g., compensatory education.

A study by Parelius (1968) concerned the position of the special education director as perceived by the director and superintendent. A total sample of 55 directors and superintendents responded to a questionnaire based upon eight critical task areas, developed by the Southern States Cooperative Program in Educational Administration in 1955. Results indicated that within groups, role consensus was moderate for directors and high for superintendents, with regard to role-expectation statements for the role of director for special education. There were no significant differences between directors and superintendents on the combined role-expectation statements. It was recommended that directors have administrative authority over instruction, pupils and professional personnel, facilities, and organizational development and community relations. Little confidence was placed in the authority of the special education administrator to control transportation, finance, and business management. Parelius' findings were in partial conflict with those of Taylor (1967); in the earlier study, more than 70% of the special education directors perceived a need to be involved in budget preparation and management.

In another study, Hill (1967) compared the amount of agreement between superintendents and directors of special education in terms of their perception of major administrative tasks and major responsibilities for certain administrative functions. A sample of 53 superintendents and 60 directors of special education was drawn from 10 of the largest school districts in seven southeastern states. The subjects responded to an instrument developed by Hill, composed of 55 specific administrative tasks. Hill found no major disagreement between superintendents and directors of special education in their perceptions of administrative tasks or major responsibilities of the special education director.

Edgington (1968) studied five different types of personnel: assistant superintendents, building principals, psychologists, teachers, and special education administrators. He wanted to determine similarities or differences in perception of program philosophy, the degree of interaction between each of these groups of personnel, and the type of administrative structure in a number of school districts. Five respondents came from the 18 California school districts with the largest number of educable mentally retarded children. Data were obtained through personal interview. Results of this study were also used in the development of a set of guidelines to resolve administrative problems in programs for the retarded.

Results indicated differences of opinion in critical problem areas. There was a major tendency among the respondents not to hold certain concepts for one another's roles. While the personnel felt that administrators in special education encountered unique problems, they were, in fact, the same problems faced by other areas of administration. From the study it was found that (a) 16 of the 18 districts had an organizational chart delineating roles and responsibilities, with the greatest concern being the line-staff delineation of the director of special education; (b) generalists, or assistant superintendents, mentioned that principals and directors chiefly effected changes in their behavior, while directors cited principals and teachers as primary motivators of change in their role implementation.

Sloat (1969) attempted to differentiate special education personnel from general education administrators and supervisory leadership personnel on the basis of perceived task, skill emphasis, and certain demographic characteristics. In addition, differences in special education leadership personnel were analyzed. From each administrative group (special education administrator, general education administrator, supervisory personnel), 30 leadership personnel responded to a Likert-type scale rating 36 tasks. The tasks were weighted according to the type of task (administrative or supervisory) and type of skill (human, conceptual, or technical).

When Sloat compared special education leadership personnel to other leadership groups, he found that the former tended to be somewhat younger, had less administrative experience, and came from special education teaching ranks (60%), especially the secondary ranks. As a group, they tended to interact more often with a variety of professionals in other disciplines in education, both within and outside of their school districts. They generally had had master's or post-master's training, held more teaching certificates, but had fewer administrative and/or supervisory certificates. These results were consistent with the summary compiled by Kohl and Marro (1971) of special education administrators as compared with the general education administrators.

Two distinct groups of special education leadership personnel were identified after task analysis of the skill-perception ratings. The first group, called Special Education-Unique (U), was found to have very high clustered scores, and the responses of the second group, Special Education-Combination (C), clustered with a majority of the administrative and supervisory responses. U-type leaders perceived their job to be equally important in all facets of public school administration. This group tended to be older and had less formal training than the C-type leader. They had been in their positions longer, were less status-oriented, and were employed most often in small to medium-sized districts.

The C-type leader, on the other hand, perceived his role more like that of a majority of administrators and supervisors in general education. When this group was further subdivided, it was found to be more closely in line with the personnel task choices of supervisory personnel. Burrello (1969) found that special education administrators under 44 years of age tended to have higher status needs and deferred less to others. Sloat (1969) recommended that a replication of this study be done, using larger samples of subjects to verify the reliability of the judges' rating and the validity of self-perceived task-importance scores. Also, he recommended that preparation programs include an emphasis on supervisory training and that more attention be given to human relations skills.

Another study of tasks and skills was performed by Sage (1968), comparing special education administrators and building principals. The investigator utilized a 12-celled grid developed by Hemphill, Griffiths, and Fredericksen (1962), in order to classify a random sample of responses from members of the Council of Administrators of Special Education and the statements of knowledge and function listed in the professional-standards report of the Council for Exceptional Children (1966). Seventy-nine administrative function from the professional-standards report were classified by 12 doctoral students in terms of the 12-celled grid.

The analysis scheme has two dimensions. The first contains four categories to classify problems encountered by the school administrator: improving educational opportunities, obtaining and developing personnel, maintaining effective interrelationships with the community, and providing and maintaining funds and facilities. The other dimension includes three types of skills suggested by Katz (1955) as required in administrative functioning: technical, human, and conceptual.

The major factor which distinguishes roles, when evaluated from either source of data, is in the educational-program technical cell. Sage (1968) found that this role, "having greater involvement with improving educational opportunity and greater requirement for technical skills to have accomplished the task," is reflected by the special educator's concern for "securing services, which for the general administrator are sufficiently well-established to be operating under their own momentum [p. 71]." When the results were used to compare the special educator with the general educator, the same factor was reflected: the special educator tended to focus upon the technical details of providing and improving services and programs for handicapped children. Sage also found that size of district was a variable which contributed to the differentiation he found. This was similar to the findings of Downey (1970) but contrary to those of Courtnage (1967) and others.

In another study by Harris (1969), the present role and specific activities of directors of special education in Michigan were compared with other general education administrators. The study compared the perceptions of administrative tasks and level of preparation of special education administrators in both local and intermediate school districts, and those of intermediate superintendents and elementary and secondary building principals. A total sample of 182 school administrators responded to a three-part survey, designed to elicit responses regarding administrative activities and personal and school-wide data. Harris found that administrative activities of intermediate directors of special education were more like those of intermediate superintendents, while local directors behaved more like building principals in terms of their administrative duties. Both types of special education administrators stated that they spent most of their time in staff relations and in other areas of personnel administration. All groups believed that they should be spending more time in the areas of curriculum and instruction.

These two groups could also be distinguished by different kinds of preparation. Special education administrators tended to major in special education, while general educators majored in educational administration. Special education administrators tended to have a shorter tenure of office and fewer years in leadership experiences. These results were similar to those obtained by Sloat (1969) and Kohl and Marro (1971).

Lamb (1970) studied groups, not focusing on administrative tasks and skills but on values and attitudes held toward exceptional children. The major purpose of his study was to investigate the administrator's and supervisor's knowledge of, and attitude toward, exceptional children in two county-wide systems which followed different educational philosophies. These two Florida counties were contiguous and ranked third and fourth in the state in population. One county represented a highly integrated approach to special education, while the other maintained an almost completely segregated approach. The total sample consisted of 163 respondents, building principals, supervisors, county level administrators, and others.

The groups were surveyed by means of a questionnaire designed to measure the amount of knowledge and attitude toward exceptional children. A personal data form was completed by all respondents. It was concluded that there were no significant differences in the accepting attitude of administrators and supervisors toward exceptional children that could be related to identification with either an integrated or a segregated approach. On the general information inventory, however, the results indicated that personnel in the integrated county system tended to be more knowledgeable about the education of exceptional children than administrators and supervisors in the county system which operated programs in separate facilities; this difference was significant at the .05 level.

Research group 3: Between-group studies of organizational climate

Three studies analyzed different components of administrative behavior within an intermediate school district by investigating the relationships between the director of special education and his level of training and experience with the perceptions of staff, with regard to organizational climate and preferred climates.

Birch (1970) sought to determine whether there were differences in the perceptions of organizational climates and preferences for organizational climates between directors of special education and their staff, and between staff in individual districts. The population for this study (as well as for the other two to be reported) consisted of directors and staff of 29 intermediate school district special education departments in Michigan. The 528 participants, comprising eight categories of personnel, were directors, supervisors, school diagnosticians, school social workers, speech therapists, itinerant consultants, teachers for the physically handicapped, and teachers for the homebound and hospitalized. The instrument used to collect the data was the organizational-climate-description questionnaire (OCDQ) developed by Halpin and Croft (1963) for use in elementary schools. The OCDQ contains 64 items and assesses eight dimensions of organizational climate. The dimensions of disengagement, hindrance, esprit, and intimacy described the behavior of the group; production emphasis, thrust or modeling behavior, and consideration described the behavior of the leader. In order to make these items appropriate for use in an intermediate school district, the items were revised and factor-analyzed; the resulting factors were compared with the orginal OCDQ. This procedure found that original and revised OCDQ to be statistically similar.

In Birch's study, personnel were asked to give their perceptions of the present organizational climate and indicate their preferences for a new or different climate. The findings were as follows: There were no significant differences between categories of personnel with respect to organizational climate perceived or desired. There was close agreement between the directors as a group and the staff as a group, in the perception of the present organizational climate and that which they desired. Where differences between staff and director's perceptions of organizational climate were found, they were seen to be the function of the individual district and not of the group to which the individual belonged. The degree of thrust and production emphasis demonstrated by directors of special education departments was less than desired by their staffs. The special education staff also preferred to have higher esprit. Finally, a majority of the district directors preferred less hindrance and greater esprit and consideration than they perceived.

Spicknall (1970) used the same population sample in a follow-up study to investigate the relationship between organizational-climate variables and communication variables and the adoption of innovative special education programs, practices, and procedures. In addition to the OCDQ, Spicknall developed an innovativeness scale, whose score was based upon the adoption of 19 programs, practices, and procedures in each of the intermediate school districts. All of these practices had been adopted by less than 50% of the districts in the population. He also developed a communication-variables questionnaire which scored the use of mass media, interpersonal sources of information, professional involvement of staff and director, staff and director cosmopolitanism, and opinion leadership of director; a personal data sheet also was included.

The relationships between the innovativeness and the communication variables were measured by a multiple-linear-regression analysis. The professional involvement accounted for almost 20% of the variance in innovativeness. Only the communication variable was found to have a significant relationship with innovativeness, at the .05 level. Of the other 17 relationships between innovativeness and organizational climate that were tested, only four variables were found significant: (a) Innovativeness of intermediate special education departments was positively related to the size of the school-aged population of the intermediate school district; i.e., larger school-aged populations were associated with higher innovativeness. (b) Innovativeness in intermediate special education departments was positively related to the esprit score on the revised OCDQ; i.e., higher morale or esprit was associated with higher innovativeness. (c) Innovativeness in intermediate special education departments was related positively to the thrust score on the revised OCDQ; i.e., higher thrust was associated with higher innovativeness in intermediate special education departments. (d) Innovativeness in intermediate special education departments was positively related to the professional involvement of the special education staff.

The third study in this group (Clark, 1970) was primarily concerned with the relationships between organizational-climate factors measured by the same instrument and variables associated with academic training, professional experience, age, tenure, and sensitivity training of the intermediate directors of special education. The results follow: (a) No relationships were found between scores on any of the OCDQ factors and the following variables: amount of course work in education, special education or educational administration, director's reported undergraduate grade-point average, amount of sensitivity training of the director, his age, length of tenure of the director, previous employment of the director. (b) There were statistically significant correlations found at or beyond the .05 level in the following instances: a positive correlation between recency of degree earned and hindrance indicated that directors who recently received their highest academic degrees were perceived by the staff to be relatively more hindering than facilitating with regard to task accomplishment. (Earlier, Newman [1970] had suggested that a study be made of the relationship between special education teaching experience and administrative functioning.) According to Clark (1970), elementary grade teaching and total amount of teaching experience both correlated negatively with consideration, while secondary grade teaching was negatively correlated with thrust. This suggested that directors who have had these teaching experiences are perceived by their staff to be relatively less considerate and to have less thrust. Nonclassroom special education experience correlated negatively with aloofness, suggesting that directors who have had this experience are perceived to be less aloof or impersonal. Negative correlations appeared between noneducational administrative experience and esprit, production emphasis, and thrust. This suggests that morale is lower in staffs where directors have had such experience. These directors were also perceived by their staffs to be ineffective in moving the organization, whether by close supervision or by example. A positive correlation was found between internship experience and production emphasis, which suggests that directors who have had this experience are perceived to be highly directive and to be closely supervisory of their staff.

Research group 4: Studies of factors used in determining administrative structure of special education services

A fourth group of studies, undertaken between 1964 and 1970, dealt with the development and growth factors which affect special education in different geographical settings, from sparsely populated rural county school units to more populated urban school districts.

The four most prevalent types of special education administrative structures were found to be (*a*) large local school districts, the major providers of services for the handicapped populations; (*b*) smaller contiguous districts, which enter into cooperative agreements with the larger system; (*c*) smaller districts, which band together; (*d*) a number of smaller districts, which defer to the larger intermediate or regional unit and which may be defined in terms of degrees of autonomy.

Bowers (1970) identified three types of intermediate units: a dependent intermediate unit (Type 1), in which policy making, decision making, and program development remain in the hands of the local districts; a semi-independent intermediate unit (Type 2), in which the regional unit has some responsibility and authority but is closely bound to the desires and recommendations of local educators and citizenry; and an independent intermediate unit (Type 3), in which complete physical and policy autonomy exist.

What criteria are used to select the appropriate administrative structure in rural sparsely populated areas and in suburban or metropolitan areas? Both Bowers (1970) and Chalfant (1965, 1967) found that urbanization, educational level of the community, socioeconomic status, rural occupations, financial ability, and population growth were major criteria in the planning of special education services in county units with low incidence of handicap. Bowers, among others, applied these criteria and found that the independent intermediate unit (Type 3) was considered to be the most efficacious to meet the needs in rural and sparsely populated areas. He also indicated that this type of organizational unit suffered in attitudinal criteria, in that local educators found communication with this type of district was difficult and, in fact, a barrier in the establishment of a regional program, since these programs were not as sensitive to local needs and desires as a Type 2 program.

Other studies have considered community and school factors which affect the development of special education services. In a survey of school superintendents in Kentucky, Edwards (1964) found that the climate of opinion within a local school district toward services for educable mentally retarded can be defined by the professional educator's recognition of need, the local district's assessment of need, and community recognition of need. She also collected data on the existent classes in the local districts and predicted the number needed to reach a full-service objective. She found, in analysis of superintendents' responses, that there was a relationship between the presence of existing programs and predicted needs for classes of educable mentally retarded children. The presence of programs apparently influenced local awareness of needs more than the predicted size of the need for programs. Frazee (1967) used an urban sample of 92 Illinois school districts (average daily attendance 10,000 +), which were divided into three groups: 26 high school districts, 30 elementary districts, and 36 unit-school districts. He found that three school factors (size of pupil population, staff ratio, escalating costs) and two community factors (presence of slums, number of elderly) correlated with growth of special education, as measured by the number of professional special education personnel per 1,000 pupils in the average daily attendance. Growth of special education was not limited by financial resources in urban areas. Conclusions have limited generalizability, since the ratio of state to local funds needed to support programs for the handicapped varies significantly in different states.

Bentley (1970) found that cost factors for each area of exceptionality varied across school districts from five different states and that the relationship between state reimbursement and local contributions was the primary factor for the observed differences. He also found that personnel costs in administrative, instructional, and supportive areas, as well as supplies, equipment, operation maintenance, and transportation costs, were the main cost differentials which maintained themselves across all major categories of exceptional-child programs and regular school programs.

SPECIAL-GENERAL EDUCATIONAL ADMINISTRATION AND THEORY

The need for theory in special education administration was first recognized by Connor (1963) and later by others such as Willower (1970) and Kohl and Marro (1971). In response to this need, this section is devoted to an examination of the motivation and need for theory as a guide to research and practice in special education administration. An examination will be made of the assumption upon which administrative theory is based and of the relationship between special education and general education administration. In conclusion, a social-systems theory of administration will be outlined, and research questions derived from theory will be presented in relation to the area of special education administration.

Why a theory of administration for special education? Halpin (1958) cautioned those interested in theory development to examine their motives. He asked: "Are we seeking a better 'understanding' of theory, or are we trying to promote the 'idea' of theory? [p. 14]."

In this chapter, the concern is with the former question. Even while selecting a particular theory to illustrate the use of theory and to present research questions, the author recognizes the truth in Halpin's comments: "Neither a particular theory nor the idea of theory are things to be sold, to be marketed as an advertiser might market a new breakfast cereal [p. 14]." A number of theories may serve equally well; here, the conceptualization of Getzels and Guba (1957) and its elaboration by Getzels et al.

(1968) have been selected for illustrative purposes. Their work on educational administration as a social process meets the criteria of science – objectivity, reliability, operational concepts, systematic structure, and comprehensiveness.

Griffiths (1959) presented a four-step criterion for a theory of administration and its value. First, theory provides guidance for action. Both anticipated and unanticipated consequences of action should be accounted for. "Theory does this by directing attention to processes and relationships rather than techniques [p. 25]." Second, theory provides guidance in the collection of facts in two ways: (*a*) Facts are sought to enhance concepts upon which a theory is built; and (*b*) facts are suggested by theory and give meaning to and validate it. Third, theory should guide the researcher through suggesting testable hypotheses. It is this function of theory which leads to the development of empirical laws from which principles may be derived. Fourth, theory should enhance our understanding of the administration process. According to Thompson (1958), "The focus of an adequate theory will be on processes rather than on correlations [p. 32]."

An example of an empirical test of theory was reported by Barrett (1970). Initially, Barrett provided an excellent overview of a number of theoretical frameworks which deal with how organizations integrate the goals of individuals with the objectives of the organization. These theoretical frameworks became the focus of his empirical study, which dealt with "understanding conditions conducive to simultaneously satisfying individual needs and achieving organizational functioning [p. 3]."

The three models are described and presented in terms of a general theoretical model. The first, the exchange model, deals with the relationship between personal goals and organizational objectives, rather than with an integration of the two dimensions. The model can be best characterized as a bargaining relationship between the individual and organization. The two mechanisms used within the model to provide incentives for the individual to meet organizational objectives are the offering of monetary rewards in exchange for services and the provision of opportunities for informal social relations. Examples cited by Barrett are considerate treatment from superiors and opportunities to engage in informal social relationships with peers.

Barrett's second model is the socialization model. Within this model, goal integration is achieved by encouraging individuals to adopt a positive frame of reference toward organizational objectives and by discouraging participation in activities which do not lead to organizational effectiveness. The two major socialization mechanisms operative in this model are (*a*) leader socialization: a formal leader not only explains, but also demonstrates by his own actions, the kind of behavior he wishes his followers to emulate; it is hoped that the individual members of the organization will internalize his behavior; i.e., adopt organizational objectives and accept them as personal individual goals; (*b*) peer socialization: this mechanism operates in the same fashion, as an inducement to adopt organizational objectives.

Barrett also described a model he labeled "the accommodation model." Here, individual goals are taken into account in determining organizational objectives and the mechanisms or procedures for obtaining them. Objective building begins with individual goals, and the organization is so structured and operated as to meet simultaneously the expressed goals of individuals within the organization.

The two mechanisms described within the accommodation model are (*a*) role or job design: the personalization of roles becomes a primary tool so that roles can be divided in a number of ways to meet individual objectives; (*b*) participation: regardless of their level within the organization, individuals play a role in setting objectives and ordering priorities, seeking solutions to problems, and making the final decisions within the organization. The process of participation which Barrett discussed relates to goal integration in two ways:

The process of participating will be directly satisfactory to individuals whose personal goals it includes, if they are in control or contributing to policy formation. . . . Participation also allows the individual to represent his own unique needs and issues in the processes which actually define the nature of the organization [p. 12].

The results of Barrett's study, involving 178 refinery employees at all levels of management and skill, will not be presented here. To restate the focus of the study, it dealt with testing mechanisms within the three theoretical models and with the degree of goal integration achieved in organizational units. The second focus of the study was on the degree of goal integration and the quality of functioning of the organizational units, as reflected in their communication, coordination and control processes, innovation, and self-rated effectiveness. It also dealt with reactions of individuals to the membership in the organization, reflected in their levels of motivation, satisfaction, commitment to the organization, and freedom from job-related tensions.

Generally, Barrett's study indicated that:

Goal integration mechanisms associated with the three general models described above differ in the strength of their relationships to the goal integration present in the units. Mechanisms associated with the exchange model show inconsistent, generally low and sometimes negative relationships at a level of goal integration present. These exchange mechanisms, it appears, are clearly ineffective means of generating high levels of goal integration in organizations. Mechanisms associated with the socialization or accommodation model, on the other hand, reveal significant positive relationships to goal integration, the accommodation mechanisms showing the highest relationships of all. The use of socialization and accommodation mechanisms, therefore, would seem to be an effective means of generating high levels of goal integration in organizations [p. 99].

This study exemplified an empirical study to test the operational mechanisms, as described by three commonly identified theoretical frameworks in the area of administration. It represented an attempt to test the explanatory power of various theoretical frameworks, with regard to goal integration of organizational and individual expectations.

Assumptions: Special-general education administration

The theoretical model selected to illustrate the use of theory in research in special education administration is the social-system model described by Getzels and

Guba (1957). This model is concerned with the conceptualization of organizations as social systems, and, like the theories described by Barrett, has its basis within concepts upon which the exchange, socialization, and accommodation models are built: role effectiveness and efficiency, leadership, and so forth. The social-system theory, like Barrett's set of conceptualizations, is concerned with the meshing of organizational objectives and personal needs.

Before describing the social-system model of Getzels and Guba, it is necessary to list some assumptions regarding the relationship between special education and general education administration:

Educational administration is not significantly different from other types of administration, e.g., hospital, business, or public administration. Special education and general education administration are essentially similar. Griffiths (1959) indicated that "no strong case can be made for the exclusive study of adjectional administration (hospital versus educational administration) and no case at all can be made for the exclusive study of subadjectional administration (educational versus special or vocational administration) [p. 72] ."

The administration of special education programs can be studied within a social-system model, regardless of level and its constituent parts (classroom, school, local and intermediate school district) and its relationship to general education classroom, individual schools, and school districts.

The social-system model

The basic model, administration as a social process within a social-system context, was first described by Getzels and Guba (1957) and later by Getzels et al. (1968). The latter is the primary reference for the brief description of the model.

First, the model can be examined from three vantage points: structurally, functionally, and operationally. Structurally, administration is seen as a "hierarchy of superordinate-subordinate relationships within a social system [p. 52]." Functionally, this hierarchy of relationships is a locus for allocating and integrating roles and facilities, in order to achieve the goals of the system. Operationally, the administrative process takes effect in situations involving person-to-person interactions. The authors indicated that for general analytical purposes, the social system as they conceived it involves two classes of phenomena, which are at once "conceptually independent and phenomenologically interactive [p. 56] ." These are the institutions, with certain roles and expectations which will fulfill the goals of the system; and the individuals, with certain personalities and dispositions, inhabiting the system, whose observed inter-actions comprise what they call social behavior.

The first class of phenomena has been described as a normative or nomothetic dimension, which considers the social system whose components parts are the institution's role and expectation, each term serving as the analytical unit to determine the preceding. Briefly, these three terms are described in the following fashion: The institution is composed of people who have been structurally organized into roles which are normative in nature and maintained within prescribed parameters, in order to insure the attainment of institutional goals and objectives.

The role is considered the most important analytical unit of the institution. Roles are thought to represent position, offices, or statuses within institutions. They are defined in terms of role expectations, which call for normative rights and duties. Role expectations are affected by both formal structured norms and by informal structure within the system. Roles can be more or less flexible, tend to be complementary, and vary in scope.

Expectation is defined as those "rights and duties, privileges and obligations – in a word, those prescriptions that delineate what a person should and should not do under varied circumstances as the incumbent of a particular role in a social system [p. 64]." The normative or nomothetic dimension can be depicted in the following manner: social system → institution → role → expectation → institutional goal behavior.

The second class of phenomena, described as the personal or idiographic dimension, also contains analytical units, each term being defined by the previous one; they are the individual, his personality, and his need dispositions. In the personal dimension the individual, like the institution, consists of his component parts – in this case, personality and need dispositions. The personality is conceived in a dynamic fashion; the individual is not considered a passive actor but rather an active and stimulus-seeking person. Need dispositions are conceived as the forces within the individual. They are conceptualized as "goal oriented and influence not only the goals which individuals will try to attain in a particular environment, but also the way in which he will perceive it and cognitize the environment itself [p. 75]." Need dispositions, in their conceptualization, are perceived as patterned or interrelated. They can be organized in a hierarchical fashion, described by Maslow's need theory. It can be said that this dimension is represented in the following manner: individual → personality → need disposition → individual goal behavior. The authors summarized their description of the two dimensions of behavior in the social system by suggesting that "the one is conceived as a rising in institutional goals and fulfilling goal expectations, the other as rising individual goals and fulfilling personality dispositions [p. 78]."

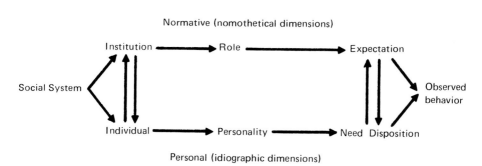

Figure 1

Getzels' and Guba's Description of Educational Administration as a Social Process

Reprinted from Getzels, J.W., & Guba, E.G. *School Review,* 1957, **65**, 423-444, with permission.

The social-system model described above was selected for its ability to generate testable hypotheses related to issues in educational administration. There are five areas in which the model provides certain conceptual and methodological advantages: (*a*) problems related to sources of organizational conflict; (*b*) problems related to adaptation and adjustment in social systems; (*c*) issues such as effectiveness, efficiency, and satisfaction and morale; (*d*) the nature of authority, leadership-followership styles, or superordinate-subordinate relationships; and (*e*) the problem of organizational change. The investigators indicated that these terms are not necessarily unique to this specific problem but have been recurrent themes in the literature of administration.

FUTURE RESEARCH WITHIN THE SOCIAL-SYSTEM MODEL FOR THE FIELD OF SPECIAL EDUCATION ADMINISTRATION

The problems in research and practice of special education administration can be conceptualized within a social-system model. Much of the previous research cited — within-group and between-group, relative to the role of the special education administrator — fits appropriately within this model. Previous research studies, however, were primarily descriptive of role and attitudes of others toward the role incumbent. They focused primarily on correlational studies, not on the processes of administration. Research questions presented below have been selected because they are major problems of concern to both practitioner and researcher. The practitioner needs guides to staff development, behavior relationships, and satisfaction and morale. The researcher in special education administration needs to develop a more generalized model of the practice of administration and to validate this theory in administrative practice.

Organizational change

Organizational change poses one of the severest tests of the ability of a systematic model to deal with present organizational structure and problems. Any model must be able to describe and predict for existing structures and to account for the process of change. Getzels et al. (1968) said that "no aspect of behavior of social systems is less well understood than the sources of change, or for that matter, failure to change [p. 150-151]."

Organizational change can come from within as well as without the social system. Special educators are faced today with the problem of change from two external sources: legislative and judicial mandates for providing services for handicapped children. In the first area, we can look to the number of states that are moving from permissive legislation regarding the provision of services to handicapped children to the passage of mandatory special education laws.

A number of issues related to criteria in the development of special education programs were suggested by Edwards (1968), Chalfant (1965, 1967), Frazee (1967), Bowers (1969), and Bentley (1970), under either permissive or mandatory special education laws. Both Bowers and Chalfant implied a significant issue which needs further study in terms of organizational change under either type of state law. Chalfant (1967) stated:

Where population density can be controlled, researchers should focus on such intangible variables as local leadership and community pressure groups who probably stimulate or repress the development of special education programs [p. 56].

In order to look at these attitudinal issues, it will be necessary to conduct participant-observer field studies where significant pressure groups are identified, both external to and within the social system itself, in order to determine opposing and supporting forces which would affect the development of special education services. Hall (1970) suggested that the Lewinian force-field analysis technique may be useful in helping decision-making community groups and institutional groups to determine perceived forces involved in changing the system's approach to service delivery to handicapped youngsters.

The force-field analysis technique has been utilized in a number of educational, health, industrial, and community settings to assist in group or individual problem identification and analysis; to delineate parameters of the problem in order to identify priorities, so that meaningful action can be accomplished within a reasonable time frame; to identify appropriate methodology to facilitate maximum level of participation and implementation; and to establish a set of evaluation criteria to determine level of effectiveness at each subsequent decision point.

Where problem situations occur, *a level of activity* is operant that is different from what may be desired. Such a level of activity (i.e., level of program integration of handicapped children due to mandatory special education in the total school program) may be occurring at different levels of frequency, depending upon the individuals, group or organization, and their reaction to a number of pressures. These influences are, in Lewinian terms, forces which "may be both external to. . . and internal to. . . the person(s) or situation in question [p. 2]." Lewin described them as the driving force and the restraining forces. The former promotes the occurrence of the activity, i.e., late-program integration of handicapped children; the latter inhibit or oppose the occurrence of the same activity level. An activity level (rate of program integration in school district) is the *result* of the simultaneous influence of both the driving and restraining forces.

The two force fields push in opposite directions and while the stronger of the two will tend to characterize the problem situation, a point of balance is usually achieved which gives the appearance of habitual behavior of a steady state condition. Changes in the strength of either of the fields, however, can cause a change in the activity level of concern. These apparently habitual ways of behaving or frozen attitudes can be changed (and related problems solved) by bringing about change in the relative strengths of Driving and Restraining Force Fields [Hall, 1970, p. 1].

Within this construct, other conflicts that arise between the community and the institution, or internally between others in the social system, too, can be further delineated. Further investigations can be pursued. Institutional and individual

247

Special Education Administration

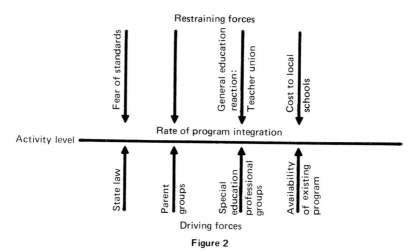

Figure 2

The Lewinian Force-Field Analysis

Reprinted from Lewin, K. *Human Relations,* 1947, **1**, 5-41, with permission.

expectations of individuals or groups within the school setting can be conceptualized as driving or restraining force fields which effect organizational change.

The second major area of concern for special educators with regard to organizational change has been the increasing litigation around the country regarding the inappropriateness of placing blacks, poor whites, and other minority youngsters into programs for the educable mentally retarded, and, most recently, suits involving the exclusion of emotionally disturbed children from services within the public schools. While most of these suits have ended in stipulated agreements between local school districts and the plaintiffs, they have made a significant impact in changing the complexion of special education service-delivery systems and their relationship to the larger systems.

Questions arising from litigation have become a major source of study for students of organizational change in special education and include the following: (*a*) How will general educators accept and implement responsibility, enforced by the courts, to provide educational services for youngsters who have been considered inappropriately placed in programs for the educable mentally retarded and emotionally disturbed? (*b*) What role should special education play in helping to design new programs to meet the needs of these youngsters within the regular school program? (*c*) What role will opposing forces play from within or outside the institution, in order to facilitate the change or resist the change?

Getzels et al. (1968) argued that responses to change may

take the form of a reaction or accommodation or some combination of the two. Reaction operates to retain congruence by bringing the changing element back to where it was; accommodation operates to retain congruence by bringing the other elements into some appropriate alignment with the changing elements [p. 154].

Whatever process, reaction, or accommodation is initiated, often there is a defensive

248

reaction from those who advocate the return of these youngsters to regular education, as well as from those who advocate maintaining the status quo within special and general education.

Research questions significant to the study of the administrative process, in terms of the implications of the stipulated agreements that grow out of the litigation, are presented below as issues in organizational change, organizational conflict, problems related to adaptation and adjustment in the social system, superordinate-subordinate relationships, and leader-follower relationships as well as issues related to effectiveness, efficiency, satisfaction, and morale. The issue of litigation provides us with a series of researchable questions to which students of educational administration might well address themselves.

Concerning problems related to sources of organizational conflict, the study of conflict between roles and within roles might be pursued in the following manner: The research question is, How does the institutionalized response pattern with the social system alter as a function of issues raised by the litigation? The referral process for youngsters who have been considered mildly retarded is no longer a viable option for the regular classroom teacher who has difficulty with such a child. The child may exhibit some difficulties in learning and may have some problems in adjustment, evidenced by his behavioral manifestations and reactions to the classroom environment. Mercer (1970), for example, charted the referral process from the regular classroom teacher to actual placement in the special education classroom. The regular education teacher, after having exhausted her own resources, generally called upon the building principal, who in turn requested psychological testing, after which a case conference was generally held and the decision to place or not to place was made.

Because of recent litigation, this process may be altered. The regular classroom teacher may now be forced to develop or seek out other resources, in order to help her deal with youngsters whom, heretofore, she has been referring out of her classroom because of the child's apparent or real inability to cope with the general education curriculum. The school curriculum, by the way, may be the real basis for both the child's and the teacher's problem. Revising the curriculum might be considered as one indication of organizational change in the structure, due to external and internal pressures to maintain children within the mainstream. Specifically, this issue involves the question of how role expectations are shaped and adapted, in order to adjust to external and internal pressure for change. Change in both institutional and personal role expectations for a variety of professionals may surface.

We might look at changes within roles. School psychologists may become a primary resource to classroom teachers, not to assist in the removal of the child but to play the role of consultant to the classroom teacher; in fact, many school psychologists have already begun to do this. One may also see that the role of the school psychologist may change from a primary participant in the decision-making process to a consultant to parents. Special resource personnel within special education may well be pressed into further service to work with children they have not been working with before. The ramifications of the relationship between teachers also become a significant area of study as one traces the development of new roles for special education personnel, from providing direct instructional services to children to providing instructional and management consultation to the regular classroom teacher through demonstration and other forms of direct service and in-service training.

In regard to issues of examining change, Miles (1967) indicated that one way of considering change targets is to examine *relationships* that are considered crucial in the school, rather than separate roles, groups, or persons. He cited relationships discussed earlier, i.e., the relationship between the central office personnel and the building principal, the principal-teacher relationships, and the teacher-teacher relationships. More important, he suggested major change goals which may appropriately be considered and operationalized in resolving these issues: increasing internal interdependence and cooperation, adding adaptation mechanisms and skills, developing stronger data bases requiring stances toward change, and continuing the commitment to organizational and personal growth and development.

Research questions resulting from Miles's perspective include the following:

1. With regard to interdependence, how does the pressure to maintain handicapped children within the regular classroom affect the relationships between regular teacher and special teacher?

2. Can we see a difference in the amount of cooperative planning between ancillary personnel and the classroom teacher?

3. Do we see a more frequent call for instructional or mental health consultation services?

4. What is the nature of the requested service?

5. Will differences in pre- and postapplication of behavior treatments for youngsters become internalized?

6. How much interdependence exists between the building principal and the director of special education?

7. Do we see more joint conferencing/action/evaluation?

8. Is there more joint planning of in-service training programs for regular classroom teachers?

9. Are special education personnel being retrained through in-service efforts within the school district, so that they may act as consultants to the regular classroom teacher?

10. What new models or service options are developed in response to the need to maintain previously excluded youngsters?

11. What models or service options are more effective, as rated by teacher, administrator, parents, and children, for different types of learning or behavioral problems?

12. Do we see a difference in the kind of services that a director of special education provides to the building principal? Does the former become more of a

consultant to the principal, rather than an administrator supervising programs for the educable mentally retarded within the principal's building?

In terms of adaptation mechanisms, Miles was chiefly concerned with "how school systems develop, test, and institutionalize the adaptive mechanisms they must have in order to cope effectively with accelerated change [p. 24]." Miles's other two concerns were implicit within his strategy to test and institutionalize through system development and personnel development, on an adequate data base.

At a crucial juncture in the delivery of special education services, what role might special education play in facilitating organizational change within education? Special education that is conceptualized as experimental education suggests a new role for the field. Within this schema, special education would primarily serve as a change-managing unit within the schools. Its primary functions would include (a) problem identification and specification involving individual or groups of children, teachers, administrators, and supervisors; (b) analysis of a problem situation into component parts; (c) cooperative setting of priorities and parameters for problem resolution; (d) design of strategies to collect data to generate alternative solutions within school and community context; (e) identification of human and fiscal resources and inputs; (f) pilot testing and selection of appropriate intervention in terms of benefit/cost analysis; and (g) establishment of evaluation outcome criteria and evaluation procedures. The remaining functions are primarily related to testing system responsiveness, to accepting innovation, and to seeking adaptation and institutionalization through demonstration and in-service training activities. These latter functions also should be conceptualized in terms of expected outcomes according to some predetermined evaluation criteria.

Miles (1967) recommended a research and demonstration council of personnel to stimulate planning, development, and testing of new models of service delivery to children, teachers, administrators, and other staff personnel. Special education could refine and define its role as a subsystem, from an instructional role to an internal consultant role to the range of staff mentioned above. Certain instructional responsibilities would remain for those children with sensory and severe organic deficits which demand a highly structured environment managed by personnel with special technical skills.

In terms of subordinate-superordinate relationships (i.e., teacher-to-principal relationships), alterations may also occur. The traditional placement process may be changed. Hanson (1970) and Skay (1970) offered some evidence that this has already begun to occur. The teacher no longer goes to the building principal; ancillary personnel, where available, are often first sought out for assistance in designing educational prescriptions, developing management techniques, or providing mental health or social work services to the teacher, family, and child. Hanson's research indicated that where building programs have a large number of ancillary personnel, larger numbers of children are being retained within regular programs. However, other research by Skay indicated that many regular classroom teachers have been disenchanted with the nature of the ancillary services. This research raises other kinds of questions with regard to the degree of satisfaction or the degree of effectiveness of existing services being offered by special education personnel to general educators.

A number of research questions emerge:

1. What role does the principal play in securing effective support services for his teachers, who must now provide for children they have traditionally excluded from their regular programs?

2. Will regular education teachers refer all children with learning problems to supportive service personnel, if available, or continue to refer only certain children (as Skay found in his study of the referral process)?

3. What implications does the amount of special help requested by regular teachers have on the principal's perception of teacher effectiveness?

4. Will the principal-teacher relationship be affected, as evidenced by differences in perceptions of organizational climate in the school building?

The two remaining areas of research inquiry deserving mention, within the social-system model, relate to leader-follower styles and issues such as effectiveness, efficiency, and satisfaction or morale. Studies in leader-follower relationships were previously restricted to the personality traits of the leader (Stodgill, 1948). Since 1950, however, the research emphasis has switched from a "search for personality traits to a search for leadership behavior that makes a difference in the performance or satisfaction of the follower [Bowers & Seashore, 1966, p. 239]."

Bowers and Seashore reviewed leadership research since 1950 and found that four aspects emerge, forming what may be called the basic structure of leadership. They are:

1. *Support:* behavior that enhances someone else's feeling of personal worth and importance.
2. *Interaction facilitation:* behavior that encourages members of the group to develop close, mutually satisfying relationships.
3. *Goal emphasis:* behavior that stimulates an enthusiasm for meeting the group's goal or achieving excellent performance.
4. *Work facilitation:* behavior that helps achieve goal attainment by such activities as scheduling, coordinating, planning, and by providing resources such as materials and technical knowledge [p. 247].

Research relating leadership and organizational effectiveness usually begins with the selection of criteria of effectiveness, such as follower satisfaction or morale. The next step involves relating leadership to the criteria selected. Bowers and Seashore recommended that a better strategy would be to obtain

(a) measures reflecting a theoretically meaningful conceptual structure of leadership; (b) an integrated set of systematically derived criteria; and (c) a treatment of these data, which takes account of the multiplicity of relationships and investigates the adequacy of leadership characteristics in predicting effectiveness variables [pp. 249-250].

Within the social-system model, the nature of the leader-follower relationship depends in part on the operating style within the particular social system. Getzels and Guba (1957) described three distinct types of leader-follower styles — the nomothetic, the idiographic, and the transactional — within their social-system model. Each style represents a different focal point in terms of how to achieve the same or similar goal.

A further delineation of these three styles can be found in Blake and Mouton's (1964) discussion of a managerial grid. The grid focuses on five "ideal types" of leadership and/or supervisory behavior, based upon two dimensions of goal orientation of the leader: task dimension, or concern for production; and personal dimension, or concern for people.

Within any of the conceptualizations of leader-follower styles cited above, it is crucial to establish a set of criteria. In the social-system model, effectiveness cannot be merely the observed behavior of the leader and his follower. Effectiveness is perceived as a function of the "congruence of behavior with expectations," and both should be assessed. It is situational both in origin and at the point of assessment. Efficiency is perceived as personal in origin and is described as the function of the "congruence of behavior with need dispositions [Getzels & Guba, 1957, pp. 435-436]."

Using our previous examples of organizational changes confronting special and general education today, we might undertake the study of leader-follower relationships in terms of different leadership styles and their implications for achieving the stated goal. When the leader (principal or director of special education) is confronted with a problem situation, such as the assimilation of large numbers of handicapped children into regular classes from self-contained special education classes, his leadership style may generate particular response patterns on the part of subordinates, peers, superordinates, and parents. By determining the expectations held for his behavior in terms of these significant others and tracing his own decision-making pattern, one should be able to determine which leadership styles correlate highest with the predetermined level of expected effectiveness.

To determine the level of efficiency, one must search for the relationship of behavior to the needs and expectation dimensions in the model. When the leader's behavior conforms to his followers' need system, and programs are implemented with a minimum of strain (i.e., children are returned appropriately, with proper support to both sets of teachers and children), the behavior can be viewed as efficient. However, if his behavior conforms to the expectation dimension (i.e., maintaining the status quo, little integration) and it is in conflict with the need dimension, the behavior that is observed will be considered inefficient by the role incumbents.

To determine the level of satisfaction achieved, one must simultaneously study the institutional expectations and individual need dispositions of the role incumbents and how the leader selects alternative courses of action in order to produce maximum levels of effectiveness and efficiency.

Bowers and Seashore (1966) were quoted earlier with regard to the components of a strategy relating leadership behavior and organizational effectiveness. They noted that the multitude of relationships between criteria and the adequacy of leadership characteristics in predicting effectiveness, efficiency, and satisfaction need inclusion in studies of leader-follower behavior.

One example of the need to examine the relationship of criteria can be found in Halpin's (1966) discussion of the research on leader behavior within the social system. Effective leadership is a function of high performance on both dimensions of initiating structure (nomothetic) and consideration (idiographic). He indicated, however, that there is "some tendency for superiors and subordinates to evaluate opposite the contribution of the leader behavior dimensions to the effectiveness of leadership [p. 98]." Superordinates are generally more interested in seeing the leader implement the organizational expectations, while subordinates prefer the leader to extend more consideration to their need dispositions. Halpin concluded by saying: "This difference in group attitude appears to impose upon the leader some measure of conflicting role expectations [p. 98]."

In terms of Bowers and Seashore's second point concerning the adequacy of leadership characteristics in predicting organizational effectiveness, they indicated that "relationships exist not only between leadership or non-leadership variables and criteria, but also among leadership and non-leadership variables [p. 259]." In this conceptualization, prediction becomes a search within a complex chain of events and arrangements of concepts.

Within the social-system model, examples of chains and constructs which may be helpful in relating leadership behavior and issues of effectiveness, efficiency, and satisfaction or morale are discussed below.

Personality needs of the individual role incumbent (director of special education or principal) and the goal congruence of the individual and the organization (school system) demand further study.

Results from Sloat (1969), Burrello (1969), Clark (1970), and Kohl and Marro (1971) suggested that special education administrators tended to be younger than their general education administrative counterparts and had fewer years of experience; and that special educators within the groups could also be differentiated by the younger administrators having higher levels of activity and higher needs for recognition and status. These results were derived from self-report inventories, questionnaires, and perceptions of subordinates.

With regard to congruence between expectations, a crucial variable was found to be significant in studies by Sage (1968), Burrello (1969), Downey (1970), and Bowers (1970). This is related to the nature and type of organizational setting in which administrators of special education programs function. Specifically, within a longitudinal study, the issue could be stated in the following fashion: Younger administrators with higher needs for recognition and status, exhibiting a higher level of activity than their older counterparts, will not sustain their need preferences and will reduce their level of activity over time. Getzels et al. (1968) described this as the socialization of the individual over time within the social system. A second study is suggested in which administrators of both local school districts and intermediate units would be differentiated on the basis of need for independence, to determine if they can sustain this need value or if they become socialized within the institutional expectations of an individual district or intermediate program.

A measure of the perceived openness or closedness of the organizational climate in which the leader and role incumbent work would assist in making predictions of organizational effectiveness. Can differences in leadership styles (nomothetic, idiographic, or transactional) be identified on the basis of organizational climate? What observed differences can be identified in follower groups within climates, differentiated on an open-closed continuum?

Examples of teacher satisfaction and morale have been reported. Hammer (1970) indicated that special education teachers were less satisfied with their working conditions, opportunities for advancements, and other such factors, as compared with regular class teachers. It would be helpful to examine the personality of the special education teacher and the role expectations held for him by both special education administrators and the building principal, to determine congruence between their expectations and their relationship to level of performance. These issues could also be studied with regard to totally segregated versus more integrated programs, to determine satisfaction and the level of effectiveness in perception of working conditions. Both studies should include measures of climate in order to determine if climate factors account for constricting role descriptions (Halpin, 1966). Closed climates would tend to be more constricting than open climates.

SUMMARY

This chapter has provided a rationale for the selection and organization of research in special education administration and for new research directions in the field. It has listed some assumptions regarding the relationship between special education and general education administration; provided criteria for the selection of the social-system model; and described in some detail a theoretical framework or conceptual model which has received a great deal of attention in educational administration and which the author feels can channel special education administration research into new directions. Crucial issues on mandatory special education and its effects upon the school system, as well as implications of litigation for special education, have been briefly discussed; these topics were selected both because they are relevant to practitioners and researchers and because they serve as excellent examples of the effect of organizational change on institutional objectives (defined in roles) and individuals within the social system (defined in need dispositions). Research questions have been raised within the framework of the model regarding inter-role conflict, adaptive mechanisms, issues in morale and satisfaction, and organizational change in general. New criteria and research methodology for further consideration have been suggested for the field of special education and its practitioners.

The social-system model was selected because it has generated provocative research hypotheses and questions. It is by no means the only conceptual mode that should be encouraged and used. The development of a theory base for research in administration, however, is necessary if this field is to move onward to the point where it can predict kinds of behavior which will occur under specific conditions and within different organizational structures.

The author has indicated categorically that the need for theory to guide research is as great in special education as it is in general education. The purpose has been to enrich our understanding of administration, not to devise or promulgate a particular theory of administration. Finally, it has been suggested that pressing issues within the field of special education could be conceptualized within a social-system model in order to assist both researcher and practitioner.

References

Barrett, J.H. *Individual goals and organizational objectives: A study of integration mechanisms.* Ann Arbor, Mich.: Institute for Social Research, 1970.

Bentley, R.W. *An exploration of relationships between expenditures for educational programs for exceptional children and expenditures for regular educational programs.* (Doctoral dissertation, University of Wisconsin) Ann Arbor, Mich.: University Microfilms, 1970, No. 71-3449.

Birch, E.L. *A study of the differences between perceived and desired organizational climate in special education staffs of selected intermediate school districts in Michigan.* (Doctoral dissertation, Michigan State University) Ann Arbor, Mich.: University of Microfilms, 1970, No. 71-2034.

Blake, R.R., & Mouton, J.S. *The managerial grid: key orientations for achieving production through people.* Houston: Gulf, 1964.

Bowers, D.G., & Seashore, S.E. Predicting organizational effectiveness with a four factor theory of leadership. *Administrative Science Quarterly,* 1966, 2, 238-263.

Bowers, N.E. *The development and application of a set of criteria for use in the establishment of a comprehensive regional special education program.* (Doctoral dissertation, University of Illinois) Ann Arbor, Mich.: University Microfilms, 1969, No. 70-13, 251.

Burrello, L.C. *The development and validation of the Behavior Preference Inventory based upon Rotter's social learning theory for use with special education administrators.* (Doctoral dissertation, Syracuse University) Ann Arbor, Mich.: University of Microfilms, 1969, No. 70-14, 718.

Chalfant, J.C. *Factors related to special education services in Illinois.* (Doctoral dissertation, University of Illinois) Ann Arbor, Mich.: University Microfilms, 1965, No. 65-11, 752.

Chalfant, J.C. *Factors related to special education services.* Washington, D.C.: Council for Exceptional Children, 1967.

Clark, A.L. *A study of the relationships between organizational climate factors and the academic preparation, professional experience, and other related variables of intermediate district special education directors in Michigan.* (Doctoral dissertation, Michigan State University) Ann Arbor, Mich.: University Microfilms, 1970, No. 71-2044.

Connor, L.E. Preliminaries to a theory of administration for special education. *Exceptional Children,* 1963, 33, 431-436.

Council for Exceptional Children and National Education Association. *Professional standards for personnel in the education of exceptional children.* Washington, D.C.: Author, 1966.

Courtnage, L.E. *School administrators' attitudes and opinions concerning the public school's responsibility in providing education for exceptional children.* (Doctoral dissertation, Colorado State College) Ann Arbor, Mich.: University Microfilms, 1967, No. 67-13, 672.

Downey, R.D. *A study of the leader behavior of special education administrators in Illinois public schools.* (Doctoral dissertation, Southern Illinois University) Ann Arbor, Mich.: University Microfilms, 1970, No. 71-9983.

Edgington, H.J. *The administration and supervision of programs for the educable mentally retarded.* (Doctoral dissertation, University of Southern California) Ann Arbor, Mich.: University Microfilms, 1968, No. 68-12, 030.

Edwards, S.A. *Indices of community readiness for special classes for the educable mentally retarded in Kentucky.* (Doctoral dissertation, Teachers College, Columbia University) Ann Arbor, Mich.: University Microfilms, 1964, No. 65-4726.

Frazee, V.F. *School and community characteristics related to special educational services in urban communities.* (Doctoral dissertation, University of Illinois) Ann Arbor, Mich.: University Microfilms, 1967, No. 68-1751.

Getzels, J.W., & Guba, E.G. Social behavior and the administrative process. *School Review,* 1957, **65**, 423-444.

Getzels, J.W., Lipham, J.M., & Campbell, R.F. *Education administration as a social process.* New York: Harper, 1968.

Griffiths, D.E. *Administrative theory.* New York: Appleton-Century-Crofts, 1959.

Gulick, L., & Urwick, L. (Eds.), *Papers on the science of administration.* New York: Institute of Public Affairs, 1937.

Hall, J. The effective organization. In *Models for management.* Conroe, Tex.: Teleometrics, 1970.

Halpin, A.W. (Ed.) The development of theory in education administration. *Administrative theory in education.* Chicago: Midwest Administration Center, 1958.

Halpin, A.W. *Theory and research in administration.* New York: Macmillian, 1966.

Halpin, A.W., & Croft, D.B. The organizational climate of schools. *Administrator's Notebook,* 1963, **11**(44), 1-14.

Hammer, R.E. *Job satisfaction of special class teachers in Iowa: An application of the Hertzberg two factor theory.* (Doctoral dissertation, University of Iowa) Ann Arbor, Mich.: University Microfilms, 1970, No. 70-23, 896.

Hanson, R.M. *Factors affecting elementary principals' decisions to maintain handicapped children in the regular class.* (Doctoral dissertation, Syracuse University) Ann Arbor, Mich.: University Microfilms, 1970, No. 71-11, 008.

Harris, G.A. *An investigation of the preparation patterns and administrative activities of special education directors in Michigan.* (Doctoral dissertation, Michigan State University) Ann Arbor, Mich.: University Microfilms, 1969, No. 69-20, 869.

Hemphill, J.K., Griffiths, D.E., & Fredericksen, N. *Administrative performance and personality.* New York: Bureau of Publications, Teachers College, Columbia University, 1962.

Hill, R.A. *Tasks of the special education director as defined by superintendents of schools and by directors of special education.* (Doctoral dissertation, University of Georgia) Ann Arbor, Mich.: University Microfilms, 1967, No. 67-16, 226.

Katz, R.L. Skills of an effective administrator. *Harvard Business Review,* 1955, **33**, 33-42.

Kohl, J., & Marro, T. The special education administrator: A normative study of the administrative position in special education. Final Report, 1971, Grant No. OEG-0-70-2468 (607), Bureau for the Education of the Handicapped, U.S. Office of Education.

Lamb, J.R. *A comparison of administrators' and supervisors' knowledge of and acceptant attitude toward exceptional children in two Florida counties using diverse organizational patterns.* (Doctoral dissertation, Syracuse University) Ann Arbor, Mich.: University Microfilms, 1970, No. 70-15, 233.

Lewin, K. Frontiers in group dynamics: Concept, method and reality in social science and social change. *Human Relations,* 1947, **1**, 5-41.

Meisgeier, C.H., & Sloat, R. Special education administration and supervision: A review of relevant literature. In C.H. Meisgeier & J.D. King (Eds.), *The process of special education administration.* New York: International Textbook, 1970.

Mercer, J. The ecology of mental retardation — the challenge of mental retardation in the community. In J. Cohen (Ed.), *Proceedings of the 1st Annual Spring Conference of the Institute for the Study of Mental Retardation and Related Disabilities.* Ann Arbor, Mich.: University of Michigan Press, 1970.

Miles, M.B. Some properties of schools as social systems. In G. Watson (Ed.), *Change in school systems.* Washington, D.C.: National Training Laboratories, 1967.

Newman, K.S. *Tasks of the administration of programs of special education in selected public school systems with pupil populations between 13,000 and 30,000.* (Doctoral dissertation, Arizona State University) Ann Arbor, Mich.: University Microfilms, 1968, No. 68-15, 012.

Newman, K.S. Administrative tasks in special education. *Exceptional Children,* 1970, **34**, 521-524.

Parelius, A.M. *A study of the role expectations of special education directors in Oregon.* (Doctoral dissertation, University of Oregon) Ann Arbor, Mich.: University Microfilms, 1968, No. 70-9463.

Reynolds, M.C. Foreword. *Review of Educational Research,* 1969, **9**, 4.

Rotter, J.B. *Social learning and clinical psychology.* Englewood Cliffs, N.J.: Prentice-Hall, 1954.

Rucker, C. *Administration of special education dissertations, completed and in progress.* Columbus, O.: General-Special Education Administration Consortium, University Council for Educational Administration, 1971.

Sage, D.D. Functional emphasis in special education administration. *Exceptional Children,* 1968, **35**, 69-70.

Skay, D.J. *A study of referral procedures for elementary special education placement in the Minneapolis Public Schools.* (Doctoral dissertation, University of Iowa) Ann Arbor, Mich.: University Microfilms, 1970, No. 70-23, 948.

Sloat, R.S. *Identification of special education and other public school leadership personnel through task and skill area delineation.* (Doctoral dissertation, University of Texas) Ann Arbor, Mich.: University Microfilms, 1969, No. 70-10, 863.

Spicknall, H.W. *The relationships between innovativeness, organizational climate factors, and communications variables in intermediate school district depart-*

ments of special education in Michigan. (Doctoral dissertation, Michigan State University) Ann Arbor, Mich.: University Microfilms, 1970, No. 71-2169.

Stodgill, R.M. Personal factors associated with leadership: A study of the literature, *Journal of Psychology,* 1948, **25**, 35-71.

Taylor, F.D. *The position of administrator of special education in unified school districts in California.* (Doctoral dissertation, University of Southern California) Ann Arbor, Mich.: University Microfilms, 1967, No. 68-1202.

Thompson, J.D. Modern approaches to theory in administration. In A.W. Halpin (Ed.), *Administrative theory in education.* Chicago: Midwest Administration Center, 1958.

Voelker, P.H., & Mullen, F.A. Organization, administration and supervision of special education. *Review of Educational Research,* 1963, **33**, 5-19.

Willenberg, E.P. Organization, administration and supervision of special education. *Review of Educational Research,* 1966, **36**, 134-150.

Willower, D.J. Special education: Organization and administration. *Exceptional Children,* 1970, **34**, 591-594.

THE ROLE OF LITIGATION IN THE IMPROVEMENT OF PROGRAMMING FOR THE HANDICAPPED

Julius S. Cohen, Ed.D

Henry DeYoung, M.A.

Institute for the Study of Mental Retardation and Related Disabilities
University of Michigan

Education in America has been regarded as the means through which both status and economic advancement may be achieved. When it was recognized that certain children could not profit from general education programs, or that certain children represented problems to other children, teachers, or the school system itself, special approaches were developed. Special education is presumed to remove selected children from the mainstream of general education in order to provide a specialized and more individualized curriculum that will help them meet the demands of adult society in the most adequate ways possible.

Inquiries into the effectiveness of this approach have questioned its validity and the true impact of special education programs on the lives of children. It has been suggested that children placed in such segregated special classes do not improve significantly; that the programs therein do not meet their needs and frequently are nothing more than holding operations, maintaining children in school until they can legally drop out. Concern has been expressed about the racial and social-class imbalances which special class programming has created.

Another major concern has been residential facilities for the retarded, where commitment usually results in lifelong placement, even for the mildly retarded and nonretarded inappropriately placed in these human storehouses. The educational programs within such facilities have typically been outside the authority, control, or concern of educators in the community, e.g., in public schools. There has been little educational control exercised by state departments of education over program length, content, or staff in institutions. Education codes have not applied to residential programs.

During the decade of growth that started with Public Law 85-926 in 1958, colleges and universities rapidly expanded their special education training programs. Unfortunately, at this time, questions concerning the appropriateness and impact of special education were not answered or were not even heard. There was a great rush to obtain traineeships for growing numbers of students interested in entering the field, to improve diagnosis and testing skills as part of the labeling process for handicapped children, and to provide teaching techniques and approaches designed to perpetuate the system of "special education." These activities provided the trained manpower and initiated an almost inexorable sequence of events that led to increasingly expanded allocation of public education funds for the establishment and maintenance of separate systems for handicapped children.

Until the rights of individuals were brought into sharper focus by the civil rights activists, little concern was expressed within the educational establishment about the right of children *not* to be labeled, the right of due process, and the right of a child to challenge a system that purports to be operating in his interest. Student rights had been ignored in practice, and limits were not clearly established by the courts. Children were removed from the mainstream of education and assigned to special programs. To some observers, these assignments often seemed to be a function of race or class differences, rather than individual needs.

It is apparent that education does not equally benefit all school children. Those who are most disadvantaged are children who are poor and culturally or racially different. The treatment of the handicapped within public education programs, too, suggests that they are often viewed as not worth educating — in effect, as children lacking human values equal to those of "normal" children. The situation is the educational equivalent of that which prevailed in American history when each black was counted as 3/5 of a person.

In addition to often segregating, as opposed to educating, the handicapped, there has been inadequate provision of services, even based on the segregation model, in schools. During the 1968-1969 school year, 19 states were reported as serving less than 31% of their handicapped populations, and 11 states as serving 20% or less (Weintraub, Abeson, & Braddock, 1971). Educators apparently have used the law and school regulations to develop special programs, to establish criteria for transferring children into such programs, to exclude children from regular and special programs, to establish the qualifications of teachers, to limit class size, and in fact, to do almost everything except guarantee sufficient and appropriate educational experiences for handicapped children.

Increasingly, parents are using the law and litigation to insure the rights of their children to an adequate education and treatment. Moreover, these rights are being demanded so as to limit as little as possible the right of individuals to be served within the educational mainstream. The United States Supreme Court, in its ruling in *Brown v. Board of Education* (1954), indicated:

In these days it is doubtful that any child may reasonably be expected to succeed in life if he is denied the opportunity of an education. Such an opportunity, where the state has undertaken to provide it, is a right which must be made available to all on equal terms.

The response of those in the educational system — administrators, teachers, psychologists, and others — to such demands will be critical in determining what effect current litigation trends ultimately will have on special education programming.

It is when the special education program and the process impinge upon the rights of the individual, and when the needs of systems rather than of children are being met, that litigation can be expected to occur. Redress to the courts by parents and other concerned individuals can be viewed as a threat by educators. It can also be seen as a method to help them meet the needs of children.

This chapter reviews the early court rulings which led to special placement. It considers some of the basic litigation in general education and the most significant cases affecting special education. The cases *against* testing, labeling, and placement and *for* the right to education and treatment are presented. There follows a discussion of the implications of litigation for practitioners and for trainees, as well as a consideration of what may be anticipated in the future.

EARLY COURT RULINGS

In this country, special education programs for the deaf are over 110 years old. Programs for the mentally retarded (MR) are about 75 years old. Other special programs for children who have been identified with one label or another are more recent. The system of special programs permitted the schools to label and isolate certain children. In addition to their option of segregating children into special education classes, the schools also have long enjoyed the right to select those children whom they felt were suitable for participation in the educational process. Schools could refuse to educate those children who did not fit appropriately within their expectations and norms. What is appropriate and acceptable still varies over time and location and according to the staff and students involved. Traditionally, the use of schools and teachers to obtain an education has been viewed as a privilege, not a right.

In 1893, a Massachusetts court ruled that a student could be expelled if he displayed continuous disorderly conduct "either voluntarily or by reason of imbecility [*Watson v. City of Cambridge*, 1893]." The determination of what constituted disorderly conduct was, of course, made by school personnel. The Wisconsin Supreme Court in 1919 said that a school could exclude a child, even though he was academically and physically capable of functioning within the school program, if his presence had a deleterious effect on the other children and the teachers; this decision was handed down in *Beattie v. State Board of Education,* 1919. The ease with which this ruling could be applied to children who were disturbing to the teacher or other school officials is obvious; the ruling implies that the rights of individual children to attend schools are of lesser importance than the overall good of the system.

In the *Beattie* case, students were expelled because they displayed continuous disorderly conduct or had:

...a depressing and nauseating effect on the teachers and school children. The rights of a child of school age to attend the schools of the state could not be insisted upon, when its presence therein is harmful to the best interest of the school.

Using these cases as precedents, the schools have kept the handicapped, disadvantaged, and/or undesirables out of school.

The school thus was given the role of plaintiff, prosecutor, judge, and jury in situations where a child's suitability for a program or for school itself is to be determined. Consistent with the decisions in these cases, schools have kept many disabled and/or deviant children out of regular educational programs. The children might be placed in special education tracks or excluded entirely, whichever was better for the system or cheaper for the school. Special education programs expanded according to the individual resources in, and pressures felt beyond, states or localities; little attention, in any case, has been given to the plight of those excluded from school or those for whom the schools have denied any responsibility, with children in public residential facilities virtually ignored.

In an article surveying the situation and reported in the *New York Times* (October 9, 1971) it was estimated that over 60% of the nation's retarded children do not receive a public education. This same report indicated that in Pennsylvania, one-half of the 100,000 retarded children of school age were not receiving a public education. A review in Michigan estimated that during 1971, 100,000 students were waiting for placement in the too-few special education programs (Detroit *Free Press,* June 15, 1971). In Massachusetts, a report based on a statewide study showed that there were 1,372 emotionally disturbed children eligible for programs for the disturbed who were excluded from school. Many had been on the waiting list for more than 2 years (Boston *Globe,* December 23, 1971).

Such reports merely focused on the size of the population not being served and the extent of its needs. Not included, but necessary, are considerations of the quality of the programs that *are* being offered, and the extent to which they protect the rights of the individual.

STUDENT RIGHTS

With the overthrow of the concept of "separate but equal" by the Supreme Court in the *Brown* case, there has been a steady growth in the number of cases brought before the courts to insure the protection of student rights and the provision of adequate education for all children. The *Brown* decision indicated that under the law, separate but equal education is, by its nature, inherently unequal. This finding was challenged in *Stell v. Savannah-Chatham County Board of Education* (1963), where the opponents of desegregation offered psychological and educational "evidence" that segregation had a more beneficial effect on black children than integration. The Court agreed with the evidence presented in this case; however, on appeal this decision was reversed on the basis that *Brown* had established as a matter of *law*, rather than as a matter of *fact*, that segregation is inherently unequal. Thus, under the law, segregated programs cannot be justified, even on the basis that they provide a more adequate educational and psychological experience for the students.

In *Gault (In re Gault*, 1967), the Court held that if a juvenile is to be denied the constitutional protections of due process on the theory that the entire juvenile court system and related rehabilitory institutions are created for his benefit, and on the supposition that there is in reality no adverse party but simply a variety of parties seeking the juvenile's best interest, then the system must, in fact, reflect those values. The Supreme Court found, in essence, that although the juvenile court theory is laudable in intent, in practice it has led, in many cases, to situations similar to those occurring with adult criminals; incarceration rather than education or treatment is the final result. Since this is so, specific constitutional guarantees must be provided even within such children-serving systems.

Gault enumerates four constitutional guarantees for the citizenry: (*a*) the right to be notified of specific charges, (*b*) the right to cross-examine witnesses, (*c*) protection against self-incrimination, and (*d*) the right to counsel. What this case really says is that a juvenile who happens to be part of a system that purports to exist for his benefit cannot be deprived of his rights simply because he has not achieved adult status. The decision is basic to many of those presently being brought in the special education area and is becoming increasingly important to those who wish redress against schools on grounds that they have deprived children of their right to a basic education or have acted in a discriminatory manner. Rather than impartially serving children and providing programs and experiences based on ability, the socioeconomic, cultural, and racial biases of schools are expressed by tracking, special class placement, and exclusion. Such practices by the educational system are being challenged with growing frequency through the courts.

In *Tinker v. Des Moines Independent Community School District* (1969), the students were recognized as persons with full rights under the United States Constitution. The decision did not dispute that school authorities have power over the student's conduct in school, but it indicated that these powers are limited by the Bill of Rights and that no school official can exercise authority inconsistent with fundamental constitutional safeguards. The Court indicated that neither students nor teachers lose their constitutional rights and freedoms when they enter a schoolhouse.

Slowly, the rights of all children under the law are being defined. As these rights become clearer and as the laws are enforced, adequate protection is offered to the students in the school. Since "special education" children are part of the total student body, these decisions affect children in special education programs as well as those in state residential facilities for the retarded and the mentally ill.

LITIGATION ARGUMENTS IN SPECIAL EDUCATION

As the legal rights of children in regular programs in schools have been clarified, there has been an increasing focus on the rights of the handicapped and of those assigned to special programs. In recent years, parents have been trying to secure equal educational opportunities for their handicapped children, as guaranteed in *Brown*. There has been concern with the potentialities of testing, labeling, and placement for being injurious to children, both in stigmatizing them and segregating them from the mainstream of education. The primary instruments schools have used have been ability tests, which discriminate against poor children and children from various racial or cultural minorities. These tests, standardized as they are on the dominant white culture of the country, do not provide an adequate measure of the ability of children with differing experiential backgrounds. It should not be surprising that when a psychologist who can speak only English administers a standard version of the Wechsler Intelligence Scale for Children (WISC) to Mexican-American and Indian children, the children do poorly on the test. It is not unusual, either, that the results of these tests are used to label, separate, and subsequently track these students to various special education programs or even to deprive them of formal schooling entirely. In the series of court cases which have attacked the entire process, there have been five basic arguments presented, as outlined below (Ross, DeYoung, & Cohen, 1971).

Inappropriate tests

First, for many children, intelligence tests standardized on white middle-class students do not accurately measure the learning ability of the plaintiffs. The tests are heavily verbal and rely on experience with standard English. Moreover, many of the questions assume a certain life style. Children from families that deal with cash or barter as the primary means of meeting their needs probably do not know what a bank check is. This bit of ignorance does not make the child less intelligent, but may well contribute to his being labeled retarded. Unfortunately, the test scores often are used as the primary, if not sole, criterion for establishing a diagnosis of mental retardation – with all the consequences of such a diagnosis.

Incompetent administration

In a second argument, the plaintiffs contend that the administration of tests is often performed incompetently. They emphasize that the tester must be fully aware of the cultural backgrounds and the primary language of the children being tested. Without this knowledge and orientation, the examiner is functioning incompetently, no matter how experienced and skilled he is with the instrument.

Lack of parental involvement

The third point is the need for full and informed involvement of the parents in the placement process. Testing and placement are often done without the parents' knowledge or consent, and parents are denied an opportunity to participate in the placement decision. What is demanded is parental involvement *prior* to the school reaching any decisions. Professional educators should not be permitted to "con" parents into agreeing with the change of status of the student *after* a decision has been made to place him in a special class. In such situations, parents are told that special classes are smaller, that the teacher can provide more individual help, and even that the placement is temporary, i.e., until the child improves in his performance. They are not told that once a child is labeled retarded and placed in a special education class for the retarded, there is a high likelihood that he will remain in such circumstances for the remainder of his school career.

Special education is inadequate

The fourth point is a direct challenge to special education itself, and holds that such programming is inadequate. In this argument, the plaintiffs usually contend that placement is permanent and that the program does little to develop necessary educational and vocational skills. The special class becomes an educational burial ground and insures lower socioeconomic status for its graduates. It separates children from the regular classroom and keeps them segregated. Plaintiffs challenge special education as being inherently inadequate in the same manner as the situation ruled on in *Brown*.

The placement stigmatizes

The fifth argument is that improper placement in special classes causes irreparable personal harm. Special class placement is seen as injurious to the child's self-concept and to the way in which his peers and teachers view him. Further, the stigma of the label far outlasts the school experience. A recent Supreme Court case considered whether due process must be followed before the state stigmatizes a citizen (*Wisconsin v. Constantineau,* 1971). In this case, the police had posted a notice in all retail liquor establishments forbidding sales to Mrs. Constantineau because of her excessive drinking. This was done without prior notice to her and without a hearing. The Court wrote: "The only issue present here is whether the label or characterization given a person by 'posting,' though a mark of illness to some, is to others such a stigma or badge of disgrace that procedural due process requires notice and an opportunity to be heard." The labels that are applied to the handicapped child are much more demeaning, and their effect on the child much more debilitating, than posting an adult as an excessive drinker. Moreover, depriving a child of an appropriate education is more serious than losing public access to alcohol. Plaintiffs are demanding the protection of due process.

CASES IN SPECIAL EDUCATION

The first court challenge to the use of testing to label and place school children was made in Washington, D.C., in the case of *Hobson v. Hansen* (1967). *Hobson* charged that in the Washington school system, children were tracked into four groups on the basis of various tests. The tests were said to be primarily verbal, culturally weighted, and therefore inappropriate for use with a large portion of the school population. Once a child was placed in a track, there was very little likelihood of his being reevaluated and placed in a different (higher) track. Judge Skelly Wright, in his decision, deemed that this practice was illegal and in violation of the equal-protection clause of the United States Constitution, and *ordered the abolishment of the tracking system.* This decision was appealed in *Smuck v. Hobson* (1969), but the Court of Appeals affirmed the lower court action.

Tracking or ability grouping was also challenged in *Spangler v. Board of Education* (1970) in the Federal District Court for the District of Southern California. A group of black students charged that as a result of the use of intelligence tests, a racial imbalance existed in the facilities of the Pasadena School District. Without contest, it was admitted that IQ tests were inaccurate and unfair, and the practice was stopped.

In *Diana v. Board of Education* (1970), nine Mexican-American public school students, aged 8 through 13, claimed that they had been improperly placed in classes for the mentally retarded on the basis of inaccurate test scores. The plaintiffs held that the intelligence tests ignored any learning abilities in Spanish and, because of the test standardization, did not relate to the Spanish-American culture. The case was settled out of court.

The stipulated agreement which was reached in *Diana* resulted in radical changes in the school code in California, with the establishment of new policies and procedures for the identification and assessment of minors and for placement in special education programs for the educable mentally retarded (EMR) (Rice, 1971). The new policies and procedures require that children of all ethnic, socioeconomic, and cultural groups be provided with equal educational opportunities, and that they not be placed in classes or other special programs for the EMR if they can be served in regular classes. The policies and practices require that each school establish a screening and referral process. Further, the policies require that before a minor is placed in a special education class, (*a*) the parent or guardian must give written permission for individual psychological evaluations; (*b*) an individual case study must be undertaken and must include educational history, in-school achievement data, psychometric assessment, developmental history, peer relationships, health history, psychological adjustment, social, economic, and cultural background information, and other pertinent information; (*c*) a local admissions committee must be established; (*d*) a conference must be held with the parent; and (*e*) written consent for special placement must be secured. It is further recommended that the school establish procedures to assist the student in his new special education placement. To permit monitoring of local programs, an annual report must be provided to the Department of Education, including the ethnic breakdown of children placed in special education classes, and there must be an annual review and complete reevaluation of all students enrolled in special education classes. The ratio of minority children in these classes may vary up to 15% from their frequency in the general school population. This allows a high variance, especially when there are relatively few minority children in the school. For example, if the school population is 5% black, the special education program could contain 20% black children and still be within acceptable limits.

Charging that Mexican-American children were being placed in inadequate special education classes on the basis of culturally biased intelligence tests and without parental involvement in the process, *Arreola v. Board of Education* (1968) asked the California Superior Court for relief against the identification and placement of such children. This case has not been settled; it appears moot, based on the stipulated agreement in *Diana* and the resultant changes in the state school code.

In *Covarrubias v. San Diego Unified School District* (1971), the plaintiffs were 12 black and five Mexican-American pupils in classes for the EMR in the San Diego Unified School District. While similar to *Diana, Covarrubias* introduced two new concepts. First, it requested that in addition to adjusting for language differences, revised tests to be used within the state must recognize the cultural influences of the black ghetto. It went further than the previous case, in that punitive damages were asked to redress, in part, the aggravated wrong done to the children. This case is still pending.

In a Boston case, *Stewart v. Phillips* (1970), the plaintiffs argued in Federal District Court for the District of Massachusetts that the improper placement of poor or black students on the basis of tests which do not accurately measure their learning ability, and the denial of educational programs for their specific educational needs, abridge their rights to equal protection and their rights to due process under the Fourteenth Amendment. The plaintiffs in *Stewart* have extended the concern about test bias in *Covarrubias* by asking that intelligence tests recognize not only the influence of black culture in determining learning ability, but that they also be sensitive to the influence which poverty has on educational potential. In *Stewart,* the plaintiffs demanded participation in the decision-making process prior to placement in special education classes; they have also asked punitive damages. A final decision in this case is still pending. However, during the past year, Massachusetts school officials cooperated with the plaintiffs in developing new state regulations for the placement of children into special classes. Generally, these new regulations meet the demands made in *Stewart.*

The use of standardized tests in the placement of Mexican-American and Yaqui Indian school children in classes for the EMR was challenged in Arizona (*Guadalupe v. Tempe Elementary School District,* 1971). This suit went further than the ones cited above, asking that not only should children already in classes for the retarded be reassessed, but also that the *defendants be enjoined from administering tests to students who may do poorly on them because of their cultural backgrounds.* Further, they asked that no child be placed in a special education class before the age of 10. In a stipulated agreement dated January 24, 1972, it was agreed that (*a*) intelligence testing should be in the child's primary language; (*b*) cultural background and home experiences must be considered in the placement process; (*c*) the parents and a team of professionals must have a part in the placement process; and (*d*) the school must demonstrate compelling educational justification if the proportion of any ethnic or language group in special classes differs significantly from the proportion of that group in the total school population. In addition to providing parents with full access to their children's school records, the parties agreed that all children whose first language is other than English will be reassigned from the classes for the retarded to regular classes by October 1973.

While there has been a court decision in *Hobson* and in *Spangler,* all of the other cases have either been settled out of court or are still pending. *Covarrubias* and *Stewart* have asked for money damages as high as $20,000 per student. It is doubtful that the courts will grant major money damages of this type, but it is too early to make a prediction. However, it is noteworthy that most of the cases are being settled out of court. This does not permit a judicial decision which might possibly allow for punitive damages. Instead, the defendants are reaching settlements by agreeing to changes demanded by the plaintiffs in the testing, labeling, and placement procedures.

The most pervasive changes have been in the California school code and derive, to a large extent, from *Diana.* As a result, thousands of children have been returned to the regular classrooms. Children are being tested in their primary language and, at least in theory, the needs of these children are being met in accordance with the agreements, the new laws, and education department regulations.

However, a closer look at the situation presents a dismal picture. Children being returned to the regular classes are provided little of the necessary additional support, enrichment, and remedial services which will redress the effects of their prior educational experiences and permit them to function at the level of other students in the regular classes. Apparently, they are not expected to do well, and many will not. It seems certain that the blame for their failure will be placed on the children, rather than on a system that will not modify itself and its resources to meet their particular needs.

On November 18, 1971, *Larry P. v. Riles* was filed in the United States District Court for the Northern District of California. The plaintiffs were six black elementary school students from the San Francisco Unified School District, representing a class of black children in California wrongly placed and retained in classes for the mentally retarded. The plaintiffs are members of families whose primary culture is the contemporary black American culture and whose language skills vary from standard English. The brief asserted that the plaintiffs are not and have never been retarded; that the special education classes provide minimal training in reading, spelling, and mathematics; and that improper placement in one of these classes can be tantamount to a life sentence of illiteracy and public dependency. The plaintiffs were independently retested by black psychologists from the same cultural backgrounds, and the resultant IQ scores ranged from 79 to 104. These scores are above the retarded level.

The plaintiffs charged inadequacies in the recently modified procedures, especially in meeting the needs of the class they represent. A central concern was that biased tests are still being used to place minority children in special classes. Blacks, who represent 9.1% of the school children in California, represent 27.5% of the children in MR programs, a variance almost within the permitted 15%. It was charged that no meaningful efforts have been taken to insure that psychological assessments are conducted by persons adequately prepared to evaluate cultural factors. In San Francisco, where 28.5% of the school population is black, 60% of all children in the EMR program are black, and there is only one black examiner. *Larry P.* asked that the children be returned to regular classrooms and provided with intensive and supplemental individual training to bring them to the achievement level of their peers. Moreover, they requested that all indications of retardation be removed from the school records.

In summary, *Larry P.* reflects the concern that despite the proposed changes in the California education code, black children continue to be injured by special class placement. It is an effort to halt the use of standard tests of intelligence in the intellectual assessment of black children. The state contended that the lawsuit is premature, in that it was filed shortly after the new regulations went into effect. The state also contended that other factors may contribute to the imbalance in enrollment, e.g., dietary deficiencies leading to low ability and/or performance.

In a suit filed on January 23, 1972, *Arnold v. Tamalpais Union High School District,* it was charged that the district did not follow and is not following the regulations set forth by the state in accordance with the *Diana* agreement. The plaintiffs charged that the district failed to carry out duties provided under the California education code and the regulations adopted by the superintendent of public instruction. Charges include (*a*) failure to maintain an active screening and referral process to reach all minors who would benefit from a properly run special education program for EMR children; (*b*) failure to administer intelligence tests properly as required by law, or to complete comprehensive individual evaluations of children enrolled in the program; (*c*) failure to consult with the parents of enrolled children or to make regular home visits; (*d*) failure to secure the permission of parents for the testing, enrollment, participation, or removal of children from the program; (*e*) failure to make substantial efforts to integrate EMR children into modified regular school classes with supplementary teaching support; (*f*) failure to place certain EMR children with adequate test scores in regular academic classes; and (*g*) failure to adequately supervise and staff the program with qualified and certified teachers to insure the quality of the educational content. In sum, the plaintiffs indicated the failure of the district to provide the adequate and appropriate services as defined by the law. They asked that the district be ordered to comply with the state education code, that the violations cease, and that the district pay $600,000 damages. Apparently, once rights are defined in the courts, careful monitoring and perhaps additional litigation will be required to insure the provision of those rights.

THE RIGHT TO EDUCATION AND TREATMENT

There has been a dramatic shift in the emphasis of the litigation during the past few years. These suits focus on the responsibility of the state to provide the special programs required by children and to allocate funds equitably to schools within a district and between districts in the state. The plaintiffs in these suits are usually the more severely handicapped – those excluded from schools, those in ghetto schools where the expenditures per pupil are below the average for the district or state, or those in residential facilities for the handicapped.

Historically, parents have been successful in changing school codes so as to provide better education for their children. As early as 1911 in New Jersey, 1917 in New York, and 1920 in Massachusetts, mandatory legislation was passed which required school districts to provide classes for the mentally retarded. Programs for other disabilities were provided for in later legislation. Other states have followed this pattern. However, many districts stand in violation of the law and do not provide such programs. Children are excluded, placed on waiting lists and never admitted to schools, or are otherwise unable to gain access to the limited number of existing programs. Through the courts and the legislatures, parents are forcing schools to provide whatever specialized instruction is needed to benefit the child.

As an example of legislative action and community pressure, during 1971 Michigan passed a mandatory special education bill which requires each district to serve all its handicapped children by 1973. No longer will some 100,000 students be excluded from schools in Michigan because the districts do not provide suitable programs for them. Pressure is also being applied on legislators in other states to provide similar guarantees for handicapped children. However, greater and more immediate pressure is being applied through the courts.

The effects of the *Beattie* decision, which permitted exclusion of certain children from regular classes, were modified somewhat in 1967 when the attorney general of Wisconsin stated that while schools have the right to exclude or to suspend a child, such a removal from the school does not conclude the state's responsibility for the child; i.e., if a child is excluded or suspended, the responsibility for his public education rests with and must be provided by the school.

A landmark decision by Judge D. Frank Willkins in *Wolf v. Legislature of the State of Utah* (1969) resulted from a suit regarding the exclusion of two trainable mentally retarded (TMR) children. The Court ruled that "education ... is a fundamental and inalienable right and must be so if the rights guaranteed to an individual under Utah's Constitution and the United States Constitution are to have any real meaning." This ruling, in effect, made education mandatory for all children in the state of Utah. Similar suits have been filed in California (*Alexander v. Thompson,* 1970) and elsewhere.

The *Pennsylvania Association for Retarded Children v. Commonwealth of Pennsylvania* (1971) was also a landmark case in establishing the right to education. The plaintiffs charged that they have been excluded or excused from attendance in public school, have had their admission postponed, or otherwise have been denied free access to a public education because they are retarded. It was charged that they may represent as many as 53,000 individuals. Included in the class are inmates of the state residential facilities for the mentally retarded. (The reader is urged to obtain a copy of the brief and read pages 9-20, which contain short summaries of the *noneducation* of each of the 13 plaintiffs. It is an indictment of common special education practices.)

On October 7, 1971, a consent agreement was signed by the parties establishing the precedent of the "right to education" for all of the retarded children of Pennsylvania. The court order indicated that all children can benefit from education and have a right to it. The agreement gave the state 90 days to identify every retarded child of school age not in school, and ordered the state to begin teaching all of them no later than September 1972. Thus, Pennsylvania must place all retarded children into special or regular classes, unless exceptional handicaps require training elsewhere. In the latter event, the state still maintains a responsibility to insure that the child obtains adequate programming. A hearing board was established to insure that each child has effective access to a free public program. Revisions and clarification of the school code also were ordered to insure adequate protection of the rights of these children and their parents. Masters were appointed by the Court to implement the ordered relief and to assure that it is extended to all members of the class entitled to it. The masters have the responsibility to oversee the process of identification, evaluation, notification, and compliance presented in the court order. Thus, in one action, the Court has redefined the role and the responsibility of the schools and has ordered compliance with a program which will insure the right to an education for children traditionally ignored by the education system.

Two suits were filed in Wisconsin during 1970. In *Doe v. Board of School Directors of the City of Milwaukee* (1970), a temporary injunction was placed on the Board of School Directors to prohibit the school from placing MR children on the waiting list for special education. A similar temporary restraining order was placed on the system in *Marlega v. Board of School Directors of the City of Milwaukee* (1970) when the Court considered exclusion from school for medical reasons. The Court directed that a due process hearing must include (*a*) specification of the reasons for exclusion; (*b*) a prior hearing; (*c*) the rights to be represented by counsel, to confront and cross-examine witnesses, and to present evidence and witnesses on the child's behalf; (*d*) a stenographic record of the hearing; (*e*) a final decision in writing stating in detail the reasons for any exclusion; and (*f*) *a specification of available public education alternatives.* In each of these Wisconsin cases, the courts are bringing into focus the school's ongoing responsibility to provide an education for these children.

In Washington, D.C., *Mills v. Board of Education of the District of Columbia,* 1971, was filed to secure the equal right to education for *all* District children who are excluded or otherwise denied access to instruction and training. The plaintiffs included, but were not limited to, children who are profoundly and severely retarded, children with learning disabilities, children labeled emotionally disturbed, and children who have been referred to the juvenile correction system and are awaiting disposition on their cases. This case is a successor legal action to the *Hobson* intervention, in which Judge Wright noted that the District [of Columbia] Board of

Education has a moral and legal duty to educate the plaintiffs' children. In *Hobson,* Judge Wright ruled that the four-level tracking system used by the District was illegal and must be abolished.

The *Mills* case highlighted the existence of a fifth track — one for those who are in a state of nonattendance in the schools. Their education is delayed, deferred, or denied by the school by a variety of means. *Mills* asked that the school meet its responsibility of providing these children with an education. The Court ordered that the plaintiffs in the case be enrolled immediately in a publicly supported education program suited to their needs. It is of considerable note that among the plaintiffs were two profoundly retarded children with IQs below 25.

In *McMillan v. Board of Education of State of New York* (1970), the plaintiffs were brain-injured children who sought an injunction to prohibit enforcement of a $2,000 ceiling on state payments for each child in an approved private school, and to require the defendants to provide an adequate number of special classes within the public schools. Some relatively well-off parents are able to use the option of private schooling and to pay the difference between state support and actual tuition costs; however, for those children whose parents cannot afford this, there is the waiting list or outright exclusion. These children are being kept out of special classes by a lack of space. In New York State, it is estimated that there are approximately 600 of these minimally brain-injured children on waiting lists. It should be noted that the technique of the waiting list insures nonattendance of the children, "cools off" the parent with the hope of eventual placement, and leaves the impression that the schools are doing something.

The same situation is true in Massachusetts, where it is charged that at least 1,371 emotionally disturbed children, although eligible to participate in appropriate educational programs, were not placed. Instead, they were entered on a waiting list. *Barnett v. Greenblatt,* 1971, challenged the arbitrary and irrational manner in which emotionally disturbed children are denied the right to an education by being classified emotionally disturbed and excluded both from the public schools and from alternative educational programs in day or residential schools. In these cases, the basic right to an education was being asserted.

The precedent established in the *Pennsylvania Association for Retarded Children* case suggests the urgent need for educators to address themselves to children who, to a large extent, have been ignored by programs which seem to be more designed to meet the needs of those operating the educational system than those enrolled in it. The policy of meeting the needs of those children who most closely fit the predetermined role of the "student" often means that poor, disadvantaged, black, Mexican-American, Indian, and other minority groups are not served. Schools serving these children do not receive a fair share of the public monies available; their families are unable, both because of a lack of money and information about their rights, to obtain adequate services through the primary or alternate systems.

The use of the property tax to support public education has come under attack.

Opponents of the system point to the fact that in wealthy districts, more dollars per student are generated at a lower tax rate than in poor districts. This imbalance is seen as denying students in poorer districts equal protection of the law. A similar picture has been shown when examining schools within a single district, and concern about this injustice has led again to the courts.

Litigation has been brought to insure equality of educational expenditures and to correct other injustices. For example, the Washington, D.C., system no longer may spend more money in some schools than in others, as all schools must have within 5% of the mean pupil expenditure. This ruling has come as a result of *Hobson v. Hansen-II* (1971), which showed that expenditures per pupil in predominantly "black schools" were significantly lower than in schools with a larger portion of white students. A similar case was brought in California (*Mission Coalition Organization v. San Francisco Unified School District,* 1970). However, this point may be moot because of the *Serrano v. Priest* (1971) decision by the California State Supreme Court that unequal expenditures per district are unconstitutional. A similar action was taken in the Federal Court in Texas with similar findings.

These rulings should have special impact on districts in which unusually high proportions of the student population are labeled and placed in special programs. It now appears that the white, wealthy, suburban districts will not be able to use their greater tax base to provide enriched programs while the poor districts, both urban and rural, cannot provide adequate education for all children. With property tax being ruled out as the fiscal base, it may be hoped that a more equitable statewide distribution of education funds will permit the establishment and operation of programs adequately designed, conceptually sound, and geared toward the varied needs of the many populations to be served. This may also have the serendipitous effect of making the white suburban "golden ghetto" less attractive if, in fact, the variation in quality of school programs is diminished.

THE RIGHT TO TREATMENT IN RESIDENTIAL FACILITIES

Perhaps the most significant recognition of the rights of the retarded has come as a result of *Wyatt v. Stickney* (1971). Due to a general cutback in expenditures in the state of Alabama, the Department of Mental Health ordered a staff reduction in the state residential facilities for the mentally ill and the mentally retarded. *Wyatt* was filed originally on behalf of residents at Bryce Hospital, a facility for the mentally ill. The case was broadened to include Searcy Hospital and Partlow State School and Hospital for the Mentally Retarded. On December 10, 1971, the Federal District Court for the Middle District of Alabama directed that a hearing be conducted "for the purpose of allowing the parties and *amici* the opportunity to present proposed standards which would meet medical and constitutional requirements for the operation of the three mental institutions herein concerned and to present evidence by experts in support thereof." By a subsequent order, the Court continued the mental retardation aspects of the case until February 18, 1972.

The hearings on the conditions at Partlow were held before Judge Frank Johnson on February 28, 29, and March 1, 1972. On March 2, 1972, Judge Johnson issued an interim emergency order and directed that immediate steps be taken to protect the lives and well-being of the residents of Partlow. The Court stated that the evidence elicited from the hearing concerning the mental retardation components of *Wyatt* vividly and undisputedly portrayed Partlow State School and Hospital as a warehousing institution which, because of its atmosphere of psychological and physical deprivation, was wholly incapable of furnishing treatment and habilitation to the mentally retarded and was conducive only to the deterioration and debilitation of the residents.

The interim emergency order included (*a*) hiring, within 30 days, 300 additional residential-care workers, including professionals of the various disciplines, on a temporary or permanent basis, with the defendants not being required to comply with the state merit system or any other formal procedure in hiring; (*b*) engaging, within 10 days, a team of physicians to conduct appropriate immunization for all residents; (*c*) employing, within 15 days, a team of physicians to examine every resident as to the appropriateness of any anticonvulsives and/or behavior-modifying drugs, with a view to immediately revamping Partlow's entire drug program. These and other measures were designed to provide immediate protection of the lives of the inmates of Partlow. However, the Court further announced that in order to safeguard the constitutional rights of the mentally retarded in Alabama, massive reform is needed in almost every area of Partlow's operation. The Court stated that it intends, in due course, to enter a final order in this case granting plaintiffs appropriate relief.

In a posttrial memorandum on adequate habilitation for the mentally retarded, the plaintiffs substantiated the lack of a habilitation program at Partlow and requested that the Court establish constitutionally required standards for adequate habilitation for the mentally retarded and set up machinery to assure prompt implementation of such standards. The parties agreed upon a set of standards for adequate habilitation. In the area of education, it was agreed that a master's degree in special education from an accredited program is necessary to qualify one as an MR professional. They agreed that residents have a right to the least restrictive conditions necessary to achieve the purposes of habilitation, and that to this end every effort should be made to move the individuals toward the highest level of independent living. They further agreed that the residents have a right to receive suitable educational services, regardless of chronological age, degree of retardation, or accompanying disabilities or handicaps. The institution was required to formulate a written statement of educational objectives consistent with the institution's mission and to provide school-age residents with a full and suitable educational program. The minimum standards which were set (*a*) stipulated 6 hours per day as the minimum length of the school day; (*b*) limited class size to 12 mildly retarded, 9 moderately retarded, or 6 severely/profoundly retarded per class; and (c) established a school year of 9 to 10 months for the mild and moderately retarded, and 11 to 12 months for the severely and profoundly retarded. The educational program, in conjunction with the long-range habilitation plan, is designed to assist the residents in moving toward their highest practicable level. The Court issued an order and decree on April 13, 1972, directing the implementation of the habilitation plan.

In a similar case, residents of the Belchertown State School for the Retarded in Massachusetts sought to enjoin the operation of that facility for failing to provide adequate treatment (*Ricci v. Greenblatt,* 1972). The Federal District Court issued a temporary and preliminary restraining order (a) requiring the defendants, within 30 days, to make a complete evaluation of the medical needs of each resident; (b) prohibiting the transfer of any resident or the admission of any new persons to that facility until a plan for the orderly reduction of the population can be presented to the Court, together with evidence that all the residents receive adequate treatment and enjoy humane living conditions; (c) revoking the administrative prohibition of filling vacant positions in the Belchertown State School; and (d) requiring the formulation of a comprehensive treatment plan for all residents which will provide for adequate and proper therapeutic services as follows: medical, dental, educational, nutritional, physical, occupational, psychological, social, recreational, speech, and vocational.

On March 17, 1972, a lawsuit was filed against the state of New York regarding conditions at the Willowbrook State School (*New York State Association for Retarded Children, Inc., v. Rockefeller,* 1972). The suit charged widespread physical abuse, inhumane and destructive conditions, severe overcrowding and understaffing, involuntary servitude, extended solitary confinement, and an almost total absence of therapeutic care. The suit asked the federal courts to declare that conditions at Willowbrook violate the constitutional rights of the children and that Willowbrook does not meet constitutionally minimal standards of care, treatment, habilitation, and training. Among other items, the Court was asked to set minimum standards and to order state officials to meet those standards. They cited that no schooling whatever is provided for 80% of the school-age residents and that no adult education is provided for 96% of the adult residents. The plaintiffs are utilizing the memorandum of agreement developed in *Wyatt,* which established the staffing and programming standards for habilitation, care, treatment, education, and training of the mentally retarded.

The plaintiffs, apparently concerned that the state, in an effort to improve appearances at Willowbrook, would transfer residents to institutions for the mentally ill and other facilities where they would not receive adequate treatment, requested a restraining order on the transfer of residents from the Willowbrook State School to any other institution or facility. The Court issued that order on March 17, 1972.

Assuming that *Ricci, Barnett,* and the *New York State Association for Retarded Children, Inc.,* cases are decided for the plaintiffs, as were *Wyatt* and *The Pennsylvania Association for Retarded Children,* and that these cases become prototypes for similar cases across the country, the increased demand for educational services and qualified personnel will be tremendous. It will no longer be possible for schools to get rid of their problems by referring them for "long-term care" or by excluding them from school facilities. With the strong likelihood that education will be mandated within the residential facilities across the nation, public school educators must directly face their responsibilities for the retarded population. Well-planned, closely coordinated, and integrated programs are necessary to create optimal opportunities for retarded children in residential facilities; these programs must use public education facilities in the community and, whenever possible, move on to full community-programming status. Unless this becomes an integral part of the planning, public education may continue not to meet the needs of this portion of its student population.

Ideally, the education of the child should remain the responsibility of his local school district, and plans should be developed to insure an adequate education experience. The funds which the district spends to educate each child should follow the child to wherever his program places him. Today, it generally is to a district's financial benefit to exclude a child or refer him to an institution or other program, rather than provide the expensive services required. However, the assignment of the average per-pupil expenditure to the facility in which the child is actually enrolled — local school, private school, or residential institution — could promote a greater concern by the school regarding its responsibility for each child and could improve the quality of the programs.

IMPLICATIONS FOR PRACTITIONERS

Many practitioners question the viability of the court decisions. They indicate that the courts are not administrative bodies responsible for implementing the change, do not understand the problems that result within the educational system from the ordered changes, and cannot provide the long-range monitoring which is required. Judges also indicate that the most appropriate place for reform in educational decisions is in the school, not in the court. Judge Wright stated in *Hobson*:

It is regrettable, of course, that in deciding this case this court must act in an area so alien to its expertise. It would be far better indeed for these great social and political problems to be resolved in the political arena by other branches of government. But these are social and political problems which seem at times to defy such resolution. In such situations, under our system, the judiciary must bare a hand and accept its responsibility to assist in the solution where constitutional rights hang in the balance.

Judge (now Chief Justice) Burger's dissenting opinion in *Smuck* also raised critical comments on the extent to which the judiciary can accomplish change within the educational system. Educators should be aware that in the area of providing equal educational opportunities, as in the area of desegregation, court decisions may be extremely difficult to work with and may be ordered with little lead time. In *Hobson*, Judge Wright ordered in June 1967 that the track system be abolished; a compliance report was due the following October. In *Wyatt,* massive changes were ordered to occur within 30 days. It is noteworthy that 200 staff had been recruited and employed by the end of the first week and that despite years of abuse and neglect, the state was able to comply with other aspects of the emergency order.

School personnel involved in court cases may not receive what they consider sufficient time to carry out court orders. In *Diana,* the stipulated agreement order was signed in February 1970. This was, in large measure, translated into law through Chapters 1569 and 1543 of the Statutes of 1970 of the Education Code of the State of California. These were revised by Senate bill 33 in the spring of 1971, to help insure that the intent of the stipulated agreement be met while protecting the rights of individual children. Relatively immediate and major changes were required in the California system by the start of the 1972-1973 school year. Sufficient time has not passed to determine the extent to which educators in this state were able to meet the challenges of the new procedures.

As decisions regarding change within the education system continue to be reached through the courts, educators will have to adjust to performing while under the scrutiny of, and within the time limits set by, the courts. If, however, there is agreement that the responsibility for change lies within the profession, then the professionals must assume the leadership in implementing change as rapidly as possible. The changes must provide for the specific and individual needs of the student while protecting his rights. The educators must provide good educational experiences with as little denial as possible of the individual's freedom and rights to a general education. It is indeed unfortunate that the reimbursement policy in many states encourages the local district to maintain segregated, self-contained classrooms. Such programming emphasizes the differences between children in special classes and those in regular classes. Moreover, for those children who require only additional support and instruction within the regular placement, special class placement represents an excessive infringement on their right to be maintained in general education.

There is a great deal of discussion and disagreement on the effectiveness of testing, the impact of labeling, and even the value of special education programs in preparing handicapped children for adult roles. The psychologists defend the tests, maintaining that they represent the best instruments available and that they predict success in school. Teachers defend their use of the scores because they often are the primary data that the psychologists supply. Until recently, no one defended the students and prevented them from being whipsawed between these points. The courts are examining the situation and, in large measure, are placing responsibility on the school personnel for what is being done *to* children by those who claim to be doing things *for* children. While the usual approach of the professional is to carefully define the situation and then spend considerable time researching the problems, the immediate need is for positive action. As adversaries, educators may be confronting people who place emphasis on change and provision of rights now − not after the research findings are published. The plaintiffs in a case may be individuals who disagree with expert opinion and its application and who wish to offer other experts and other information. In most situations today, the schools present a closed system to them, and the courts represent their one available resource. However, if the schools provided administrative recourse where a full and impartial hearing was available to the dissatisfied, where the concerns of the individual would be weighted with the concerns of the system, and where resolutions were reached cooperatively, then there would be no need for recourse to the courts. Resolution could be kept within the expertise of the educational system. If the system is unable or unwilling to provide these procedures, then the individuals who, under law, must have an opportunity to be heard, will be heard in the courts. If the plaintiffs assert a violation of constitutional rights, the court must determine whether such constitutional rights have been in fact violated, even if this involves the weighing of difficult technical and unfamiliar knowledge. One of the strongest implications of these court cases for the education profession is the necessity of marshaling legal evidence for use in the courtroom in such a way that it is impervious to attack by the opponent's counsel and expert advisors (Nordin, 1971).

It is noteworthy that most of the cases in this area do not go to judgment, but are closed as a result of a stipulated agreement. In a stipulation, both parties agree to certain facts and specify future actions. In almost every instance, the stipulated agreements have contained all of the demands of the plaintiffs — and the defendants have agreed to them. If the agreements reflect the injustices accurately, then why did the defendants wait until they were brought into court to agree to perform their professional responsibilities? Could they be blindly following past practices? Is their behavior a function of discrimination? of nonprofessionalism? Are the defendants merely expressing a lack of respect for the rights of students because students are seen as individuals who have no power base or spokesmen? Whatever the reasons for this behavior so fully documented in court, there is still an opportunity to assume professional leadership.

While theoretical discussions about the effectiveness of the court rulings and the impact of legal decisions on the educational system may continue, it is significant that in some of the cases money damages have been asked. The frequency of malpractice suits against physicians and lawyers demonstrates the impact that the threat of money damages can have on professional practice in any area. While a continued number of litigation cases may cause change, real change in professional practice may result more quickly from the possibility of monetary damages. This would be especially true if individual responsibility is established for those who claim special expertise in working with the mentally retarded — the psychologist, the school diagnostician, the special educator, and others involved in service to the handicapped.

With damage suits as a possibility, the psychologist may be more concerned that the intelligence test is appropriate for the subject; the teacher more concerned that the results are used correctly and the program specifically designed for the child;

and the administrator more concerned that all the safeguards of due process are provided and that the facility adequately provides equal opportunities for every student.

Much depends on the posture assumed by the majority of educational leaders in the field. The response must be in terms of correcting the injustices being done to students, rather than preparing a defense for the individual practitioners or the system. It is sad to hear educators speculate on what could be done to protect themselves and their programs from suit. The sound answer is to operate the programs so that the needs and rights of the student are being met; the answer that educators present, however, is to develop procedures and practices so that the program is covered under the law.

A corollary has been speculation on the impact of the appointment of Chief Justice Burger and other Supreme Court justices who are regarded as more conservative than the members they replaced. Such speculations emphasize the Court's historical policy of not becoming involved in the administration of public education; its willingness to accept the expertise of educators; earlier court decisions which have supported exclusion or the rights of the group over those of the individual; and the probability that with the new, more conservative orientation of the Supreme Court, decisions may increasingly support the status quo.

These discussions fail to recognize the changes that are occurring which represent an increased emphasis on the rights of the individual. Some professionals are willing to testify and challenge the position taken by representatives of programs or facilities which are being sued. There also may not be a full recognition of the importance of the specific court selected to hear the case. This important tactical decision is made by the plaintiff's attorney. Using previous decisions and other information known about court members, the attorney can select the court which he feels is most appropriate and most receptive to the plaintiff's position. This could very well be a state rather than a federal court.

IMPLICATIONS FOR TRAINING PROGRAMS

Recently, one of the authors was invited to meet with a class of undergraduate students in special education to discuss the impact of litigation and legislation on special education programming. As the class was assembling, the instructor was listing topics on the board for several following class sessions. One of the items was intelligence testing. When asked about the focus of this session, the instructor indicated that its purpose was to familiarize the students with the Wechsler Intelligence Scale for Children (WISC) and the Stanford-Binet, and to make them aware of the standard framework within which such instruments are used in diagnosing children with retardation.

It is appalling that at this time, with the tests under such heavy attack, student training still focuses on the standardized administration of these instruments. Perhaps the student will be told that the tests are standardized on white children and that they have a cultural bias; however, they will probably also be told that they do predict academic success and are the best tools available. Students must be exposed to a broader perspective than this. Ideally, they should have a full understanding of the impact of various practices on children and the opportunities that the students have, as teachers, to effect change.

The application of the "disease model" to the educational system results in a need to identify the pathology in the individual, provide a label for the condition, and attempt to treat the labeled condition. Students are taught on the basis of norms and normative behavior. Alternate modes of behavior are not perceived merely as being different, but rather as deviating from the norms. This deviancy and the resultant problems are seen as residing in the individual child, not in the system, the teachers, or the society. Without exposure to a broader view, teachers will continue to be prepared for, and will maintain, a special education system which many hold to be injurious to children.

Teacher-training programs must introduce an ecological view that emphasizes four points: First is the importance of observing human behavior in its natural setting. The testing situation is a highly structured and artificial one, which attempts only to get a small sampling of the individual's behavior. There is little or no effort at obtaining data on the individual's functioning in the broader life arena. Thus, it is possible for a child to obtain poor test scores (usually indicative of low achievement) and yet function adequately in the community, using skills that are not evidenced in school and test data.

Second, there is the need to focus on the interactive nature of behavior. Rather than view the performance of a child in isolation, one should view it as a function of the interaction between him and others in the environment, with the environment having varied effects on his output. One must examine the impact of family members and significant persons in the community. This does not preclude looking at the teacher or other professionals who may have positive or deleterious effects on an individual. For example, when a child is having problems, the professionals often recommend that the family obtain counseling or therapy. One might ask how often such counseling or therapy is needed by members of the professional team and how often it is recommended.

Third, the influence of the setting must be evaluated carefully; behavior that appears deviant or maladaptive when viewed in isolation may, in fact, be highly adaptive for a particular setting. Unfortunately, the training of education students does not emphasize skills permitting such analysis; nor does it provide an orientation encouraging consideration of the influence of the setting on children's behavior. As a result, the pressure of the system is on forcing change within the child, rather than within the environment.

Fourth, students must be able to objectify and qualify their observations so that helpful data can be available for program development for a particular child. The tendency is to recall and record negative information but to overlook or minimize more positive data. Teachers' anecdotal records have relatively little value because they are not obtained in a routine way to sample broadly the individual's functioning, including all aspects of behavior.

The focus of training must move from the traditional segregated special class emphasis of special education. State financing still places priority on the establishment of self-contained special classes limited to children of a single-ability classification or disability type, despite the growing evidence of legal and educational pressures toward serving children within regular programs as much as possible. Students must be made aware of other program and role options which are developing, e.g., serving as a resource for regular classroom teachers, operating a resource room, and working as an itinerant teacher. The trained special education person of the future may be more of a consultant, advisor, or tutor of exceptional children in regular classrooms, rather than a traditional special class teacher. He will have to be a far more sophisticated and adaptable professional.

It has become apparent to the authors, from their direct involvement in the development of some of the legal cases and extensive contacts with the lawyers involved, that many lawyers have become very knowledgeable about the educational system and the ways in which it deals with handicapped children. Teachers must develop an equal awareness of the legal system. Teacher trainees must be made aware of the meaning and importance of the litigation cases and must be taught techniques of marshaling legal evidence for use in courts so as to make it truly reflective of the educators' positions. As Virginia Davis Nordin (1971), a lawyer, stated:

The implications of these findings for educators are interesting in their practical effect. They imply ... that an educator who wishes to use the judicial process to change the educational system must be prepared to understand the laws of evidence and to present persuasive, factual data and scientific studies which can be substantiated by recognized methods, and also be prepared to cross examine expert witnesses on the other side along these same lines. Indeed regardless of their own desires, many educators may soon be forced to understand the workings of the courts [p. 100].

PROLOGUE

This final section of the chapter is entitled "Prologue" because the authors feel strongly, and evidence suggests, that the court actions discussed in this chapter are merely a beginning. The chapter has reviewed the litigation especially pertinent to the area of special education and the implications of the court orders and agreements which have been reached. The focus of the cases has moved from basic rights under the Constitution — the right to equal educational opportunities with the informed involvement of the parents — toward an expression of the recognition of the basic right to an education for all children. It should be expected that this movement will continue, and educators must be ready to provide positive responses to these pressures.

Most impressive to the authors has been the increasing number of cases being filed and the growing awareness of the rulings. In the 3 months between February and

May of 1972, several additional cases were filed, and the emergency interim order and the order and decree in *Wyatt* were issued. By the time this is read, many additional cases will probably have been filed and additional decisions reached. These cases and decisions must affect the way in which special education programs are operated and the format within which its staff functions. It is imperative that personnel in the field maintain an up-to-date awareness of these forces and initiate planned modifications which meet both the legal and human implications of these decisions. There is a strong positive leadership opportunity for those willing and able to assume this role.

References

Alexander v. Thompson, 313 F. Supp. 1389 (S.D. Cal. 1970).

Arnold v. Tamalpais Union High School District, Civil Action No. 61215 (Superior Ct. Marin Cty., Cal. 1972).

Arreola v. Board of Education, Case No. 160-577 (Superior Ct., Orange Cty., Cal. 1968).

Barnett v. Greenblatt (U.S. District Ct. 1971).

Beattie v. State Board of Education, 169 Wis. 231, 172 N.W. 153 (1919).

Boston *Globe* (December 23, 1971).

Brown v. Board of Education, 347 U.S. 483, 74 S. Ct. 686, 98 L. Ed. 873 (1954).

Covarrubias v. San Diego Unified School District, Civil Action No. 70-30d (S.D. Cal. 1971).

Detroit *Free Press* (June 15, 1971).

Diana v. Board of Education, Civil Action No. C-70-37 (N.D. Cal. 1970).

Doe v. Board of School Directors of the City of Milwaukee (U.S. District Ct. E.D. Wis. 1970).

In re Gault, 387 U.S. 1, 87 S. Ct. 1428, 18 L. Ed. 2d 527 (1967).

Guadalupe v. Tempe Elementary School District, Civil Action No. 71-435 (D. Ariz. 1971).

Guadalupe v. Tempe Elementary School District, Stipulation and Order (January 24, 1972).

Hobson v. Hansen, 269 F. Supp. 401 (D.D.C. 1967), cert. denied, aff'd sub. nom., 393 U.S. 801, 89 S.Ct. 40, 21 L.Ed. 2d 85 (1967).

Hobson v. Hansen-II, 320 F. Supp. 720 (D.D.C. 1971).

Larry P. v. Riles, Civil Action No. 71-2270 (N.D. Cal. 1971).

Marlega v. Board of School Directors of the City of Milwaukee, Civil Action No. 70-C-8 (E.D. Wis. 1970).

McMillan v. Board of Education of State of New York, 430 F. 2d. 1145 (2d Cir. 1970).

Mills v. Board of Education of the District of Columbia, Civil Action No. 1939-71 (D.D.C. 1971).

Mission Coalition Organization v. San Francisco Unified School District, Civil Action No. 70267 (N.D. Cal. 1970).

New York State Association for Retarded Children, Inc. v. Rockefeller (U.S. District Ct., E.D. N.Y. 1972).

New York State Association for Retarded Children, Inc. v. Rockefeller, Temporary Restraining Order (March 17, 1972).

New York Times (October 9, 1971).

Nordin, V.D. Comment on a paper by Dr. Whelan and Mr. Jackson. In J.S. Cohen (Ed.), *Confrontation and change: Community problems of mental retardation and developmental disabilities.* Ann Arbor, Mich.: Institute for the Study of

Mental Retardation and Related Disabilities, 1971.

The Pennsylvania Association for Retarded Children v. Commonwealth of Pennsylvania, Civil Action No. 71-42 (E.D. Pa. 1971).

Ricci v. Greenblatt, Civil Action No. 72-496F (E.D. Mass. 1972).

Rice, P. *Special education memorandum.* Sacramento, Calif.: California Department of Special Education, August 31, 1971.

Ross, S., DeYoung, H., & Cohen, J.S. Confrontation: Special education and the law. *Exceptional Children,* 1971, 4(7), 5-12.

Serrano v. Priest, 96 Ca. Rptr. 601, 5 Cal. 3d 584 (1971).

Smuck v. Hobson, 408 F. 2d 175 (1969).

Spangler v. Board of Education, 311 F. Supp. 501 (S.D. Cal. 1970).

Stell v. Savannah-Chatham County Board of Education, 220 F. Supp. 667 (S.D. Ga. 1963).

Stewart v. Phillips, Civil Action No. 70-1199F (D. Mass. 1970).

Tinker v. Des Moines Independent Community School District, 393 U.S. 503, 89 S.Ct. 733, 21 L. Ed. 2d 731 (1969).

Watson v. City of Cambridge, 157 Mass. 561, 32 N.E. 864 (1893).

Weintraub, F., Abeson, A., & Braddock, D. *State law and education of handicapped children: Issues and recommendations.* Arlington, Va.: Council for Exceptional Children, 1971.

Wisconsin v. Constantineau, 39 U.S. L.W. 4128 (January 19, 1971).

Wolf, v. Legislature of the State of Utah, Civil Action No. 182646 (3d Judicial District Ct. Utah. 1969).

Wyatt v. Stickney, 325 F. Supp. 781 (M.D. Ala. 1971).

Wyatt v. Stickney, Interim Emergency Order (March 2, 1972).

Wyatt v. Stickney, Post trial Memorandum on Adequate Habilitation for the Mentally Retarded (March 14, 1972).

Wyatt v. Stickney, Order and Decree (April 13, 1972).

SPECIAL EDUCATION IN EASTERN EUROPE

Ivan Z. Holowinsky, Ed.D.

Rutgers University

We are witnessing the emergence of considerable interest on the part of American educators and psychologists in education and educational research in foreign countries. This review attempts to bring to the American reader some understanding of the magnitude of problems related to special education in Eastern Europe. It is difficult to interpret comparative educational and research problems in other countries. It is even more difficult to interpret research and practice in special education in the East European countries which, for a number of years, were cut off from normal contact with their West European and American counterparts. A survey of special education in Eastern Europe is complicated by such factors as unavailable source materials, inadequate translation of terminology, problems in interpretating classification systems, and obscurities due to the absence of common criteria such as standardized intelligence and educational tests.

Because of these difficulties, most of the educational and research trends reported in this chapter deal specifically with special education in the Soviet Union and Poland, although these countries also present difficulties in obtaining source material and the interpretation of available data.

Special education in Eastern Europe can be adequately interpreted only in the light of historical educational trends and current political realities. For example, an American educator, accustomed to frequent articles and research in this country emphasizing emotional disorders in children, will be surprised to find very few studies on this topic in Soviet publications. This lack reflects a trend in Soviet defectology, which tends to view children's disorders as problems of education and faulty learning habits, rather than as the manifestations of illness or "defect." The trend is based upon Vygotsky's teachings: Vygotsky believed that emotional development is primarily the result of cultural and environmental factors which could be significantly influenced by educators and teachers. This primarily environmentalistic notion, based in turn upon Pavlovian psychology, is the cornerstone of Soviet pedagogy.

Understanding of special education in the Soviet Union is complicated by the fact that we are dealing not with a cultural and national unity but rather with a multinational and multicultural political system. Problems of special education in the Russian Republic are different from problems found in Kazakhstan, Latvia, Ukraine, or other national republics. Not only are there national, cultural, and linguistic differences, but the educational services themselves differ in various parts of the Soviet Union. Professor Vlasova recently indicated (1971) that there are whole regions and republics within the Soviet Union without special education services. The historical development of special education in the United States and the Soviet Union has been markedly different. Its development in the United States has been characterized by considerable diversity in programs, terminology, methods, and degree of efficiency, with much depending upon the initiative of various individuals. This growth has had a spontaneous quality about it, although directions and goals have had similar casts from time to time. In the Soviet Union, however, special education as well as education in general is highly centralized. Curriculum, research efforts, terminology, and so forth, are developed, modified, and guided by the Institute of Defectology of the Academy of Pedagogical Sciences. Furthermore, the Academy of Pedagogical Sciences has a distinct political role and has been affected in the past by ideological struggles (Little, 1968). During the first few years following the revolution, a strong movement based upon European and American influence emerged among Soviet educators. This movement, described as "pedalogy," attempted, among other things, to identify and assess individual differences in abilities. However, strong opposition to pedalogy soon developed; among its most vocal critics were such renowned Soviet educators as Makarenko and Medinsky. Professor Medinsky (1954), in particular, criticized intelligence and achievement tests. In his words:

Intelligence and achievement tests were made with such calculations that the children of the indigent parents should appear as weakly endowed and nonachieving. Those tests claiming objective proof were in reality the means to enable the children of the bourgeois to continue their education and to except the children of toilers [p. 179].

On July 4, 1936, the Central Committee of the Communist Party took the official position that pedalogy was founded on a pseudo-scientific anti-Marxist thesis. They condemned those pedalogists who grouped children in the category of backward, "transferring them from normal educational institutions to specialized auxiliary schools [Shore, 1947, p. 178]." Such strong, dogmatic statements from official sources hampered the development of evaluation and testing for many years; even today, individual intelligence testing is virtually unknown in the Soviet Union. This factor must be constantly kept in mind; in large part, it is the relative absence of quantitative criteria for the measurement of intellectual abilities and differences that makes it difficult to translate terminology used in the U.S.S.R., and to directly compare American and Soviet programs dealing with various levels of intellectual functioning.

COMPARATIVE TERMINOLOGY AND CLASSIFICATION

Special education in Eastern Europe reveals two strong influences in terminology and classification. Throughout the Soviet Union, as well as in Bulgaria, terminology prevails that was developed by the Institute of Defectology of the Academy of Pedagogical Sciences in Moscow. However, in such countries as Poland, Romania, Czechoslovakia, and Yugoslavia, one can still see strong West European (primarily French) influences. Within the Soviet Union, two different terms are used to describe children who have intellectual and educational difficulties: "oligophrenics" and *umstvenno otstaly* (mentally backward). The Russian term which most closely approximates "mental retardation" is "oligophrenia." No lesser authorities than Vlasova and Pevzner (1967) still subdivide oligophrenia into traditional groups: idiots, imbeciles, and *debeles* (French term for "feeble-minded"). This suggests that oligophrenia, as a concept, covers the range of profound, severe, moderate, and mild retardation in the U.S.S.R. The major criterion for oligophrenia classification is evidence of organic or neuropathological insult. Pevzner (1970a) stated that oligophrenia is characterized by developmental lack of learning abilities, primarily thinking, and that it is basically due to biological defects of the central nervous system, especially of the most complex and later-developed brain structures. She suggested that one should exclude from oligophrenic classification most types of retardation related to metabolic disorders, schizophrenia, epilepsy, and psychotic episodes, as well as mental retardation due to localized defects and environmental factors. The oligophrenic classification implies inadequate development of all upper layers of the cortical hemispheres, resulting in inadequacies of all higher neurological activities. Etiopathogenesis of oligophrenia can be described by three factors: time, etiology, and location of the damage.

In the Soviet Ukraine, acceptable terminology for intellectual subnormality is *rozumova vidstalist.* This can be translated as intellectual backwardness as well as mental retardation. Since only small numbers of mildly retarded individuals show organic etiology, it can be safely assumed that most of those classified in the United States as retarded, with unknown etiology, would not be so classified in the Soviet Union. It is obvious that differences in terminology directly influence the estimated number of retarded individuals within a general population; this accounts for the fact that while in the United States the estimated incidence of retardates within the general population varies from 3% to 5%, the Soviet Union estimates only .5% to .7% of its general population as being mentally retarded. Owing to the Soviet criterion of organicity in the definition and diagnosis of oligophrenia, there are probably many children attending Soviet regular schools who, according to the AAMD criteria, would be classified as mildly retarded. On the other hand, one may assume that many other youngsters in Soviet special auxiliary or helping schools probably are not retarded. This latter assumption is based on the fact that educational underachievement is the criterion for admission to an auxiliary school, and any child who fails to be promoted twice in a row may be a candidate for such a school. Children placed in auxiliary schools are described as *umstvenno otstaly* (Vlasova, 1971). However, when we consider that the term "oligophrenia" covers the range from profound through mild retardation, *umstvenno otstaly* appears to describe children who, in English, could be called "intellectually backward" or "slow learners."

Owing to the stringent requirement for diagnosis of oligophrenia, children who are functionally retarded in the Soviet Union and Poland are described simply as "pseudooligophrenics (Dziedzic, 1969)." This diagnosis is related to inadequate diagnostic tools and techniques – an understandable assumption, since the basis for diagnosing a child as oligophrenic is objective evidence of cortical damage. Dziedzic (1969) also argued that pseudooligophrenic children should be placed, as a rule, in regular schools. Since the U.S.S.R. lacks standardized tests to assess the level of intellectual functioning, Pevzner (1970a) emphasized the need for qualitative rather than quantitative diagnosis.

Although, as indicated, individual intelligence testing as practiced in the United States is virtually unknown in the Soviet Union, recently the Institute of Defectology developed differential diagnostic approaches to distinguish between mentally retarded, mentally backward, and temporarily developmentally retarded (Vlasova, 1971). Unfortunately, the author could not obtain more definite information concerning this interesting approach. The whole field of defectology (Vlasova & Pevzner, 1967) is concerned with etiological factors related to various aspects of the psychophysical development of children, e.g., the auditory-language, visual-perceptual, intellectual, and emotional areas. Vlasova and Pevzner (1967) used the term "emotional-volitional" to describe certain behavioral-psychological functions. Use of the word "volitional" is in line with the Russian school of thought that views human emotional development as a complex dialectical process.

As mentioned earlier, Soviet terminology, although used extensively in Eastern Europe, has been questioned by some writers. Doroszewski (1969) argued against acceptance of the term "defectology" in Poland. For support, he cited such authorities as Maria Grzegorzewska, who apparently has been opposed to the general use of the word. Doroszewski suggested that such terms as "special pedagogy" or "therapeutic pedagogy" should replace "defectology," despite its frequent use in Eastern Europe.

SPECIAL EDUCATION CURRICULA

As noted, special education organization and curricula in Eastern Europe, and especially within the Soviet Union, are highly centralized. This centralization is symptomatic of the totalitarian regime to such an extent that Stalin himself has been given the credit for the development of Soviet defectology.

U.S.S.R.

The Larger Soviet Encyclopedia (1952) describes the development of special education within the Soviet Union as follows: "Soviet defectology has been guided by the genius of Stalin, his teachings about language and thinking, and also by teachings of the great Russian physiologist Pavlov [Vol. 14, p. 171]."

According to Medinsky (1954), progress of defectology in the Soviet Union can be related to the efforts of Zenkov, Rau, Azbukin, and Kovalenko. Defectology eventually developed into the following branches: typhlopedagogy (education of the blind), surdopedagogy (education of the deaf), oligophrenopedagogy (education of the mentally retarded) and logopedicpedagogy (speech correction and therapy) (Medinsky, 1954; Vlasova, 1971). In the Soviet Union, the Institute of Defectology of the Academy of Pedagogical Sciences has the responsibility for providing curricula, textbooks, teaching aids, and equipment for the entire system of Soviet special education.

The Institute of Defectology became part of the Academy of Pedagogical Sciences in 1944. Since 1966 it has been elevated to the status of an all-union institution (Little, 1968). The institute conducts research in many areas of defectology, psychology, psychoneuropathology, neurophysiology, and so forth (Vlasova, 1971).

The Psychological Institute of the Ukrainian Soviet Socialist Republic in Kiev is noted for its efforts in learning research and mental development (Proskura, 1969). It published, in collaboration with the Institute of Pedagogy and Psychology of the Ukrainian Soviet Socialist Republic, a monumental work under the direction of A.I. Diachkov entitled *Principles of Assessment and Education of Atypical Children* (Vlasova, 1971).

Training of defectologists is conducted primarily in Moscow, Leningrad, Kiev, Minsk, and Sverdlovsk. Until 1959 defectologists were also trained in the area of general education, but since 1959 their training has been exclusively specialized. At the present time, the training of defectologists requires 4 years of full-time study. The required curriculum includes general and pathological anatomy, physiology, neuropathology, and psychopathology of childhood.

Special education schools in the Soviet Union are generally of two types; (a) separate schools for children with serious physical and mental defects (such as schools for the blind, deaf-mute, and oligophrenic); and (b) auxiliary schools, within public school systems, for intellectually backward children as well as children with minor defects. The schools for children with serious physical and mental defects have become special institutions in which the pupils receive general education and vocational training.

The program in special (auxiliary) schools is arranged in such a way that a pupil is expected to complete it in 12 years of schooling, reaching a competency level equivalent to eighth grade. It takes 8 years to complete the program from first to fifth grade, and 4 years from sixth to eighth grade. The curriculum of separate schools for the mentally retarded is similar to the curriculum of the first 4 years of normal school but is covered within 7 years. Visually handicapped children undergo 12 years of schooling within the Soviet Union; deaf children attend school for 13 years (Levin, 1963).

It is difficult to obtain reliable data on how children are placed into auxiliary schools. However, Vlasova and Pevzner (1967) reported on a survey, conducted in 1964 in the Russian Republic, which indicated that in 250 auxiliary schools more than 90% of the pupils in the first and third grades of those schools were placed there after failing 2 or 3 years in regular public school programs. The data published by UNESCO (International Directories of Education, 1968) indicated that at that time in the Soviet Union there were 1,290 separate schools for the mentally retarded; 115 for the blind and partially sighted; 235 for the deaf and hard-of-hearing; 46 for the orthopedically handicapped; and 25 for children with speech defects.

Poland

In Poland, special education efforts are coordinated by the Governmental Institute of Special Education. This institute was established officially in 1922 (Lipkowski, 1970). It was the first of its kind in Poland, and is one of the oldest in Europe. The institute conducts research in special education and trains professional workers. Polish special education has a long history: In 1967 Polish educators marked the one hundred fiftieth anniversary of the establishment of their first special school, the so-called Institute of Deaf-Mute and Blind in Warsaw (Lipkowski, 1968). The main credit for the growth of special education in Poland is given to Maria Grzegorzewska, who was significantly influenced in her work by the writings of Seguin (Dziedzic, 1968). The intellectually subnormal population in Poland is estimated at from 1.3% (Lipkowski, 1968) to 1.8% (Dziedzic, 1968). The number of special education schools is estimated by Lipkowski to be 508, while a UNESCO report (1968) estimated 234 special schools plus a considerable number of special classes within public schools. Curriculum in Polish special schools consists of the Polish language, geography, music, history, and nature study (Stolkowski, 1970).

Hungary

In Hungary, as of 1968, approximately 20,000 youngsters attended special education programs. Programs are divided according to the chronological age of the child as per the following manner: Children between 3 and 6 years of age attend preschool special education classes. Children between 6 and 14 years of age attend special classes for the retarded in supplementary schools. Moderately retarded children between 6 and 8 years of age attend preparatory schools, and mildly retarded children between 8 and 16 years of age attend the so-called practical schools (Dziedzic, 1968).

Czechoslovakia

In Czechoslovakia, the number of mentally retarded children is estimated at 34,589, and all other categories of the handicapped at 54,607; together these groups comprise 2.3% of the general population (Lipkowski, 1968). Compulsory education for the handicapped was introduced in 1960 for the chronological age span of 6-15 years. Preschool education for the blind and deaf between 3-6 CA was mandated in 1968 (Lipkowski, 1968). Mentally retarded children can be admitted to special schools at 6 years of age upon the recommendation of classification committees consisting of a school principal and a special educator, as well as a physician (Dziedzic, 1968).

Yugoslavia and Bulgaria

In Yugoslavia, special schools are part of the general public education from 3 to 18 years of age. In 1963 Yugoslovia recorded 22 special schools, 217 special classes, 15 so-called "children's homes" or institutions with 1,982 youngsters, 11 diagnostic centers, and 4 prevocational training institutes (Dziedzic, 1968). As estimated by Lipkowski (1968), mentally retarded youngsters in Bulgaria numbered 11,380, and other handicapping categories numbered 12,940, comprising together an estimated 1.1% of the general population served in 83 schools. Special preschools exist for children 4 to 7 years of age. Children between 7 and 15 years of age attend eight grades in supplementary schools (Dziedzic, 1968).

Romania

Preschool special education classes for MR youngsters of 4-7 CA have also been established in Romania. Youngsters of 7-14 CA attend elementary special education schools, while older children attend residential special vocational schools (Dziedzic, 1968).

The youngsters are selected for special schools by evaluation committees consisting of a pediatrician, neurologist, psychologist, psychiatrist, special class teacher, and general education teacher. Since 1959 industrial establishments have been requested to reserve from 3% to 5% of their available positions for the handicapped and graduates of special schools (Lipkowski, 1968). The UNESCO (1968) report listed 96 schools for the handicapped, including 34 schools for the mentally retarded.

RELEVANT RESEARCH

In this section an attempt will be made to review the studies published in East European journals that have direct or indirect implications for special education. The review is limited by the lack of original journals from these countries. It was possible to obtain only incomplete sets of the following publications: *Voprosy Psychologii, Defectologia, Sovetskaia Pedagogika,* and *Szkola Specjalna.* Two other factors complicate the interpretation of studies published in Soviet journals. First, very little attempt is made to arrange articles according to content, and one can find, in a single issue, an article dealing with problems of a field-crop leader's activity as well as a highly technical piece on "Changes of Constant Potential in the Human Cortex and Deep Brain Structures Caused by Emotional Reactions." Second, Soviet publications deal with concepts that American psychologists might find less than "scientific" (e.g., "gnostic self-regulation," Pushkin, 1969). Soviet writers reject dogmatic materialism, which, according to Piaget (1971), "has no connection with dialectical materialism, which is indeed a kind of evolutionist constructivism and not at all reductionist in principle [p. 46]."[1] Soviet defectologists view the individual not just from an ontogenetic point of view, but also as a product of phylogenetic development and sociohistorical conditioning (Vygotsky, Luria, Zaporozetz, and Tsvetkova). Their view of complex disorders is positivistic in nature; i.e., they believe in the possibility of restructuring defective functioning (Tsvetkova, 1972). Emphasis is usually placed on basing the retraining process upon the strengths rather than the weaknesses of the individual (Zykov, 1970). Visual modalities, for example, are stressed when teaching concept formation to deaf children (Glovackaya, 1970) or slow learners (Pinski, 1970). Auditory and tactile approaches have been used by Bubnova (1970) in investigating formation of special images in visually handicapped sixth graders in tasks involving ability to "visualize" geographic concepts such as land masses, seas, and rivers. Recognizing the need for ambidexterity in a technological society, with its emphasis upon mechanized and automatized production, Mavrov (1969) conducted a study which attempted to determine whether it is possible to teach right-handed children to use the left hand equally well.

The considerable interest in handicapped children in East European literature has concerned questions of speech and language development, as well as speech and communication disorders. Classical in this area have been the contributions of Vygotsky (1939, 1962), who is also widely known in Western scientific literature.

Speech development of young children 12-16 months of age was investigated by Popova (1968), who studied speech interaction in different situations: When children simply had an opportunity to imitate adults, their speech production was inferior to the speech of children who had an opportunity to act with an object and address an adult. In situations of independent play, when there was no contact with adults, the level of speech activity decreased. Tonkova-Iampolskaya (1968) investigated the development of speech intonation in children 2 years of age. The intonation was electro-acoustically analyzed and was found to have certain physical characteristics that conveyed emotionality. Even in the cry of the newborn child, a certain intonational pattern can be traced similar to an intonation of displeasure in older children and adults. In associating with adults and experiencing their vocal expression, other kinds of intonational manifestations appear in children: an intonation of calm cooing, beginning from the second month of life, and an intonation of pleasure from the third month. From the seventh month an intonation of request appears, and from the beginning of the second year of life, an intonation of question. The patterning of children's intonations is not identical to that of adults, but there is a considerable

---

[1]"Evolutionist constructivism" is a term apparently coined by Piaget to describe a scientific process or point of view which attempts to explain psychological and cognitive phenomena as a result of constructive phylogenetic development. The term "reductionist," according to Piaget, "manifests itself nowadays in more subtle form when people try to reduce psychology to physiology pure and simple [p. 46]."

similarity. Kononova (1968) studied vocal reactions in children during the first year of life. The highest number of vocal reactions appeared in so-called "social situations," e.g., in contact with other individuals. The study also demonstrated that a child's motor activity stimulates positively his vocal reactions. Markova (1969) conducted a study of the mastery of syllabic composition of words in children. From her results it appears that in children, the ability to reproduce syllabic structure precedes ability to accurately reproduce phonetic content.

Speech disorders associated with aphasic conditions were investigated by Luria (1962), Tsvetkova (1972), Ianakiev, Ovcharova, Raichev, and Televa (1968). Luria's classical contribution on speech disorders is contained in his book on the higher cortical functions of man. He contributed to our understanding of the complexity of feedback mechanisms in perceptual and cognitive functioning. Tsvetkova (1972) suggested the use of a kinesthetic-motor training approach in retraining aphasic patients. Differential diagnosis, establishing essentially two kinds of aphasic conditions, has been proposed in a study by Ianakiev, Ovcharova, Raichev, and Televa (1968). Another study, with possible pragmatic application to teaching speech skills to deaf-mutes, was presented by Volkova (1961). She suggested that in addition to visual analyzers, tactile analyzers should also be used. Volkova claims that deaf-mute individuals can perceive, through their skin, differences in the character of the streams of air created when pronouncing different vocal sounds. Stimulation of speech development in mentally retarded children was the concern of Ulianova's (1970) study. She used various objects of nature, such as plants, animals, and birds, in order to increase children's vocabulary. She achieved positive results with the use of concrete examples.

Basic to our understanding of learning disorders are studies dealing with information processing, storage, and information retrieval. Malkov (1969) studied the optimum functioning of the nervous system, or its inadequate functioning, as it relates to attention concentration. He described concentration of attention as the optimum focus of the degree of excitation in the brain cortex. His work appears to be related to studies on concentration done in this country. Malkov's study found a statistically significant correlation between the optimum functioning of the nervous system and concentration of attention. The neurophysiological basis of limits of attention and memory span were investigated by Chuprikova (1968). She found that Ss who were memorizing visual stimuli experienced an increase in excitability in those points of the visual analyzer (visual nerve pathways) which corresponded to the projection of incoming stimuli. She observed that the increase in the number of simultaneously presented stimuli resulted in a gradual decrease of excitability. This suggested to Chuprikova an inverse relationship between the intensity of attention and its span. In her opinion, the phenomenon of inverse relationship is the result of the involvement in the perceptual act of separate objects of inductional inhibition. She emphasized that the most important function of the inhibition consists of focusing and sharpening excitation coming to our central nervous system.

Related to studies of attention is research on short-term memory. An investigation of the relationship between visual and auditory memory was reported by Luria and Klimkovsky (1968). Their study showed that for optimum results in memorizing, a high degree of interdependence between visual and auditory modalities was necessary. A significant disturbance in the process of memory was found in patients with lesions of the left temporal regions. The authors attributed this disturbance to the pathologically increased retroactive inhibition. Pathological inhibition, in their judgment, appeared to be related directly to the negative effects of the lesion.

The relationship between the ability to memorize words and the frequency of their use was investigated by Bolshunov and Soloviev in association experiments (1968). Experiments on memorizing series of words of different familiarity levels showed that word frequency in association experiments correlated positively with memorizing words, and that the more frequently used words were more easily combined in habitual groups [p. 76]. This finding suggested that similarity or communality is one of the most important factors in the association process.

Psychophysiological correlates of problem-solving activity were investigated by Zinchenko (1968). On the basis of registration and analysis of the eye movement routes in the problem-solving process, he formulated a hypothesis that there were different phases of the process. Motor activity of the eyes was interpreted as a means of manipulating or recreating the image.

Makhlakh (1969) suggested in his study the existence of different psycho-physiological bases for visual and verbal types of memory. His hypothesis, if substantiated by other studies, would explain some of the complexities of the problems found in learning disorders.

Retrieval of information, or memory, is an integral part of complex cognitive operations, since it relates to learning, mental development, or intellectual subnormality. This problem has been investigated in Eastern Europe from various viewpoints. An attempt was made by Pushkin (1969) to investigate, from a psychophysiological point of view, the dynamics of cognition involved in the process of solving a problem. In his study, he referred to "a phenomenon of mental gaze," which was investigated by a transducer fixed on the pupil of the eye and stabilized in reference to the retina. Pushkin demonstrated several phases of activity in the process of problem solving. Three basic movement patterns were observed, and there were high correlations between quantitative indices of three kinds of movements; these findings implied to Pushkin the existence of a single complex process which he termed "gnostic self-regulation."

Problem solving as it relates to developmental aspects was investigated by Leites (1969); he suggested that developmental levels of knowledge in problem solving help to determine the nature of general capacities. The study employed three specific age groups (CA 8-9; CA 12-13; CA 15-16), with different clusters of abilities being identified in addition to a general progression of abilities. The development of mental operations in younger children (CA 5-7) was studied by Zarandia (1971), who sought to determine whether the mental operations of contemporary children mature sooner than similar operations in children of the same chronological age who were 5-7 years in 1928. Zarandia's study was a follow-up of Urnadze's study (1966). His results showed that the mental operations of generalization and definition are formed earlier in present-day children than in those who were studied in 1928.

Classification of the properties of objects in preschool children was studied by Venger (1970). His purpose was to determine whether a process of complex serial classification and systematization follows uniform development, or whether there is a separate pattern of development for sensory and intellectual problem solving. The children (CA 3-7) were given tasks consisting of passive and active systematization (serialization). "Passive" was defined as being based upon concrete visual examples; "active" was defined as involving multiple classification and serialization. Venger concluded that "the assimilation of passive systematization is a result of the perfection of perceptual actions with colors and hues, whereas the assimilation of active systematization involves the learning of intellectual operations that do not depend on the material on which the teaching is brought about [p. 86]."

The relationship between the general level of mental operations and specific abilities in first-grade children (CA 7-8) was investigated by Dubrovina (1970). Specific abilities studied were related to mathematics, grammar, and visual imagery. A positive correlation was found between general level of mental abilities and performance on the specific tasks.

There has been considerable emphasis in East European research on the theoretical and pragmatic problems of mental retardation (oligophrenia). Noted among the contributions have been those of Pevzner and Luria. Luria's theories covering the second signaling system has received particular attention abroad (Balla & Zigler, 1971; Milgram, 1971). (Readers interested in current Soviet thinking on mental retardation are referred to *Soviet Education* [Special Education in the Soviet Union], 1971-1972, **14**, November, December, January; and especially to articles by Babenkova & Iurovskii [1971], Kuzmaite [1970], Pevzner [1970], Rubinshtein [1970], and Zubrimin [1971], which also appear in *Defectologia*.)

An interesting study was conducted in Poland by Kostrzewski (1970); he attempted to determine the process of intellectual development in individuals with complete and incomplete trisomy of chromosomes, Group G in the karyotype. The purpose of the study was to determine whether the mental age of persons with Down's syndrome rises systematically with chronological age, or whether deterioration occurs between CA 12 and 15. The study raised an interesting question as to whether clinical groups of individuals with Down's syndrome could be differentiated further, according to the pattern of intellectual development. Initial impressions, based on two groups of subjects (incomplete and complete trisomy) suggested that individuals with incomplete trisomy possess higher IQs and MAs than individuals with complete trisomy of chromosome G in the karyotype.

Of considerable potential interest and pragmatic applicability for compensatory education are studies dealing with the role of teaching or training in the acquisition of abstract concepts. Venger (1970), in his study on the mastery of classification of external properties of objects by preschool children, suggested possible techniques to increase the information-processing capacity of children. Venger's paper deals with part of a large research program currently directed by Zaporozetz. Early education, prior to CA 5, of children with Down's syndrome was reported by Tsykoto (1970). This article described the educational use of toys, colors, and geometrical forms as preparatory activities leading toward the teaching of basic academic skills.

The extent to which teaching can enhance serial learning was investigated by Proskura (1969) and reported in the United States by Holowinsky (1970). The purpose of Proskura's research, conducted at the Psychological Institute of the Ukrainian Soviet Socialist Republic, was to investigate serial learning based upon Piaget's original notion of conceptualization. The subjects were youngsters born in the Ukrainian Republic. The study results led to some conclusions concerning the cross-cultural applicability of Piaget's developmental sequence. Before attempting to ascertain whether the children used trial and error or conceptualization in their problem-solving attempts, it was determined whether the child understood the meaning of such concepts as "larger" and "smaller." As a next step the children were told that they would be given sticks of various lengths and that they would be asked to arrange them in order of length. However, prior to actual performance, the children were asked to draw on a piece of paper how they would arrange the sticks in the serial order. Many of the 3- and 4-year-olds may not have understood the assigned task, for they created all kinds of familiar objects out of the sticks. The experiment itself consisted of two parts: In the first, the level of serialization operations in normal situations (without prior instruction) was investigated at all age levels. The performance of the children at various age levels compared closely to the original Piagetian theory of concept development. Most of the performance of preschool children was based on trial and error; the children did not reveal a capacity for conceptual serialization. The study showed definite positive progression with age, and it indicated that, regardless of training or instructions, 3- and 4-year-olds are incapable of abstract generalizations.

How to improve logical memorizing in preschool and elementary school children was studied by Smirnov, Istomina, Maltseva, and Samokhvalova (1969). This study revealed that children were capable of logical memorizing to a much greater extent than expected, provided a definite strategy for teaching each method was applied. The complete process of teaching included two stages: (a) teaching logical operations and (b) teaching how to use these actions with mnemonic purpose.

The role played by teaching in the acceleration of mental development has also interested Polish educators and psychologists (Grzywak-Kaczynska & Walesa, 1969; Walesa, 1970). Walesa (1970), in his theoretical work on the study of experimental teaching of logical operations in children, compared Piaget's theories with those of Galperin. It appeared to him that there are essential differences between the two theorists in terminology and in the emphasis on various aspects of intellectual development. The author recommends adaptation of Piaget's theory as a base from which to study experimental teaching, although he also feels that the use of Galperin's theory seems more promising.

In an extensive experimental study (241 subjects), Grzywak-Kaczynska and Walesa (1969) investigated the influence of teaching on the acceleration of children's mental development. Two matched groups were selected. The experimental group was taught 6 successive days, twice daily, 20 minutes per lesson. Both the experimental and the control groups were tested three times; at the end of the experiment and 1 month later, the results showed statistically significant improvement in children who were taught, but also indicated the importance of developmental maturation; for example, the accelerated learning of 4-year-old children appeared to be superficial and vanished with time.

Few studies are found in Eastern Europe, especially in the Soviet Union, which deal with problems presented by socially and emotionally maladjusted children and juvenile delinquents. Reluctance to acknowledge behavioral disorders of primarily social etiology stems from the Soviet belief that in a classless, ideal Marxist society, such problems do not exist. The need for such denial seems obvious when one considers that basic to the Marxist concept of personality is an assumption that personality is socially determined. Soviet psychologists strongly maintain that Freudian psychology and "personalism" are "irreconcilable with principles of Soviet psychology [Budilova & Slavskaya, 1969 p. 138]." After more than 50 years of supposedly ideal socialism, an admission that socially maladjusted children or juvenile delinquents exist would run contrary to the dogmatic assumptions. By the recent admission of Soviets themselves (Zubin, 1969), such children are studied "extremely insufficiently." More studies are found dealing with serious emotional disorders. Such conditions are attributed almost exclusively to organic (biological or physiological) etiologies (Vlasova & Pevzner, 1967).

In some countries of Eastern Europe, e.g., Poland, psychologists and educators are less reluctant to discuss programs for juvenile delinquents (Kozielowa, 1970; Kwinta, 1968). Occasionally one even finds statistical data on numbers and status of juvenile delinquents or socially maladjusted youngsters (Nurowski, 1969).

CONCLUSION

The organization, programming, and development of special education in Eastern Europe, and especially in the Soviet Union, strongly reflect ideological and political reality. However, this is by no means uniform, and in some East European countries (e.g., Poland, Czechoslovakia, and Romania), one can see a strong influence of Western traditions and trends. Therapeutic education, preschool education, and the relationship between teaching and mental development are distinctly emphasized. Very few studies deal directly with socially related character and emotional disorders. More systematic periodic research is needed to obtain clearer pictures of current trends as well as the strengths and weaknesses of East European and Soviet special education.

References

Babenkova, R.D., & Iurovskii, S. Spatial organization of movements by mentally retarded schoolchildren, *Defectologia,* 1971, **3**, 30-34.

Balla, D., & Zigler, E. Luria's verbal deficiency theory of mental retardation and performance on sameness, symmetry and opposition tasks; a critique. *American Journal of Mental Deficiency,* 1971, **75**, 400-413.

Bolshunov, I.V., & Soloviev, V.M. The relationship between the memorization of words and the frequency of their use in association experiments. *Voprosy Psychologii,* 1968, **6**, 71-76.

Bubnova, T.V. Formation of spatial image in visually handicapped school children. *Defectologia,* 1970, **4**, 13-20.

Budilova, E.A., & Slavskaya, K.A. Problems of personality in the works of Rubinshtein. *Voprosy Psychologii,* 1969, **5**, 137-143.

Chuprikova, N.I. On neurophysiological bases of the limits of attention and memory span. *Voprosy Psychologii,* 1968, **2**, 23-37.

Doroszewski, W. Problems of terminology. *Szkola Specjalna,* 1969, **1**, 1-4.

Dubrovina, I.V. An investigation of elementary manifestations of specific mental abilities in junior school children. *Voprosy Psychologii,* 1970, **6**, 94-102.

Dziedzic, S. Educational care of the severely retarded. *Szkola Specjalna,* 1968, **3**, 206-222.

Dziedzic, S. Pseudo-oligophrenia. *Szkola Specjalna,* 1969, **31**(4), 359-366.

Glovackaya, Y.I. Concept formation in deaf second grade school children based on the concrete practical operation with objects. *Defectologia,* 1970, **3**, 36-39.

Grzywak-Kaczynska, C.H., & Walesa, G. Influence of teaching on the acceleration of the development of logical faculties of children. *Roczniki Filozoficzne,* 1969, **17**(4), 79-97.

Holowinsky, I. Seriation action in preschool children. *Journal of Learning Disabilities,* 1970, **3**(9), 34-35.

Ianakiev, M., Ovcharova, P., Raichev, R., & Televa, T.S. Some quantitative linguistic characteristics of aphasics. *Voprosy Psychologii,* 1968, **3**, 90-93.

International directories of education (special education). Paris: UNESCO, 1968.

Kononova, I.M. Vocal reactions in children of the first year of life and their relationship with various patterns of behavior. *Voprosy Psychologii,* 1968, **5**, 119-127.

Kostrzewski, J. The dynamics of intellectual development in individuals with complete and incomplete trisomy of chromosomes group G in the cariotype. *Roczniki Filozoficzne,* 1970, **28**(4), 55-81.

Kozielowa, S. Personality characteristics of socially maladjusted children and educational work in institutions for juvenile delinquents. *Szkola Specjalna,* 1970, **31**(3), 217-232.

Kuzmaite, L.I. Some aspects of personal relations among junior mentally retarded schoolchildren. *Defectologia,* 1970, **3**, 30-36.

Kwinta, M. My educational experience in institutions for juvenile delinquents. *Szkola Specjalna,* 1968, **29**(3), 251-255.

Larger Soviet Encyclopedia. (2nd ed.) Moscow: Government Printing Office, 1952.

Leites, N.S. The problem of general capacities in developmental aspects. *Voprosy Psychologii,* 1969, **2**, 15-24.

Levin, D. *Soviet education today.* London: Macgibbon & Kee, 1963.

Lipkowski, O. Current status and developmental tendencies of special education in Europe. *Szkola Specjalna,* 1968, **3**, 223-238.

Lipkowski, O. New structure and new goals of the Governmental Institute of Special Education. *Szkola Specjalna,* 1970, **3**, 193-195.

Little, R.D. The Academy of Pedagogical Sciences; the political role. *Soviet Studies* (University of Glasgow), 1968, **19**(3), 387-397.

Luria, A.R. *Higher cortical functions in man.* Moscow: Moscow University Press, 1962.

Luria, A.R. Psychological studies of mental deficiency in the Soviet Union. In N.R. Ellis (Ed.), *Handbook of mental deficiency.* New York: McGraw-Hill, 1963.

Luria, A.R., & Klimkovsky, M. On the model organization of short-term memory. *Voprosy Psychologii,* 1968, **5**, 81-84.

Makhlakh, E.S. On the relationship between visual and verbal types of memory. *Voprosy Psychologii,* 1969, **1**, 125-127.

Malkov, N.E. The strength of the nervous system and the concentration of attention. *Voprosy Psychologii,* 1969, **2**, 75-82.

Markova, A.K. Mastery of the syllabic composition of words at an early age. *Voprosy Psychologii,* 1969, **5**, 118-126.

Mavrov, E. An ambidexterity in schoolchildren. *Voprosy Psychologii,* 1969, **3**, 99-109.

Medinsky, Y.N. *Public education in the USSR.* Moscow: Foreign Language Publishing House, 1954.

Milgram, N. Cognition and language in mental retardation: A reply to Bella and Zigler. *American Journal of Mental Deficiency,* 1971, **76**(1), 33-41.

Nurowski, E. Certain aspects of referral problems of juveniles referred to institutions for juvenile delinquents. *Szkola Specjalna,* 1969, **30**(3), 204-210.

Pevzner, M.Z. Etiopathogenesis and classification of oligophrenia. (Translated by G. Malawko) *Szkola Specjalna,* 1970, **4**, 289-293. (a)

Pevzner, M.Z. Principal directions of research in oligophrenia. *Defectologia,* 1970, **2**, 40-45. (b)

Piaget, J. *Biology and knowledge.* Chicago: University of Chicago Press, 1971.

Pinski, B.I. Tasks of correctional-educational work with mentally retarded children of school age in the labor training process. *Defectologia,* 1970, **1**, 13-19.

Popova, M.I. Some features of speech manifestations in the children of the first-half-year of the second year of life. *Voprosy Psychologii,* 1968, **4**, 116-122.

Proskura, E.V. The role of teaching in the formation of seriation action in pre-school children. *Voprosy Psychologii,* 1969, **15**, 37-45.

Pushkin,V.N. On the study of thinking as a process. *Voprosy Psychologii,* 1969, **6**, 20-34.

Rubinshtein, S.Y. S.S. Vypotsky on the emotional development of mentally retarded children. *Defectologia,* 1970, **5**, 3-10.

Shore, M. *Soviet education, its psychology and philosophy,* New York: Philosophical Library, 1947.

Smirnov, A.A., Istomina, Z.M., Maltseva, R.P., & Samokhvalova, V.I. The formation of methods of logical memorization in children of pre-school age and in juvenile school children. *Voprosy Psychologii,* 1969, **5**, 90-101.

Stolkowski, W. Textbooks for special schools. *Szkola Specjalna,* 1970, **31**(4), 359-366.

Tonkova-Iampolskaya, R.V. Speech intonation development in children of the first two years of life. *Voprosy Psychologii,* 1968, **3**, 94-101.

Tsvetkova, L.S. Basic principles of a theory of reeducation of brain-injured patients. *Journal of Special Education,* 1972, **6**, 135-144.

Tsykoto, G.V. Family education of young mentally retarded children. *Defectologia,* 1970, **1**, 78-84.

Ulianova, T.K. Some method of speech development in the mentally retarded schoolchildren during the study of objects of the environment. *Defectologia,* 1970, **3**, 50-54.

Urnadze, D.N. *Psychological studies.* Moscow: Education Publishing, 1966.

Venger, N.B. On the assimilation of the systematization of external object properties in children under school age. *Voprosy Psychologii,* 1970, **4**, 77-86.

Vlasova, T.A. Toward the new achievements of the Soviet defectology. *Defectologia,* 1971, **3**, 3-12.

Vlasova, T.A., & Pevzner, M.S. *For teachers, about children with developmental anomalies.* Moscow: Academy of Pedagogical Sciences, 1967.

Volkova, K.A. What must be taught in lessons in speech skills in schools for deaf-mute. *Soviet Education,* 1961, **4**(1), 33-35.

Vygotsky, L.S. Thought and speech. *Psychiatry,* 1939, **2**, 29-54.

Vygotsky, L.S. *Thought and language.* (Trans. by E. Haufmann & G. Vakar) Cambridge, Mass.: MIT Press, 1962.

Walesa, G. Theoretical basis of the study of experimental teaching of logical operations to children. *Roczniki Filozoficzne,* 1970, **28**(4), 45-54.

Zarandia, M.I. On the development of mental operations in the children of pre-school age. *Voprosy Psychologii,* 1971, **5**, 100-109.

Zinchenko, V.P. Perceptual and mnemic elements of creative activity. *Voprosy Psychologii,* 1968, **2**, 3-7.

Zubin, L.M. Psychological aspects of the problem of pedagogically neglected children and juvenile delinquents. *Voprosy Psychologii,* 1969, **3**, 132-142.

Zubrimin, Iu.K. Cooperative efforts of physicians and special educators toward treatment of severely retarded children, *Defectologia,* 1971, **2**, 30-34.

Zykov, S.A. Concrete practical activities in the development of deaf children. *Defectologia,* 1970, **2**, 56-64.

SUBJECT INDEX

A

Achievement ratio, 3
American Educational Research Association (AERA), 207, 220
Associative-ability — see Jensen's associative-ability and cognitive-ability theory
Autistic children, behavior modification in special education, 75-77

B

Behavior modification in special education, 51-88
  autistic children, 75-77
  children with speech disorders, 77-80
    articulation, 79, 80
    stuttering, 78, 79
  development of a behavior-modification program, 55-58
  disadvantaged children, underachievers, and children with learning disabilities, 72-75
    academic skills, 72-75
    classroom deportment, 75
  emotionally disturbed, 67-72
    antisocial behavior, 71, 72
    classroom behaviors, 69-71
    hyperactivity, 67-68
    social behaviors, 68
  generalization, 80-86
    procedures to augment response maintenance, 83-86
    response generalization, 83

stimulus generalization, 81-83
mentally retarded, 58-67
  classroom behavior, 63, 64
  disruptive and destructive behaviors, 61, 62
  language development, 62, 63
  occupational and work-related behaviors, 64-66
  self-care behaviors, 58-61
  social responses, 66
principles of operant conditioning, 53-55
training staff, attendants, and teachers, 86, 87
Behaviorally disordered, contemporary issues in education of, 137-155
  definition of problem, 137-144
    crisis of identity, 139-144
  implications, 153-155
  public school intervention approaches for, 144-153
    affective curriculum experience, 147, 148
    behavior-modification approaches, 149-153
    core conditions of teacher-pupil relationships, 146, 147
    learners as teachers, 148, 149
Behavioristic task analysis, 107, 111
Bias of intelligence tests and testing, 162-168
Biculturation, 168
Bilingualism, Mexican-American and Spanish-speaking children, 175

C

Cases in special education, litigation, 267-271

Cognitive-ability — see Jensen's associative-ability and cognitive-ability theory

Council of Administrators of Special Education (CASE), 233, 236

Culture-fair tests, 169-172

D

Direct *versus* inferential measurement, 110

Dyslexia, specific reading retardation, 7-9

E

Eastern Europe — see Special education in Eastern Europe

Educational program evaluation, 217-220

Emotionally disturbed, behavior modification in special education, 67-72

I

Imitate, teaching to, trainable-level retarded students, 112-116

Impact of educational research on changes in educational practice, 203-223
  educational program evaluation, 217-220
  implications for researchers, 216, 217
  importance of educational research, 206-211
  process of educational change, 211-216
    characteristics of, 211
    personal and political factors in, 214-216
    studies of, 212
  program packaging and dissemination, 220-223

Importance of educational research, 206-211

Indians — see North American Indian children

Instructional determinism, 109

Instructional empiricism, 109

Instructional environmentalism, 108

Instructional programs for trainable-level retarded students, 103-131 behavioristic task-analysis, 107, 111
  direct *versus* inferential measurement, 110

instructional determinism, 109

instructional empiricism, 109

instructional environmentalism, 108

instructional technology, 111-131
  imitate, teaching to, 112-116
  language, 130
  mathematics, 124-127
  prevocational behavior, 127-130
  reading, 116-124
longitudinal objectives of instructional programs, 106

Instructional technology, 111-131
  imitate, teaching to, 112-116
  language, 130
  mathematics, 124-127
  prevocational behavior, 127-130
  reading, 116-124

Intelligence testing of ethnic minority-group and culturally disadvantaged children, 161-191
  bias of intelligence tests and testing, 162-168
  culture-fair tests, 169-172

  Jensen's associative-ability and cognitive-ability theory, 184-186
  Mexican-American and Spanish-speaking children, 173-183
    bilingualism, 175, 176
    inappropriateness of intelligence tests, 177, 178
    performance on the WISC, 181-183
    rapport, 177
    research studies on sociocultural factors, 174, 175
    speech difficulties, 176
    translating a test, 178-181
  modifying test procedures, 172, 173
  Negro examinees and examiners' race, 169
  North American Indian children, 183, 184
  Value and validity of intelligence tests, 186-188

J

Jensen's associative-ability and cognitive-ability theory, 184-186

L

Language, instructional technology, trainable-level retarded students, 130

304

Mission Coalition Organization v. San Francisco Unified School District (1970), 275
Pennsylvania Association for Retarded Children v. the Commonwealth of Pennsylvania (1971), 272
Serrano v. Priest (1971), 275
Wolf v. Legislature of the State of Utah (1969), 272
right to treatment in residential facilities, 275-278
New York Association for Retarded Children v. Rockefeller (1972), 277
Ricci v. Greenblatt (1972), 277
Wyatt v. Stickney (1971), 275-277
student rights, 264, 265
In re Gault (1967), 265
Stell v. Savannah-Chatham County Board of Education (1963), 264, 265
Tinker v. Des Moines Independent Community School District (1969), 265

S

Secondary retardation, 185
Society for the Psychological Study of Social Issues, 166
Sociocultural factors, Mexican-American and Spanish-speaking children, intelligence tests, 174, 175
Special Education Administration Consortium, 229, 230
Special education administration, research and theory in, 229-256
future research within social-system model, 246-255
organizational change, 246-255
review of research on administration and supervision of special education, 230-241
between-group studies, 234-237
between-group studies of organizational climate, 237-240
studies of factors used in determining administrative structure of special education services, 240, 241
within-group studies, 231-233
special-general educational administration and theory, 241-246
assumptions, 243, 244
social-system model, 244-246

Special education combination, 235-236
Special education in Eastern Europe, 287-299
comparative terminology and classification, 288-290
relevant research, 293-299
special education curricula, 290-293
Bulgaria, 293
Czechoslovakia, 292
Hungary, 292
Poland, 292
Romania, 293
USSR, 290-292
Yugoslavia, 293
Special education-unique, 235, 236
Special-general educational administration and theory, 241-246
assumptions, 243,244
social-system model, 244-246
Specific reading retardation, 1-38
association of reading problems with antisocial behavior, 32-34
concepts, 4-9
definition of, 2-4
developmental delay, 16-22
audiovisual integration and sequencing, 17
choreiform movements, 20
"maturational delay", 21
motor impersistence, 20
motor incoordination, 20
perceptual difficulties, 19
right-left awareness, 18
specific developmental functions, 20
dyslexia, 7-9
genetics, 26, 27
handedness, eyedness, and footedness, 15
neurological aspects, 21-26
delayed physical maturation, 26
disorder, 21
electroencephalographic findings, 23
minor signs, 22
perinatal complications, 23
postnatal disease, 24
prevalence, 9-11
cross-cultural differences, 11
school influences, 30
sex distribution, 11
social and familial influences, 28-30
educational interest and opportunities in the home, 29
family disruption, 30
family history of reading difficulties, 30

AUTHOR INDEX

A

Abercrombie, Davis, & Shackel (1963), 26

Adams (1969), 216

Ali & Costello (1971), 172

Allen, Turner, & Everett (1970), 75

Altus (1953), 181

Anastasi (1961), 189

Anastasi & Cordova (1953), 175, 177, 181

Atchison (1955), 170

Ayres & Torres (1967), 23

Azrin, Bugle, & O'Brien (1971), 59

Azrin & Foxx (1971), 59

B

Bailey, Wolf, & Phillips (1970), 71

Baratz & Baratz (1971), 142

Barclay & Yater (1969), 171

Barnes (1971), 162, 189

Barrett (1970), 242, 243

Barrish, Saunders, & Wolf (1969), 70

Barton (1970), 62

Barton, Guess, Garcia, & Baer (1970), 60

Bellamy & Brown (1972), 124-127

Belmont & Birch (1965), 15

Belmont & Birch (1966), 15

Belmont, Birch, & Belmont (1968), 18

Bensberg, Colwell, & Cassel (1965), 59

Bentley (1970), 241

Birch (1970), 238

Birch & Belmont (1964), 17

Birnbrauer (1968), 61

Birnbrauer & Lawler (1964), 63

Bishop (1970), 212

Blank & Bridger (1966), 17

Blank, Weider, & Bridger (1968), 17

Blatt (1971), 137

Bolshunov & Soloviev (1968), 296

Bowers (1970), 240

Bowers & Seashore (1966), 252, 253

Brady (1971), 78, 79

Brim (1965), 186

Brown, Bellamy, Bancroft, & Sontag (1972), 123

Brown, Bellamy, & Sontag (1971), 107, 111

Brown, Bellamy, Tang, & Klemme (1971), 115

Brown & Elliott (1965), 69

Brown, Fenrick, & Klemme (1971), 120

Brown & Foshee (1970), 116

Brown, Hermanson, Klemme, Haubrick, & Ora (1970), 119

Brown, Huppler, Pierce, Johnson, & Sontag (1972), 116

Brown, Huppler, Pierce, York & Sontag (1972), 121

Brown, Jones, Troccolo, Heiser, & Bellamy (1972), 121

Brown & Pearce (1970), 65

Brown & Perlmutter (1971), 120, 122

Bruininks & Feldman (1970), 187

Buchan (1971), 215

Burchard (1967), 71, 72

Burchard & Tyler (1962), 71, 83

Burrello (1969), 233, 236